SECOND EDITION

INVESTIGATING DIFFERENCE

SECOND EDITION

INVESTIGATING DIFFERENCE

Human and Cultural Relations in Criminal Justice

The Criminology and Criminal Justice Collective
of Northern Arizona University

Prentice Hall
Upper Saddle River, New Jersey
Columbus, Ohio

Library of Congress Cataloging-in-Publication Data

Investigating difference : human and cultural relations in criminal justice/ The Criminology
and Criminal Justice Collective of Northern Arizona University.—2nd ed.
  p. cm.
Includes bibliographical references and index.
ISBN-13: 978-0-205-61021-1 (alk. paper)
ISBN-10: 0-205-61021-8 (alk. paper)
  1. Criminal justice, Administration of—United States.   2. Discrimination in criminal justice
administration—United States.   3. United States—Social conditions.   I. Northern Arizona
University. Criminal Justice Collective.
  HV9950.I58 2009
  364.97308—dc22

2008021707

Editor in Chief: Vernon Anthony
Senior Acquisitions Editor: Tim Peyton
Editorial Assistant: Alicia Kelly
Media Project Manager: Karen Bretz
Director of Marketing: David Gesell
Marketing Manager: Adam Kloza
Marketing Coordinator: Alicia Dysert
Production Manager: Kathy Sleys
Creative Director: Jayne Conte
Cover Design: Margaret Kenselaar
Cover Illustration/Photo: Alexis West
Full-Service Project Management/Composition: Shiny Rajesh/Integra Software Services

Credits and acknowledgments borrowed from other sources and reproduced, with permission, in this
textbook appear on appropriate page within text.

Pearson Education Ltd., London
Pearson Education Singapore, Pte. Ltd
Pearson Education Canada, Inc.
Pearson Education–Japan
Pearson Education Australia PTY, Limited
Pearson Education North Asia, Ltd., Hong Kong
Pearson Educación de Mexico, S.A. de C.V.
Pearson Education Malaysia, Pte. Ltd.
Pearson Education Upper Saddle River, New Jersey

Prentice Hall
is an imprint of

www.pearsonhighered.com

10 9 8 7 6 5 4 3
ISBN-13: 978-0-20-561021-1
ISBN-10:   0-20-561021-8

*For our Criminology and Criminal Justice students,
past, present, and future.*

CONTENTS

FOREWORD

This is an important book!

As its title suggests, *Investigating Difference: Human and Cultural Relations in Criminal Justice* tackles the tough questions that lie at the intersections of criminal justice and difference. In contrast to typical treatises on diversity, *Investigating Difference* goes well beyond superficial discussions of race and gender. Reflecting a deep understanding of privilege, this text considers the now familiar categories of difference while reframing the dialogue in terms more innovative, more provocative, more integrative, and ultimately, more productive.

Constituted primarily of faculty in the Department of Criminology and Criminal Justice (CCJ) at Northern Arizona University (NAU), the Criminal Justice Collective is a network of scholars devoted to improving the criminal justice system as well as criminal justice education. In its first edition, *Investigating Difference* sold steadily and was adopted as a key text in educational program across the United States. As the then Dean Susanna Maxwell wrote in the foreword to the first edition, "Consistent with their collective commitment to making a difference, all proceeds from the sale of this book will benefit educational and student projects within the department [of Criminology and Criminal Justice at NAU] and not the individual authors" (xvii). True to their pledge and their principles, to date, the Criminal Justice Collective has contributed over $14,000 in royalties to scholarships and other forms of support for NAU students. I have no reason to doubt that this new and updated edition will reach an even wider audience.

As Nielsen, Jones, and Perry imply in the introduction to this edition, understanding diversity is no longer optional; mere awareness of difference is no longer sufficient. Misunderstanding difference is at the root of injustice, while understanding difference is the key to progress toward "a more perfect union" and a more civil and compassionate society.

Again, this is an important book. But readers beware, reading this book may:

- Disrupt long held beliefs,
- Heighten dissatisfaction with the status quo,
- Alter familiar patterns of thinking and acting, and
- Increase intolerance for prejudice, discrimination, and injustice.

Consider yourself forewarned!

Michael R. Stevenson, Ph.D.
Dean, College of Social and Behavioral Sciences
Northern Arizona University
December 2007

ACKNOWLEDGMENTS

This is the second edition of *Investigating Difference: Human and Cultural Relations in Criminal Justice*. When we wrote the first edition, we never suspected that the book would ever be popular enough to have a second edition. As with the first book, this has been a collaborative effort of the faculty members of the Department of Criminology and Criminal Justice at Northern Arizona University—and a few special others. Therefore, our first expression of gratitude is to the departmental members who directly contributed to this project by sharing their expertise in their chapters, and to those who contributed indirectly by offering support and encouragement. The scholarly expertise, creativity, and collegiality of the good folks in the department made this project not only possible, but absolutely enjoyable. We would especially like to acknowledge the contributions of Dr. Barbara Perry, one of the original editors of this collection, who had the bad grace to move back to Canada and is now Professor of Criminology, Justice and Policy Studies at the University of Ontario Institute of Technology. She worked diligently for us on this volume as well. We would also like to acknowledge the extraordinary and extra-departmental contributions of Dr. Karla Hackstaff (NAU Department of Sociology and Social Work), Dr. Cynthia Baroody-Hart (San Jose State University, Justice Studies Program), Dr. Carole Mandino (NAU's Northern Arizona Gerontology Institute), Paula Rector (Missouri State University), and Dr. Brian Smith (Department of Sociology, Anthropology, and Social Work at Central Michigan University). Without the support and active push of our Chair, Dr. Nancy Wonders, this book would likely not have been produced—thank you! We would also like to thank Dr. Michael R. Stevenson, the Dean of the College of Social and Behavioral Sciences at NAU, for his support and participation in the book. This is reflective of his commitment to diversity initiatives throughout the college.

The cover art was created by Alexis West, who designed the cover art for the first edition also.

We would also like to acknowledge graduate student Kenneth Cruz, who assisted with online research for some of our authors; Ann Lewis and Cathy Spitzer, our hardworking and exceedingly patient administrative staff; and April Tuftee, Merry Tyminski, and Briana Leyba, our student workers who did way too much photocopying throughout the editing process. Thank you so much for your cheerful assistance, "can-do" attitude, and fast work.

Finally, we would like to thank David Repetto, formerly of the Allyn & Bacon Criminal Justice Division, who immediately saw the potential of a revised edition and patiently worked through the initial administrivia with us, and Tim Peyton and Alicia Kelly of Prentice-Hall who took over our project and encouraged us with amiability and enthusiasm.

We are pleased to tell you that all royalties from this book go into the "Investigating Difference Scholarship Fund," which benefits both undergraduate and graduate students through recognition of their scholarly accomplishments, funding for travel to attend and present papers at conferences, and funding to support graduate student research projects.

Lynn Jones and Marianne O. Nielsen
May, 2008

ABOUT THE COVER ARTIST

Alexis (Kathleen) West is a freelance graphic artist, photographer, color field painter, and writer. She spends her summers "chasing smoke" as a Public Information Officer at wildfire incidents. West's photography has been featured in *Crime, Media, and Culture* (Sage Press, UK) and *Les Cashiers de la Femme* (Toronto University, Canada). Her writing has been published in several U.S. literary magazines, most recently *The Strange Fruit*, Seattle. West completed an M.S. in Professional and Technical Communications at the University of Montana, and an M.S. in Criminal Justice from Northern Arizona University. West's trademark is ALXS. Her work can be viewed at www.alxsw.com.

SECOND EDITION

INVESTIGATING DIFFERENCE

PART ONE

Framing Difference

CHAPTER 1

Introduction
Investigating Difference

Marianne O. Nielsen, Lynn Jones,

Barbara Perry

The United States is one of the most diverse countries in an increasingly diverse world. Improved transportation and communication systems have led to increased interaction, both temporary and permanent, with people seen as "Others." Immigrants, refugees, visiting students and business people, tourists—all have brought their differences to our country. We are also becoming more conscious of our long-resident groups that are nonetheless considered different: Native Americans, Latino/as, African Americans, religious groups, the disabled, gays and lesbians, women, the elderly, the young. It is a relatively rare individual who cannot claim membership in one or more categories of difference.

Difference has been one of the great strengths of the United States in the past, and in our increasingly small world, has the potential to be our greatest strength in the future. Relatively recently in historical terms, the United States fought in World War II to stop the mass killing of millions of people who were considered different—Jews, Gypsies, gays, and others who were not deemed sufficiently "Aryan" by the Nazi party. It is one of the great paradoxes of human nature that perceptions of difference can lead to fear and hate, terror and bloodshed, but perceptions of difference can also lead to strength and hope, discoveries and innovation, as different groups come together to stop the slaughter. Integral to ending that war were the Navajo Code Talkers, the (African American) Tuskegee Airmen, the 442nd Regimental Combat Team (RCT) of Japanese Americans who suffered 9,486 casualties (Muller, 2003), and the women working, perhaps for the first time outside the home, in munitions factories and flying transport planes.

This strength based in difference is available to us not only in times of disaster and conflict, but in everyday accomplishments, both historically and in today's society: in science, with individuals as diverse as Albert Einstein (German American), Stephen Hawking (disabled), Carolyn Shoemaker (female), and Steven

Chu (Asian American); in political leadership, with President John F. Kennedy (Catholic), President Franklin Delano Roosevelt (disabled), Justice Ruth Bader Ginsburg (second woman and first Jewish woman to serve the U.S. Supreme Court), Secretary of State Condoleeza Rice (African American female), civil rights leaders César Chávez (Latino) and Martin Luther King (African American), and Nobel Peace Prize winner Elie Wiesel (Jewish); in economic development, by such business leaders as Sergey Brin (Russian immigrant co-founder of Google), Oprah Winfrey (African American female owner of one of the country's largest entertainment businesses), and William B. Fitzgerald (African American bank founder); in professional sports, with golfers Tiger Woods (mixed race) and Michelle Wie (young female Korean American), and Boston Red Sox player Jacoby Ellsbury (Navajo); and in the arts, with performers such as Academy Award–winning actors Denzel Washington, Jamie Foxx, Morgan Freeman, Forest Whitaker, Halle Berry, and Jennifer Hudson (African American); Celine Dion and Alanis Morrisette (French Canadian and female); Burning Sky and Carlos Nakai (Native American); Salma Hayek, Christina Aguilera, Jimmy Smits, and Jennifer Lopez (Latino/a); Rosie O'Donnell and Ellen DeGeneres (lesbian); Tom Cruise and Ray Charles (disabled), and so many others that all the pages of this whole book could be used just to list them. These people, of course, have many other identities than those by which they are identified here, and certainly, many of them are the rarest members of our society, the famous and the rich. We see them on the covers of magazines and profiled on television shows, and often it is their "difference" that becomes part of the story. It is important to remember that these individuals had to work hard, often against great social odds, to win such honors or leadership positions. Most importantly, the knowledge, skills, experience and talent they have provided to this country are representative of the human resources that are plentiful among the "ordinary" people perceived as different.

Among an ordinary college or university population, for instance, the diversity of the student body and the faculty plays a significant role in the recruitment and retention of individuals of any background. Northern Arizona University (NAU) has made some improvements in diversity since the publication of the previous edition of this book. Our student body's diversity has increased since the previous edition, now with 12% Latino/a (from 9%), 6% Native American (no change), 2% Asian American (from 1.5%), and 3% African American (from 1.4%) (NAU PAIR, 2007a student data). This student body is a fairly good representation of the general population of the northern part of the state of Arizona. No doubt our student body is quite different from the student body at any other university, and we make every attempt to highlight the strengths in our diversity. This year, NAU ranked first nationally for the total degrees awarded to Native Americans, with 253 graduates at the undergraduate, master's, and doctorate level (Integrated Postsecondary Education Data System Report, 2007). Even though criminal justice is a field still dominated by men, female students comprise 63% of the student body at NAU and hold a slight majority (51%) among criminology and criminal justice majors over the last several years (NAU PAIR, 2007b department data).

As a society, we need the wisdom to see all groups and identities as the resources they are, and ensure that there exist equitable opportunities to participate and contribute for the benefit of us all.

One of the objectives of this book is to present diversity as a resource to the criminal justice system, not as a problem to be solved, or a situation to be managed, or an inconvenience to be tolerated. It should be recognized and celebrated. This approach to dealing with diversity should be reinforced throughout our educational system. It can and should begin with our classrooms, which are as diverse as our society.

Support for diversity education is growing rapidly within the criminal justice field. Significant changes in student demographics, shifts in cultural values, pressures from university administration and criminal justice agencies, and interests of faculty have led to criminal justice and criminology programs reviewing and revising their curricula. As a result, universities and colleges around the country are adding courses on topics such as gender, race and ethnicity, cultural diversity, and social inequalities (Nielsen and Stambaugh, 1998). NAU and the Department of Criminology and Criminal Justice, we would like to think, are leaders in this movement. In the department, we have enhanced the difference offerings of our curriculum since the time of the last edition, including recent course additions on global justice, and on immigration and human rights.

NAU offers special events and films on women's and gender issues, and students are active in advocacy organizations such as Associated Students for Women's Issues (ASWI) and PRISM (GLBTQ). We have an Institute for Native Americans, a major in Applied Indigenous Studies, Native American Student Services, a Latin American Studies minor, the Martin-Springer Institute, which runs programs based on lessons of the Holocaust to promote tolerance, and some relatively new student organizations such as TASH (disability advocacy) and the MARS project (Men Against Rape and Sexism). These are just a few of the programs, resources, and educational opportunities that are available to our students, faculty, and to the wider community(ies) that surrounds us. Our students in criminal justice use these resources to prepare themselves to be more effective criminal justice personnel. They learn Spanish or Navajo if they want to be police officers or lawyers in the Southwest; they take classes about women's issues to provide better services for female victims of violence; and they intern with DNA People's Legal Services or the county Victim/Witness program and any number of other community service groups to learn more about issues from the community's point of view.

In turn, we use the students' experiences and ideas about difference as teaching resources. Historically, attending college was for men and the wealthy. While barriers to education still exist for many in society, we see colleges opening to more and more individuals. Looking beyond categories such as race and ethnicity, gender, and social class, we might view the "difference" among students along other lines. Consider the various personal identities and group memberships found among students at a university, such as: single parent, fraternity member, student athlete, graduating senior, transfer student, "townie" or commuter, criminal justice major (or other major), intramural champion, member of the Dean's list, and more. Their family background, life experiences, and occasional resistance to valuing difference can all become part of our teaching tools when used with respect and sensitivity by their instructors (see Nielsen and Stambaugh, 1998). In a similar vein, difference can also be a resource for training academies, community colleges, and organizational training departments.

Difference is not just an educational resource; it is also a service resource. Personnel from diverse backgrounds bring knowledge and skills into organizations and jobs; this knowledge and these skills are becoming essential for effective service provision and good community–criminal justice system relations. Individuals with knowledge of cultural differences in attitudes toward authority, family structure, and communication styles; community leadership structures; and community issues are not only more likely to gain the cooperation of community members, but are also more likely to be able to protect the public and themselves.

We must recognize that we are united in our diversity. It is one of the traits that makes this country a relatively peaceful, healthy, and safe place to live. Arthur Solomon (1994:127), an Anishnabe elder, teacher, and poet, states it elegantly in a passage from a poem about healing in Native communities:

> Our strength is in our togetherness.
> Our weakness is in our aloneness.
> As long as we don't care about each other and for each other
> we will all be alone and we will be destroyed *one by one*.

In stark contrast to those who see difference as the very source of our strength, there are those who see that difference as the cause of all problems in society. Their negative responses can vary from prejudice and avoidance, to hate crimes such as lynchings, homicide, and other attempts at the physical extermination of the group. There is a dark side to difference, in that it is feared and rejected by many groups and individuals.

In the years since the first edition, we have seen a number of cases in which difference turned negative with fear and hate and violence. One general example is the terrorist attacks of September 11, 2001, and the resulting anti-Muslim and anti-Arab sentiments, which led to hate crimes and support for profiling at airports, to name a few specific reactions. In 2006 in Jena, Louisiana, black and white students became divided over sitting under a shady tree: white students sat there while black students sat inside; a black student's request to sit under the tree was approved, but then three nooses were hung from the tree, leading black students to respond violently when the white students' behavior was labeled a "prank." The resulting criminal justice response to the black students was thought to be racially biased, triggering national protests. As these examples illustrate, an exclusionary and negative view of difference is not just a thing of the past.

The United States remains a country in which decisions must be made about the meaning of difference. We can accept, celebrate, and use difference as a resource as we have done so ably in the past, or we can use power, coercion, and hate to try to eradicate diversity from our country as many fundamentalist, militant, and radically conservative groups and individuals advocate—as happened in the recent examples discussed previously. Unfortunately, the criminal justice system often has contributed to attacks on difference. In the past, for example, laws were used to exclude immigrant groups such as Jews and Japanese; they restricted the rights and justified the exploitation of African Americans and Native Americans; and they put women, gays and lesbians, and children "in their place"—that is, ensured they did not have the rights and protections granted to males, heterosexuals, or adults. While some groups have gained rights under the law, new groups face exclusion or discrimination and often have to fight the same battles as those before them. Legislators cannot be given the whole blame, of course; police and courts enforced these laws, and the correctional system punished the transgressors. The criminal justice system is a powerful arm of the status quo. Its function is to ensure conformity to the laws. Sometimes, as members of groups perceived as different are well aware, the laws were unjust or enforced differentially, and sometimes the criminal justice system went beyond enforcing conformity to the law by enforcing conformity to values and norms not regulated by law.

Legal changes began to gather momentum with the civil rights era and the criminal justice system began to change, too; though many would argue that the changes came with reluctance and resistance. It could be argued that a second wave of changes began within the criminal justice system in the late 1980s and early 1990s. Racism in the criminal justice system hit the 6 o'clock news with the videotaping of the beating of Rodney King. On the witness stand, again in prime time, Officer Mark Fuhrman of the LAPD proved racism was thriving within the ranks of the police force. The trial of O. J. Simpson split the country's view of criminal justice along black/white lines. The criminal justice system's historical role in the oppression of diverse groups once again became part of the public consciousness.

Following the terrorist attacks of September 11, 2001, the public's attention to difference on both a global and local scale was heightened. As noted in Chapter 10 (Perry) and Chapter 16 (Perry and Morgan), racial and religious difference became an apparent motivation for hate crimes, discrimination, harassment, and profiling of Muslim Americans, people perceived to be of Arab descent (consider the case of Balbir Singh Sodhi, a Sikh Indian) (Lewin, 2001), and some Asians. Immigration issues resurfaced as part of the national security debate, and large-scale political demonstrations advocating for the rights of immigrants took place in spring 2006. Difference and the associated meanings for different groups continue to demand our attention in the pursuit of justice.

The criminal justice system is responsible for protecting and serving the public, yet justice professionals are sometimes not aware that this public holds many different views on crime and the criminal justice system itself, based on history and their own life experiences. Rather than try unsuccessfully and with futility to coerce groups to conform and assimilate, a more effective and practical alternative is to invite and encourage difference, to use difference, and to incorporate difference as a normal part of criminal justice.

In recent years, governments, organizations, and courts acted to protect difference. In 2007, the U.S. Supreme Court restored judicial discretion to depart from sentencing guidelines out of disagreement with Congress's view that crack cocaine offenses deserved much longer sentences than powder cocaine offenses—a question that involves issues of race and class (Greenhouse, 2007); 12 American Indian tribal nations in Arizona successfully challenged in court the use of reclaimed water at a ski resort on their sacred land as a violation of their religious freedoms; voting rights of racial and ethnic minorities have been further protected with changes in election procedures and technology, and lawsuits; the people of New Orleans are now being supported through oversight investigations into the governmental response to Hurricane Katrina; and the Violence Against Women Act (VAWA) was renewed with funding.

If we wish to celebrate and use our differences, then we must protect and defend them. To live up to this ideal of criminal justice service provision, difference must become part of criminal justice educational and training curricula, not in token two-hour modules but woven into the tapestry of the whole curriculum. As Gould states later in this book (Chapter 20), diversity education and training must be required early and often throughout criminal justice careers. Diversity must become part of hiring and promotional criteria. It must become part of organizational culture, leadership style, and management practices. It must become so all-encompassing that it becomes "normal" and familiar.

Most of all, difference must be respected—in our families, in our workplaces, and in our day-to-day interactions any place we find ourselves. As the centuries-old knowledge of Indigenous peoples tells us:

> Receive strangers and outsiders with a loving heart and as members of the human family. . . . All the races and tribes in the world are like the different coloured flowers of one meadow. All are beautiful. As children of the Creator they must all be respected. (Bopp *et al.*, 1988:82)

This book is our contribution to this essential effort.

THIS BOOK

In designing the book, we decided there would be three main "through-lines" that all the chapters would share. In the new edition, we have added a fourth through-line to reflect the changing society in which we now live. The first of these is that all *issues are presented in an historical context*. This kind of historical approach is necessary because the present can only be understood as the product of the past. History teaches us that the social world is "two-sided"; we create it and we are created by it (Abrams, 1982). We can better understand group formation, individual actions, and the structures within which they occur by using an historical approach. We cannot understand current events in the criminal justice system, for example, without recognizing that they are the results of processes that happen over time, and that these processes are shaped by the social, cultural, and historical contexts within which they occur (Clemens, 2007).

A second through-line is that the authors use a *paradigm of power and powerlessness*. As Wonders explains in Chapter 2, difference is a social construction, and some groups within society have more power than others in defining who is different and who is not. Power, or lack of power, is one of the most important factors in defining how various groups will be treated by the criminal justice system. Based on their race, gender, age, or sexual orientation, will they face positive or negative discrimination, or no discrimination at all? Will they have the resources to "buy justice"? Or will they even understand the workings of the wheels of justice in motion?

The third through-line is that a balanced view must be taken of each diverse group so that *each is discussed not only as offenders and victims, but that their contributions as service-providers, policy makers, and innovators are also recognized and discussed.*

The disciplines of criminology and criminal justice have been guilty in the past of perpetuating stereotypes of dangerous minority offenders; passive female or elderly victims; and tough, male police officers who form the "thin blue line." These are stereotypes because they are simplistic, inaccurate generalizations. A more realistic portrait is one of rich complexity, as the criminal justice system interacts with all the diverse groups that comprise its environment and its internal human subsystems.

New to this edition is an emphasis on *how and why difference matters*. Many authors had previously included in their chapters arguments for understanding the significance of difference; in this edition, we added a new section with topics that specifically illustrate how difference matters in today's criminal justice system. Also new to this edition is the fourth through-line of *globalization*. It is increasingly difficult to discuss issues of difference within a boundary of one nation; individuals are more and more connected across national identities and within global communities. The field of criminology and criminal justice has moved increasingly to an emphasis on global inequalities and the international context for crime and victimization, and many authors have included these themes where relevant.

In keeping with the emphasis of the book on maintaining a balance in how we perceive the relationship between the criminal justice system and diverse groups, a final through-line is that the book identifies trends in how these various issues are being handled in innovative ways (see Part Four below).

The new edition of this book is divided into four main parts. Part One, Framing Difference, provides a theoretical and empirical framework for the discussions of the categories of difference that make up the majority of the book. This section begins with an overview of how difference is conceptualized within our society, and more specifically within the criminal justice system, in Chapter 2 by Wonders. Chapter 3 by Gould describes the two main standards of "normal" within our society and within the justice system: being white and being male. Chapter 4, by Nielsen and Maniglia, identifies the importance of positive intercultural and interpersonal communication. Part Two, Categories of Difference, describes the experiences of 12 diverse groups with the criminal justice system. We start this section with a chapter on social class (Michalowski, Chapter 5) since it acts as a theoretical and structural framing of the later chapters. In addition, this section contains chapters on Native Americans (Nielsen and Robyn, Chapter 6), immigrants (Perry, Fernandez, and Costelloe Chapter 7), African Americans (Smith, Chapter 8), Latino/as (Fernandez and Alvarez, Chapter 9), and Asian Americans (Perry, Chapter 10). There are also chapters on women (Hackstaff and Rector, Chapter 11), gays and lesbians (Perry, Chapter 12), the elderly (Mandino, Chapter 13) and youth (Maniglia, Chapter 14), persons with disability (Baroody-Hart and McDowell, Chapter 15); and religious groups (Perry and Morgan, Chapter 16).

Part Three, How Does Difference Matter?, is newly added for the second edition. In this section, the authors of three new chapters use specific topics and criminal justice contexts to illustrate the ways in which difference matters in the criminal justice system. Chapter 17 by Costelloe discusses moral panics in relation to immigration. Catlin's chapter (Chapter 18) shows how difference plays an important role in the setting of the courts. Schehr's chapter (Chapter 19) on wrongful conviction shows how difference plays a role in the many mistakes made in the justice system.

Part Four presents two chapters on important strategic trends in dealing with difference. There are chapters on cultural diversity training (Gould, Chapter 20), and the relationship between crime workers and crime victims (Jones, Morgan, and Perry, Chapter 21). In the concluding chapter, the many strategies presented throughout the book, regarding the social and political action that various diverse groups have developed to further their equality within the criminal justice system, are woven together (Jones, Perry, and Nielsen, Chapter 22).

This outline hints at two of the important strengths of this book. The first is that this book presents a perspective on the relationship between difference and the criminal justice system that is "outside the box"—different from the one usually presented in criminal justice and criminology courses. Although groups based on race, ethnicity, and gender are important parts of the discussion, so are groups such as the disabled, religious minorities, and the elderly, who are often mentioned only in passing in more traditional courses on diversity and criminal justice. It is still rare to find books that cover the range of categories of difference found here. Second, the authors of these chapters, in the majority of cases, are scholars active in carrying out research agendas on the groups they write about, or are teachers of courses on difference and criminal justice. At NAU, this book continues to be used in a required junior-level undergraduate course called "Investigating Difference" (CJ 345), which has been recently taught by Fernandez, Jones, Maniglia, Nielsen, and Wonders. The faculty and students at NAU continue to prioritize community outreach and involvement, and we feel that this book reflects this real-world perspective and the needs and interests of our community members.

References

Abrams, Philip. 1982. *Historical Sociology*. West Compton House: Open Books.

Bopp, Judie, Michael Bopp, Lee Brown, and Phil Lane. 1988. *The Sacred Tree*, Special edn. Lethbridge, AB: Four Worlds Development.

Clemens, Elisabeth S. 2007. Towards a Historicized Sociology: Theorizing Events, Processes, and Emergence. *Annual Review of Sociology* 33: 527–549.

Greenhouse, Linda. 2007. Justices Restore Judges' Control Over Sentencing. *New York Times*. December 11, Section A, 1.

Integrated Postsecondary Education Data System Report. 2007. *Status and Trends in the Education of Racial and Ethnic Minorities*. http://nces.ed.gov/pubs2007/minoritytrends/ind_6_25.asp

Lewin, Tamar. 2001. Sikh Owner Of Gas Station Is Fatally Shot In Rampage. *New York Times*. September 17.

Muller, Eric L. 2003. *Free to Die for Their Country: The Story of the Japanese American Draft Resisters in World War II*. Chicago, IL: University of Chicago Press.

NAU Planning and Institutional Research (PAIR) data on Current Student Characteristics for Fall Semester (2007a). http://www4.nau.edu/pair/StudentCharacteristics/CurrentStudent/CurrentsStudentCharacteristics.asp

NAU Planning and Institutional Research (PAIR) data on Current Student Characteristics by Department for Fall Semester (2007b). http://www4.nau.edu/pair/StudentCharacteristics/CurrentStudent/StudentDept.asp

Nielsen, Marianne O., and Phoebe M. Stambaugh. 1998. Multiculturalism in the Classroom: Discovering Difference from Within. *Journal of Criminal Justice Education* 9 (2): 281–291.

Solomon, Arthur. 1994. *Eating Bitterness: A Vision Beyond the Prison Walls*. Toronto: NC Press.

CHAPTER 2

Conceptualizing Difference

Nancy A. Wonders

Despite the critical role that difference plays within the criminal justice system, it is rare for either practitioners or scholars to spend time investigating difference. It is often taken for granted that the differences between people are natural and obvious and, therefore, uncontroversial. Yet, little about difference is actually either natural or obvious. And difference is far from uncontroversial. Over the last decade, there has been an explosion of work on difference and identity. This scholarly work has highlighted the complex nature of difference; it also contains lessons that are invaluable for those seeking to understand the place of difference within the criminal justice system.

In this chapter, I outline some of the important insights about difference that have emerged from the contemporary literature on difference and identity. My objectives are to explore "difference" as a topic of study, to forge conceptual links between the concept of difference and justice issues, and to introduce some of the common themes regarding difference that are discussed in the chapters in this volume. The subsections that follow offer answers to these questions: What is difference, and where does it come from? Why do some differences matter, while others do not? What is the relationship between law and difference? Why study difference within the field of criminal justice?

DIFFERENCE IS SOCIALLY CONSTRUCTED

Most people think that the most important differences between individuals are fundamentally biological. Race, ethnicity, sexual orientation, gender, age, and even social class are frequently viewed as inherited traits—what sociologists call *ascribed characteristics*. In this view, people are "black" because they were born with dark skin; "white" because their skin is lighter in color. People are designated "female" or "male" because they are born with particular genitalia. What is most interesting about biology, however, is not how different we all are from each other, but rather how remarkably similar most people are in both design and function.

Indeed, the biological differences that do exist between people rarely matter in themselves; instead, they are made to matter through the process of social interaction. To say that *difference is socially constructed*, then, is to say that the meaning attached to difference, including biological difference, is created by people in interaction with each other. From this perspective, difference is a social process that can be understood only historically, contextually, and culturally—we are all "doing difference" all the time (West and Fenstermaker, 2002). To reiterate an earlier point, "difference" is the term used to describe the social and cultural *meanings* attached to human variation.

Of course, there are biological differences between us. Some people have larger noses, smaller feet, larger breasts, or lighter skin. However, biological differences do not come with instructions telling us how to deal with or respond to them. In fact, if biology were destiny, we probably would not spend so much time and money dressing our boys in blue and our girls in pink, because boys would be "naturally" masculine and girls "naturally" feminine, regardless of the color of their clothes or other markers used to signify their sex to the rest of the world. Nor would Jews have been made to wear yellow stars during World War II so that they could be identified easily. Nor would we emphasize the importance of eating certain kinds of traditional foods or engaging in particular cultural celebrations. Instead, we put enormous energy into constructing and enforcing gender, ethnic, sexual orientation, race, and other differences as a kind of insurance against "nature." Race, ethnicity, social class, sexual orientation, and even age reflect the *meaning* we give them rather than natural facts about our biology. Some additional examples may help to illustrate this point.

Today, it is frequently assumed that women are naturally more interested than men in fashion and beauty, and that these interests are associated with femininity and femaleness. It is important to remember, however, that in Victorian England, it was men who wore wigs, high heels, stockings, and frilly blouses. Instead of exhibiting femininity, this set of differences was strongly associated with masculinity and power. Only "real men" wore wigs! Biology is clearly not destiny. For this reason, many scholars (e.g., Lorber, 2007) find it useful to make a distinction between "sex" and "gender": *sex* refers to human variations in bodies, hormones, genitalia, and reproductive abilities (which have relatively limited consequence since reproduction directly affects only a small portion of the human life cycle), whereas *gender* refers to the social characteristics, statuses, and legal identities that have come to be loosely associated with sex (e.g., femininity and masculinity). Sexual variation exists, but it is the meaning that is made out of that variation through the construction of gender that has the greatest consequence for individual life chances. Importantly, children must be taught how to act in gender-appropriate ways. The behaviors associated with each gender, however, have changed over time as society has changed, and are not determined by biological differences. History reveals that:

> Sex categorization involves no well-defined set of criteria that must be satisfied to identify someone; rather, it involves treating appearances (e.g., deportment, dress, and bearing) as if they were indicative of an underlying state of affairs (e.g., anatomical, hormonal, and chromosomal arrangements). The point worth stressing here is that, while sex category serves as an "indicator" of sex, it does not depend on it. Societal

members will "see" a world populated by two and only two sexes, even in public situations that preclude inspection of the physiological "facts." . . . Gender, we argue, is a situated accomplishment of societal members, the local management of conduct in relation to normative conceptions of appropriate attitudes and activities for particular sex categories. From this perspective, gender is not merely an individual attribute but something that is accomplished in interaction with others. (West and Fenstermaker, 2002: 65)

In other words, we are all constantly "doing gender" by acting in ways that signal to others how we ought to be categorized and by reacting to others in ways that define them as "male" or "female" (Fenstermaker and West, 2002). We "do" gender every day by dressing, sitting, talking, and acting in ways that create and reinforce gendered patterns of behavior. In fact, we are often confused and bothered by individuals who do not act consistently with our own expectations of appropriate "female" or "male" behavior, or whose dress or physical features seem inconsistent with their gendered behavior; for example, women who are unusually tall or masculine or men who are unusually petite. Indeed, such inconsistencies have often led to prejudice and discrimination against individuals in the justice system and in the larger society for their failure to communicate their sex and gender "appropriately" and consistently with dominant expectations (Belknap, 2007).

Similarly, it was often assumed historically that race reflected biological differences between people. Yet, the anthropological evidence is clear that race is not a biological difference; there are no genetic markers that clearly differentiate where "white" or "black" begins. Instead, *race* is a social construction, given meaning by people in the context of social interaction and history (Ore, 2008; Winant, 2004). Pieter-Dirk Uys (1988), a satirist from South Africa, illustrates the historic flexibility of race in the following remarks, which appeared in the *New York Times*:

Let me quote from one of our few remaining daily newspapers, the Government Gazette: "Nearly 800 South Africans became officially members of a different race group last year, according to figures quoted in Parliament and based on the Population Registration Act. They included 518 colored who were officially reclassified as white, 14 whites who became colored, 7 Chinese who became white, 2 whites who became Chinese, 3 Malays who became white, 1 white who became an Indian, 50 Indians who became colored, 54 coloreds who became Indian, 17 Indians who became Malay, 4 coloreds who became Chinese, 1 Malay who became Chinese, 89 blacks who became colored, 5 coloreds who became black." I couldn't make it up if I tried.

This example illustrates the changing nature of race over time and the fact that racial categorization depends heavily upon who is doing the defining. A person considered black in the United States may not be considered so in South Africa or in Brazil; "indeed, some U.S. blacks may be considered white in Brazil" (Telles, 2006:79). Throughout history, race as a category of meaning has changed to fit changing circumstances. Like gender, the meaning of race is constructed through human interaction.

Ethnicity, or socially constructed cultural affiliation, is similar in this regard, as evidenced by the historical process by which immigrants to the United States, particularly non-Hispanic whites, were able to transform themselves from Italian, Irish, or Japanese ethnic groups into "Americans" and more specifically into "White" Americans (Roediger, 2006). The fact that ethnic and racial identities reflect a long process of historical construction was explicitly recognized in the year 2000 when the U.S. Census, our national strategy for counting race and ethnicity, moved beyond the six racial categories listed and allowed individuals to check more than one category of identification, creating a new "multiracial" category. Research has found that individuals who self-identify in one racial group but who are routinely misclassified by others experience adverse psychological consequences (Campbell, 2007). Thus, because ethnicity and race have been made to matter in our society, it is important to respect how individuals *self*-identify.

Even social class differences cannot be explained merely by external variation in wealth or income. *Social class* is also a social construction linked to history and culture, and one's class identity can be understood only in relationship to others. Social class is evidenced through barometers such as material success and social location in the economic system, but it is also characterized by the presence or absence of particular styles of speech, behaviors, and attitudes. As Langston (2004:141) argues, "class is also culture":

> . . . class is how you think, feel, act, look, dress, talk, move, walk; class is what stores you shop at, restaurants you eat in; class is the schools you attend, the education you attain; class is the very jobs you will work at throughout your adult life. We experience class at every level of our lives; class is who our friends are, where we live and work even what kind of car we drive, if we own one, and what kind of health care we receive, if any. Have I left anything out? In other words, class is socially constructed and all encompassing. When we experience classism, it will be because of our lack of money (i.e., choices and power in this society) and because of the way we talk, think, act, move—because of our culture.

Because class is cultural, individuals who are poor have a difficult time becoming middle class even when they obtain more money. Being middle class means learning how to "act" middle class—to "walk the walk" and "talk the talk." Growing up poor creates a distinct cultural disadvantage given that "proper" behavior, dress, and linguistic style in much of the world of work and within the justice system is determined by those from higher social classes. There is a well-documented history of discrimination against lower-class individuals within the criminal justice system, beginning with the creation of laws specifically designed to control the "dangerous classes" and affecting virtually every stage of the criminal justice system (Reiman, 2006; Shelden, 2007). As will be illustrated later in this volume, the price for class differences can be high.

As these examples illustrate, the construction of difference reflects an historical process of human interaction and negotiation. All differences have a cultural component that carries enormous weight in shaping attitudes and behavior. In this sense, who others "think" we are may matter more than who we "really" are. This is a particularly important point for justice workers. Police officers may think of themselves as caring citizens trying to help others, but this matters little if citizens "think" police officers are "pigs" and, therefore, act toward them with hostility. A young man wearing baggy pants and a bandanna may think of himself as a hardworking student, loving son, or good friend, while others consider him to be only a gangbanger. Being regarded as "black" or "white," "gay" or "straight," or "female or male" carries the weight of the culture behind it. For this reason, it is important to realize that saying that difference is socially constructed is not the same thing as saying that individuals construct their own identities. We each have some control over how we will be viewed in the world, but mostly the identity choices available to us result from *structured social inequality*—which is to say that our choices are constrained and structured by our culture, the historical time period into which we are born into, previous patterns of inequality, social institutions, and where in the society we are located. You might think of yourself as without a race or gender, for example, but try getting everyone else to treat you that way and see how far you get!

Understanding that difference is socially constructed is a critical first step toward ensuring justice in a democratic society. We all bear some responsibility for the differences between us, and for the real consequences those differences have for human lives. It is especially important for those who work in the justice system to understand the role they play in giving differences meaning and making some differences matter.

DIFFERENCE ASSUMES A NORM OR STANDARD THAT REFLECTS POWER RELATIONS AND PRIVILEGE WITHIN THE CULTURE

Because differences are socially constructed though a process of human interaction, power plays an important role in determining how differences will be defined and which differences will be made to matter. Not surprisingly, some people have more *power* to define differences than do others. In general, history evidences a process whereby those with greater power become the standard of comparison against whom everyone else is measured. It is through this process that difference comes to have meaning.

Difference can only exist where there is a *norm* or standard against which everyone else is compared. Difference always implies a contrast and frequently it depends upon the construction of a two-part *dichotomy*.

> Difference is constructed when a continuum is turned into a dichotomy, such that one part of the dichotomy is represented as better than the other. So we take the continuum of age, create the categories of "adult" and "child," and privilege adults over children. We take the continuum of skin color, invent racial categories based on how closely skin color resembles blackness or whiteness, and then privilege whiteness. Difference is a linguist construction in which the *relationship* between two halves of the dichotomous construction is ignored, while the binary construction is elevated in importance . . . (Wonders, 1998: 117)

So we can understand the concept "man" only by understanding the concept "woman." We can understand "black" only because we can conceptualize "white."

Over time, these dichotomies come to take on a life of their own—to seem "natural," even biologically based.

Yet, social scientists have provided compelling evidence that virtually all human variations fall along a continuum rather than into two (or more) discrete boxes. People are not "black" or "white" but instead exhibit a huge range of skin colors, making racial designations based on skin color exceedingly arbitrary. People are not just "heterosexual" or "homosexual," since a large number of individuals have same-gender sexual experiences at some point during their lives without ever considering themselves gay or lesbian. Indeed, ". . . contemporary youths are increasingly adopting alternative labels . . . or rejecting sexual identity labels altogether, in an explicit acknowledgement of these labels' arbitrary nature . . ." (Diamond, 2003:491). Similarly, biological genitalia and body function provide a relatively weak basis for dichotomizing either sex or gender, since physical variation, even on such narrow criteria as breast size, the capacity for menstruation, and the size of one's external genitalia, is very high among humans and over the life course (Fausto-Sterling, 2000).

Not only is dividing social reality into dichotomies fundamentally inaccurate, it can have very harmful consequences. This is especially true when one half of the dichotomy is valued while the other half is devalued, a tendency that is all too common. *Devaluation* of social identities is expressed in a myriad of ways, through structural barriers to housing and employment, neighborhood segregation, interpersonal violence, and hate crime (Perry, 2001). The destructive impact of this devaluation has been well documented in research. For example, "Blacks and those in lower socioeconomic positions are less satisfied with their personal lives, housing, incomes, jobs, free time and standard of living. They also tend to be less satisfied with the way things are going in the country" (Hurst, 2004:236). Another example of this devaluation can be found in research on girls, which sadly has found that "even by the end of grade school, girls begin to evaluate themselves more negatively than do boys" (Chesney-Lind and Irwin, 2008:70). This *internalization* of negative societal messaging also has adverse consequences for justice in the United States. Some scholars, for example, argue that citizen perceptions that justice workers regard women and people of color as second-class citizens may reduce reliance on the police by the very groups most likely to experience certain kinds of personal victimization (Belknap, 2007; Gabbidon and Greene, 2005).

Clearly, dichotomizing differences into two parts or groups does not mean that each part is viewed as equal. Not only is one group often devalued, the other group obtains greater privilege, in part because it comes to be viewed as somehow more "normal." This phenomenon, known as *normative privilege*, ensures that the standard for evaluation reflects and maintains the already existing privilege of the more powerful group. As a result, we have a tendency to focus on only one portion of the dichotomy when discussing difference. The more privileged groups often remain invisible. When we discuss "race," most people assume we are only talking about people of color. When the issue of "gender" is raised, people assume it is a women's issue. But to the extent that a society divides people into categories, then *everyone* is subject to the impact of categorization. Some people benefit, some do not, but everyone is affected.

In this volume, the authors have chosen to devote relatively more time to description and analysis of groups within the United States that have historically been disadvantaged and marginalized within our culture and within the justice system. The increased attention to these groups is regarded as a needed antidote to the lack of attention to these groups within the criminal justice literature. However, the chapters that follow also investigate the behavior of those groups who have historically been privileged by justice practices in the United States. We believe that issues of difference do not belong to only one group; they are human issues that ought to concern us all.

DIFFERENCE MATTERS

Although the meanings attached to differences are socially constructed (rather than natural or biological), once differences are created they have real consequences for human lives and for the justice system. Because difference construction is a historical process, the place and time period into which we are born will have a lot to do with defining which characteristics will matter to the larger society. To be born with dark skin in the United States means something different today than it did during most of the 1800s, when slavery was commonplace. Those born without eyesight earlier in the twentieth century had significantly different life chances than those born without eyesight today. But in every case, once society has decided that a particular characteristic or set of characteristics warrants differential treatment, those viewed as having those characteristics will have a difficult time escaping categorization, prejudice, stereotyping, and discrimination.

Categorization is the process by which society decides which individuals fit into the boxes used to create difference. Once categories are created and given significant societal consequence, it becomes extremely important to decide who fits into which category. That is why so many individuals in South Africa had their race changed— different racial categories are linked to different privileges and opportunities in South African society. It's also why we work so hard to be sure that "boys will be boys." Research has evidenced that males experience greater privilege in our society in numerous areas, including in employment, education, and economic opportunity (Levit, 2000). Once society has created categories, enormous effort goes into forcing people into one category or another. Through the process of *socialization*, children are taught which categories they fit into, as well as how to behave consistently with those identities. Key agents of socialization, including parents, the media, schools, peers, and important social institutions, such as religion, all participate in socializing children to internalize the differences that are assigned to them from birth. Socialization is a form of *soft social control* that helps to ensure that cultural attitudes about difference will be internalized and passed down from generation to generation. As will be seen shortly, the justice system and other agents of *hard social control* also have played an active role in defining and maintaining differences in our society, sometimes through force, but also via the law and justice institutions.

Two other processes that help to ensure the continuation of difference are prejudice and discrimination. Prejudice and discrimination are different, though related phenomena. *Prejudice* is a set of beliefs and attitudes about people based on their group membership. Stereotyping is closely linked to prejudice and helps to reinforce it. *Stereotypes* are based on the assumption that all individuals who belong to a particular group share the same characteristics. It is important to point out that stereotypes and prejudices can be "good" or "bad" in intent, but they are much more often bad than good in their consequences. For example, it may be that Asian Americans are stereotyped as being especially good at academics (presumably a "good" trait), but this assumption can be devastating for the Asian American youth who does not fit the stereotype, even though it is an apparently positive stereotype.

While prejudice is a set of attitudes about individuals and the groups they belong to, *discrimination* is a *behavior* whereby individuals are treated adversely because of their group membership. Discrimination serves to privilege some characteristics over others by linking particular characteristics with either positive or negative consequences. Prejudice ensures that those on one side of the dichotomies we create—male/female, dark/light, straight/gay—are viewed as "less than" those on the other end. Discrimination is the behavioral component of prejudice. When people discriminate, they act toward others in positive or negative ways based upon real or imagined group membership.

Although some people argue that people are discriminated against because they are different, it is more plausible to argue that people come to be viewed as "different" because they are discriminated against. Because privilege and opportunity often result in greater power in the society, it is in the interests of those who are privileged by the construction of difference to perpetuate differences so that they, their children, and others like them can continue to receive disproportionate benefit. Said differently, we all want to avoid the negative consequences attached to prejudice and discrimination, and at the same time we desire the advantages offered to us by our privileged statuses; thus, there is a built-in incentive to try to maintain categories that privilege some individuals and groups over others. Thus, one way to reduce the power of difference is to eliminate the discriminatory and/or privileging effects attached to a particular difference. Merely having blue eyes rather than brown eyes is a difference that does not "matter" because neither privilege nor negative consequences accrue to those with different eye colors. Other differences might matter less if we could successfully alter the dichotomous nature of the rewards attached to them.

In the chapters that follow, the authors explore the ways that difference matters within the criminal justice system, for offenders, victims, and for justice professionals. The impact of power, privilege, prejudice, stereotyping, and discrimination on the administration of justice is explored for a wide range of social groups. Importantly, strategies for reducing the adverse consequences associated with difference are also discussed.

LAW PLAYS A CRITICAL ROLE IN CREATING AND MAINTAINING DIFFERENCE; IT CAN ALSO BE USED TO AMELIORATE THE NEGATIVE CONSEQUENCES OF DIFFERENCE

Historically and contemporarily, law has played a central role in the construction and maintenance of difference. In some cases, it is obvious that law works to categorize people in ways that artificially construct difference. One good example is age. Everyone is one age or another, but the social meaning attached to age has varied over time and from culture to culture (Stearns, 2006). Less than 100 years ago in the United States, children were expected to take on the responsibilities of adulthood as soon as they were able. Until relatively recently, people of all ages worked on farms or in factories—everyone performed the work of society. This is still true in many cultures and, indeed, in some neighborhoods in the United States.

Childhood as a separate category does not exist "naturally." The meaning of childhood must be created, and this is often accomplished through legal mechanisms, such as the creation of laws regarding the age of majority. In the United States, the age of majority has fluctuated over time, ranging between the ages of 18 and 21 in the last two decades; those younger than this age were considered to be "children" under the law, with limited rights and responsibilities. The arbitrary nature of this boundary is highlighted by the contradictions it creates, such as the fact that an individual 18 years old cannot drink alcohol but can be tried as an adult in a court of law or drafted into military service. The definition of childhood and the rights and responsibilities attached to that definition also vary cross-culturally. For example, in many states in the United States, a 17-year-old can drive but not drink alcohol, while in many European countries, such as the Netherlands, the opposite is true—young people are permitted to drink well before they gain the privilege of driving.

The meaning of race and ethnicity has also been shaped by the law. Historically, legal definitions often sought to facilitate the social exclusion or social control of particular groups. During the period of slavery, the United States developed a law saying that individuals with even one drop of black blood were to be considered black (Doob, 1999). Similarly, laws passed to define who constituted an American Indian rested on "blood quantum" or "degree of Indian blood," a measure that became useful in reducing the official number of Native Americans. At the turn of the twentieth century, this standard facilitated the federal government's strategy of forced assimilation for American Indians via land seizure and acceptance of the ideology of private property (versus collectively held property). Land seized was reallocated to individuals; "each Indian identified as being those documentably of *one-half or more Indian blood*, was entitled to receive title in fee of such a parcel; all others were simply disenfranchised altogether" (Jaimes, 1992). Today, federal laws continue to set standards that define who may be considered a member of a particular Native American tribe. The rigid, legal definition of identity may one day define Native Americans out of existence, because intermarriage with other groups will ensure a dilution of the percentage of "Indian-ness" the next generation can claim. As these examples illustrate, law plays a critical role in defining difference.

Law also plays an important role in maintaining differences once they are created, and helps to ensure that differences will "matter." For example, when one man hits another man, this behavior may be prosecuted as assault in every state. However, if a husband hits his wife, in many states this behavior is defined as "domestic violence." Not only does the phrase "domestic" make the violence sound less serious, but extensive research has evidenced that the widespread attitude that violence between intimates is less serious than violence between strangers slows police response, reduces the likelihood of arrest, and reduces penalties if the perpetrator is convicted (Belknap, 2007). This differential treatment of violence against women reinforces the differences between men and women and helps to ensure that the category "woman" will be less valued than the category "man." Historically, legal restrictions on voting rights, marriage rights, and property rights for women, certain racial and ethnic groups, children, the differently abled, and for individuals with particular sexual preferences have helped to ensure that socially constructed differences would privilege some and disadvantage others.

A great deal of scholarly work has explored the link between law and difference. This work has evidenced the way that law has been used to maintain and perpetuate ageism, racism, ethnic discrimination, gender discrimination, classism, and many other differences between people as well. Some of this work is drawn upon in the chapters that follow.

It is important to point out that law is not just a vehicle for creating and maintaining difference; it can also be used to ameliorate the negative consequences associated with difference in our society. It is evident that law served to restrict the rights of huge segments of the U.S. population when the country was founded. For example, when the Constitution was written, those who did not own property, as well as women and people of color were all precluded from voting in the newly created "democracy" (Parenti, 2007). However, the law has also been used to extend rights to groups formerly disenfranchised. Although some would argue that law is a limited method for creating social change because it may not change deeply held attitudes and beliefs, it can provide important protections to those who experience inequality. As Martin Luther King (as cited in Ayers, 1993:135) said,

> The law cannot make an employer love an employee, but it can prevent
> him from refusing to hire me because of the color of my skin. The habits,
> if not the hearts of people, have been and are being altered by legislative
> acts, judicial decisions, and executive orders.

Although efforts to use the law as an instrument of social change are often controversial, it is clear that laws and policies like affirmative action, busing, and hate crime legislation will continue to have an important impact upon the meanings and consequences attached to difference in our society. For this reason, later in the book, substantial attention will be devoted to the role of law in promoting social changes and ensuring greater justice.

DIFFERENCES OVERLAP AND INTERSECT WITH ONE ANOTHER

For the most part, the chapters in this book address difference by describing the historical and contemporary experiences of particular social groups in our society: African Americans, religious minorities, women, lesbians and gays, and so forth. Yet, identity is a complex construct for most people. Although it is possible to talk generically about "women" or "Hispanics" or "heterosexuals," most people would deny that their membership in a single group defines who they are as individuals. Nor can we simply add identities together if we want to understand the complex identity of a particular individual. Understanding the experience of "blacks" in the justice system and then analyzing the experience of "women," is not the same thing as understanding the experience of "black women." Similarly, men are never just "men" or children just "children"; they always occupy many categories simultaneously. People differ from one another in many ways and they belong to many groups at the same time—in other words, individuals reflect the *intersectionality* of multiple identities.

Most of the work that has been done to understand difference within the justice system analyzes only one difference at a time, focusing on race *or* gender *or* social class. Only recently has research been conducted that tries to analyze more complex relationships between differences and the way that differences intersect with one another to shape our experience of justice. For example, in their research on the criminalization of pregnant drug users, Rector and Wonders (2004) illustrate the way that race, class, and gender inequalities intersect to ensure that poor African American women will be much more likely to be criminalized for their drug use than others because they are much more likely to seek treatment in public hospitals, to come under the scrutiny of disproportionately white caregivers, and to be held responsible for the health problems of their unborn/newborn children (in marked contrast to drug-using fathers). (See Chapter 11 in this volume.) This research is just one example of a new wave of research that explores how differences intersect to shape the experience of justice.

The organization of this book uses specific historic group identities as a heuristic device for exploring differences. However, to the extent that it is possible, each chapter will touch on some of the ways that differences overlap to affect justice experiences and outcomes as a way to remind readers that lived experiences are always a product of unique intersections between individual biographies and the larger social world.

DIFFERENCES AND THEIR CONSEQUENCES CAN BE CHANGED

Perhaps the most hopeful aspect of studying difference is realizing that because differences are constructed by people, they can be changed by people. However, this is often more easily said than done. Even if we choose to live as though our race, sex, and ethnicity are irrelevant to who we are, these characteristics will still be important in our lives if the rest of the world links arrest decisions, employment decisions, educational opportunities, and so on to our membership in certain groups. In other words, attitudinal change toward difference is often very difficult to achieve in the short run; constructing difference differently often requires a great deal of patience. However, changing behavior is often easier to accomplish. We may not be able to easily change how others will perceive us, but we can restrict their ability to use differences as a basis for discrimination. The authors of this volume are convinced that those who work in the justice system have a special obligation to ensure that their behavior promotes justice rather than injustice.

Some people today claim that focusing on differences is actually part of the problem since dividing the world into separate groups—even for analytic purposes—reinforces the differences further. This is a serious danger. When we study "race" or "ethnicity," we make them "real" for the purpose of our study. When we divide people into "Hispanic" or "female" or "white" groups, we give the meaning attached to group membership greater weight. However, an even more serious risk occurs when differences that have real consequences are ignored. This is a risk criminal justice professionals cannot afford to take. For instance, claiming that race does not "really" exist in nature does little to help us explain why the majority of those incarcerated in U.S. jails and prisons are people of color (Sudbury, 2005). For those who work daily in justice occupations, misunderstanding or ignoring difference can be a matter of life and death. Assuming that the only danger in our society comes from people who look a certain way may make us vulnerable to serious harm from those who do not fit the stereotype.

Much research, for example, has shown that the crime committed by white collar and corporate offenders is far more harmful to the public than the crime committed by traditional street offenders (Michalowski and Kramer, 2006; Reiman, 2006; see also Chapter 5 of this volume). Partly because white-collar offenders and government officials do not fit our stereotypic image of the "criminal," we have failed to respond effectively to a wide range of extremely harmful behavior, including environmental pollution, consumer fraud, and occupational injury. This is a mistake that can be remedied only by careful attention to the construction of difference and the consequences of privileging some groups over others within a democratic society.

Part of what makes talking about difference a difficult task is that there is a tendency to assume that acknowledging differences must be a bad thing. But it is too simplistic to say, "Let's just do away with difference!" Indeed, if we could do away with difference, the world would be an extremely boring place. The problem is not with difference *per se*; the difficulty arises in the meaning we make out of difference. It is not a problem that some people have lighter skin and some darker, or that some people hold one set of religious beliefs but not another. The problem is that some societies treat those with one set of characteristics or beliefs as valuable and those with another set as less worthwhile. It is this process of giving meaning to and placing value on differences that requires our attention. This is especially critical within the justice system.

DIFFERENCE AND THE PURSUIT OF JUSTICE IN A GLOBALIZED WORLD

Ultimately, the goal of studying difference within the justice system is to ensure that, as a democratic society, we do not penalize people for the differences they exhibit and that we create a justice system that does more to foster human diversity rather than to constrain it. This has never been more important than it is today, given how rapidly globalization is changing our society and our world. Globalization has brought into sharp relief many of the cultural, religious, ethnic, and social differences that divide the planet. At the same time, it has created new opportunities for cooperation, collaboration, and global engagement. The next generation of justice professionals will have to understand much more about cultural diversity, global and comparative criminology, transnational crime and justice, and human rights issues than any generation thus far if they are to effectively foster the pursuit of justice in a globalized world. The new and pressing problems of our time—terrorism, cross-border migration, identity theft, genocide, and human trafficking, just to name a few—simply cannot be understood without broad intercultural and global knowledge.

Indeed, it is our job to *investigate difference* in order to protect the rich diversity of identities, groups, and individuals on the planet, and to guarantee that justice is available to all. The authors of this book recognize that this can be difficult to accomplish on a practical level. The goals of the justice system are often contradictory, and there is no clear standard of "fairness" with which we all agree. Too often, justice practitioners lack the knowledge and skills needed to ensure that justice prevails in an increasingly multicultural society and global world. Surely, one book cannot analyze, let alone overcome, all of the challenges associated with "difference" in the criminal justice system. However, by investigating how identity and difference affect the justice process, we do hope that this book will provide a useful starting point for those committed to creating a just society.

References

Ayers, Alex. 1993. *The Wisdom of Martin Luther King, Jr.* New York: Meridian.

Belknap, Joanne. 2007. *The Invisible Woman: Gender, Crime and Justice.* New York: Wadsworth.

Campbell, Mary E. 2007. The Implications of Racial Misclassification by Observers. *American Sociological Review* 72 (5): 750–765.

Chesney-Lind, Meda, and Katherine Irwin. 2008. *Beyond Bad Girls: Gender, Violence and Hype.* London: Routledge.

Diamond, Lisa M. 2003. Special Section: Integrating Research on Sexual-Minority and Heterosexual Development: Theoretical and Clinical Implications. *Journal of Clinical Child and Adolescent Psychology* 32 (4): 490–498.

Doob, Christopher Bates. 1999. *Racism: An American Cauldron.* New York: Longman.

Fausto-Sterling, Anne. 2000. *Sexing the Body: Gender Politics and the Construction of Sexuality.* New York: Basic Books.

Fenstermaker, Sarah, and Candace West. 2002. *Doing Gender, Doing Difference.* New York: Routledge.

Gabbidon, Shaun L., and Helen Taylor Greene. 2005. *Race and Crime.* Thousand Oaks: Sage Publications.

Hurst, Charles E. 2004. *Social Inequality: Forms, Causes, and Consequences.* Boston, MA: Pearson.

Jaimes, M. Annette. (Ed). 1992. Federal Indian Identification Policy: A Usurpation of Indigenous Sovereignty in North America. In *The State of Native America: Genocide, Colonization, and Resistance,* 123–138. Boston: South End Press.

Langston, Donna. 2004. Tired of Playing Monopoly? In *Race, Class and Gender: An Anthology,* ed. Margaret L. Anderson and Patricia Hill Collins, 140–149. New York: Wadsworth.

Levit, Nancy. 2000. *The Gender Line: Men, Women and the Law.* New York: New York University Press.

Lorber, Judith. 2007. *Gender Inequality: Feminist Theories and Politics.* New York: Oxford University Press.

Michalowski, Raymond J., and Ronald C. Kramer. 2006. *State-Corporate Crime: Wrongdoing at the Intersection of Business and Government.* New Brunswick, NJ: Rutgers University Press.

Ore, Tracy E. 2008. *The Social Construction of Difference and Inequality: Race, Class, Gender and Sexuality.* Boston, MA: McGraw-Hill.

Parenti, Michael. 2007. *Democracy for the Few.* Belmont, CA: Wadsworth.

Perry, Barbara. 2001. *In the Name of Hate: Understanding Hate Crimes.* London: Routledge.

Rector, Paula K., and Nancy A. Wonders. 2004. Intersecting Identities and Pregnant Drug Users: Victimization and Vulnerabilities to Criminalization. In *Victimizing Vulnerable Groups: Images of Uniquely High-Risk Crime Targets,* ed. Charisse Tia Maria Coston, 107–116. Westport, CT: Praeger.

Reiman, Jeffrey. 2006. *The Rich Get Richer and the Poor Get Prison,* 8th edn. Boston, MA: Allyn and Bacon.

Roediger, David R. 2006. *Working Toward Whiteness: How America's Immigrants Became White–the Strange Journey from Ellis Island to the Suburbs.* New York: Perseus Books.

Shelden, Randall G. 2007. *Controlling the Dangerous Classes: A Critical Introduction to the History of Criminal Justice.* Boston, MA: Allyn and Bacon.

Stearns, Peter N. 2006. *Childhood in World History.* London: Routledge.

Sudbury, Julia. 2005. *Global Lockdown: Race, Gender and the Prison-Industrial Complex.* London: Routledge.

Telles, Edward Eric. 2006. *Race in Another America: The Significance of Skin Color in Brazil.* Princeton, NJ/Oxford: Princeton University Press.

Uys, Pieter-Dirk. 1988. Chameleons Thrive Under Apartheid. *New York Times* Friday, September 23. pp. 27(N) pA35(L).

West, Candace, and Sarah Fenstermaker. 2002. Doing Difference. In *Doing Gender, Doing Difference,* ed. Sarah Fenstermaker and Candace West, 55–80. New York: Routledge.

Winant, Howard. 2004. *The New Politics of Race: Globalism Difference Justice.* Minneapolis, MN: University of Minnesota Press.

Wonders, Nancy A. 1998. Postmodern feminist criminology and social justice. In *Social Justice/Criminal Justice,* ed. Bruce Arrigo, 111–128. Belmont, CA: Wadsworth.

CHAPTER 3

Privilege and the Construction of Crime

Larry A. Gould

Rather than creating a sense of guilt or blame, the point of my work is to help those with the most power to recognize that privileging systems exist and that the existence of unearned disadvantage usually involves a corresponding existence of overadvantage.

—MCINTOSH, 2002

Following the quote above, Rothenberg (2004) suggests that it is impossible to make sense of the past or present without using race, class, gender, and sexuality as central to any description, discussion and/or analysis of crime and justice, as well as the privileges that can at times be associated with these categories; however, it is important to not blame those living in the present for the actions of the past, unless those living in the present continue to commit the errors of the past.

There are two kinds of privileges or entitlements: earned and unearned. Correspondingly, there are two types of disadvantage: earned and unearned. What is often forgotten is that some privileges that have been earned are the result of having access to unearned privileges or, stated differently, unearned privileges gained by earlier generations are often passed on to later generations in a way that unearned privileges accumulate through several generations. For example, Lopez (1996) has reviewed the history of laws and court decisions that defined who could and could not hold citizenship in the United States. These laws and court decisions were most often based on either the common knowledge or scientific evidence of who was white and who was not white (see *Ozawa* v. *United States*, 260 U.S. 178, 1922). "Common knowledge" refers to the once widely held rationale that the term "white person" had a well-settled meaning in common popular speech, while the "scientific evidence" approach relied on reference to the now very dated naturalistic studies of humankind. The advantages shared by some current citizens of the United States come as a result of their ancestors having been declared citizens because of their race, while others were denied their share because their ancestors were declared to be "not white."

Certainly, being acknowledged as white in the United States has its privilege, as does being male, being Protestant (religion can have differing impacts depending on geographic location), heterosexual, coming from a better neighborhood, having attended a better school, and/or coming from a politically/socially/economically advantaged background. None of these statuses are earned; they are all descriptions, thus ascribed. It would, almost, be possible to create a matrix of ascribed characteristics, giving some weightage to some of the characteristics that would describe a point system of unearned privilege. However, when addressing issues of privilege, it is important to be aware that many people are not aware of these and other unearned privileges and most often do not attempt to use them for personal gain or at the expense of others. We must also avoid blaming people for possessing unearned privileges or, as is noted below, we should condemn only those who make use of difference to meet their own needs, while attempting to educate all others.

Historically and today, race, class, and gender have been used as a means of assigning the "real" value of people, often without the knowledge of the people to whom the value has been assigned. Inclusion and, to some extent, exclusion from the criminal justice system as service providers, offenders, and victims may result from the application of characteristics that provide unearned or undeserved status. For instance, racial profiling, while a somewhat new term, is definitely a very old practice. The ability of a person to even move about in a free society has been defined by that person's race and gender (Meeks, 2000).

White males have tended to occupy most of the most powerful and privileged positions in our society. White males dominate our corporate structure, public bureaucracies, and other organizations; thus, they are in a position to make the decisions that have major consequences for American society (Murray and Smith, 1995). As noted by Schaef (1992:36), "The legal system is a game, and white men know how to play it to win. After all, they made the rules." Historically, much of the power of white males was achieved by basing voting rights on property ownership. This attitude was no more readily apparent than in the case of *Elk* v. *Wilkins* (1884), when the Supreme Court considered the question of whether Elk had been made a citizen by the Fourteenth Amendment and decided against him. "Indians born within the territorial limits of the United States . . . are no more born in the United States . . . than children of subjects of any foreign government born within the United States" (Rothenberg, 2004:487). This meant that minorities and women were systematically excluded from the power base (Murray and Smith, 1995). One of the effects of the dominant position that white males hold in our society is that they have become the baseline against which they themselves measure all other groups, but more importantly they have become the baseline against which criminality has been constructed.

In Chapter 2, Wonders discussed how the concepts of race, class, and gender are key to the principles of social organization and to the human interaction process (Chow, 1996). The construction of race, class, and gender is also central to the development of oppressive ideologies (Lieberson and Waters, 1988; Mann and

Zatz, 2002; Rothenberg, 2004; Rubin, 1998; Winant, 1997). Making use of difference (real or constructed) is an essential step in the racist and sexist process, which leads to the devaluation of groups typified as being "different" by the dominant group (Rubin, 1998; Walker, Spohn, and Delone, 1996; Yinger, 1994). Differences attributed to moral sensibilities have alternately been treated as either innate or acquired, as have cultural/value differences. It is common for a dominant group to use these categories in combination to devalue members of the less dominant group(s). White, male, middle-class, Protestant, heterosexuals of European descent (most likely northern European) usually set the "standard" against which others have been and continue to be judged (Foner, 1998; Sacks, 1998).

Although Wonders (Chapter 2) is correct in her views of how characteristics can impact the way in which individuals or groups are viewed, there is an additional ingredient that needs to be added to the process of inclusion and exclusion. There is a pattern running through the matrix of white male privilege, a pattern of assumptions about status which are passed on to white males at birth (Krugman, 2002). As noted by McIntosh (1998), the cultural turf is theirs by fact of their skin color and genitalia. These attributes serve as assets in terms of access to education, career opportunities, and making the social systems work to their advantage. McIntosh refers to this form of privilege as *unearned advantage*. Power from unearned privilege can look like strength when it is, in fact, permission to escape or to dominate.

The white privilege that results from *unearned entitlements* can lead to *unearned advantages* (McIntosh, 1998). These unearned advantages can privilege an individual in their interactions with the justice system in ways that are sometimes difficult to understand, particularly if one is white. Thus, being a white male privileges an individual by providing an invisible set of assets that can be used to their advantage every day. McIntosh (1998) notes that white, particularly white male, "privilege is like an invisible weightless knapsack of special provisions, maps, passports, codebooks, visas, clothes, tools and blank checks." The irony is that white males are all-too-often unaware that they occupy privileged positions (Murray and Smith, 1995; Rubin, 1998; Sacks, 1998).

The outcome of these privileges can be measured in many ways, both related to and outside of the justice system. Statistically, white males constitute 39.3% of the population in the United States, but account for 82.5% of the Forbes 400 (individuals with a net worth of at least $265 million), 77% of members of Congress, 92% of state governors, 70% of tenured college faculty, almost 90% of daily newspaper editors, and 77% of television news directors. It is interesting to note that these statistics have not changed since first writing this chapter for the first edition of this book (about 9 years ago). The effect of this is to place white males in a particularly powerful position so that they can make the rules by which others must play the game. As the reader reviews the information in this chapter, there is another set of statistics which is equally impressive, including the following: 94% of serial killers have been white males; 96% of those individually accused of environmental crimes have been white males; and the vast majority of those accused and/or arrested for sexual abuse are white males. Most whites in the United States think that racism does not affect them because they are not people of color, they do not see "whiteness" as a racial identity (McIntosh, 1998).

One factor clearly emerges from all the interlocking forms of oppressions: they take both active forms that we can see and embedded forms that, as a member of the dominant group, one is taught not to see. That is, whites, as an ethnic group, do not see themselves as racist because they are taught to recognize racism only as individual acts by members of white society, never in the form of the invisible system that confers unsought racial or sexual dominance on the group at birth (McIntosh, 1998).

The criminal justice system, a white-male–controlled group of organizations, has played an important role in maintaining the status quo of the dominant group(s) by using the law to maintain, among other things, social differentiation. Martin and Jurik (1996) suggest that *social differentiation*, or the practice of distinguishing categories based on some attribute or set of attributes, is a fundamental social process and the basis for differential evaluations and unequal rewards. Given the mission of the criminal justice system—to control conduct that violates the criminal laws of the state (Martin and Jurik, 1996)—and the vast discretion accorded to the members of the system (police, courts, and corrections), it has become a powerful gatekeeper in determining which groups and individuals are going to have their visibility raised as the result of some action or inaction on the part of the system. For instance, the "Jim Crow" laws (1867–1965), which were designed to maintain the separation of blacks from whites and to control the behavior of blacks in the South, are an example of the types of law used to subordinate other groups. Another example of laws used to subordinate groups are those that prohibited Irish and Italian Catholics from teaching in public schools or even entering certain trades.

There are many myths and misperceptions concerning the involvement of the majority population as offenders, victims, and service providers in the criminal justice system. These myths have often been perpetuated by the majority population to either create the image that they were the protectors of the moral fiber of the country or to hide the fact that they were responsible for a much greater proportion of the crime problem than they wished to acknowledge. This chapter focuses on the involvement of majority population members in the criminal justice system, but first we discuss how the "majority population" (Franklin and Moss, 1994; Wirth, 1945) is defined and how "image of whiteness", or "visibility" (i.e., being different from the majority population) (McIntosh, 1998; Stanko, 1990) either increases or decreases the chance that an individual will become an offender, victim, or service provider. This chapter also reviews the majority population(s) in terms of both their efforts to protect their status and the perceptions that these efforts have created.

CONTINUUM OF DISCRIMINATION OR DISPARATE TREATMENT

Discrimination or disparate treatment exists on a scale, the polar ends of which are systematic discrimination and pure justice (Walker, Spohn, and DeLone, 1996). *Systematic discrimination* refers to the type of discrimination that occurs at all levels of a social system including the criminal justice system. It is evident at all times and all places within the system, including arrest, prosecution, and sentencing. *Institutionalized discrimination* involves racial disparities in outcomes that result from established (institutionalized) policies. It is often the case that such policies are not directly related to race or gender, but involve *de facto* practices that become codified, and thus sanctioned, by *de jure* mechanisms. Two examples of this type of treatment are the "poll" or voting tax and the height/weight limitations to be considered for employment as a police officer.

Until the 1960s, in many parts of the South, one of the requirements to vote included the payment of a poll tax. If the individual was unable to pay the tax, that person could not vote. Blacks, even though they might have been registered to vote, were often unable to vote because they could not afford the poll tax. Secondly, women and some members of minority groups were frequently excluded from joining police forces because they did not meet the minimum height and weight requirements to be police officers. The height and weight requirements were usually based on the average height and weight of northern European white males.

Contextual discrimination involves discrimination in certain situations or contexts. One of the most common examples is the victim–offender relationship and its outcome in death penalty cases. Controlling for other causal factors, the likelihood of a black receiving the death penalty for murdering a white is much greater than the likelihood of a white receiving the death penalty for murdering a black. Individual discrimination results from discriminate treatment of disadvantaged or minority group members by an individual most frequently acting alone. The acts of this individual do not represent the general patterns of the rest of the criminal justice agency. For example, a police officer, parole officer, prosecutor, or judge may single out a minority group member for harsher treatment. Pure justice refers to a system in which there is no discrimination at any time or place in the criminal justice system.

MAJORITY POPULATION DEFINED

A full explanation of the term "Anglo-Saxon" is beyond the limited scope and space of this chapter (see Aguirre and Turner, 1998); however, a short description will be useful. For our purposes, the term Anglo-Saxon or WASP (White Anglo-Saxon Protestant) refers to a person of northern European cultural and social institutional heritage. This category, while a mix of ethnic backgrounds, is usually dominated by the English and to some extent other northern Europeans. It should be noted that the term English, as opposed to British, has been deliberately used here. British is a term most often used to refer to the Commonwealth, including parts of Ireland, Scotland, and Wales, whereas English is a term used to refer to a specific subdivision of that Commonwealth. More specifically, the term WASP refers to an ethnic complex consisting of northern European ethnic stock with light skin, most often with Protestant religious beliefs, Protestant-inspired values based on individualism, hard work, savings, and secular material success, and English cultural traditions (language, laws, and beliefs) and institutional structures (politics, economics, and education) (Aguirre and Turner, 1998).

It is, of course, interesting to note that many of the Anglo-Saxons who arrived in the United States in the various waves of immigration were themselves members of a subordinate group and, thus, the victims of disparate treatment in the countries from which they came. Examples include the Puritans, the Quakers, many debtors, and landless workers. The Anglo-Saxons established themselves in what is now the eastern United States, putting into place the cultural and institutional structures by which all later groups would be compared and evaluated, and would have to compete within. The elite members of this group tend to be overrepresented by the descendants of those who arrived prior to the American Revolution. This observation is contextually important because it was the elite members of this group who came to have the power to influence beliefs and, thus, the development of policy regarding how people are either rewarded or punished for violating the rules and standards set by the dominant group (Aguirre and Turner, 1998). The dominance of white ethnic groups, especially those in the Anglo-Saxon core as well as others who have adopted this core culture, is reflected not only in their economic well-being (Aguirre and Turner, 1998), but in the laws, mores, and cultural means by which the effects of differences are emphasized in the United States. The core group is generally considered to be composed of groups from England and Germany, but includes those of Scottish (Protestant), Irish (Protestant), Dutch, and Scandinavian descent. An example of those groups that have been assimilated, for the most part, into the core includes the Irish (Catholic), Italians, and Jews. Most research suggests that the members of the original core, and later immigrants who were absorbed into this core, do much better politically, economically, and educationally than do other groups, particularly those groups that can be singled out based on skin color or facial configurations.

WHITE ETHNIC GROUPS

Biological differences, as noted by Wonders in Chapter 2, are superficial, often inaccurate, and mostly difficult to use as markers of boundaries between peoples; nevertheless, they are important sociologically because they allow for the social construction of difference (Lopez, 1996). It is interesting to note that current genetic research suggests that there is only eight-tenths of 1% (0.8%) difference in the genetic makeup between individuals and, of that small amount, only six-tenths accounts for racial differences. It is unfortunate that many people continue to believe that members of other racial or ethnic groups are biologically distinctive; thus, they tend to respond to them as being different, and most often as being inferior. It is quite common that people associate superficial biological differences with variations in psychological, intellectual, and behavioral makeup, and in cultural and/or ethnic difference. Because of this, they all too often feel justified in using discriminatory behavior (Aguirre and Turner, 1998). The important thing to note is that manner of dress, body type, and facial configuration, as they all relate to either positive or negative attributes, are social constructions *defined by the dominant group based on their own physical appearance.* It is the mark of the dominant group that they have the power to define not only what constitutes difference, but also the intensity and methods of discrimination. Given the present levels of discrimination, whether systematic, institutional, contextual, or the result of individual acts perpetrated on currently disenfranchised groups (African Americans, Hispanics, Asians, Native Americans), it is often forgotten that similar discrimination was faced by the newly arrived Irish (Catholic), Italians, and Jews, who are now members of the core, of just a century ago. One of the reasons, among many, that the former groups are less assimilated is their *visibility*; that is, their outward appearance is sufficiently different from the latter group that they do not fit the "image of white."

The dominant group uses several methods by which it can either establish or rationalize its superiority over other groups, one of which is reliance on the belief in a natural hierarchy. This was the method most often used by the "core" group in earlier American history. It should be noted at this point that this is also the method used by white supremacist groups today. Historically, and contemporarily, dominant and "wannabe" dominant groups often absolve themselves of the racist or sexist connotations in the way difference is defined. Belief in, and use of, the nature/biology paradigm performs a critical function in the role of absolution. Absolution in this case is gained through one or more of the following means, all of which avoid any condemnation of the majority group for the problems of the disadvantaged group(s). First, it implicitly and explicitly defines a hierarchical order as natural. That order is, of course, represented as the natural order of things, with the dominant group at the top. It is suggested here that other groups are atavistic throwbacks to earlier forms of human evolution. Second, it holds the victim(s) responsible for their own condition, thus absolving the dominant group from any responsibility for the conditions of the subordinate group. The dominant group suggests that no better can be expected of the subordinate classes because they do not know any better, and even if they did, it would not matter because they could not act any better anyway. Third, it forestalls efforts to change the ranking of the groups, whether racial, ethnic, religious, or gender related, by portraying the differences as one of kind, not degree (Miller and Levin, 1998). Again, the argument of the dominant class is that other groups are most likely genetically different, and thus they are different species rather than simply people with different cultural values.

VISIBILITY

Each of us also has "ascribed characteristics," such as race, gender, age, and outer appearance of social class. These ascribed characteristics often affect the way in which others react to us and, in turn, how we react to others. In general, the lesser an individual's appearance mimics the characteristics associated with the appearance of northern Europeans, the more visible that individual becomes (Lopez, 1996; Meeks, 2000). Conversely, the more closely an individual "fits" the profile of northern Europeans in terms of ascribed status and the more "standard" that individual's appearance is in terms of dress, skin color, and so on, the more invisible they become.

Research on crime, deviance, and living on the fringe tends to focus on acts or behavior committed by groups other than the "invisible white." Moreover, for crimes in which Euro-Americans (typically northern Europeans and also now Irish, Italians, and Jews) are most likely to be the offenders (e.g., white-collar crimes, arson, driving under the influence, burglary, and serial murders), race is usually not mentioned as a factor in the crime (Ellis, 1988; Hackett, McKillop, and Wang, 1988; Kunen, 1990; Miller and Levin, 1998; Podolsky *et al.*, 1990; Van Biema, 1995) On the other hand, it is quite typical for researchers to mention, either as a means of comparison or as an example, the race of either the individual offender or the group of offenders when talking about street crimes, drugs, violent crimes, and crimes of passion (Ellis, 1988; Hackett, McKillop, and Wang, 1988; Van Biema, 1995; Walker, Spohn, and DeLone, 1996). This typification of offenders has created a widely shared stereotype of what the potential offender might look like. While typification is also based on ethnicity, gender, manner of dress, styling of hair, or body ornamentation, the most common characteristic on which it is based is race. For example, even though African Americans are more likely to be the victims of crime, whites express higher levels of fear of crime. Crime, for whites, tends to be a code word for fear of social change (Rosenbaum, Lewis, and Grant, 1986; Walker, Spohn, and DeLone, 1996).

Miller and Levin (1998) suggest that the imagery of crime that has been created by the media and ourselves is that the only true victims of crime are innocent whites caught in the crossfire or preyed upon by others. This further suggests that the "imagery also implies that whites who do commit violent crimes are somehow unique—they don't reflect white culture and society more generally" (Miller and Levin, 1998). Of particular note is the case of Susan Smith, a white female living in Union, South Carolina. The nation was ready, on face value, to believe her story of a demonic, carjacking, black devil when, in fact, she was the murderer of her own sons (Rome, 2002). The media focus on street crime typically does not pay attention to the participation of whites in those activities, even though evidence suggests that the majority of participants are white (Miller and Levin, 1998; Walker, Spohn, and DeLone, 1996). Researchers, the media, politicians, and the police have helped create, for the rest of us, an image of a potential offender who is non-white, young, and male (Rosenbaum *et al.*, 1986; Walker *et al.*, 1996).

As previously noted, "difference is socially constructed"; that is race, ethnicity, sexual orientation, gender, age, and social class take on social content that is out of context with their real meaning. The perception of difference and how it is constructed either increases or decreases the visibility of an individual or group. There appears to be one set of rules for middle-class whites and another for minority members and for whites who did not sufficiently fit the image of white. It is, however, important to note that there are many varieties of "whiteness" (Winant, 1997) and that over time many but not all newly arrived groups have been assimilated into the core (Curtis, 1971). Among the groups that have been mostly assimilated are the Irish, the Jews, and the southern and southeastern Europeans, predominately composed of Italians.

THE CATHOLIC IRISH, ITALIANS, AND JEWS

When the Catholic Irish, Italians, and Jews began to arrive in large numbers in the United States in the nineteenth century, the dominant Anglo-Saxon population undertook to portray the new immigrants as distinct and biologically different races. Members of these groups became the targets of discrimination as the result of their religions, their poverty, and their willingness to work for lower wages than earlier immigrants. Much of the stereotyping of the Irish that occurred in America resulted from the British construction of the image of the Irish in Ireland. The Irish, often for their own self-protection, formed groups, some of which became a part of the criminal class. This served as evidence to the dominant classes that the Irish could never be anything more than a bunch of thugs. They were stereotyped as being apelike, drunken, hostile, and immoral (Curtis, 1971) and were viewed as the "missing link" between apes, Africans, and the English (Aguirre and Turner, 1998). Catholic Irish were excluded by Protestant employers from anything but unskilled work as a result of the belief (misbelief) in their racial inferiority, low intelligence, pugnaciousness, and unreliability (Aguirre and Turner, 1998; Lieberson and Waters, 1988). One of the stereotypes about the Irish that seems to endure is their involvement in graft, corruption, and other forms of criminal activity associated with big-city or local politics

(Aguirre and Turner, 1998). It is noted, however, that success at the local political level did not translate into success at higher levels, where the Catholic Irish were excluded from the judiciary and executive branches of government until the 1930s. One of the arguments (excuses) for excluding the Irish from higher positions was that they owed their allegiance to the Pope in Rome, not to the United States.

The experience of the Italian immigrants was similar to that of the Catholic Irish. There was some immigration of the more highly educated Italians from northern Italy in the early part of the nineteenth century. The northern Italians assimilated more easily than the later arriving southern Italians, who were less educated, less skilled, and of generally darker complexion. Southern Italians were often portrayed as a distinct "race," with lower intelligence, a different set of cultural values, and criminal tendencies, as well as being oversexed and Catholic (Gambino, 1974; Kamin, 1974; Lopreato, 1970; Tomasi and Engel, 1970). Italians were also viewed as being ingratiating, jealous, racist, and physically tough (Gambino, 1974). They are often credited in the movies with having invented organized crime in America, but it should be noted that up to the time of prohibition, Irish and Jewish Americans controlled most of the organized syndicates. While organized crime was a means for upward mobility in a hostile society, the crime rates for Italians were actually quite low (Lopreato, 1970).

As was the case with the Irish and the Italians, but for a much longer period, Jews have been considered a separate "race." The basis for this is, of course, social and cultural, not biological. Most often, Jews are identified by religious beliefs with a foundation in the Torah, or the first five books of the Bible (Aguirre and Turner, 1988). An additional source of Jewish identity is the awareness of a shared history of persecution and the sense that they constitute a community with traditions that are very different from those of Protestants or Catholics (Aguirre and Turner, 1988). However, it is the very organization, networks, and shared beliefs that have allowed them to survive extremes in discrimination.

Some of the negative perceptions that have been used to stereotype Jews include beliefs that they are money-grubbing, materialistic, sly, involved in a "Jewish conspiracy" to control all governments, and that they control all of the banks. Despite a record of economic and academic success, Jews have been underrepresented in many occupations, professions, and high-level positions due to discriminatory practices that result from the negative perceptions listed above (Alba and Moore, 1982; Zweigenhaft and Domhoff, 1982).

The Irish, the Italians, and the Jews began to make strides economically, educationally, and socially by the turn of the century; however, they came into serious conflict with the African Americans who were migrating north. African Americans were viewed as a threat to the Irish-developed unions because they were used as strikebreakers and would work for lower wages. African Americans still suffer from the legacy of this hostility (Bonacich, 1976), as noted by the school busing riots in Boston and the attacks on blacks in predominantly Irish neighborhoods (Bensonhurst). Additionally, blacks are still excluded from, or only included in limited numbers in, certain Irish-controlled labor unions and trades. The Catholic Irish have more easily assimilated into the mainstream of American society and are today virtually indistinguishable from the descendants of the Anglo-Saxon core in terms of their place in the American socioeconomic hierarchy (Aguirre and Turner,

1988; Lieberson and Waters, 1988). This is in large part due to their ability to become invisible or blend in with the Anglo-Saxon core, that is, the fact that they are white.

THE TYPICAL OFFENDER, VICTIM, AND SERVICE PROVIDER: GATEKEEPING

Gatekeeping of one sort or another is common within virtually any society. By *gatekeeping* we mean that access to or exclusion from the resources or rewards in the society are often closely guarded. The various organizations in the criminal justice system often participate in the gatekeeping process by determining who becomes a police officer, lawyer, correctional officer, or a member of many of the other professions in the system. Criminal justice organizations also determine who will be accorded the official status of victim and offender.

Members of criminal justice organizations, either consciously or unconsciously, use many standards, including visibility, as measures of who gets to be a member (Farmer, 1999; Meeks, 2000). Many ascribed statuses such as height, weight, physical ability not related to job expectations, gender, and race have at one time or another been used to either include or exclude a person as an offender, victim, or service provider. What this means is that as an individual's ascribed status approximates or resembles that of those people already in the criminal justice organization, there is an increased likelihood of that individual being accepted as a new member. Conversely, the greater the difference of the individual's ascribed status from that of the majority of the members of the criminal justice organization, the less likely that individual is to be included as a member of the organization. Gould (1997) found that black female police officers had the greatest difficulty in entering the police force and, if they were hired, they had an increased likelihood of leaving the force within a few years. Other examples of exclusion and inclusion based on ascribed status include the following: women have been excluded from policing as a result of the perception that an officer must be physically strong; blacks have been arrested out of proportion to their representation in the population due to their race; Latinas have been accorded less status in the justice system as compared to white women; and blacks have been excluded from law schools.

The Irish, Italians, and Jews (males) have been more successful in moving into criminal justice organizations as service providers than blacks, Latinos, Native Americans, and Asians. Blacks, Latinos, Native Americans, and certain groups of Asians have had a greater likelihood of being included as offenders, and these same groups have often not been accorded an equal status as victims when compared to whites. In part, these differences can be attributed to the visibility of blacks, Latinos, Native Americans, and Asians when compared to the Irish, Italians, and Jews.

White America has been successful in creating the image of the black man, and, to a lesser extent, the black woman as the universal bogeyman (Fishman, 1998), while whites, males in particular, have been imaged (falsely) as the universal good guy (Hamm, 1998). Whites, particularly white women, are most often portrayed as the victims of crime (Castro, 1998; Harjo, 1998), while minorities are most often portrayed as the offenders (Castro, 1998; Hamm, 1998; Harjo, 1998; Laidler, 1998). Whites, particularly white males, have been advantaged in terms of their employment as service providers (Martin and Jurik, 1996). In the next three subsections of this chapter, we will review some of the descriptive statistics associated with the gatekeeping practices of criminal justice organizations.

THE TYPICAL OFFENDER?

The crimes that receive the most attention, particularly from the media, politicians, and criminal justice policy makers, are the so-called "street crimes" such as murder, robbery, and rape (Meeks, 2000; Rodriguez, 2002; Walker *et al.*, 1996). For all too many people, particularly those of European heritage, the image of the criminal is a young African American (in some areas of the country, a young Latino) male armed with a gun who commits a robbery, rape, or murder. In other words, the term "crime" is synonymous with "minority crime" (Walker *et al.*, 1996). It thus comes as something of a surprise to many to learn that the majority of violent crimes are committed by young white males (Hamm, 1998). It is somewhat uncomfortable for many, particularly whites, to learn that they account for 54% of the yearly arrests for murder, rape, robbery, and aggravated assault (Donziger, 1996; Miller, 1996) and 66.9% of all crime is committed by whites (Bureau of Justice Statistics, 1997). While much of the other violent crime is committed by young black males from urban areas (Boyum and Kleiman, 1995; Fagan, 1992), it is interesting to note that much of that violence is related to trade in crack cocaine and heroin, a market largely supported by middle-class white males (Chambliss, 1994).

It is very easy for the majority group to blame those people who look and act different for crime problems, while ignoring the fact that white males are responsible for the vast majority of white-collar crime (see Chapter 5). The vast majority of bank frauds, insider trading, junk bond deals, environmental crime, and savings and loan frauds have been committed by white males. The Charles Keating (Lincoln Savings and Loan Association) scandal in Arizona cost investors more money than was stolen in all banks robberies in at least the last 20 years. In 1986, Michael Milkin was indicted for insider trading, racketeering, market manipulation, price fixing, and other criminal stock market activities. The results of his activities led to large-scale layoffs, loss of savings for thousands of individuals, and the firing of many people. The damage done to the ordinary citizen by white-collar crime committed by white males has a much greater impact than all other crimes put together. The difficulty of the majority white community in accepting the image of offenders as being white, whether it be for violent crimes or for white-collar crimes, results in a misplaced fear and certainly a prejudicial response to white crime. When former Governor of Arizona Fyfe Symington was on trial for fraudulent schemes, his biggest defenders in the community were older white retirees, many of whom were demanding that the government go after real crimes such as drug users and burglars. What this means is that if television and movies, along with the news media, were to portray offenders in proportion to their actual numbers, they would have to give more play to white crime. In addition, many middle-class whites would have to rethink the image of the criminal most likely to be of threat to them. In short, the image of the stereotypical criminal would have to be adjusted.

THE TYPICAL VICTIM?

The white majority, when it thinks of the victim of crime, is more likely to imagine a person very much like themselves. As already noted here, our perception of crime and the criminal is, to a large extent, shaped by the media, whether it is the nightly news, news documentaries, films, and/or television. Often, the assumption of too many of the dominant-group members of our society is that the typical crime is a violent crime, that the typical victim is white, and that the typical offender is African

American, Latino, or some other non-white. There is compelling evidence to suggest that this picture is inaccurate on all counts. A review of the *Sourcebook* (Bureau of Justice Statistics, 1995) provides the following picture.

The homicide (victim) rate for African Americans (34.0 per 100,000 persons) was seven times greater than was the rate for whites (4.9 per 100,000 persons). For males between the ages of 14 and 17 the difference was even greater (65.9 for African Americans and 8.5 for whites).

African American–headed households have higher victimization rates for burglary (69.3 per 1,000 for blacks and 44.3 per 1,000 for whites), household larceny (218.5 per 1,000 for blacks and 203.5 per 1,000 for whites), and motor vehicle theft (22.2 per 1,000 for blacks and 12.1 per 1,000 for whites).

Victimization rates for crimes of violence were 88.7, 100.1, and 110.8 per 1,000 persons age 12 and older for whites, Hispanics, and African Americans, respectively. The victimization rate for African Americans for robbery was 15.6 and for whites 4.7. African Americans were about three times more likely to be the victims of robbery than were whites.

The stereotypical victim is often portrayed as either a white female or an elderly white person. While this does hold true for certain crime types, it does not hold true for those crimes listed above. The image of the "victim" has led to an inordinate fear of being the victim of those crimes listed above, by both the elderly and females; thus it has played a significant role in how these people conduct their lives.

Minority victims of crime are often discounted by the criminal justice system and the dominant members of our society. It is sometimes hard for whites to develop sympathy for members of other racial groups who have been victimized. As a young police officer in the early 1970s, I was counseled that "the only reason that we make reports on niggras [*sic*] killing niggras is that the district attorney needs the easy convictions." In this sense, minority victimization tends to be invisible to whites. Because the vast majority of police officers are white, the insensitivity to minority needs as crime victims tends to be very broad and runs very deep. The dominant members of the society find it difficult to be sympathetic to the problems of members of the minority community. This can be demonstrated by the number of police officers, amount of resources, types of crime on which the officers focus, and attention paid to the needs of middle- and upper-class neighborhoods as compared to minority neighborhoods. A group of white kids walking the streets in a white neighborhood is most often viewed as kids having fun, while a group of black or Latino kids walking in their own neighborhood is often viewed as a gang. White communities have greater political power to demand police protection and get results than do minority communities, even though minority communities suffer greater rates of crime.

THE TYPICAL SERVICE PROVIDER?

Each of the criminal justice professions (police, corrections, and those associated with the legal profession) is currently dominated by whites (males) of European extraction, including the Irish, Italians, and Jews. As the "controllers" within the justice system, whites, particularly white males, have variously excluded females and members of the less dominant ethnic groups from entry into these professions. Currently, white males constitute 75.2% of all full-time police officers in local police departments

(Bureau of Justice Statistics, 1997), 60% of all full-time correctional employees (Martin and Jurik, 1996), and 60% of enrollees at ABA-approved U.S. law schools (Abel, 1989). While the number of black police officers in the 50 largest cities has increased since 1983, in some cases by as much as 128%, they are still underrepresented. Even when blacks do become police officers they suffer from double marginality (Alex, 1969). Black officers must deal with the expectation that they will give other blacks a break, while often experiencing overt racism from white police officers. Another problem is the difficulty that black officers have in attaining command positions despite the growing numbers of black officers on most police forces.

Latinos have also made some gains in terms of their representation on police forces, although these gains are generally not as dramatic as those made by blacks. Additionally, the changes for Latinos have been very uneven nationwide, with some cities showing gains while others have shown losses in the number of Latino officers employed (see Chapter 9).

While courts have repeatedly supported the addition of women to the ranks of policing by striking down entrance requirements that were intended to keep all but a few women from qualifying as successful candidates, their numbers have grown to only about 9% of all sworn officers (Daum and Johns, 1994; Martin, 1988). Women also continue to be underrepresented in the senior administrative ranks, and they are often assigned duties that underutilize their skills (Garrison, Grant, and McCormick, 1988; Martin and Jurik, 1996). Surveys of male officers indicate that only one-third accept women on patrol, and that less than half of the male officers believe that women can handle the physical requirements of the job as well as men (Brown, 1994).

For the Anglo-Saxon core and for the later arriving Irish, Italians, and Jews, employment in the justice system, particularly in policing, has been either a means of controlling local neighborhood politics or a means to move up the ladder of success in America. This means that it has been important to control entry into the justice system so as to, either knowingly or unknowingly, maintain the privileges that are attached to being white. Along with control of entry into the justice system comes the means to control who gets arrested and for which crimes. Again, we can see that control of the arrest process privileges those ethnic groups who play a dominant role in the justice system.

CONCLUSION

It is vital that we not place the blame for unearned privileges on white males or, for that matter, on any present-day category of people. That blame should only be reserved for those who do not recognize the extent of those privileges and more importantly do not wish to seek change in the system.

The core members of the dominant group have long since ceased to be in the numerical majority; however, they, and those who have been assimilated into that core, still tend to be in the political and economic majority. By the year 2035, whites will be in the numerical minority in the United States, and white males will be less than 25% of the population, but will still control 70 to 80% of the wealth.

If the criminal justice system continues to not represent the minorities—that is, the peoples who are currently in the category of more visibility—what will this mean for the effectiveness and reputation of the criminal justice system? It is not only necessary that the deliberate disadvantaging of groups cease, but also that the more insidious advantaging of one group over another cease. For the system to continue to function and, better yet, to improve the delivery of its services, it will be necessary for the "visible" to become "invisible" in terms of how victims are treated, how service providers are hired, and how offenders are treated.

For the institutional discrimination to end, for unfair economic competition to assume some sense of fairness, and for Social Darwinist ideologies to be relegated to the dustbin, the barriers that have to this point either prohibited or reduced the likelihood of non-white minorities from entering the justice system on a level-playing field with whites must be removed.

References

Alba, Richard, and Gwen Moore. 1982. Ethnicity in the American Elite. *American Sociological Review* 47: 373–383.

Abel, Richard L. 1989. *American Lawyers*. New York, NY: Oxford.

Alex, Nicholas. 1969. *Black in Blue: A Study of the Negro Policeman*. New York, NY: Appleton-Century-Crofts.

Aguirre, Adalberto, and Jonathan Turner. 1998. *American Ethnicity: The Dynamics and Consequences of Discrimination*, 2nd edn. Boston, MA: McGraw-Hill.

Bonacich, Edna. 1976. Advanced Capitalism and Black-White Race Relations in the United States: A Split Labor Market Interpretation. *American Sociological Review* 41: 34–51.

Boyum, David, and Mark Kleiman. 1995. Alcohol and Other Drugs. In *Crime*, ed. James Q. Wilson and Joan Petersilia, 47–94. San Francisco, CA: Institute for Contemporary Studies.

Brown, Mary. 1994. The Plight of Female Police: A Survey of NW Patrolmen. *Police Chief* 61: 50–53.

Bureau of Justice Statistics. 1995. *Sourcebook of Criminal Justice Statistics, 1994*. Washington, DC: U.S. Department of Justice.

Bureau of Justice Statistics. 1997. *Sourcebook of Criminal Justice Statistics, 1996*. Washington, DC: U.S. Department of Justice.

Castro, Diego. 1998. Hot Blood and Easy Virtue: Mass Media and the Making of Racist Latino Stereotypes. In *Images of Color: Images of Crime*, ed. Coramae Richey Mann and Marjorie S. Zatz, 134–144. New York: Roxbury Publishing.

Chambliss, William J. 1994. Why the U.S. Government Is Not Contributing to the Resolution of the Nation's Drug Problem. *International Journal of Health Services* 24: 675–690.

Chow, Esther Ngan-Ling. 1996. Transforming Knowledge: Race, Class and Gender. In *Race, Class & Gender: Common Bonds, Different Voices*, ed. Esther Ngan-Ling Chow, Doris Wilkinson, and Maxine Baca Zinn. Thousand Oaks, CA: Sage Publications.

Curtis, Lewis P. 1971. *Apes and Angels: The Irish Victorian Caricature*. Washington, DC: Smithsonian Institution Press.

Daum, James, and Cindy Johns. 1994. Police Work from a Woman's Perspective. *Police Chief* 61: 46–49.

Donziger, Steven R. 1996. *The Real War on Crime: The Report of the National Criminal Justice Commission*. New York, NY: Harper Perennial.

Ellis, David. 1988. Hedda's Hellish Tale. *Time*, December 12, 32.

Fagan, Jeffrey. 1992. Drug Selling and Licit Income in Distressed Neighborhoods: The Economic Lives of Street-Level Drug Users and Dealers. In *Drugs, Crime and Social Isolation*, ed. Adele V. Harrell and George E. Peterson, 78–101. Washington, DC: Urban Institute Press.

Farmer, John J. 1999. *Final Report of the State Police Review Team*. New Jersey Department of

Law and Public Safety, Office of the Attorney General.

Fishman, Laura. 1998. Images of Crime and Punishment: The Black Bogeyman and White Self-Righteousness. In *Images of Color: Images of Crime*, ed. Coramae Richey Mann and Marjorie S. Zatz, 109–126. New York, NY: Roxbury Publishing.

Foner, Eric. 1998. Who is an American? In *Race, Class, and Gender in the United States: An Integrated Study*, ed. Paula S. Rothenberg, 4th edn., 84–91. New York, NY: St. Martin's Press.

Franklin, John H., and Alfred A. Moss, Jr. 1994. *From Slavery to Freedom: A History of African Americans*, 7th edn., New York, NY: Knopf.

Gambino, Richard. 1974. *Blood of My Blood: The Dilemma of Italian-Americans*. Garden City, NY: Doubleday.

Garrison, Carole, Nancy Grant, and Kenneth McCormick. 1988. Utilization of Police Women. *Police Chief* 55: 32–33.

Gould, Larry. 1997. Can Old Dogs Be Taught New Tricks? Teaching Cultural Diversity to Police Officers. *Policing* 20: 339–357.

Hackett, George, Peter McKillop, and Dorothy Wang. 1988. A tale of abuse. *Newsweek*, December 12, 56.

Hamm, Mark S. 1998. The Laundering of White Collar Crime. In *Images of Color: Images of Crime*, ed. Coramae Richey Mann and Marjorie S. Zatz, 244–256. New York, NY: Roxbury Publishing.

Harjo, Suzan Shown. 1998. Redskins, savages and other enemies: A historical overview of American media coverage of native people. In *Images of Color: Images of Crime*, ed. Coramae Richey Mann and Marjorie S. Zatz, 30–46. New York, NY: Roxbury Publishing.

Kamin, Leon J. 1974. *The Science and Politics of I.Q.* New York, NY: John Wiley and Sons.

Krugman, Paul. 2002. The Sons Also Rise. *New York Times*, November 22.

Kunen, James S. 1990. Risen from Near Death, the Central Park Jogger Makes her Day in Court One to Remember. *People*, July 30, 32.

Laidler, Karen J. 1998. Immigrant Bashing and Nativist Political Movements. In *Images of Color: Images of Crime*, ed. Coramae Richey

Mann and Marjorie S. Zatz, 169–178. New York, NY: Roxbury Publishing.

Lieberson, Stanley, and Mary C. Waters. 1988. *From Many Strands: Racial and Ethnic Groups in Contemporary America*. New York, NY: Russell Sage.

Lopez, Ian F. Haney. 1996. *White by Law: The Legal Construction of Race*. New York: New York University Press.

Lopreato, Joseph. 1970. *Italian Americans*. New York, NY: Random House.

Mann, Coramae R. and Marjorie S. Zatz. 2002. *Images of Color: Images of Crime*, 2nd edn., Los Angeles, CA: Roxbury Publishing.

Martin, S. 1988. Female Officers on the Move? A Status Report on Women in Policing. In *Critical Issues in Policing*, ed. B. Dunham and J. Alpert, 23–45. Grove Park, IL: Waveland Press.

Martin, S. and Jurik, N. 1996. *Doing Justice, Doing Gender*. Thousand Oaks, CA: Sage Publications.

McIntosh, P. 1998. White Privilege, Color, and Crime: A Personal Account. In *Images of Color: Images of Crime*, ed. C. R. Mann and M. S. Zatz, 207–216. New York, NY: Roxbury Publishing.

McIntosh, P. 2002. White Privilege, Color, and Crime: A Personal Account. In *Images of color: Images of crime*, ed. C. R. Mann and M. S. Zatz, 45. New York, NY: Roxbury Publishing.

Meeks, K. 2000. *Driving While Black*. New York: Broadway Books.

Miller, J. G. 1996. *Search and Destroy: African–American Males in the Criminal Justice System*. New York, NY: Cambridge University Press.

Miller, J. and Levin, P. 1998. The Caucasian Evasion: Victims, Exceptions, and Defenders of the Faith. In *Images of color: Images of crime*, ed. C. R. Mann and M. S. Zatz, 217–233. New York, NY: Roxbury Publishing.

Murray, C. B., and Smith, J. O. 1995. White Privilege: The Rhetoric and the Facts. In *Multiculturalism from the Margins*, ed. D. A. Harris, 139–154. Westport, CT: Bergin & Garvey.

Podolsky, J. D., Balfour, V., Eftimiades, M., and McFarland, S. 1990. As the Central Park Jogger Struggles to Heal, Three Attackers

Hear the Bell Toll for Them. *People,* September 30, 47.

Rodriguez, L. J. 2002. The Color of Skin is the Color of Crime. In *Images of Color: Images of Crime,* ed. C. R. Mann and M. S. Zatz, 33–45. New York, NY: Roxbury Publishing.

Rome, D. 2002. Murderers, Rapists, and Drug Addicts. In *Images of Color: Images of Crime,* ed. Coramae R. Mann and Marjorie S. Zatz, 2nd edn. Los Angeles, CA: Roxbury.

Rosenbaum, Dennis, D. A. Lewis, and J. Grant. 1986. Neighborhood-Based Crime Prevention: Assessing the Efficacy of Community Organizing in Chicago. In *Community Crime Prevention: Does It Work?,* ed. Dennis Rosenbaum, 103–134. Newbury Park, CA: Sage Publications.

Rothenberg, Paula S. (Ed.). 2004. *Race, Class, and Gender in the United States: An Integrated Study,* 6th edn. New York, NY: Worth Publishers.

Rubin, Lillian, 1998. Is This a White Country, or What? In *Race, Class, and Gender in the United States: An Integrated Study,* ed. Paula S. Rothenberg, 4th edn., 92–99. New York, NY: St. Martin's Press.

Sacks, Karen B. 1998. How Jews Became White. In *Race, Class, and Gender in the United States: An Integrated Study,* ed. Paula S. Rothenberg, 4th edn., 100–115. New York, NY: St. Martin's Press.

Schaef, Anne W. 1992. *Women's Reality: An Emerging Female System in a White Male Society.* San Francisco: HarperCollins.

Stanko, Elizabeth. 1990. *Everyday Violence: How Women and Men Experience Sexual and Physical Danger.* London, UK: Pandora.

Tomasi, Silvano, and Madeline Engel (Ed.). 1970. *The Italian Experience in the United States.* New York, NY: Center for Migration Studies.

Van Biema, David. 1995. Abandoned to her Fate. *Time,* December 11, 50.

Walker, Samuel, Cassia Spohn, and Miriam DeLone. 1996. *The Color of Justice: Race, Ethnicity, and Crime in America.* New York, NY: Wadsworth Publishing.

Winant, Howard. 1997. Behind Blue Eyes: Whiteness and Contemporary U.S. Racial Politics. In *Off White: Readings on Race, Power, and Society,* ed. Michelle Fine, Lois Weis, Linda C. Powell, and L. Mun Wong, 40–56. New York, NY: Routledge.

Wirth, Louis. 1945. The Problem of Minority Groups. In *The Science of Man in the World Crisis,* ed. Ralph Linton, 23–54. New York, NY: Columbia University Press.

Yinger, J. Milton. 1994. *Ethnicity: Source of Strength? Source of Conflict?* Albany, NY: SUNY Press.

Zweigenhaft, Richard, and B. William Domhoff. 1982. *Jews in the Protestant Establishment.* New York, NY: Praeger.

CHAPTER 4

Talking Through Our Differences

Intercultural and Interpersonal Communication

Marianne O. Nielsen

Rebecca Maniglia

In contrast to the diversity in the offender population, on the whole, criminal justice practitioners are members of privileged groups. On average, they are white, male, physically able and middle class. This lack of commonality means that intercultural and interpersonal communication skills take on a special significance in providing justice services, especially when coupled with the power differential between criminal justice practitioners and their clients.

For example, police officers are the gatekeepers to the criminal justice system. It is "an accepted fact" for most officers that citizens will be uncomfortable communicating with them (Womack and Finley, 1986:145). Many citizens see the police as representatives of the dominant society and as authority figures who have the power to determine their security, peace of mind, freedom, and even their chances of dying. This power is not limited to the police. Lawyers, prosecutors, judges, correctional officers, and parole and probation supervisors make decisions daily that can have the same impact.

Criminal justice practitioners, like ordinary citizens, often feel uncertainty and anxiety in communicating with strangers, particularly when those exchanges cross the boundaries of difference (i.e., race or gender). The power they wield, however, gives them an added responsibility in dealing with their own negative reactions. They must ensure they have the skills to communicate effectively with those in the diverse systems in which they serve. Equally important, they must communicate with enough competence that understanding becomes a two-way street. This chapter, or indeed any book on intercultural or interpersonal communication, cannot provide "the" answer for handling all intercultural interactions effectively and appropriately;[1] it does, however, provide useful information about the knowledge and skills needed to do so, and the issues that can arise in communication.

Interpersonal communication is usually understood as verbal and nonverbal exchanges between two or more people on a specific topic. Improving intercultural communication skills can be a vital strategy for maintaining effective interpersonal communication. This is usually done through two kinds of intercultural communication training: culture-specific and culture-general (Hammer, 1989). Culture-specific training focuses on building communication competence in just one culture, as when an American Drug Enforcement Agency officer studies Colombian culture. In contrast, culture-general skills are ones that can be generalized to intercultural interactions regardless of the culture (Hammer, 1989). While intercultural communication is the focus of this chapter, most of the skills described are equally applicable to interpersonal communication with members of other groups (see Milhouse, 1993).

COMMUNICATION COMPETENCE IN CRIMINAL JUSTICE

Communication is the process that occurs between two or more individuals who use words and/or nonverbal signals to construct the reality of their interaction and to attach meaning to the messages they transmit (Gudykunst, 2003). Competent communication is about developing a shared reality or negotiating "mutual meanings, rules, and outcomes that are 'positive' " (Gudykunst and Nishida, 1989:36). It has been said that effective communication is primarily about minimizing misunderstanding (Gudykunst, 2003), but communication is seldom perfect. Both partners in the interaction bring to it their individual personalities, life experiences, and social and cultural roles. This means they may misinterpret the meaning of the other's words or actions (Gudykunst, 2003). One common area of misinterpretation is culture.

Many people are unaware of, uncomfortable with, or unable to discuss the dynamics and implications of cultural differences. This lack of knowledge or interpersonal comfort can lead to tension or conflict as people interpret others' words and behaviors incorrectly, become frustrated, make negative judgments about others, and eventually cut off the interaction. They may even end up avoiding situations of intercultural communication in the future (Cushner and Brislin, 1996). In the case of criminal justice members, they may even choose to become aggressive in their interactions with those outside of their own culture (Gundersen and Hopper, 1984). One way to avoid these scenarios is to develop the knowledge and skills to operate effectively and appropriately in intercultural interpersonal interactions or to become competent communicators.

---

[1] It should be noted that while this chapter discusses the aggregate-level characteristics of some groups, there is a great deal of individual variation within each group. It should also be noted that most of the work in intercultural and interpersonal communication has been done from a Eurocentric point of view (Martin, 1993).

Rewards of Competent Communication

Competent communication has many rewards. First, competent communicators learn about someone else's cultural concepts and gain insight into a world very different than their own. For example, the Cree Indians, one of the largest indigenous groups in Canada, have no word for or concept of "guilt". What does this suggest about their view of crime? What might be the repercussions of this when they appear as an accused in court? Similarly, the Cree have no gender pronouns. What might be the impact of this linguistic difference if a Cree is asked to give testimony about the identity of an offender?

Second, competent communicators may gain a new perspective on their own culture. For example, if the Japanese have many words for rice because of its centrality to their diet, what might this say about all the words Americans have for guns? Similarly, what does it mean that Americans have gender pronouns when the Cree don't? Do Americans attach status and prestige to gender in ways that are different from other cultures? How does this affect how women are treated in the criminal justice system?

Third, competent communicators are more likely to make decisions that take into account the perspectives of all parties to the interaction. Actions taken by a police officer, for example, in handling a domestic violence dispute will be more likely to calm the situation than inflame it if the police officer has some knowledge of the culturally defined domestic roles of the spouses, their attitude toward authority figures, and their normal tone of verbal and nonverbal communication.

Womack and Finley (1986) believe that good communication has a number of other benefits to the criminal justice system generally, including allowing for better community relations, a decrease in misunderstandings, tensions, and conflicts among coworkers from different backgrounds, and increased self-esteem among criminal justice members as they become better able to handle intercultural interactions.

CRITICAL KNOWLEDGE ABOUT COMMUNICATION

In order for criminal justice personnel to achieve intercultural communication competence, it is important to have knowledge about certain key influences on communication, including the impact of diversity on communication, the power of nonverbal communication, and the importance of the situational context.

The Impact of Diversity on Communication

There are many kinds of diversity that can influence communication. In this section we will look at just three: gender, culture, and power/status. While these three are among the most important for criminal justice personnel, it should be recognized that many kinds of diversity influence communication, including race, education, physical abilities, and age. Similarly, categories of diversity intersect with one another to create an even broader form of influence.

GENDER. Communication research across settings and populations has found communication differences between men and women. Aries (1996: 189) says these findings include

> [m]en show a greater task orientation in groups, women a greater social-emotional orientation; men emerge more often as leaders in initially leaderless groups; men interrupt more; women pay more attention to the face needs of their conversational partners; women talk more personally with their close friends.

The meanings connected with these differences are socially constructed and often based on gender stereotypes. For example, a man's statement might be interpreted as assertive whereas the same statement from a woman may be interpreted as aggressive or even "bitchy."

According to Aries (1996:195), "gender differences cannot be understood without putting them in the context of gender inequalities in society." Women in American society are still perceived and treated as having a lower status than men, and dominant–subordinate status can have a great deal of influence on communication. Interestingly, when men and women are given the same status, few gender differences in communication emerge. In criminal justice, the few that do exist may have positive consequences. For example, female police and correctional officers are more willing to use reason, less likely to provoke hostilities, more likely to diffuse tensions, and more likely to mediate conflict than their male counterparts (Martin and Jurik, 2007).

Verbal and nonverbal communication can be difficult to interpret. There are a wide array of variables that can influence an interaction, including the class and status of the partners, sexual orientation, age, ethnicity, and individual style. Situational factors such as the relationship between the partners, the setting, the topic, and the length of the interaction can also influence the degree to which gender differences have impact (Aries, 1996). In addition, there are cultural variances in the proper tone of conversation, the kind of touch allowed (if any), and the appropriate personal distance between men and women. There are also cultural differences in the level of appropriate intimacy in the topic and in the expectations of response. These differences could lead to misunderstandings or even to accusations of sexual harassment if one of the partners in the interaction is seen by the other as "stepping over the line" (Cushner and Brislin, 1996).

In order to deal competently with communication differences, people need to learn as much as possible about the expectations of the groups with which they interact. They also need to learn to recognize indicators of power differences and understand that they have evolved as the result of group history. Communicators should not take such changes personally and should always keep their interactions respectful and professional. Finally, competent communicators need to recognize that job-related differences in male and female communication may even be advantageous to the criminal justice system.

CULTURE. Cultural groups can be differentiated along a number of standard dimensions. While various typologies have been developed to describe these,[2]

---

[2] See Gudykunst and Nishida (1989) for an overview of theoretical frameworks for intercultural communication.

probably the best known is Hofstedes' (2005). Hofstede and Hofstede differentiate cultures by their individualism/collectivism, their high and low power distance, their uncertainty avoidance, and their approach to masculinity and femininity.[3] As they explain,

> Individualistic cultures emphasize the individual's goals while collectivistic cultures stress that group goals have precedence over individual goals. High power-distance cultures value inequality, with everyone having a "rightful place," and the hierarchy reflects existential inequality. Low power-distance cultures, in contrast, value equality. Uncertainty avoidance involves the lack of tolerance for uncertainty and ambiguity. Cultures high in uncertainty avoidance have high levels of anxiety, a great need for formal rules, and a low tolerance for groups that behave in a deviant manner. Masculinity involves valuing things, money, assertiveness, and unequal sex roles. Cultures where people, quality of life, nurturance, and equal sex roles prevail, on the other hand, are feminine (Gudykunst and Nishida, 1989:21–22).

Another important typology differentiates between high context and low context cultures (Hall, 1976). In high context cultures, much of meaning is implicit and is communicated by context and nonverbal nuances or signals. In low context cultures, meaning is given directly, with little reliance on context or nonverbal signals. African American, Native American, and Latino/a subcultures within the United States are relatively high context, while European-based cultures (i.e., the dominant "white" culture) are low context. As most criminal justice personnel are trained to be low context in their communication, knowing where a group fits in this typology can be useful for trying to anticipate and prevent cultural conflict.

POWER AND STATUS DIFFERENCES. Groups with subordinate status have developed specialized ways of communication based on their past interactions with members of the dominant group. Orbe (1998:16–17) presents a long list of these, including diverting communication away from potentially dangerous topics, remaining silent when offensive statements are made, downplaying or ignoring differences, ridiculing self, confronting, educating others, imposing a psychological distance through verbal and nonverbal strategies, and avoiding communication altogether. The individual strategy used will depend on the perceived gain or cost for the subordinate member of the interaction (Orbe, 1998).

Individuals employed within the criminal justice system may experience an instantaneous change in status that may affect how communication is perceived and carried out. There may be potential differences in naming, respect, and nonverbal communication. For instance, a Latina lawyer may be treated with more deference in court than she receives in the supermarket. Likewise, a native African employed within the system may experience black–white discrimination in ways that are unfamiliar.

---

[3] It should be noted that some theorists find Hofstede and Hofstede's use of the terms "masculine" and "feminine" sexist and stereotypical, and substitute the term "gender," which is still a questionable term (see Hecht, Andersen, and Ribeau, 1989).

The Importance of Nonverbal Communication

According to Henderson (1994), about 70 to 80% of communication is nonverbal. Knowledge of what nonverbal communication conveys, while not always reliable, is an important tool for criminal justice personnel. Most nonverbal communication is spontaneous, unconscious, and subtle (Andersen, 1994:229). The manner of speaking communicates as much as the words; it just does not communicate the same thing in every culture. Characteristics that may vary across cultures and between groups include: tone, placement of emphasis, volume, pitch, quality (e.g., clear versus slurring), and duration (Henderson, 1994). The following are seven key areas for understanding nonverbal communication.

Silence makes many Americans nervous. Citizens from the northeast are taught to finish other people's sentences, to interrupt, and to leap immediately into any space in a conversation. Similarly, some racial or ethnic populations, such as African Americans or Italians, are known for loud, expressive dialogues. Rather than being markers of impoliteness, these represent speech patterns or learned cultural behaviors. In contrast, many Native American and Asian peoples are taught to wait a space after another person has stopped talking. The length of the silence reflects the importance they give to the other person's words. In a meeting between individuals from these cultures, we might observe a significant cultural clash in communication, with some populations feeling they have no room to present their concerns because others are imposing their point of view through aggressive communication.

Gestures and movements are among the most important aspects of nonverbal communication. There are over 100,000 different gestures used around the world, and most have meanings that vary from culture to culture. A simple example is the head nod used in the United States to signify agreement. In Greece, depending on the exact movement, a nod might actually mean "no" (Henderson, 1994).

Personal space or "zones of territory" also vary across cultures, class, and gender. Generally, if a person invades the space of another, it may cause discomfort, but people in some cultures prefer to stand closer than others. High contact is desirable in Latin American, African, Arabian, and southern European cultures, while noncontact or low contact is preferred by Asian and northern European cultures (Henderson, 1994).

Touching is also viewed differently by low contact and high contact cultures. Touching includes kissing, embracing, hugging, hand shaking, and general touch. Touching varies not only by culture but by the gender and status of the persons in the interaction, the timing of the interaction, and the private or public location of the interaction (Henderson, 1994).

Eye contact standards can also vary. Cultures vary in how long people make eye contact, how intensely, when, what part of the body is looked at, and how much blinking is done (Henderson, 1994). Some cultures consider extended direct eye contact as a sign of honesty while others see it as disrespectful.

Movement while speaking can also vary. In some cultures people may walk away and return to emphasize agreement (Henderson, 1994). In others, individuals talking to authority figures are expected to stand still and upright.

Symbols are a special category of nonverbal communication. Examples include flags, ankhs, crosses, Stars of David, badges, uniforms, jewelry, scout patches, head coverings, colored ribbons, political cartoons, and thousands of others. Each group has symbols that have special meanings to its members. Some of these are easy to recognize and understand; others are not. Some are used to draw a group together (flags), while others divide or exclude (swastikas). In the criminal justice system, much gang identification relies on the colors and styles of clothing worn. Police uniforms are also symbolic—of assistance to some, while of oppression and tyranny to others.

Competent communicators must learn the nonverbal signals of cultures or cocultures that they interact with frequently but must be very careful in using them as they may not have a full appreciation of the subtleties.

Situational Context

To understand each other, partners in an interaction must know something about social, cultural, and personal context. Without context, "behavior is just noise" (Cushner and Brislin, 1996:13). Each participant in an interaction operates within the context of their own life experience, status, motivations, culture, and group history. This means that a wide range of factors can affect an interaction, including the physical and emotional setting in which the interaction occurs (i.e., in a dark park late at night or in a crowded mall) or the characteristics of the participants (i.e., their numbers, attractiveness, prototypicality, personality, temperament, and mood) (Giles and Franklyn-Stokes, 1989). The historical relations between the groups the participants represent can also matter as can personal status or power. If one group is or has been dominant and the other subordinate, power and status can influence the context of the interaction.

The participants' knowledge of the language is also an important factor. It may be taken for granted that both parties understand the meanings of words, when they may not. Words and concepts can have subtly different, slightly different, or even drastically different meanings (Cushner and Brislin, 1996:289). For example a "date" with a prostitute is not the same as a "date" to the movies, and "snow" as in precipitation differs from "snow" as in heroin. The nonverbal communication that accompanies words may also completely change their meaning. For example, "mother" can change meaning depending on the tone of voice or hand gesture that accompanies it. While a nonnative English speaker may possess a working knowledge of the language, there is a chance that they are not familiar with the nuances of English words and expressions. The English phrase "see you later," for example, has led to accusations of American insincerity, since it does not necessarily express the intent to see you later, but is simply a ritual parting phrase (Cushner and Brislin, 1996).

The purpose of the interaction can also affect communication. Some cultures have high regard for the ability to debate, while others use silence to communicate respect. Some have a great enjoyment of small talk, while some have very little use for it. Some use talk as a form of social control; others use it as a means of establishing affiliations. Even knowing how to agree or disagree may be an important skill.

What each participant considers appropriate behavior or presentation of self is also important (Henderson, 1994). This may include greetings (e.g., handshakes versus bowing), showing affection, covering the head or legs, the formality or informality of dress, removal of shoes on entering a room, how to sit "properly," how to criticize, how to give and receive compliments, and recognizing symbols of marriage (jewelry, hairstyle, clothing style).

CRITICAL ISSUES IN COMMUNICATION

There are many communication issues that may lead to difficult situations for criminal justice members. We will look at five that have had a great deal of impact on the system.

Stereotyping

In order to psychologically process all the information they receive, people learn to place others in abstract social categories based on easily identified characteristics (Gudykunst and Gumbs, 1989). In this country, these characteristics include skin color, sex, presence or absence of disabilities, and apparent age, but stereotypes can also be based on accent, social class, and/or ethnicity. Stereotypes attribute certain behaviors to all members of a certain category, allowing for no individual variation. Positive stereotypes are formed about in-groups such as family, friends, and members of the same class or race (i.e., they are all intelligent, talented, and kind), while negative stereotypes are formed about out-groups (i.e., they are all criminal, lazy, and greedy) (Gudykunst and Gumbs, 1989). Categories and placements in them are learned through jokes, ethnophaulisms (rude names), epithets (expressions), stories, and the media.

Stereotypes can prevent individuals from interacting with each other or even cause them to be afraid of each other. People are often concerned that if they try to learn more, they will embarrass themselves by saying or doing something "stupid." Yet, they may also find that the "Other" is an individual just like them, with similar family problems and career hopes. The only way to understand this, however, is to see people as individuals, overcome stereotypes, and not see others as homogeneous members of some group of strangers. This requires true, meaningful communication.

Ethnocentrism

Ethnocentrism is the tendency to judge others by the standards of one's own group and to form a negative opinion as a result of such comparisons (Hofstede and Hofstede, 2005). Often when individuals are faced with cultural practices different from their own, their reaction is to compare the practice unfavorably with what they are familiar and, therefore, not participate. Not surprisingly, such negative responses may be interpreted as disrespectful. Similarly, if someone criticizes what is perceived to be American culture, Americans may react poorly, while in these situations it is best not to assume disrespect was intended (Argyle, 1982).

Naming

Meanings of names change over time and in different regions of the country or the world, and the process of naming is influenced by the power dynamics present. Oppressed groups that have historically been named by those in power may have strong feelings about labels. For instance, the labels "African American" and "black" are often used interchangeably, while they may have particular connotations to those in that racial group. Likewise, the term "Hispanic" is commonly used to group individuals whose roots may be in countries as varied as Mexico, Argentina, Puerto Rico, and Spain. The fact that members of the dominant group do not understand why the name they use for the minority group is offensive or limiting is a sign of the social distance between members of the minority and dominant groups. It symbolizes the traditional indifference of the dominant society to the concerns of minority groups (Herbst, 1997:258).

Members of named groups may also choose to use naming as a means of "talking back" to the dominant society, for example using names like "gringo" or "round eyes" for Americans, who are members of the privileged white group. Oppressed groups may also adopt the derogatory names for their own purposes—"self-definition, solidarity, or irony" (Herbst, 1997:256, xii; Orbe, 1998:16–17)—such as the use of the term "queer" by the GLBT (Gay, Lesbian, Bisexual, and Transgender) community.

Further, many people have trouble understanding that words and expressions (such as "acting like a wild Indian" in reference to a rambunctious child) have connotations which can make them ethnic, racial, or gender slurs. Connotations are the "emotional and cognitive associations of words" (Herbst, 1997:256), and it is the connotations that are offensive more so than the words themselves. The words "restrict, misrepresent, or distort how people are known" (Herbst, 1997:ix) and as such, they are an element of stereotyping. Names reveal societal and individual attitudes about groups. They develop in response to the changing needs of their users and the evolving needs of the society in which they are used. "In the United States the vast array of abusive ethnic words reflect the society's complexity, increasing ethnic diversity and fast-paced social change" (Herbst, 1997:255). Derogatory names may hinder the political interests of groups, are ideologically loaded, mark boundaries between "us" and "them", create distance between the speaker and the group spoken of, "keep people in their place" and justify discrimination in the minds of the people discriminating (Herbst, 1997:ix, 256). They are also used to chastise people who are perceived as straying from acceptable intercultural behavior or who are assimilating too far into the dominant society of which they are not a part (Herbst, 1997:x).

Humor

Humor can be used for many social purposes, including as an information-gathering tool, as a means of giving information, as a means of anxiety management, for social control, and as a means of preserving the status quo (Foot, 2006). The first three purposes suggest that humor can be a vital strategy for criminal justice personnel developing intercultural and interpersonal communication. It can be used as a means of diffusing tense situations, as a means of coping with embarrassment, or for gathering information. It can, however, also be a risky tool. Humor targeting group membership, such as ethnicity, race, or gender can lead to serious problems. These jokes are based on stereotypes and serve (perhaps unintentionally) as a means of social control and of preserving the status quo. Jokes reinforce the characteristics and "place" of some groups within society; that is, they reinforce prejudice. As Foot (2006:271) states, "Because the joke is a socially acceptable form, the message it conveys is extremely powerful and the recipient or target, however much offended, can hardly denounce it without standing accused of the greatest crime of all—lacking a sense of humor."

In terms of using humor, it is important to remember that a great deal of humor relies on shared cultural and linguistic experiences. It is often not the words that are funny, but the understanding that goes with them. In other words, humor is highly culture-specific (Hofstede and Hofstede, 2005). It is probably best to follow the advice given by Hofstede and Hofstede, (2005:329) who suggest, "In intercultural encounters the experienced traveler [or criminal justice practitioner] knows that jokes and irony are taboo until one is absolutely sure of the other culture's conception of what represents humor."

Translation

Translation is an intervening variable in communication between two primary parties. Because translation is an active process in which the translator must make a series of decisions and judgments, it has the potential to affect the decisions or knowledge of criminal justice personnel. Cultural orientation can make direct translations meaningless or alter their meaning. Many legal concepts cannot easily be translated into some languages, and translating the underlying ideology of concepts is even more difficult. In these cases, the translator must not only translate, but also interpret. As a result, the translation has the potential to influence the results of the interaction (Banks and Banks, 1991).

With the changing population demographics in this country, the need for translation has increased geometrically for criminal justice service providers (Banks and Banks, 1991). Sanders (1989) reported that over 43,000 requests for translation services in 60 languages were made annually in federal courts and that New York City courts alone needed interpreters about 250 times *a day*. Translators trained in legal terminology can be invaluable; however, there is no standard certification required by the U.S. justice service (Banks and Banks, 1991) even though some individual states have language skills tests for translators.

CRITICAL SKILLS

Which skills are important and how to develop them has been the subject of many publications on improving intercultural and interpersonal communication (Hammer, 1989; Henderson, 1994). Gudykunst (2003) suggests that competent communicators must have the motivation, knowledge, and skills to communicate. They are motivated by the fulfillment of certain needs that arise in interaction. These include a need for predictability, a need to avoid anxiety, and a need to sustain self-concept. Knowledge means knowing about the other person's group and knowing what needs to be done in order to communicate in an effective way. Gudykunst describes six skills that are particularly important. In order to reduce anxiety, communicators must have the ability to be mindful, tolerate ambiguity, and manage anxiety; in order to reduce uncertainty, communicators must be able to empathize, adapt their behavior, and make accurate predictions about and know explanations for others' behavior (2003:253–270). Listening, asking questions, and conflict management are subsumed among these skills, but because of their importance to criminal justice personnel, they are discussed separately.

Being mindful means that communicators must be aware of their own communication behavior and the process of communication, rather than focusing on their feelings or on the outcome. It also means being open to new information and other people's perspectives. *Tolerating ambiguity* means having the skill to deal successfully with situations in which a lot of information needed for effective communication is missing. People with a low tolerance for ambiguity may try to find information that supports their previous conceptions, while people with a high tolerance try to gather objective information. *Managing anxiety* means being able to control bodily symptoms of anxiety, as well as control worrying thoughts. People who are involved in an interaction with unfamiliar, "weird" people may feel uneasy, tense, and worried. They may fear that their self-concept will be damaged, that there will be negative behavioral consequences (e.g., that they will be exploited or be harmed), and that they will be negatively evaluated by their group or the other group. It is important to remember that a moderate amount of anxiety actually aids performance while too much or too little hinders communication.

Practicing empathy means trying to take the perspective of the other in order to understand the other's feelings and point of view. This is not to be confused with sympathy, which is trying to imagine how *you* would feel in the other's situation. *Adapting* is being able to perceive different situational contexts and choose the verbal and nonverbal communication strategies that are most appropriate and effective. *Making accurate predictions and explanations* for others' behavior requires knowing that all cultures have rules of thought, feeling, and behavior, but that these vary from group to group. Effective communicators do not assume the other is using a particular set of rules but try to determine what rules are underlying the communications and use these to predict and explain behavior.

Listening, according to Gudykunst (2003), is a process in which individuals take in new information, check it against what they already know, and select information that is meaningful. It is a skill that does not come naturally and needs to be practiced. This is a particularly important skill for criminal justice personnel who must gather information and make decisions about how to deal with people. In the dominant American culture, "active listening" is the recommended strategy. *Active listening* involves three skills: attending skills comprised of the nonverbal body language, posture, and eye contact we maintain in interactions; following skills, which are the verbal and nonverbal ways we indicate to the person we are listening; and comprehending skills, which comprise the ways we ensure that we are understanding the speaker. Active listening may not be appropriate with all groups, however. Some cultures find asking questions disrespectful. Also, verbal indicators of "following" may be seen as interruptions and lead to the cessation of talk, while the "attending" skill of maintaining eye contact might be interpreted as a challenge.

In American culture, *asking questions* is the simplest way of gathering information. However, within some cultures, it is considered rude. This can be especially problematic for criminal justice personnel with investigative roles. For instance, in some Native American cultures, asking questions, especially of elders, is impolite and will not likely elicit a response. These situations require alternative ways of requesting information, such as saying, "I wonder if . . . " or "someone told me . . . ," pausing, and allowing the person time to offer information if they wish to do so. Other times it is the content of the question that is unintentionally rude as each group has topics that are not acceptable in conversation. For instance, most Americans are uncomfortable talking to casual acquaintances about their sexual relations. Finally, who is asking the question may also be an issue. In many Australian Aborigine cultures, there is "men's" knowledge and "women's" knowledge, and it is inappropriate for a man to share men's knowledge with a woman no matter what her occupation, and vice versa.

Conflict management is another important skill for criminal justice personnel. Conflict is handled differently by various cultural groups. Individualistic and collectivistic cultures, for example, handle conflict differently. Members of collectivistic cultures are more likely to try to smooth over the conflict or to avoid it altogether, whereas members of individualistic cultures are likely to try to control the conflict situation and/or treat conflict as a problem to be solved (Gudykunst and Nishida, 1989). Criminal justice practitioners need to know the appropriate strategies for different groups.

TRANSLATING COMMUNICATION COMPETENCE INTO ORGANIZATIONAL SUCCESS

Criminal justice organizations employ and must provide services to a diverse population. The cultures represented in the organization will influence management and leadership styles and overall organizational culture (Tayeb, 1996:101; Hofstede and Hofstede, 2005). Some cultural values and behaviors will have more impact than others. For instance, Tayeb (1996) suggests that organizations are particularly affected by their employees' attitudes toward power, tolerance of ambiguity, individualism, collectivism, commitment, and interpersonal trust.

Issues in intercultural and interpersonal communication within organizations are similar to those between individuals. Not surprisingly, the prejudices found in society at large are also present in the work place (Henderson, 1994). Coworkers may act in a discriminatory manner, or managers may refuse to recruit, hire, or promote members of various categories of difference.

There are, of course, also problems in communication. Racial groups interacting within the workplace, for example, may assign different meanings to verbal and nonverbal communication (Asante and Davis, 1989). Some occupations also have specialized argots that act as a communication code for practitioners (e.g., police officers using radio codes in casual conversation). These may be very difficult for new staff members to understand, especially if they come from a group that has been traditionally excluded from the occupation. There are also language usages that are exclusive to one category of individuals, leaving others out. For instance, the use of sports metaphors during planning meetings may isolate those without such knowledge.

Organizations have three options in managing their diverse workforce: they can ignore its diversity; they can recognize its diversity but not use it; or they can use its diversity as a rich resource for the provision of services. Organizations that ignore or resist diversity will find that they are denied the benefits of a fully productive diverse workforce. Further, discrimination is against the law, and companies that allow discrimination will not only lose offended customers and staff, but may well find themselves the target of lawsuits. Organizations which actively use their workforce diversity are more competitive and are more creative in problem solving and have fewer internal conflicts (Tayeb, 1996). This means that effective interpersonal and intercultural skills are valuable not only for the individuals, but also for their organizations. As a result, many organizations, including criminal justice organizations, are suggesting and even requiring that their employees take part in initiatives that will develop their communication skills.

A number of strategies can help organizations develop and make better use of the communication skills of their employees. First, management's encouragement or discouragement of diversity affects the behavior of everyone within the organization. If competent intercultural and interpersonal communication is to be part of the organizational culture, it must occur with the cooperation and active participation of senior administration (Henderson, 1994). Second, managers must learn both verbal and nonverbal communication skills in order to teach others. These managers use their skills to learn about their employees' values, motivations, communication styles, attitudes, and needs (Henderson, 1994). Third, intercultural and interpersonal communication initiatives must be based on the objectives and commitments of the organization. Policy must provide clear direction for the initiatives' objectives and how they are to be reached. Employees should be part of planning these initiatives and must feel there will be personal benefits for participation (Henderson, 1994). Fourth, policies concerning bias-free written and spoken language should be implemented. Terminology used should reflect the occupation or task, not the personal characteristics of the staff member; for example, referring to "the secretary" instead of "the girl." Similarly, proper titles or proper names should be used rather than slang names.

Finally, organizations can create programs that develop employee competency in language proficiency, negotiation, and general communication (Tayeb, 1996). Ideally, training programs should meet the needs of the trainees and their organization. There is a wide range of training programs from which to choose (Cargile and Giles, 1996). One of the most effective is the "culture-general assimilator," which presents a series of critical incidents in which intercultural communication did not work. Participants choose from a set of answers until they find the correct explanation for the failure (see Cushner and Brislin, 1996). This training method is particularly appropriate for criminal justice personnel, who must provide effective services in a wide range of job scenarios every day. Hargie (2006) recommends that training in communication skills is best carried out through "microtraining"—that is, carried out in small groups over short periods of time and focusing on only one skill at a time. Skills are identified, training sensitizes staff to those skills, and then participants are given opportunities for skill practice and to receive feedback. Evaluation of the program focuses on the impact of the new skills on client groups. Other training methods include lectures, role plays, field trips, and experiential games (Cargile and Giles, 1996).

Organizations can evaluate the intercultural competence of their employees based on three very straightforward criteria: whether or not employees feel comfortable and satisfied with intercultural or interpersonal interactions; whether the employee is rated as a competent communicator by members of various difference categories; and whether the employees are rated by a supervisor as effective in dealing with members of other groups (Argyle, 1982). Being able to establish meaningful interpersonal relationships with members of other groups has also been suggested as an indicator of competence.

In summary, to be effective, intercultural communication initiatives must be well planned, must occur organization-wide, must be coordinated from the top, must be on-going, and must include nonverbal communication (Henderson, 1994). In this diverse world, there is little doubt that increased competence in intercultural and interpersonal communication skills is of benefit to both individuals and organizations within the criminal justice system.

References

Andersen, Peter. 1994. Explaining Intercultural Differences in Nonverbal Communication. In *Intercultural Communication: A Reader*, ed. Larry A. Samovar and Richard E. Porter, 7th edn., 229–239. Belmont, CA: Wadsworth.

Aries, Elizabeth. 1996. *Men and Women in Interaction.* New York: Oxford University Press.

Argyle, Michael. 1982. Intercultural Communication. In *Cultures in Contact*, ed. Stephen Bochner, 61–79. Oxford: Pergamon Press.

Asante, Molefi K., and Alice Davis. 1989. Encounters in the Interracial Workplace. In *Handbook of International and Intercultural Communication*, ed. Molefi Kete Asante and William B. Gudykunst, 374–391. Newbury Park: Sage Publications.

Banks, Anna, and Stephen P. Banks. 1991. Unexplored Barriers: The Role of Translation in Interpersonal Communication. In *Cross-cultural Interpersonal Communication*, ed. Stella Ting-Toomey and Felipe Korzenny, 171–185. Newbury Park: Sage Publications.

Cargile, Aaron C. and Howard Giles. 1996. Intercultural Communication Training: Review, Critique, and a New Theoretical Framework, In *Communication Yearbook 19*, ed. Brant R. Burleson, 385–423. Thousand Oaks: Sage Publications.

Cushner, K., and Richard W. Brislin. 1996. *Intercultural Interactions: A Practical Guide*, 2nd edn. Thousand Oaks, CA: Sage Publications.

Foot, Hugh C. 2006. Humour and Laughter. In *The Handbook of Communication Skills*, ed. Owen

D. W. Hargie, 3rd edn., 259–285. London: Routledge.

Giles, Howard, and Arlene Franklyn-Stokes. 1989. Communicator Characteristics. In *Handbook of International and Intercultural Communication*, ed. Molefi Kete Asante and William B. Gudykunst, 117–144. Newbury Park: Sage Publications.

Gudykunst, William B. 2003. *Bridging Differences*, 4th edn. Thousand Oaks, CA: Sage Publications.

Gudykunst, William B. and Lauren L. Gumbs. 1989. Social Cognition and Intergroup Communication. In *Handbook of International and Intercultural Communication*, ed. Molefi Kete Asante and William B. Gudykunst, 204–224. Newbury Park: Sage Publications.

Gudykunst, William B., and Tsukasa Nishida. 1989. Theoretical Perspectives for Studying Intercultural Communication. In *Handbook of International and Intercultural Communication*, ed. Molefi Kete Asante and William B. Gudykunst, 17–46. Newbury Park: Sage Publications.

Gundersen, D. F., and Robert Hopper. 1984. *Communication and Law Enforcement.* Lanham, MD: University Press of America.

Hall, E. T. 1976. *Beyond Culture.* New York: Anchor/Doubleday Books.

Hammer, Mitchell. 1989. Intercultural Communication Competence. In *Handbook of International and Intercultural Communication*, ed. Molefi Kete Asante and William B. Gudykunst, 247–260. Newbury Park: Sage Publications.

Hargie, Owen D. W. (Ed.). 2006. Training in Communication Skills: Research, Theory and Practice. In *The Handbook of Communication Skills*, 3rd edn., 473–482. London: Routledge.

Hecht, Michael L., Peter A. Andersen, and Sidney A. Ribeau. 1989. The Cultural Dimensions of Nonverbal Communication. In *Handbook of International and Intercultural Communication*, ed. Molefi Kete Asante and William B. Gudykunst, 163–185. Newbury Park: Sage Publications.

Henderson, George. 1994. *Cultural Diversity in the Workplace*. Westport, CT: Quorum Books.

Herbst, Philip H. 1997. *The Color of Words*. Yarmouth, MA: Intercultural Press.

Hofstede, G. and Hofstede, G. J. 2005. *Cultures and Organizations*, 2nd edn. New York: McGraw-Hill.

Martin, J. N. 1993. Intercultural Communication Competence: A Review. In *Intercultural Communication Competence*, ed. R. L. Wiseman and J. Koester, 16–29. Thousand Oaks: Sage Publications.

Martin, S. E. and Jurik, N. C. 2007. *Doing Justice, Doing Gender*, 2nd edn. Thousand Oaks: Sage Publications.

Milhouse, V. 1993. The Applicability of Interpersonal Communication Competence to the Intercultural Communication Context. In *Intercultural Communication Competence*, ed. R. L. Wiseman and J. Koester, 184–203. Thousand Oaks, CA: Sage Publications.

Orbe, M. P. 1998. *Constructing Co-Cultural Theory*. Thousand Oaks: Sage Publications.

Sanders, A. L. 1989. Libertad and Justicia for All. *Time*, May 29, 65.

Tayeb, M. H. 1996. *The Management of a Multicultural Workforce*. Chichester: John Wiley and Sons.

Womack, M. M. and Finley, H. H. 1986. *Communication: A Unique Significance for Law Enforcement*. Springfield, IL: Charles C. Thomas.

PART TWO

Categories of Difference

CHAPTER 5

Social Class, Crime, and Justice

Raymond J. Michalowski

> *The crime that I've always been fighting is violent crime—the rapists, the murderers, the child molesters, the bank robbers. Those are the people who are a danger to society. The issue we are dealing with here has to do with nuances of financial reporting, no theft of money or anything like that. So, it's different.*

With these words, J. Fyfe Symington, millionaire, land developer, and former governor of Arizona, rejected the idea that the financial misdealings that led to his 1997 prosecution for felony fraud constituted *real* crime (Nachtigal, 1998). By claiming that his crimes were not a "danger to society," Symington dramatized how *social class* influences the way crime and criminals are defined in the United States.

Typically, when people of high social status commit crimes in the course of business or government—even serious offenses that might costs victims millions of dollars or even their lives—they do not see themselves as *real* criminals. They are also seldom treated as real criminals by the press or the public. More importantly, many harmful acts that can be committed *only* by people of high social status are never defined as crimes. Millions of Americans have contracted chronic or fatal diseases because corporate managers or government officials either knowingly or negligently exposed them to environmentally hazardous substances, deliberately hid the truth about the risks these substances posed, or both (for details see Braithwaite, 1984; Hawkins, 1997; Kauzlarich and Kramer, 1998; Michalowski and Kramer, 2007; Mintz, 1985; Rebovich, 1992; Wright and Smye, 1996). Even so, corporate decision-makers are rarely charged with criminal offenses for the illness and death resulting from this type of wrongdoing (Hills, 1987; Stitt and Giacopassi, 1995). Instead, we reserve the label of "real crime" for behaviors typically associated with people of lower social status, even when their offenses are relatively minor or lack immediate victims, such as drug use or prostitution (Chambliss and Seidman, 1982; Michalowski, 1985; Websdale, 2001).

Social class is a critical component of *social difference* in the United States. Social class combines with other elements of identity such as gender, race, and age to create multifaceted social identities. No woman ever appears on the street or in the U.S. justice system as just a woman. Every woman bears the signs of her class, her race, her ethnic identity, and any other markers of social differentiation she might possess, such as youth or disability. The same is true for men. There may be middle-class Italian-American men, Latino working-class men, and White Anglo-Saxon Protestant upper class men, but there are no men who represent nothing but their male gender. Among the many elements that constitute an individual's social identity, social class membership is one of the most determinative of a person's life chances. It may be difficult to belong to a socially devalued minority, but it is significantly less difficult to be a rich member of that minority than a poor one.

This chapter explores how social class, as one of the central factors shaping the social meaning of *identity* and *difference* in the United States, helps ensure that both the majority of people who are victims of crime and the majority of those who are arrested, go to court, and find their way to America's currently overcrowded prisons and jails come from the poorest segments of the U.S. class structure (Beck and Glaze, 2004; Pastore and Macquire, 2007; Western, 2007). Specifically, I will focus on three aspects of the relationship between social class, differences, and crime: (1) how social class shapes the definition of crime, (2) how social class influences patterns of victimization and wrongful behavior, and (3) how fundamental changes in our society are presently altering the way the criminal justice system deals with lower income populations. Before examining these topics, it is useful to explore the meaning of *social class*.

UNDERSTANDING SOCIAL CLASS

When people talk about social class, they frequently use terms like "upper class," "middle class," "lower class," "working class," and "underclass." These terms characterize social groups according to their access to economic, social, political, cultural, or lifestyle resources.

Economic resources consist of the wealth and/or income controlled by different social groups. Social resources constitute the degree to which groups can exert political influence and/or cultural authority. Political influence refers to the ability to directly shape the actions of governmental institutions as political leaders or governmental functionaries, or indirectly through positions of power outside of government. Cultural authority is the ability to shape popular consciousness through access to mass media, education, or other platforms of public communication.

Finally, "lifestyle" resources refers to the degree to which group-based patterns of behavior and belief are valued or devalued within a society. These include such things as modes of speech, style of dress, expressed attitudes and values, and preferred and/or available pleasures. As both William Wilson (1987) and Philippe Bourgois (1994) have shown in their studies of ghetto youth, the less individuals can look, talk, dress, and act in the approved middle-class manner, the less likely they are to be hired, even when they have the necessary skills for a job.

There have been many attempts to create precise definitions of the U.S. class structure by attempting to determine where one class ends and another begins (see, for example, Bartley and Briggs, 1979; Szymanski, 1983; Wright, 1985; 1996). Rather than treat social classes as distinct groups bounded by precise lines, however, I want to suggest that the central elements of social class in the form of economic, cultural, and political resources intersect to place individuals somewhere along a social class continuum that ranges from the least to the most advantaged Americans.

The uppermost reaches of social class formation in the United States are inhabited by individuals who (1) enjoy large annual incomes; (2) control substantial wealth, not only in the form of real estate and material objects, but also in the form of financial securities such as stocks, bonds, and hedge funds; (3) exert substantial influence over making and implementing laws and governmental policy; (4) are able to use wealth and political power to shape the content of mass media; and (5) live the kinds of lifestyles that many people envy and would like to emulate. Nearer the bottom are individuals who (1) earn relatively low annual incomes, (2) own little material property and almost no financial securities, (3) enjoy little influence over government or media, and (4) whose style of speech, dress, conduct are often viewed as maladjusted or "dangerous" by those from more advantaged sectors of the society. Between these two poles is a broad range of individuals who enjoy differing configurations of economic, social, and lifestyle resources that afford them less than elites but more than the worst off.

The criminological significance of this differential distribution of resources is how it influences justice processes. Specifically, the social class system in America enables resource-advantaged groups to implement definitions of crime and justice that ensure elite-caused harms will rarely be treated as crime, while harms more common among less advantaged group—so-called "street crimes"—will be criminalized and vigorously punished.

WHY DO WE HAVE SOCIAL CLASSES?

The United States, like most of the world, is based on a political-economic system organized around free-market competition, that is, around *capitalism*. One of the essential features of competitive market systems is that some people will win a larger share of the society's resources than others. There are many factors that can influence why some people obtain more than others. Some are healthier than others. Some start life with more cultural advantages than others. Some have more hope. Some work harder than others. And so on. Whatever the *individual* reasons for success or failure, however, they are not the cause of inequalities among large social groups.

When societies are organized around private production and economic competition, the division of society into haves, have-somes, and have-nots is an inevitable structural outcome. In modern, capitalist societies this outcome is the result of political-economic processes through which the state facilitates private profit-making while managing social tensions over the redistribution of that profit in ways that tend to favor wealthier social groups (Poulantzas, 1975). In the absence of radical redistribution policies, these processes promote the formation of social classes in which members of more advantaged classes typically enjoy a larger share of the society's benefits than those who have more limited access to economic and social resources. Consequently, in capitalist societies the lazy son of a rich man will almost always end up better off than the lazy son of a poor man, and in most cases, even the *hard-working* son of a poor man will end up poorer than the lazy son of a rich man.

The division of society into social classes has both current and cumulative impacts on equality. The more resources individuals bring to the game, the more they can win, because economic growth does not benefit all social classes equally.

The period between 1979 and 2005, for instance, was one of substantial economic growth in the United States (see Figure 5.1). By 2005, however, the after-tax income of the richest 5% of the U.S. population, that is, the segment whose income derives mostly from investments, had grown by 81%, while the after-tax income of the poorest 20% of the population *declined* by 1%, and the middle fifth—the core of America's hard-working middle-class—experienced 15% income growth, barely one-fifth of the income growth among the top 5% of income earners (U.S. Bureau of the Census, 2006; Wolff, 2000). In other words, during one of the strongest periods of income growth, income inequality increased (Bernstein, McNichol and Lyons, 2006; Johnston, 2007).

In addition to shaping the allocation of financial wealth, economic inequality ensures the continuation of social class distinctions by determining access to *social capital*, that is, the non-monetary resources and skills that enable individuals to do well in competitive societies. Children who grow up in financially advantaged homes in neighborhoods with high-quality schools, and who enjoy important developmental experiences such as early exposure to reading, writing, analytic reasoning, the arts, and travel will typically do better in school, pursue higher levels of education, obtain better jobs as adults, and earn more money in their lifetime than those who grow up in households that cannot provide these benefits (Lusane, 1991; Macleod, 1995). It is true

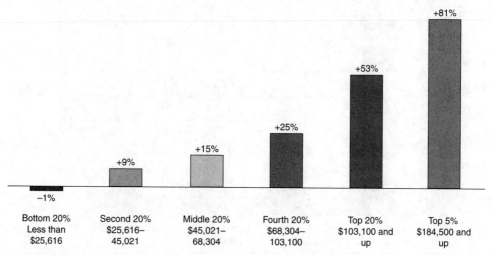

FIGURE 5.1 Change in Real Family Income by Quintile and Top 5%, 1979–2005.

Source: U.S. Census Bureau. Historical Income Tables—Table F3. http://www.census.gov/hhes/www/income/histinc/h01ar.html

that some individuals who are born poor succeed beyond expectations, while some who have every advantage fail. For most of the people, most of the time, however, their social class origins will shape much of the character of their adult lives.

The process of uneven competition ensures that income and wealth will concentrate within relatively small segments of the population, ensuring the continuation of social class differences. In 2005, for instance, the richest 5% of the American population owned 70% of everything of value in the nation, and one-third of this was owned by only *one-half of one percent* of the population (Figure 5.2). This left less than a third of the nation's wealth (29%) for the remaining 95% of the U.S. population (U.S. Bureau of the Census, 2006).

While an uneven distribution of wealth and cultural advantages is inevitable in competitive market societies, just how uneven this distribution will be is the result of political forces. Governmental policies can either intensify or mitigate class inequalities. Progressive taxation of income and capital gains can be used to finance programs that help improve the chances of the less-well-off while reducing the income and wealth gap between social classes. Alternatively, governments can pursue policies that make the poor poorer and the rich richer, such as regressive sales taxes and reducing their spending on social programs that would close the wealth gap.

Government policies can also increase or decrease the criminogenic consequences of income and wealth inequality by choosing to pursue preventative or punitive justice strategies. Preventative strategies such as pre-school education of poor children (e.g., Head Start), housing subsidies, and income support policies for poor families will help reduce the negative effects of income and wealth inequality, lessening the number of low-income children for whom hopelessness becomes a pathway to delinquency, drug use, and maybe even adult crime. Punitive strategies, meanwhile, attack the crime problem through "get tough" tactics such as determinate

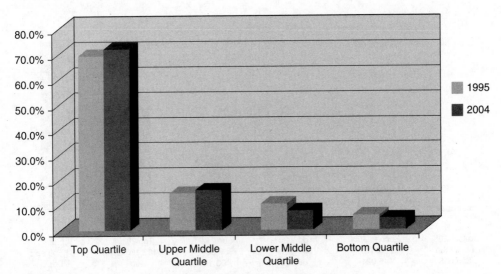

FIGURE 5.2   Percentage Shares of U.S. Household Wealth, 1995–2004.

Source: Di, Z. X. 2007. *Growing Wealth, Inequality, and Housing in the United States.* Cambridge, MA: Joint Center for Housing Studies, Harvard University.

sentencing, "wars" on crime and drugs, and removal of rehabilitation programs from prisons. These have the effect of increasing rather than decreasing the number of people who will become enmeshed in the justice system.

SOCIAL CLASS AND THE DEFINITION OF CRIME

Social class divisions involve the unequal distribution of political power and cultural authority, as well the distribution of wealth. Individuals whose money comes primarily from investments or well-paying occupations have more opportunities to influence the formal institutions of government—including the justice system—than ordinary wageworkers, the poor, the unemployed, the young, or the undereducated. If you doubt this, examine the composition of the U.S. Senate, the Congress, or your state legislature, where you will find that the vast majority are either wealthy, have high-status professional careers, are business owners, or manifest some combination of these characteristics (Parenti, 1977). At the federal level, one-third of all Senators and over a quarter of all U.S. Representatives are millionaires (Santini, 2004). Conversely, factory workers, sales clerks, truck drivers, ordinary white-collar workers, house-wives, students, unemployed, homeless, or any of the other non-elite social groups that together comprise the vast majority of the American social landscape are almost entirely absent from the physical places and social spaces where laws are made. As a result, the laws and policies that shape how we define crime are more likely to reflect the values, life experiences, and interests of the upper echelons of society.

I am not suggesting that laws and policies reflect *only* the interests of upper echelons of society. There are many areas of agreement among the U.S. social classes over the definition of crime. Both the rich and the poor agree that murder, rape, theft, and burglary should be treated as crimes. It is where there is disagreement over the definitions of crime that the greater power of the affluent classes is manifest. For instance, the majority of Americans view deliberate acts of white-collar crimes that lead to death or injury as serious as street crimes that lead to death or injury, and corporate and political corruption as deserving of punishment as ordinary acts of theft (Rossi, 1974; Rebovich and Layne, 2000). Lawmakers, however, come primarily from the strata of society that has the *exclusive ability* to commit white-collar crimes. As a result, the prosecution and punishment of white collar, corporate, and political crimes has always been more lenient than the treatment of street crimes.

In addition to frequently prevailing in specific disagreements with less-advantaged classes, the resource-rich have always played an important role in shaping broadly held visions of right and wrong. As Ysabel Renee (1978) details in *The Search for Criminal Man,* throughout modern history the idea of who is "danger-ous" has shifted to reflect elite interests in criminalizing those whose behavior challenged established economic and cultural hierarchies. During the Middle Ages, when royalty and the Catholic Church constituted the ruling classes, "republicans" (those who believed in political equality) and "heretics" (those who refused to accept papal religious authority) were viewed as the most dangerous of criminals. During the early stages of mercantile capitalism, those who refused to be evicted from hereditary feudal lands, refused to work for wages, or who violated the new rules of private property were defined as dangerous and deserving of harsh punishments (Chambliss, 1964; Hall, 1935). With the rise of industrialization, the growing population of poorly paid and urbanized, industrial workers were labeled the "dangerous classes," and their pleasures, such as gambling and drinking alcohol, were defined as "vices" that should be criminalized and repressed (Brace, 1880; Helmer, 1975). Today, in an era when globalization is threatening to weaken, if not erase, the boundary lines between countries and economies, those who seek to migrate from poor to wealthy countries in order to find work are increasingly being defined as the new "dangerous" class (Michalowski, 2008).

Since the middle of the nineteenth century, the American justice system has promoted definitions of behavior and morality that paint the poorer parts of society as over-populated by dangerous people and deviant behavior, while the middle and upper classes are presumed to be primarily industrious and moral. As Edwin Sutherland (1949) noted in his landmark volume, *White Collar Crime,* when people of "high social status" do wrong in the course of pursuing profit, the legal system "administratively segregates" their wrongdoing from *crime.* Harmful behaviors committed in the pursuit of profit are typically defined as "regulatory violations," which carry neither the stigma nor the punishments associated with *real* crime (Edelhertz and Geis, 1974; Lynch, McGuerrinn, and Fenwick, 2004; Reiman, 1996). This occurs even though the damage to health, wealth, and life caused by these offenses *vastly exceeds* those caused by routine criminals from poorer social classes. As the populist folk singer of the 1930s, Woody Guthrie, wrote, "Some men rob you with a six gun, some with a fountain pen." The criminal justice system, however, is designed almost exclusively to control those who "rob you with a six gun." Those who commit corporate and political crime with a pen have little to fear from the justice system.

The long-term cultural effects of this process are substantial. Regardless of social class, many people think of the vices and street crimes of lower-income groups as the essence of *real* crime, and as the appropriate, primary focus of law. This is not, however, because street crimes are the most harmful ones occurring in the United States. It is because, by example and by rhetoric, this is the message the U.S. justice system has given us throughout our lives. We rarely hear of white-collar offenders being imprisoned for their crimes, but the media regularly treats us with stories of lower-income street criminals making the "perp walk" and being processed through the halls of justice (Altheide, 2006; Barak, 1994; Ericson, Baranek and Chan, 1991). Consequently, it is easier to believe that burglars, robbers, drug-dealers, and auto thieves pose a far greater threat to our well-being than corporate criminals. When political leaders repeatedly denounce drug users, gangs, or illegal immigrants as threats to American society, but rarely, if ever, use their cultural authority to condemn corporate officials who deliberately poison and impoverish large segments of the world's population in pursuit of "economic growth," we are likely to believe that it is more important to control young men showing gang colors than middle-aged businessmen who believe profit justifies human suffering (Michalowski, 1998). The more the criminal justice system focuses on people from poorer and culturally disdained backgrounds, the more it appears as if the poor are the crime problem.

The criminal justice system's focus on the crimes of the poor obscures the far greater harm done by white collar and corporate criminals. Consider the following: A U.S. Department of Justice study estimated that the total cost of serious crime in the United States in 1992 amounted to 17.6 billion dollars (Klaus, 1994). While this represents a substantial loss, it is only a fraction of the costs that white-collar criminals impose on the United States. According to the U.S. General Accounting Office, fraud and abuse account for 10% of the total money spent on health care in the United States, with most of this fraud being committed not by health care users, but by insurance companies, health care professionals, and health care organizations. In 1995, the cost from this one area of fraud alone was estimated to be *100 billion dollars,* nearly seven times greater than the cost of all street crimes (Davis, 1995; Thompson, 1992). According to the Association of Certified Fraud Examiners, the annual cost of all frauds within business in the United States is approximately *400 billion* dollars, *twenty-two times higher* than the total cost of serious street crime (Geis, 1998).

The typical argument posed against comparisons like those presented here are that although white collar and corporate crimes cost people money, even a lot of money, they do not cause the physical harms associated with street crime. Claims of this sort, however, fail to take into account the deaths and injuries that result each year from corporate lawbreaking in the workplace, the marketplace, and the environment, or the suffering caused every year by unaffordable health insurance, fraudulent investment schemes, and raided pension funds.

Each year between 9,000 and 10,000 people die due to work-related accidents, and according to the most conservative estimates, between 50,000 and 70,000 die from diseases contracted due to toxins in the workplace (OSHA, 1997). Using the lowest estimates, this means that at least 59,000 people die each year due to workplace hazards. Certainly, not all of these deaths result from violations of law. Some are due to worker carelessness or exposure to unknown hazards. However, according to data from the U.S. Government Accounting Office (1996), 69% of workplaces under government contract that were inspected by the Occupational Safety and Health Administration were guilty of at least one willful violation of workplace safety laws serious enough to pose a "risk of death or serious physical harm to workers." Insofar as government contractors are more closely supervised by OSHA than other workplaces, 69% of the deaths due to work-related injury or illness (41,125 deaths) is a reasonable estimate of the number of people who die annually due to corporate wrongdoing in the workplace.

If we compare these 41,125 criminal workplace deaths with the 24,330 homicides in 1990, the peak year for homicides in recent decades, we find that the odds of dying due to work hazards are almost double those of being murdered. However, since the workforce is less than one-half of the population, these figures actually mean that the chances that a worker will be killed in a job-related accident or die from a job-related illness are roughly four times greater than the likelihood of being murdered. For the friends and relatives of those killed, these deaths are very real, very painful losses made all the more so because, like homicide in the street or the home, they result from the criminal activity of others.

If we turn our attention to workplace injuries we find a similar picture. According to the FBI, in 2005 the rate of violent crime in the United States was 465 per every 100,000 people (U.S. Bureau of Justice Statistics, 2006). By comparison, the Occupational Health and Safety Administration estimated there were roughly 1,357 non-fatal workplace injuries or illnesses requiring medical care per 100,000 full-time equivalent workers (Bureau of Labor Statistics, 2006). In other words, the odds of being the victim of a serious workplace injury or illness was nearly three times greater than being the victim of a violent crime in 2005. While not all of these harms are caused by corporate illegality, the majority result from either outright violations of worker safety and health laws or corporate negligence that the power-elite have chosen not to regulate (Hillyard *et al.*, 2004).

These comparisons only touch on the ways white collar and corporate crime harm us in our everyday life. The financial costs and physical harms resulting from both illegal and tolerated environmental pollution (think global warming), the deliberate marketing of unsafe products, and the vast array of scams that take not only people's money, but destroy their financial security and emotional well-being exceed the physical and financial costs of street crime by a wide margin every year (Lynch and Michalowski, 2006; Reiman, 1996). Yet it is street crime and street criminals that the law targets most energetically. This is the long legacy of social class bias in the American system of criminal justice.

SOCIAL CLASS AND CRIMINALITY

There is considerable disagreement within criminology and criminal justice regarding whether individuals from lower classes are more likely to commit crime than those from the middle and upper classes. If we ask who is more likely to cause *harm* to the society, as discussed above, it would appear that the upper- and middle-class sectors pose the greatest danger to our health, life, and economic well-being. If we stick to the question of who commits the crimes targeted by the justice system, the picture becomes less clearer.

Annual FBI reports of the characteristics of people who are arrested in the United States provide information regarding gender, age, race, and ethnicity, but little regarding social class characteristics such as income, occupation, or residence. Consequently, the best information we have regarding the social class characteristics of those who populate U.S. prisons and jails street criminals is based on surveys of prison inmates, and interestingly, the government funds very little research into these characteristics. The last detailed survey of prisoners serving felony sentences in state penitentiaries, and this constitutes the majority of those incarcerated in the United States in any year, was conducted in 1993, suggesting that the federal government has little interest in regularly gathering information about the class and other social characteristics of prisoners.

According to the 1993 survey of prison inmates, there is little question that the vast majority of those serving time for criminal offenses come from the poorest segments of the society. The survey showed criminal offenders to be less well educated, far less likely to be employed, and earning far lower incomes than the general population. For instance, while 78% of the general population had graduated from high school, only 33% of the prisoners surveyed had done so. At a time when 7% of the total labor force was unemployed, 45% of those in prison had been without jobs at the time of their arrest. Finally, although the average yearly wage for full-time employed workers was $27,000, and even the *poorest* 10% of full-time workers earned an average of $13,000 a year, 53% of those in prison had incomes of $10,000 or less before being arrested (Bureau of Justice Statistics, 1993). More recently, a 2002 survey of inmates of local jails revealed a similar pattern. Only 57% of jail inmates held full-time employment at the time of their arrest even though the overall unemployment rate was below 5%, and over half earned less than $15,000 a year (Bureau of Justice Statistics, 2004).

Although these statistics may be somewhat skewed by the fact that better-off offenders charged with street crimes are more likely to avoid imprisonment, there is little reason to believe the degree of error is substantial. All one has to do is spend a few days in any urban police station or city court to know that very few middle- or upper-class citizens are brought to the bar of justice for common street crimes. Clearly, the criminal justice net hauls in the poorest of the poor. What this tells us about the link between social class and criminal behavior, however, remains controversial.

Attempts to explain the relationship between social class and criminality have produced three types of explanations: individual defect theories, social interaction theories, and structural outcomes theories. Currently, the favored *individualistic explanations* for higher rates of street crime among the poor focus on family failings and personal morality. *Body count,* an influential, conservative assessment of crime trends, argued that crime is the result of "moral poverty." The authors claimed that high crime rates occur when families fail to impose clear moral understandings of right and wrong on the next generation (Bennett, DiJullio, and Walters, 1996). By focusing on "street criminals," the authors make it clear that they are primarily concerned with the "moral poverty" of the poorer classes, not the moral poverty of corporate and political wrongdoers. This approach is a modern-day equivalent of the nineteenth-century writers who blamed the working class for their poverty, rather than asking why industrial workers were paid so little.

Even if the claim that the proportion of families passing on moral messages to the next generation has declined in recent decades were true, why is this? Might it have anything to do with the substantial decline in family wages among the poorest 40% of the population? Or the emergence of a new cybertech society that offers few opportunities for the children of today's inner-city poor? Explanations that focus on the belief systems of criminals tend to be circular insofar as they claim that (1) individuals commit crime because they lack good values, and (2) we know they lack good values because they commit crime. By placing the locus of responsibility for crime at the individual level, these explanations minimize the importance of societal changes that alter the context within which individuals learn their values and select their behaviors. In the end, individualistic explanations for crime are much like focusing on a ping-pong match while there are bowling balls rolling around underneath the table.

Social interactionist approaches argue that if it were not for the biased nature of the justice system, the poor would appear just as law-abiding as the affluent. They contend that "criminals" (i.e., wrongdoers who show up in official statistics) are disproportionately poor because (1) the justice system focuses on controlling poor communities, and (2) this practice increases the likelihood of future criminality by "labeling" residents of these areas, particularly young men, as "criminals" at an early age (Currie, 1993; Irwin and Austin, 1994; Matza, 1969). A typical example put forth is that the proportion of drug users among college students is no less than in poor communities, yet college students have a far lower risk of serving time as drug offenders than residents of poor communities because they are not the targets of "wars on drugs"—which are really wars on poor people (Chambliss, 1995; Currie, 1998). Although there is some merit to this approach, the question that remains is, *why* does the criminal justice system do this? Is it merely a reflection of the discriminatory attitudes of those who work in the justice system? Or are they, as good workers, simply pursuing the goals set out for them by a broader political and economic system?

Structural outcomes perspectives generally argue that poor communities *will* suffer from higher rates of criminal behavior, just as they suffer from disproportionate levels of other problems such as hypertension, alcoholism, and diabetes, not because of individual failings, but because of the physical and emotional pressures of poverty and inequality. This approach focuses on the structurally induced gap those in the poorer classes experience between their material wants and the resources they have to fulfill them. This concept of *structural strain*, first formalized by Robert Merton (1938), contends that while desires for the "good things" in life cuts across all social classes, the poor have fewer resources to obtain them. Some individuals resolve this pressure by resorting to illegal means to fulfill their culturally learned desires (Agnew, 2001; Featherstone and DeFlem, 2003; Merton, 1938; Messner and Rosenfeld, 2007). When it comes to non-utilitarian crimes such as interpersonal violence or drug use, structural outcomes models shift their focus toward how the daily frustrations of living poor can increase tendencies toward aggression, or to self-medication with illegal drugs to ease the sadness and difficulties of daily life (Bernard, 1990).

The problem with most efforts to explain the link between social class and criminality is the tendency to focus on a single level of analysis. It is more useful, however, to think about the relationship between social class and crime as an interaction between different levels of social life.

The broadest level is the organization of society according to the competitive market relations of capitalism. This leads to the division of society into social classes with differing levels of economic, social, and life-style resources, which has, in turn important behavioral, political, and justice system consequences.

At the behavioral level, resource-rich and resource-poor classes develop differing ways of life. Each group will utilize the resources available to them to resolve the problems or take advantage of the opportunities their social positions offer them. This includes differences in the typical ways members of these groups will do harm and find pleasures.

At the political level, however, resource-rich classes will be able to establish laws that define the harms and pleasures of resource-poor population as criminal, while leaving the harms and pleasures of their own groups largely beyond the scope of the criminal law. For instance, the legal system criminalizes poor citizens who "self-medicate" the sorrows of their lives with alcohol, marijuana, cocaine, crack or methamphetamine. Meanwhile, middle- and upper-class citizens with access to health insurance, doctors, and drug prescriptions who consume daily quantities of Prozac or Zoloft, face little risk of criminalization for medicating their sorrows. Similarly, when poor ghetto residents spend a few dollars playing the "numbers," the legal system defines their acts as criminal. Middle-class citizens who spend hundreds and even thousands of dollars in casinos chasing illusive dreams of a "big win" will face no such stigma. Similarly, the middle-class executive who takes a high-paying job overseas to increase his ability to move up the corporate ladder will be seen as making a wise choice. The poor immigrant who crosses the U.S. border at night to find a job to feed his family, however, will be defined as an illegal immigrant and as a threat to U.S. society (Nevins, 2001). These distinctions, like so many others, are shaped by the ability of affluent classes to determine who is and who is not a criminal threat.

This, in turn, leads to a justice system focused on poorer populations. The *face* of crime comes to be that of poor people using crude means such as theft or force to obtain some desired good, or reacting in frustration or sadness to the difficulties of their lives through drug use or violence in their personal relationships. This creates a repetitive feedback loop whereby citizens come to believe that the street crimes and vice crimes of the poor are the primary threat to social order, and so they support more repressive control of street crime. This leads to more poor people in jails and prisons, which leads to more fear of the poor, and more demands for control over their crimes, and so on.

SOCIAL CLASS AND VICTIMIZATION

While there is some debate about the relationship between social class and criminality, the linkage between social class and criminal *victimization* is well established. Since 1973, the Bureau of Justice Statistics has conducted the National Crime Victimization Survey (NCVS) which uses a representative sample of households nationwide to estimate the rate of criminal victimization in the United States each year. The data provided by the NCVS indicate that while the link between social class and victimization varies according to crime, overall, the less well off tend to bear a greater burden as crime victims, particularly with respect to crimes of violence.

According to the National Crime Victimization Survey, in 2004, households earning less than $7,500 were twice as likely to contain someone who had been the victim of a violent crime than households earning more than $75,000 (Figure 5.3). If we examine specific crime categories, we find even sharper differences. In comparison

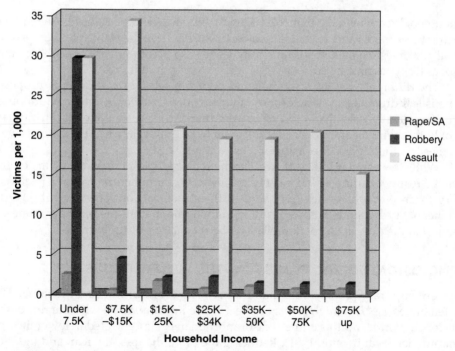

FIGURE 5.3   Violent Victimization by Household Income, 2004.

Source: National Crime Victimization Survey, Bureau of Justice Statistics, 2005, at http://www. ojp.usdoj.gov/bjs/abstract/cv04.htm.

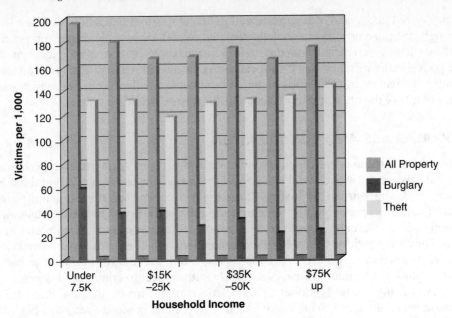

FIGURE 5.4 Property Victimization by Household Income, 2004.

Source: National Crime Victimization Survey, Bureau of Justice Statistics, 2005, at http://www.ojp.usdoj.gov/bjs/abstract/cv04.htm.

to households earning more than $75,000 annually, households earning less than $7,500 are four times more likely to contain someone who has been the victim of rape or sexual assault, 22 times more likely to contain someone who was the victim of a robbery, and twice as likely to contain someone who is the victim of assault.

The difference between the rich and poor households as victims of property crime is less dramatic, although for the more serious crime of burglary, poor households face greater risks than rich ones. According to the NCVS, for every 10 burglaries of homes with incomes over $75,000, there were 25 burglaries of poor homes with incomes less than $7,500 (See Figure 5.4).

While the popular image of street crime is often that of the poor preying on the rich, the reality of crime is that most people tend to commit crime within a relatively short distance of where they live. Thus, if the structural contradictions of poverty and inequality are more likely to result in individuals committing ordinary crimes, it means that the poor are also more likely to be the victims of street crimes.

CONCLUSION: SOCIAL CLASS AND THE FUTURE OF JUSTICE

The contemporary justice system and those who work in it face a dilemma. The United States *does have* high levels of street crime in comparison with the rest of the developed world, and this crime *is* disproportionately concentrated in lower income communities (Braithwaite, 1981). Reducing the pain, the loss, the fear, and the sadness caused by these crimes is a worthy goal for anyone who undertakes a career in criminal justice. Some important underlying features of contemporary society, however, make it a goal with a dark side.

It is not popular these days to talk about the "root causes of crime." Not talking about them, however, does not make them go away, even if business and political leaders choose to act like little children who cover their eyes and say, "You can't see me!" Whether or not we want to see it, our world is changing in ways that are increasing the production of both poor people and crimes against and by poor people. Rapid increases in hyper-technology and global competition mean that growing numbers of people are being closed off from work that pays a living wage (Rifkin, 1995; Sklar, Mykyta, and Wefald, 2002). A depressingly familiar feature of many inner-city communities is a near total absence of decent jobs. Significant numbers of people have been rendered part of a "surplus population" who are simply not needed by the work world. Equally disturbing is the fact that we have come to accept high levels of unemployment among inner-city youth as normal, just as we have come to accept homeless people as a normal feature of urban life. Yet, there was a time in living memory when neither of these things were commonplace.

As William Wilson (1996) details in *When Work Disappears,* when young people do not see adults working and being *rewarded* for legitimate work, they are more likely to pursue illegitimate routes to income, or to compensate for their lack of hope by pursuing the street comforts of alcohol, drugs, casual sex, and gang membership. This search for alternative (and often criminalized) means to material goods and social satisfaction is intensified in the contemporary world where the ability to purchase lifestyle commodities has become a key element in the construction of personal identity (see Ewen, 1988; Fiske, 1996; Unger, 1990).

Economic indicators point to a continued growth in the surplus population—what some people call the "underclass"—over the coming years, as well as increased efforts by the justice system to control this underclass (Carlson and Michalowski, 1997; Michalowski and Carlson, 1999). Historically, the United States has responded to the problem of controlling surplus populations with one of two strategies—criminal justice in the form of police and prisons, and social welfare in the form of jobs programs and cash or in-kind public assistance (Piven and Cloward, 1977). The current political climate favors a strategy based largely on using the criminal justice system, particularly prisons, to deal with the problems posed by a growing underclass. By deviantizing and criminalizing large numbers of youth from low-income (and typically racial minority) communities, often for relatively minor offenses, the justice system ensures a growing number of poor offenders, just as the poverty of their neighborhoods ensures a growing number of poor victims.

All of this poses several dilemmas for justice system workers. The first dilemma is whether working in the justice system is an honorable career devoted to protecting people from the ravages of crime, or one devoted to keeping the lid on the consequences of social class inequality so that the better-off can enjoy their larger shares of the pie in relative peace and with the confidence that *they* are not part of the problem. Of course, things are never that simple or clear cut. Crimes occur. They harm people physically and emotionally. They disrupt community life in a multitude of ways. In a society whose social structure produces high rates of crime, someone must help those who are its victims. Even if these efforts do not substantially stem the flow of crime—and there is little evidence that 35 years of a war on crime and 25 years of a war on drugs has brought many real victories—they are worth making. Every crime prevented, every victim helped, every offender rehabilitated, every addict detoxed is another human being whose suffering has been lessened. At the same time, it is important that both citizens and those who work in the justice system are not blinded by the goodness of these acts into thinking that they represent a solution to, or even major gains against, the crime problem.

The justice system helps many people, but it alone cannot produce *justice* in the society. Real justice is *social justice*. A large criminal justice system cannot compensate for a lack of social justice.

This brings us to the second dilemma facing justice system workers and others today. Should we continue to support "get tough" policies that will certainly create more jobs for justice system workers, but do so at the expense of real justice? Or should we dedicate ourselves to creating a more just society, one that can live with a smaller justice system because it is less divided by class inequalities? We can continue to treat the poor parts of our society as battle zones. This will certainly keep justice system employment high. However, if we are truly dedicated to reducing the human tragedy of crime, we need to cease the violent rhetoric of our various "wars" against crime, and begin to look for ways of reducing social inequality and creating genuine opportunities for dignified, materially adequate, and socially accepted lives for all. In the final analysis, if we want peace, we must work for social justice. The alternative is to wage a perpetually failing war against crime, drugs, and the poor.

References

Agnew, Robert. 2001. Building on the Foundation of General Strain Theory: Specifying the Types of Strain Most Likely to Lead to Crime and Delinquency. *Journal of Research in Crime and Delinquency* 38: 319–361.

Altheide, David L. 2006. *Terrorism and the Politics of Fear.* Lanham, MD: Alta Mira Press.

Barak, Gregg (Ed.). 1994. *Media, Process, and the Social Construction of Crime: Studies in Newsmaking Criminology.* New York, NY: Garland.

Bartley, Robert L., and B. Bruce-Briggs (Eds.). 1979. *The New Class?* New Brunswick, NJ: Transaction Books.

Beck, Allen, and Lauren Glaze. 2004. Correctional Populations in the United States. Washington, D.C.: Bureau of Justice Statistics.

Bennett, William J., John J. DiIulio, and John P. Walters. 1996. *Body Count.* New York, NY: Simon & Schuster.

Bernard, Thomas J. 1990. Angry Aggression. *Criminology* 28 (1): 73–96.

Bernstein, Jared, Elizabeth McNichol, and Karen Lyons. 2006. *Pulling Apart: A State-by-State Analysis of Income Trends.* Washington, DC: Center for Budget and Policy Priorities.

Bourgois, Philippe. 1995. *In Search of Respect: Selling Crack in El Barrio.* New York, NY: Cambridge University Press.

Brace, Charles Loring. 1880. *The Dangerous Classes of New York, and Twenty Years' Work Among Them.* New York, NY: Wynkoop & Hallenbeck.

Braithwaite, John. 1981. The Myth of Social Class and Criminality Reconsidered. *American Sociological Review* 46 (1): 36–57.

Braithwaite, John. 1984. *Corporate Crime in the Pharmaceutical Industry.* Boston, MA: Routledge & Kegan Paul.

Bureau of Justice Statistics, U.S. Department of Justice. 1993. *Survey of Inmates of State Prisons. NCJ 136949.* Washington, DC: U.S. Government Printing Office.

Bureau of Justice Statistics, U.S. Department of Justice. 2004. *National Crime Victimization Survey.* Washington, DC. http://www.ojp.usdoj.gov/bjs/abstract/cv04.htm.

Bureau of Labor Statistics. 2006. *Workplace Illness and Injuries: 2005.* http://www.bls.gov/news.release/pdf/osh.pdf.

Carlson, Susan, and Raymond Michalowski. 1997. Crime, Unemployment, and Social Structures of Accumulation: An Inquiry into Historical Contingency. *Justice Quarterly* 14 (2): 209–241.

Chambliss, William. 1964. A Sociological Analysis of the Laws of Vagrancy. *Social Problems* 12: 67–77.

Chambliss, William. 1995. Another Lost War: The Costs and Consequences of Drug Prohibition. *Social Justice* 22 (2): 101–124.

Chambliss, William, and Robert Seidman. 1982. *Law, Order and Power.* Reading, MA: Addison-Wesley.

Currie, Elliot. 1993. *Reckoning: Drugs, the Cities, and the American Future.* New York, NY: Hill and Wang.

Currie, Elliot. 1998. *Crime and Punishment in America.* New York, NY: Holt.

Davis, L. J. 1995. Medscam. *Mother Jones.* http://bsd.mojones.com/mother_jones/MA95/davis.html.

Di, Z. X. 2007. *Growing Wealth, Inequality, and Housing in the United States.* Cambridge, MA: Joint Center for Housing Studies, Harvard University.

Edelhertz, Herbert, and Gilbert Geis. 1974. *Public Compensation to Victims of Crime.* New York, NY: Praeger.

Ericson, Richard Victor, Patricia M. Baranek, and Janet Chan. 1991. *Representing Order: Crime, Law, and Justice in the News Media.* Toronto: University of Toronto Press.

Ewen, Stuart. 1988. *All Consuming Images: The Politics of Style in Contemporary Culture.* New York, NY: Basic Books.

Featherstone, Richard, and Mathieu Deflem. 2003. Anomie and Strain: Context and Consequences of Merton's Two Theories. *Sociological Inquiry* 73 (4): 471–489.

Fiske, John. 1966. *Media Matters: Everyday Culture and Political Change.* Minneapolis, MN: University of Minnesota Press.

Geis, Gilbert. 1998. *Association of Certified Fraud Examiners: Report to the Nation.* Austin, TX: Association of Certified Fraud Examiners.

Hall, Jerome. 1935. *Theft, Law and Society.* Boston, MA: Little Brown.

Hawkins, Mary F. 1997. *Unshielded: The Human Cost of the Dalkon Shield.* Toronto: University of Toronto Press.

Helmer, John. (1975). *Drugs and Minority Oppression.* New York, NY: Seabury Press.

Hills, Stuart L. (Ed.). 1987. *Corporate Violence: Injury and Death for Profit.* Totowa, NJ: Rowman & Littlefield.

Hillyard, Paddy, Christina Pantazis, Steve Tombs, and Dave Gordon (Ed.). 2004. *Beyond Criminology: Taking Harm Seriously.* London: Pluto Press.

Irwin, John and James Austin. 1994. *It's About Time: America's Imprisonment Binge.* Belmont, CA: Wadsworth.

Johnston, David C. 2007. Income Gap Is Widening, Data Shows. *New York Times,* March 29. http://www.nytimes.com/2007/03/29/business/29tax.html.

Kauzlarich, David and Ronald Kramer 1998. *Crimes of the Nuclear State.* Boston, MA: Northeastern University Press.

Klaus. Patsy A. 1994. *The Costs of Crime to Victims.* Washington, DC: U.S. Department of Justice, Bureau of Justice Statistics

Lusane, Clarence. 1991. *Pipe Dream Blues: Racism and the War on Drugs.* Boston, MA: South End Press.

Lynch, Michael, Danielle McGuerrinn, and Melissa Fenwick. 2004. Disappearing Act: The Representation of Corporate Crime Research in Criminological Literature. *Journal of Criminal Justice* 30: 389–398.

Lynch, Michael, and Raymond Michalowski. 2006. *Crime, Power and Identity: The New Primer in Radical Criminology.* Washington, DC: Criminal Justice Press.

Macleod, Jay. 1995. *Ain't No Makin' It: Aspirations and Attainment in a Low-income Neighborhood.* Boulder, CO: Westview Press.

Matza, David. 1969. *Becoming Deviant.* Englewood Cliffs, NJ: Prentice Hall.

Merton, Robert. 1938. Social Structure and Anomie. *American Sociological Review* 3: 672–682.

Messner, Steven F., and Richard Rosenfeld. 2007. *Crime and the American Dream,* 4th edn. Belmont, CA: Wadsworth.

Michalowski, Raymond. 1985. *Order, Law, and Crime.* New York, NY: Random House.

Michalowski, Raymond. 1998. International Environmental Issues. In *Environmental Crime,* ed. M. Clifford, 315–340. Gaithersburg, MD: Aspen Publishers.

Michalowski, R. 2008. Border Militarization and Migrant Suffering. *Social Justice* 34(2).

Michalowski, R. and Carlson, S. 1999. "Unemployment, Imprisonment and Social Structures of Accumulation: Historical Contingency in the Rusche-Kirchheimer Hypothesis." *Criminology* 37 (2): 217–250.

Michalowski, R. and Kramer, R. 2006. *State-Corporate Crime: Wrongdoing at the Intersection of Business and Politics.* New Brunswick, NJ: Rutgers University Press.

Michalowski, R. and Kramer, R. 2007. *State-Coporate Crime: Wrongdoing at the Intersection of Business and Government.* New Brunswick: Rutgers University Press.

Mintz, Morton. 1985. *At Any Cost: Corporate Greed, Women, and the Dalkon Shield.* New York, NY: Pantheon Books.

Nachtigal, Jerry. 1998. My Non-Violent Offenses "different," Symington Says: Draws Distinctions Between His Doings and Robbers, Rapists. *The Arizona Republic,* February 4, A1.

Nevins, Joseph. 2001. *Operation Gatekeeper: The Rise of the "Illegal Alien" and the Remaking of the U.S.–Mexico Boundary.* New York: Routledge.

Occupational Safety and Health Administration. 1997. *Strategic Plan.* Washington, DC: USGPO.

Parenti, Michael. 1977. *Democracy for the Few.* New York, NY: St. Martin's Press.

Pastore, Ann, and Kathleen Maguire. 2007. *Sourcebook of Criminal Justice Statistics.* http://www.albany.edu/sourcebook/.

Piven, Frances Fox, and Richard Cloward. 1977. *Poor Peoples' Movements.* New York, NY: Pantheon Books.

Poulantzas, Nicos. 1975. *Classes in Contemporary Capitalism.* Translated from the French by David Fernbach. London: NLB.

Rebovich, Donald. 1992. *Dangerous Ground: The World of Hazardous Waste Crime.* New Brunswick, NJ: Transaction Publishers.

Rebovich, Donald, and Jenny Layne. 2000. *The National Public Survey on White Collar Crime.* Morgantown, WV: National White Collar Crime Center.

Reiman, Jeffrey. 1996. *The Rich Get Richer and the Poor Get Prison: Economic Bias in American Criminal Justice,* 8th edn. Boston, MA: Allyn and Bacon.

Renee, Ysabel. 1978. *The Search for Criminal Man.* Boston, MA: Sage Publications.

Rifkin, Jeremy. 1995. *The End of Work: The Decline of the Global Labor Force and the Dawn of the Post-Market Era.* New York, NY: G.P. Putnam Sons.

Rossi, Peter. 1974. The Seriousness of Crimes: Normative Structures and Individual Differences. *American Sociological Review* 39 (1): 224–237.

Santini, Jean-Louis. 2004. Millionaires fill U.S. Congress Halls. http://www.Information clearinghouse.info/article6418.htm.

Sklar, Holly, Laryssa Mykyta, and Susan Wefald. 2002. *Raise the Floor: Wages and Policies That Work for All of US.* Boston: South End Press.

Stitt, B. Grant, and David Giacopassi. 1995. *Understanding Corporate Criminality.* New York: Garland.

Sutherland, Edwin. 1949. *White Collar Crime.* New York, NY: Dryden Press.

Szymanski, Albert. 1983. *Class Structure.* New York, NY: Praeger.

Thompson, Lawrence H. 1992. Heath Insurance: Vulnerable Payers Loose Billions to Fraud and Abuse. Report to Chairman, Subcommittee on Human Resources and Intergovernmental Operations, U.S. House of Representatives, United States General Accounting Office, Washington, D.C., May.

Unger, Peter. 1990. *Identity, Consciousness, and Value.* New York, NY: Oxford University Press.

U.S. Bureau of the Census. 2006. Historical Income Tables, F3. http://www.census.gov/hhes/www/income/histinc/h01ar.html.

U.S. Bureau of Justice Statistics. 2006. *Sourcebook of Criminal Justice Statistics.* http://www.albany.edu/sourcebook.

U.S. Government Accounting Office. 1996. Occupational Safety and Health: Violations of Safety and Health Regulations by Federal Contractrs. Washington, DC: GAO/HEHS-96-157.

Websdale, Neil. 2001. *Policing the Poor: From Slave Plantation to Public Housing.* Boston: Northeastern University Press.

Western, Bruce. 2007. Mass Imprisonment and Economic Inequality. *Social Research* 74 (2): 509–532.

Wilson, William. J. 1987. *The Truly Disadvantaged: The Inner City, the Underclass, and Public*

Policy. Chicago, IL: University of Chicago Press.

Wilson, William J. 1996. *When Work Disappears.* New York, NY: Knopf.

Wolff, Edward N. 2000. *Recent Trends in Wealth Ownership: 1983–1998.* New York: Levy Economic Institute.

Wright, Erik Olin. 1985. *Classes.* London: Verso.

Wright, Erik Olin. 1996. *Class Counts: Comparative Studies in Class Analysis.* New York, NY: Cambridge University Press.

Wright, Lesley and Marti Smye. 1996. *Corporate Abuse: How "Lean and Mean" Robs People and Profits.* London: Macmillan.

CHAPTER 6

Stolen Lands, Stolen Lives

Native Americans and Criminal Justice

Marianne O. Nielsen

Linda Robyn

Native Americans are the original inhabitants of the United States, and include American Indians, Inuit Aleutian Islanders, and Native Hawaiians, that is, they are "peoples who trace their ancestry in these lands to time immemorial" (Morse, 1989:1). They make up about 1.0% of the American population, with much higher percentages in states such as Alaska (16.0%), New Mexico (10.2%), South Dakota (8.8%), Oklahoma (8.1%), Montana (6.5%), and Arizona (5.1%) (U.S. Census, 2007). As of 2006, there were 562 federally recognized Native American Nations and Alaska villages in the United States (U.S. Department of the Interior, 2006) and about 150 tribal entities that do not have federal recognition for reasons that include not having signed a treaty, and having been unilaterally terminated as an Indian Nation by Congress (Utter, 2001).

It should be noted that many Native American Nations are called by names that are not their own, that is, the name they have now may be based on an inaccurate description (like the word "Indian" itself) or on a name that European explorers learned from unfriendly neighboring Nations (the Navajo, for example, call themselves "Diné"). In general, the most respectful name to use is the name that the Native American people in question call themselves.

Native Americans are of great importance as a "category of difference" within the criminal justice system for a number of reasons (Snipp, 1989). As the original inhabitants of this land, Native Americans have a unique legal status and have contributed to the development of American law, politics, and justice. In addition, the United States has highly held values of equal opportunity and justice, yet the history and living conditions of many Native Americans are in direct contradiction to these values. Also, Native Americans and the dominant European-based society have basic cultural beliefs about justice that are in conflict, and cause misunderstandings and injustice when they interact in the courtroom and elsewhere (Dumont, 1993). Another very important reason is that the myths and stereotypes that exist in our culture about Native Americans (see Harjo, 1998; Mihesuah, 1996; Trigger, 1985) have led and continue to lead to discriminatory actions by people in positions of authority. Also very important is that Native Americans are overrepresented as offenders in the criminal justice system, especially in some states and in some offense categories. Lastly, Native Americans are underrepresented as service providers and policy makers in the criminal justice system, meaning that Native Americans have little input into the justice policies and decisions that affect their lives and communities.

HISTORICAL CONTEXT

In discussing how the current situations of discrimination, overrepresentation, and underrepresentation came about, it is necessary to examine five important aspects of Native American history: colonization, marginalization, urbanization, cultural revitalization, and self-determination (sovereignty).

Colonization starts out as "a relationship of domination between an Indigenous . . . majority and minority of foreign invaders [who] are convinced of their own superiority and of their ordained mandate to rule" (Osterhammel, 1997:16–17). The numbers reverse over time, but the power, relationship, and attitude remain. Even so, colonization is still more than that. Colonization did in the past, and continues today, "to undermine the political, military, social, psychocultural value system, law and order, and knowledge bases of the colonized while imposing the values and culture of the colonizer" (Robyn and Alcoze, 2006:71–72). North America was invaded and eventually controlled by Europeans, as were Australia and much of Africa and Asia. There were three general "ages" of European/Native American relations in North America (Miller, 1991). In the first age, which lasted from Native American/European contact until shortly after the Revolutionary War, Native Americans and colonists lived together more or less cooperatively, with Native Americans being the dominant group during this period. The Europeans were dependent on the Native American Nations for food, shelter, trade, knowledge of the land and its resources, and military aid.

With the expansion of settlers and the need for land, the second age, which was one of coercion against Native Americans by the colonists, lasted until about World War II. Military campaigns and massacres by colonists, along with massive epidemics of foreign diseases such as smallpox and tuberculosis, and the resulting social disorganization took their toll, so that the Native American Nations, despite their active efforts, were unable to resist the colonial invasion. It is estimated that pre-contact Native American populations fall in the range of 2 to 7 million. For the contiguous United States, estimates fall between 1 and 5.5 million, with the number of Indians in the United States reaching a low point of 237,000 by 1900 (Shoemaker, 1999:3). Also see Snipp (1989).

During this era, missionaries, Indian agents, and well-meaning reformers tried to impose on American Indians what they assumed to be vastly superior European cultures, languages, religions, economies, and social structures. Alcohol and usurious credit were introduced by traders to exploit them. The reservation system relocated them onto small lots of unproductive land. Their children were stolen and put into boarding schools. Indian agents had the right to determine who married, who could work, who got farming tools and medicines, and were not above using starvation and violence to make them obey. Even so, not all Native American Nations were treated the same by the colonists; it depended on each Nation's usefulness, annoyance, or irrelevance to the increasingly dominant European-based society.

An important part of the colonization process was the development of first a religious-based ideology, then later a racist ideology of "biologically inferior" Native Americans. At first, Native Americans were seen as pagan, heathen, savages, dirty, drunken, and violent. The colonizers felt justified in denying them basic human rights and in general, treating them as less than human. The colonial ideology also had a paternalistic theme, labeling Native Americans as naive children incapable of controlling their own lives, and in need of protection and the civilizing influence of Europeans. Social Darwinism, which stated that some biological "species" of human were more highly evolved than others, gave "scientific" credence to colonial prejudices and, in their minds, justified discriminatory acts (Trigger, 1985). Just as Social Darwinism gave "scientific" support for the outright prejudice of European settlers toward Indian people, the concept of Manifest Destiny gave religious justification to this as well (Robyn, 2004:284).

The third age, which continues today, was one of confrontation between the Native Americans and the dominant society (Miller, 1991). Religious, educational, economic, and political rights are part of Native American/dominant society negotiations. Another issue involves the relationship of Indian people to their land and environment. Crimes committed by the U.S. government against Indian people are still occurring today as Indian people are criminalized for resisting huge multinational corporations in their war of aggression against Native peoples and the natural world (Robyn, 2004:283). Public awareness of Native American issues is growing. Yet now more than ever, thanks to the long-term impact of colonial processes, Native Americans are engaged in a struggle to survive as culturally distinct indigenous peoples (Boldt, 1993). This section on colonialism is, of necessity, extremely generalized and short; for excellent overviews of North American colonization, see Nies (1996), Jennings (1993), Wright (1992), and Deloria and Lytle (1983).

The main impact of the colonial processes was that many Native American Peoples became *marginalized* from what is now the dominant society in the United States. Suffering from social disorganization and without control over their own lives and resources, many Native American communities became immersed in a subculture of poverty. In 2004, more Native Americans (25.1%) lived in poverty than white non-Latinos at 8.8% (U.S. Census, 2007:16). The educational levels of American Indians and Alaska Natives were below those of the total population. Approximately 71% of Native Americans and Alaska Natives 25 and older had at least a high school education, compared with 80% of the total population (U.S. Census, 2006:8). In addition, only about 25% of Native Americans worked in management, professional related jobs compared to 38% of white non-Latinos (U.S. Census, 2007:14). High rates of suicide, family violence, and alcohol abuse are also characteristic of some Native communities (Bachman, 1992). As well, Native Americans still suffer from discrimination in employment, housing, and in general contact with the dominant society (French, 1994). These are criminogenic living conditions: that is, they put the inhabitants of these communities at higher risk of getting involved with the criminal justice system.

The impacts of these social conditions are complicated by *urbanization*. Over 60% of Native Americans live outside of the mainly rural areas officially designated "Indian" (Utter, 2001:40). Many Native Americans live in the marginalized areas of the city, although they may also be quite successful and be members of the middle and upper classes. Moving to an urban area also has a number of other possible consequences for Native Americans that could increase the likelihood of criminal justice involvement, including lack of the family, clan and friend support network found back home; lack of understanding of urban behavioral expectations; lack of knowledge about what special services, if any, are available to Native Americans; lack of contact with Nation-based spiritual and cultural life; and increased visibility to the police. Barreiro and Johnson (2005:102–103) write that the cities with the largest Indian populations were New York City (87,241) and Los Angeles (53,092). Cities with overall populations greater than 100,000 were Anchorage, AL (10.4%); Tulsa, OK (7.7%); Oklahoma City, OK (5.7%); Albuquerque, NM (4.0%); Green Bay, WI (4.1%); Tacoma, WA (3.6%); Minneapolis, MN (3.3%); Tucson, AZ (3.2%); Spokane, WA (3%), and Sacramento, CA (2.8%).

Another element that must be considered is *cultural revitalization*. While many Native American cultural practices were repressed by laws, and a great deal of knowledge was lost as the result of population decimation, a great deal of cultural knowledge also remains. Native American individuals, communities, and Nations resisted the imposition of foreign laws, religion, and government. Native American societies have been and still are extremely flexible, adaptive, and dynamic. They had to be in order to survive the active oppression they have suffered since colonialism began. Cultural revitalization is a series of movements as diverse as the communities in which they originate, with the objective of regaining (sometimes rediscovering), and re-institutionalizing the cultural traditions, ceremonies, languages, and social structures and environment that were damaged by colonialism.

There are also movements toward *self-determination*, that is, movements to regain the right of Native American Nations to control their own social institutions, including education, social services, health services, leadership, and criminal justice. American Indian Nations have the status of "domestic dependent nations," meaning that they have limited legal rights to control their own society (Pommersheim, 1995). Some of these rights have been unilaterally legislated away since the time of the Treaties, including the right to handle major crimes on the reservations. Many of these rights, such as hunting and fishing rights, and the right to establish new industries (e.g., casinos), are under ongoing attack. Many Native Americans believe that increased sovereignty will enable them to implement culturally based social processes that will more effectively deal with the social ills brought about by colonialism.

In summary, the current involvement of Native Americans in the criminal justice system can only be understood in historical context. Colonization, marginalization, urbanization, cultural revitalization, and self-determination (sovereignty) must all be taken into account when considering Native Americans, crime, and justice.

NATIVE AMERICAN OFFENDERS

Crime rates for Native Americans are extremely suspect. In the past, as Silverman (1996) points out, the FBI's Uniform Crime Reports (UCRs) sometimes missed rural areas, including American Indian Nations, where a significant number of Native Americans live. Also, "race" on the forms was usually based on the police officers' best guess. Statisticians estimate that up to 50% of Native American arrests were missing from the UCRs. There were also problems of missing information in the Census which is used to calculate the "per 100,000" part of the crime rate. There is also the decision of how to classify yourself if you are of mixed race, as are a significant (though unknown) proportion of Native Americans. Taking these factors into account, it can safely be said that past calculations of Native American crime rates have been very inaccurate.

Keeping these issues in mind, Silverman (forthcoming) reports that from 1984 to 2005, the arrest rates were 4,652 per 100,000 for all Americans with 1992 being the peak year. This breaks down to 3,975 (per 100,000) arrests for whites, 11,637 for African Americans, and 6,340 for Native Americans. Based on these figures, the Native American general crime-rate pattern (3,975 per 100,000) was higher than that of whites, but much lower than that of African Americans. As with arrest rates in general throughout the country, Native American arrest rates have dropped significantly since 1984 (Silverman, forthcoming).

For property crime, the Native American arrest rates were above the rates for the white population, but far below those of the African American population. In the area of drug abuse offenses, Native Americans had the lowest rates. It was only in the area of alcohol-related offenses (drunkenness, driving while intoxicated, and liquor violations) that Native Americans had the highest rates over whites and African Americans. Silverman (forthcoming) reports that for African Americans and Native Americans, the rate of drunkenness in 2005 was 30% less than the rate in 1984, though Native Americans continue to have the highest rate for this kind of offense. In 1984, the Native American rate was three times the average rate for all Americans, while in 2005 the Native American rate was still 2.4 times that of the average for all Americans. American Indians were arrested for DUI at a rate of 479 per 100,000 residents, compared to 332 for all races. Liquor law violation arrest rates were about 143 per 100,000 for all races, and 405 per 100,000 American Indians (Perry, 2004:vii). The total arrest rate for Native Americans in rural counties (2.9%) is much higher than in urban areas (1.3%) and suburban areas (0.8%), reflecting residence patterns (Bureau of Justice Statistics, 2003:370–372).

The stereotypes discussed earlier may inform the decisions of members of the dominant society, including criminal justice personnel. A study published in 1973 found that arresting Indians depended upon how the individual officer chose to deal with the situation. According to the study, treatment of Indians by officers ranged from indifference to brutality. Overall, in this study, officers had little knowledge of Indian cultures (Stratton, 1973, cited in Fixico, 2000:89). This issue was also raised by Lujan (1998) in her discussion of the effects of stereotyping on Native Americans. It could be, for example, that if police officers expect Native Americans to have drinking problems that they will be more likely to watch individuals who "look Indian." This decision making is based on a stereotype since the percentage of Native Americans having a drinking problem varies from Nation to Nation and, in fact, more young white people than Native American use alcohol (Mail and Johnson, 1993).

Discrimination may or may not also play a role in the sentencing of Native Americans. The evidence is contradictory. For example, Bachman, Alvarez, and Perkins (1996) in a sample of five states found a pattern of discrimination in the lengths of sentence and percent of sentence served for Native Americans in some offense categories. Yet, Hutton, Pommersheim, and Feimer (1996) found no evidence of judges discriminating on the basis of race in the sentencing of Native women. A more complex pattern was found by Bynum and Paternoster (1996) who report that Native Americans in their sample were sentenced to shorter sentences but served a greater proportion of their sentences than white offenders.

Native Americans were overrepresented as inmates. The Bureau of Justice Statistics (1999:iii) estimates that 1 in 25 Native American Indians age 18 or older is under the jurisdiction of the criminal justice system, which is 2.4 times the per capita rate of whites. Archambeault (forthcoming) writes that "Native Peoples account for about 1 to 1.5% of the total number of offenders under correctional control, and most (70–90%) of these are on probation, parole or in local/tribal jails." In addition, according to Perry (2004), Native Americans comprise about 16% of all offenders who enter federal correctional facilities annually, and have comprised about 15% of all federal prisoners since the mid-1990s. The exact number of Native Americans under some form of correctional control cannot be precisely determined due to various tribal justice systems, tribal agreements with the Bureau of Indian Affairs (BIA) police, treaty conditions, etc., but "prisons and local jails in states with large Indian populations or reservations report Indian offender populations from seven to 15 times the national average" (Archambeault, forthcoming).

According to Grobsmith (1994), the overrepresentation is even higher in a number of state correctional facilities, including those in Alaska (31.9% of prison population), South Dakota (25.4%), North Dakota (22.2%), and Montana (18.3%). Despite laws to the contrary and despite the documented effectiveness of Native American spirituality programs as a rehabilitative mechanism (Nechi, 1994), Native American inmates in some correctional institutions are still being denied access to spiritual counseling and ceremonies, and culturally sensitive drug-and-alcohol-abuse treatment programs (Waldram, 1996). As of June 2002, there were 2,080 American Indians under correctional supervision in Indian Country facilities. About 2,006 (96%) of the American Indians under correctional supervision in Indian Country were inmates, and 74 (4%) were under community supervision which included probation and parole (Bureau of Justice Statistics, 2002).

At the end of 2002, there were 26,300 Native American female prisoners in state prisons, comprising 33% of all female prisoners under state jurisdiction. As of June 30, 2004, there were 103,910 women under state and federal jurisdiction, representing a 2.9% increase from the previous year. In 1999, 1 in 10 female offenders belonged to a race other than white (other), including Native Americans, Aleuts, or Eskimos (Greenfield and Snell, 1999). Similar to Native American male inmates, Native American female inmates suffer from lack of culturally appropriate rehabilitation and treatment programming, and lack of access to spiritual guides and ceremonies.

Between fiscal years 1994 and 2001, on annual average, about 751 American Indians entered federal prison following convictions for violent offenses. In 2001,

BOP was responsible for the confinement of over 171,000 offenders. An estimated 2.4% (1,662) of the offenders entering federal prison were American Indians. The American Indian proportion was more likely to be serving a sentence for a violent offense than federal prisoners of other races. In fiscal year 2001, 55% of American Indians entering federal prison were serving a sentence for a violent crime, compared to 4% of white offenders, 13% of black offenders, and 5% of Asian offenders (Perry, 2004:20–22).

Native Americans are also overrepresented as juvenile offenders, with about 1.2% of juveniles arrested being Native American. Juveniles were most heavily overrepresented, like adults, in alcohol-related crimes. In addition, they were overrepresented in property crime arrests (1.3%) and proportionately represented in violent crime arrests (0.8%) (Bureau of Justice Statistics, 1997). As Meyer (forthcoming) writes, however, the vast majority of juvenile delinquency in Indian Country would be classified as non-serious acts, with the most common arrests for drunkenness, liquor law violations, public disorder, vagrancy, and status offenses; and even among youth who are incarcerated, relatively petty offenses seem to be the norm. Young Native Americans are more likely to be arrested in rural counties (3.1%) than in urban areas (1.0%) and suburban areas (0.5%), again, partly reflecting residence patterns (Reddy, 1995). Armstrong et al. (1996) report that substance abuse is usually associated with Native American juvenile crime, as are negative socioeconomic conditions and child abuse. About 32% of Native American children under the age of 18 live in poverty, compared to 11% of white non-Latino children (U.S. Census, 2007:16). In addition, Meyer (forthcoming) writes that the high number of alcohol-related offenses is not surprising, given the harsh social realities on reservations, which include high rates of unemployment, poverty, alcoholism, and criminal victimization.

Native American juveniles are also overrepresented in custody with 1% of juveniles in public long-term facilities being Native American, and 3% of those in open facilities (Snyder and Sickmund, 1995). Among the 70 jails in tribal areas, 10 were designated as juvenile facilities with a capacity to hold 341 inmates. As of June 2002, the juvenile jails were operating at 54% of capacity. As in all other jails in Indian Country, a majority (62%) of the offenders were held for misdemeanors, about 10% were held for felonies, and 29% for other offenses (Perry, 2004:27).

Over the period 1973 to 2002, there were 7,254 persons sentenced to death in the United States; 60 were American Indians. Between 1977 and 2002, there were 820 executions, eight of which were Indian or 13.3% of the total executed (Perry, 2004:25).

Cultural revitalization is an issue particularly relevant to juvenile crime because many community-level justice initiatives are aimed at preventing juvenile offenses. These programs are often based in traditional justice processes such as counseling by Elders, and the learning of traditional language, ceremonial and economic skills, in the belief that by learning these, young persons will feel more pride in their community and themselves. An important problem with this strategy is that many young Native Americans live in urban areas, or feel no connection to tradition because they come from families that are significantly acculturated into the dominant society.

In summary, Native American men, women, and young people are overrepresented in the criminal justice system for some offenses and in some facilities. In addition, more culturally sensitive and appropriate rehabilitation, treatment, and spiritual programming is needed for Native American offenders throughout the criminal justice system.

NATIVE AMERICAN VICTIMS OF CRIME

Native Americans have been victims of crime as Nations and as individuals. As Nations, Native Americans had their own laws and justice systems. These were not recognized as such by the invading colonists, because to do so would have consequences for the "legality" of their exploitation of the new resource-rich continent. Colonial powers consciously broke international law by staking claims and declaring ownership occupied by indigenous peoples. The colonial powers justified their actions by the "right of first discovery," which stated that "a Christian nation was divinely mandated to exercise dominion over non-Christian 'primitives' and to assert proprietary title to any 'unoccupied' land" (Boldt, 1993:3).

Second, the Treaties, legal documents signed between the colonial government and Native Nations, were broken by the colonial government when it no longer remained in its political or economic interest to honor them. This trend continues today as the American federal and state governments chip away at remaining Treaty rights. Third, laws were used to define Native American identity so that they were seen as less capable and rational than adults. In the *Cherokee Nation* case (1831), the federal government placed itself in "guardianship" over American Indians, ostensibly to protect them from unscrupulous whites; however, this relationship made it possible for the federal government to facilitate the theft of their lands and resources. Laws such as the Indian Removal Act of 1830 forced the majority of American Indian Nations in the eastern part of the country to leave their lands and move west of the Mississippi River (Deloria and Lytle, 1983). Native Americans in some states were forbidden the vote unless they could prove that they had "become civilized" by severing all ties with their Indian identity (Deloria and Lytle, 1983).

Native American individuals have also been the victims of crime, both historically and currently. Luna-Firebaugh (2007:12) writes that the murder rate in Indian Country is 29 per 100,000, compared with the national murder rate of 5.6 per 100,000. According to Perry (2004:iii), self-report studies revealed that Native Americans and Alaska Natives are victims of violent crime at a rate more than twice the national average of other U.S. racial or ethnic groups. Furthermore, rates of violence experienced by Native Americans occur across age groups, housing locations, and by gender.

On average, American Indians experienced an estimated 1 violent crime for every 10 residents age 12 or older. From 1976 to 2001, an estimated 3,738 American Indians were murdered. After 1995, this rate decreased about 45% from 6.6 to 3.6 murders per 100,000 residents in 2001. The murderer of an American Indian was most likely to be anotherAmerican Indian (58%), followed by a white (32%). Among American Indians age 25 to 34, the rate of violent crime victimizations was more than 2½ times the rate for all persons the same age. The rate of violent victimization among American Indian women was more than double that among all women. American Indians were more likely to be victims of assault and rape/sexual assault committed by a stranger or acquaintance rather than an intimate partner or family member. Overall, about 62% of American Indian victims experienced violence by an offender using alcohol compared to 42% for the national average (Perry, 2004:14).

Another disturbing fact is that Native Americans experience violence at the hands of someone of a different race, more than people of other races (70%), mainly by whites (60%) and these white victimizers are more likely to have consumed alcohol or drugs, or both (55%), before committing the offense (Perry, 2004). Individual acts of ethnoviolence, from verbal harassment to brutal assaults with weapons, are a part of everyday life for many Native Americans (Perry, 2002).

In addition to these bleak statistics regarding Native Americans as victims of violent crime are issues surrounding the ability of tribal police to arrest perpetrators of violent crimes. Because of existing case law, tribal police can arrest only tribal members and other Indians. "Non-Indian perpetrators, even if they live on the reservation or are in a personal or business relationship with an Indian, may only be detained or left to the state or federal police to be apprehended. This can cause lawlessness on a reservation that cannot be addressed by tribal police" (Luna-Firebaugh, 2007:14).

Another aspect of victimization among Native Americans in which there is very little research is the area of state-corporate crime. State-corporate crime is a hybrid of white-collar crime in that it has attributes of both corporate and government crime. Many crimes committed by the government are interlocked with corporations in the private sector. There are many links between corporate "power elites" and the government on all levels. State-corporate crime focuses on how public and private entities cooperate to further the goals of each of their institutions. This cooperation then leads to "death, injury, ill health, financial loss, and . . . cultural destruction, all the while being insulated from the full weight of criminalization for these actions" (Kramer, Michalowski, and Kauzlarich, 2002:145).

In the United States, 5% of the U.S. oil and gas, one-third of its strippable low sulfur coal, and one-half of its privately owned uranium are on Indian land (Gedicks, 1993:40). Therefore, Indian reservations are of strategic importance to both corporations and the U.S. government; and, the ability to exploit indigenous groups of people is one of the hallmarks of state-corporate crime. One common thread that runs through many of the 562 federally recognized Indian Nations is that they are poor. Unemployment, substandard health care, education, and substance abuse are but a few of the enormous problems that Indian Nations face in the United States. Given these sets of circumstances, large corporations, sometimes in cooperation with public agencies, are well positioned to exploit indigenous peoples who are on the frontline of contemporary colonial struggles. Even though desperately poor people living on many Indian reservations in this country may well receive some economic benefits from multinational intrusion on their lands initially, they are also clearly exploited and pay a high price, especially in terms of harm to health and the environment for these benefits (Robyn, 2007:2–4).

The limited existing research on Native American victimization of all types is plagued with the same methodological problems that occur with other offender statistics. This in turn affects statistics about victims. The reasons for the lack of research on Native American individual victims of crime are only speculative. However, because of historical patterns of discrimination and hostility by the colonial criminal justice system, Native Americans may perceive today's criminal justice system as hostile or indifferent, and therefore not report their victimization. The long distances from some Nations to police, schools, hospitals, and other services may not only prevent prompt assistance to victims, but may hinder reporting. Language barriers and cultural prohibitions about involving outsiders may also be factors in low rates of reporting (U.S. Department of Justice, OVC, 1992).

Victim assistance services in and around American Indian Nations are often funded by federal Office for Victims of Crime (OVC). The OVC began an initiative in 1987 to provide funding, training, and technical support to American Indian Nations, including the Children's Justice Act Partnerships for Indian Communities which provides grants for tribes to improve "the investigation, prosecution and handling of child abuse cases," Tribal Victim Assistance that makes grants available to tribal organizations to establish programs in remote communities, and grants for Counseling for Crime Victims in Indian Country by Faith-Based Organizations (U.S. Department of Justice, OVC, 2007). Community-based programs include: the Emmonak Women's shelter in Alaska; Two Feathers Native American Family Services in California; the Apache Violence-Free Living Program in Oklahoma; and the Oglala Lakota Court Appointed Special Advocate Program in South Dakota (U.S. Department of Justice, OVC, 2004). The Office on Violence Against Women (OVW) has a Safety for Indian Women Demonstration Initiative that provides grants to develop service and training programs (U.S. Department of Justice, OVW, n.d.).

In summary, Native Americans have been the victims of past and present crimes, but little research has been done to document this, and victim services programs are still in the early stages of development in and around American Indian Nations.

NATIVE AMERICAN SERVICE PROVIDERS

There is a growing recognition that the criminal justice system has failed Native Americans, and that it is not effective in handling the Native Americans in its care. One strategy is to encourage or require that non-Native criminal justice personnel at all levels of the system increase their knowledge about Native American cultures, and their inter-cultural communication skills (Ross, 1996).

Secondly, Native Americans must be more involved in operating the criminal justice system. As mentioned earlier, Native Americans are underrepresented in all aspects of justice service provision even though many justice organizations have made special efforts to recruit Native Americans. However, with the resurgence of Indian self-determination in the 1960s, more than 100 officers have been added to the Bureau of Indian Affairs, and in 1969, the Indian Police Academy came into being. In addition, through the Indian Self-Determination and Education Assistance Act of 1975 and the Indian Self-governance Act of 1994, the Bureau of Indian Affairs has turned over various law enforcement functions to the tribes making tribal police departments accountable to the tribe instead of the federal government, thus reducing much of the control of the Bureau of Indian Affairs Enforcement Services (Luna-Firebaugh, 2007:25).

In a 1991 study, the Federal Bureau of Investigation had the worst showing; they would have to hire 34 Native American men and 3 Native American women to attain population representation (0.8% of the general population). The Drug Enforcement Administration would have to hire 3 women; the U.S. Marshals Service 3 men and 1.7 women; the Bureau of Alcohol, Tobacco and Firearms 7 men and 3 women; and the U.S. Secret Service 12 men and 4 women (Reddy, 1995). While there are few figures available for state or local criminal justice services, New York City reported that in 1992, 28 of its 20,098 officers (or 0.1%) were Native American (Reddy, 1995).

Native Americans can provide criminal justice services through several different routes. The first is that they can be service providers within the European-based criminal justice system such as police, probation, and so on, usually off-reservation. Second, they could operate Native American-based or European-based justice services outside of Native American land. These organizations are relatively rare compared to similar services available to indigenous peoples in other countries, such as Canada and Australia. Indian cultural centers, of which there are dozens around the country, and local-level services such as DNA Legal Services, serving the Navajo, are examples of these kinds of services. Services may include alcohol abuse education or mental health counseling. Many of these services also suffer from lack of steady funding, making it difficult for them to respond to all of their clients' needs. Whenever possible, these organizations try to incorporate elements of their culture and practices within their organizational structure, programs, and policies.

Third, they could operate justice services on Native American land, including tribal police forces, courts, jails, probation supervision, juvenile programs, and the victims services mentioned above. With a few exceptions, Nations have limited jurisdiction over the type of offenses and the type of offenders these services can handle. While helping with more sensitive treatment and just decisions for Indian people, neither of these roles give employees sufficient options in culturally sensitive or culturally based processes or values. They could also operate Native American-based services based in socialization processes that the Nation has used since time immemorial. Navajo Peacemaking is probably one of the best known of these initiatives. With the guidance and input of a peacemaker, disputants talk over the issue and arrive at a plan for resolving it. "Offenses" that have been handled include assault, sexual assault, domestic violence, and wrongful death, as well as more common disputes over grazing rights, boundaries, and other civil matters (see Nielsen and Zion, 2005). Many Native American programs are a kind of *restorative justice* (see Hudson and Galaway, 1996) because they focus on preventing further occurrences through resolving underlying issues, and "healing" the offender, victim, and community. This kind of service provision is not only the most culturally sensitive strategy for helping many Native American offenders and victims, but may ultimately be the most effective because restorative justice approaches may help resolve the large issues of marginalization that cause Native American individuals to come into conflict with the criminal justice system in the first place.

The main hope for Native Americans to escape overrepresentation in the criminal justice system is to regain their sovereignty so that they can implement more holistic and long-range services that will end marginalization and remove criminogenic conditions. Problems surrounding available funding and other resource needs, the infrastructure of various tribes, and the size of Indian communities all need to be resolved. They need to have the choice, that is, to have self-determination, so that they can choose to utilize justice systems modeled on Western-based services (which continue to be the predominant model in most communities) or to revive and operate traditionally based, restorative justice practices.

Whether or not Native American Nations will be allowed increased self-determination by the government that has so long exploited them is the underlying question (Boldt, 1993). Because of the important natural resources that Native Americans would then control, and especially because of the massive social, economic, and political restructuring that demarginalizing Native Americans would entail, increased self-determination for Native Americans may be perceived by the government to be against the national interests of the country. If this occurs, then Native American overrepresentation in the criminal justice system can be expected to continue indefinitely.

References

Archambeault, William. 2009. The Search for the Silver Arrow: Assessing Tribal-Based Healing Traditions and Ceremonies in Indian Country Corrections. In *Criminal Justice in Native America*, ed. Marianne O. Nielsen and Robert A. Silverman. Tucson, AZ: University of Arizona Press.

Armstrong, Troy L., Michael H. Guilfoyle, and Ada Pecos Melton. 1996. Native American Delinquency. In *Native Americans, Crime, and Justice*, ed. Marianne O. Nielsen and Robert A. Silverman, 75–88. Boulder, CO: Westview Press.

Bachman, Ronet. 1992. *Death and Violence on the Reservation: Homicide, Family Violence, and Suicide in American Indian Populations.* New York: Auburn.

Bachman, Ronet, Alexander Alvarez, and Craig Perkins. 1996. Discriminatory Imposition of the Law: Does It Affect Sentencing Outcomes for American Indians? in *Native Americans, Crime, and Justice*, ed. Marianne O. Nielsen and Robert A. Silverman, 197–208. Boulder, CO: Westview Press.

Barreiro, Jose, and Tim Johnson. 2005. *America is Indian Country: Opinions and Perspectives from Indian Country Today.* Golden, CO: Fulcrum Publishing.

Boldt, Menno. 1993. *Surviving as Indians: The Challenge of Self-Government.* Toronto: University of Toronto Press.

Bureau of Justice Statistics. 1997. *Sourcebook of Criminal Justice Statistics, 1996.* NCJ-165361. Washington DC: Department of Justice.

Bureau of Justice Statistics. 1999. *American Indians and Crime, 1992–1996.* NCJ 173386. Washington, DC: U.S. Department of Justice.

Bureau of Justice Statistics. 2002. *Jails in Indian Country.* NCJ 198997. Washington, DC.: U.S. Department of Justice. http://www.ojp.usdoj.gov/bjs/pub/pdf/jic02.pdf.

Bureau of Justice Statistics. 2003. *Sourcebook of Criminal Justice Statistics.* Washington, DC: U.S. Department of Justice. http://www.albany.edu/sourcebook/pdf/t4122005.pdf.

Bynum T., and R. Paternoster. 1996. Discrimination Revisited. In *Native Americans, Crime, and Justice*, ed. Marianne O. Nielsen and Robert A. Silverman, 228–238. Boulder, CO: Westview Press.

Deloria, Jr., Vine, and Clifford M. Lytle. 1983. *American Indians, American Justice.* Austin, TX: University of Texas Press.

Dumont, James. 1993. Justice and Aboriginal Peoples. In *Aboriginal Peoples and the Justice System*, ed. Royal Commission on Aboriginal Peoples. Ottawa, ON: Ministry of Supply and Services.

Fixico, Donald. 2000. *The Urban Indian Experience in America.* Albuquerque, New Mexico: University of New Mexico Press.

French, Laurence A. 1994. *The Winds of Injustice: American Indians and the U.S. Government.* New York, NY: Garland.

Gedicks, Alan. 1993. *The New Resource Wars: Native and Environmental Struggles Against Multinational Corporations.* Boston, MA: South End Press.

Greenfield, Lawrence A., and Tracy L. Snell. 1999. *Women Offenders, Special Report.* NCJ 175688. Washington, D.C.: Bureau of Justice Statistics.

Grobsmith, Elizabeth S. 1994. *Indians in Prison: Incarcerated Native Americans in Nebraska.* Lincoln, NE: University of Nebraska Press.

Harjo, Suzan S. 1998. Redskins, Savages, and Other Indian Enemies: A Historical

Overview of American Media Coverage of Native Peoples. In *Images of Color, Images of Crime*, ed. Coramae R. Mann and Marjorie S. Zatz, 30–45. Los Angeles, CA: Roxbury.

Hudson, Joe, and Burt Galaway. 1996. Introduction. In *Restorative Justice: International Perspectives*, ed. Burt Galaway and Joe Hudson, 1–14. Monsey, NY: Criminal Justice Press.

Hutton, C., F. Pommersheim, and S. Feimer. 1996. I Fought the Law and the Law Won. In *Native Americans, Crime, and Justice*, ed. Marianne O. Nielsen and Robert A. Silverman, 209–220. Boulder, CO: Westview Press.

Jennings, Francis. 1993. *The Founders of America: From the Earliest Migrations to the Present*. New York, NY: W.W. Norton.

Kramer, Ronald C., Raymond J. Michalowski, and David Kauzlarich. 2002, The Origins and Development of the Concept and Theory of State-Corporate Crime. *Crime and Delinquency* 48:263–282.

Lujan, Carol. 1998. Or, The Only Real Indian is the Stereotyped Indian. In *Images of Color, Images of Crime*, ed. Coramae R. Mann and Marjorie S. Zatz, 47–57. Los Angeles, CA: Roxbury.

Luna-Firebaugh, Eileen. 2007. *Tribal Policing: Asserting Sovereignty, Seeking Justice*. Tucson, AZ: University of Arizona Press.

Mail, Patricia D., and Saundra Johnson. 1993. Boozing, Sniffing, and Toking: An Overview of the Past. Present, and Future of Substance Use by American Indians. *American Indian and Alaska Native Mental Health Research Journal* 5 (2): 1–33.

Meyer, Jon'a. 2009. Ha'alchini, haadaah naas-dah ("They're Not Going to be Young Forever"): Juvenile Criminal Justice. In *Criminal Justice in Native America*, ed. Marianne O. Nielsen and Robert A. Silverman. Tucson, AZ: University of Arizona Press.

Mihesuah, Devon. 1996. *American Indians: Stereotypes and Realities*. Atlanta, GA: Clarity Press.

Miller, J. R. 1991. *Skyscrapers Hide the Heavens: A History of Indian-White Relations in Canada*, Rev edn. Toronto, ON: University of Toronto Press.

Morse, Bradford W. 1989. *Aboriginal Peoples and the Law*, Rev. 1st edn. Ottawa, ON: Carleton University Press.

Nechi Institute and KAS Corporation. 1994. *Healing, Spirit and Recovery: Factors Associated with Successful Integration*. Ottawa, ON: Supply and Services Canada.

Nielsen, Marianne O., and James W. Zion. 2005. *Navajo Nation Peacemaking: Living Traditional Justice*. Tucson: University of Arizona Press.

Nies, Judith. 1996. *Native American History: A Chronology of a Culture's Vast Achievements and their Links to World Events*. New York, NY: Ballantine.

Osterhammel, Jurgen. 1997. *Colonialism: A Theoretical Overview*. Princeton: Markus Wiener Publishers.

Perry, Barbara. 2002. From Ethnocide to Ethnoviolence: Layers of Native American Victimization. *Contemporary Justice Review* 5: 231–247.

Perry, Steven W. 2004. *American Indians and Crime: A BJS Statistical Profile, 1992–2002*. NCJ 203097. Washington, DC: U.S. Department of Justice.

Pommersheim, Frank.1995. *Braid of Feathers: American Indian Law and Contemporary Tribal Life*. Berkeley, CA: University of California Press.

Reddy, Marlita A. (Ed.). 1995. *Statistical Record of Native North Americans*, 2nd edn. New York, NY: Gale Research.

Robyn, Linda. 2007. Uranium Mining on the Navajo Nation: A Case of State-Corporate Crime. A paper presented at the Annual Meeting of the Western Social Sciences Association (Calgary, Canada), April 12.

Robyn, Linda. 2004. Removal of the Southwest Michigan Potawatomi: Government crimes of oppression and cultural geno-cide. In *Victimizing Vulnerable Groups: Images of Uniquely High-Risk Crime Targets*, ed. Charisse Tia Maria Coston, 283–284. Westport, UK: Praeger.

Robyn, Linda, and Thom Alcoze. 2006. The Link between Environmental Policy and the Colonization Process and Its Effects on American Indian Involvement in Crime,

Law, and Society. In *Native Americans and the Criminal Justice System*, ed. Jeffrey Ian Ross and Larry Gould, 67–84. Boulder, CO: Paradigm Publishers.

Ross, Rupert. 1996. *Returning to the Teachings: Exploring Aboriginal Justice*. Toronto, ON: Penguin.

Shoemaker, Nancy. 1999. *American Indian Population Recovery in the Twentieth Century*. Albuquerque, NM: University of New Mexico Press.

Silverman, Robert A. 2009. Patterns of Native American Crime 1984–2005. In *Criminal Justice in Native America*, ed. Marianne O. Nielsen and Robert A. Silverman. Tucson, AZ: University of Arizona Press.

Silverman, Robert A. 1996. Patterns of Native American Crime. In *Native Americans, Crime, and Justice*, ed. Marianne O. Nielsen and Robert A. Silverman, 58–74. Boulder, CO: Westview Press.

Snipp, C. Matthew. 1989. *American Indians: The First of this Land*. New York, NY: Russell Sage Foundation.

Snyder, Howard N., and Melissa Sickmund. 1995. *Juvenile Offenders and Victims*. Washington, DC: Office of Juvenile Justice and Delinquency Prevention.

Trigger, Bruce G. 1985. *Natives and Newcomers*. Kingston, ON: McGill-Queen's University Press.

U.S. Census Bureau. 2006. *We the People: American Indians and Alaska Natives in the United States*. Washington, DC: U.S. Government Printing Office.

U.S. Census Bureau. 2007. *The American Community: American Indians and Alaska Natives: 2004*. Washington, DC: U.S. Department of Commerce.

U.S. Department of the Interior. 2006. About the Department of the Interior: DOI Quick Facts. http://www.doi.gov.facts.html (accessed October 31, 2007).

U.S. Department of Justice, Office for Victims of Crime. 2007. Office for Victims of Crime Home—Federal Assistance Division. http://www.ojp.usdoj.gov/ovc/welcovc/fcvd/welcome.html (accessed October 28, 2007).

U.S. Department of Justice, Office for Victims of Crime. 1992. *Victim Services to Serve Native Americans*. OVC Bulletin NCJ 133963. Washington, DC: U.S. Department of Justice.

U.S. Department of Justice, Office for Victims of Crime. 2004. *Victim Services: Promising Practices in Indian Country*. NCJ 207019. Washington, DC: U.S. Department of Justice.

U.S. Department of Justice, Office on Violence Against Women. n.d. Safety for Indian Women Demonstration Initiative. http://www.usdoj.gov/ovw/safety_iwdi.htm (accessed October 29, 2007).

Utter, Jack. 2001. *American Indians: Answers to Today's Questions*, 2nd edn. Norman, OK: University of Oklahoma Press.

Waldram, J. B. 1996. Aboriginal Spirituality in Corrections. In *Native Americans, Crime, and Justice*, ed. Marianne O. Nielsen and Robert A. Silverman, 239–253. Boulder, CO: Westview Press.

Wright, Ronald. 1992. *Stolen Continents: The "New World" Through Indian Eyes*. Boston, MA: Houghton Mifflin.

CHAPTER 7

Exclusion, Inclusion, and Violence

Immigrants and Criminal Justice

Barbara Perry

Luis A. Fernandez

Michael Costelloe

The bosom of America is open to receive not only the Opulent and respectable Stranger, but the oppressed and persecuted of all nations and religions, whom we shall welcome to participation of all our rights and privileges.

—GEORGE WASHINGTON, 1783

A central element of the cultural mythology of the United States is that this is a "nation of immigrants." As this chapter will demonstrate, there is some truth to this notion. Periodic waves of immigrants to these shores have transformed this country in numerous ways. However, to characterize the United States in these terms is to ignore two indisputable facts of history that are addressed elsewhere in this book: (1) that this land was inhabited and settled by Native Americans long before its "discovery;" and (2) that thousands of African "immigrants" arrived here not by choice but in chains (Rothenberg, 1997). To understand the United States as a "nation of immigrants" would render invisible the place and contributions of substantial numbers of "non-immigrants."

Having said that, we are still in a position to recognize the ways in which immigrants from around the world have helped to shape the contours of U.S. material and cultural reality. It is the rare U.S. resident who cannot trace his or her ancestry beyond the borders of this country. Each of us thus shares the legacy of immigration. With few exceptions, that legacy is one of struggle, discrimination, and violence. The plight of the immigrant—especially non-Anglo immigrants—has not always been an easy one, in light of the frequent emergence of anti-immigrant sentiment and policy that has characterized U.S. history.

IMMIGRATION PATTERNS

Patterns of immigration to the United States have been conditioned by the combined impact of "pushes" away from countries of origin (e.g., war, persecution, and economic recessions), "pulls" to the United States (e.g., democratic ideals, sanctuary, and economic opportunities), and changing immigration policies in the United States (e.g., exclusions, restrictions, and quotas).

The history of immigration to what is now the United States began with British colonization in the seventeenth century. Between 1600 and 1775, the colonizing migrants tended to be Puritans, Quakers, entrepreneurs, and unskilled or indentured laborers. By the close of the eighteenth century, the United States was peopled by a majority of Anglo-Saxon immigrant population. Of the free, non-slave, non-Native population, 60% were English, 14% Scottish (or Scots-Irish), 8.6% German, 3.6% Irish, and the remainder constituted largely by Dutch, French, and Swedes. In all then, nearly 80% of the immigrant population was from the British Isles. By virtue of their vast historical majority, then, Anglo colonizers came to set the cultural, political, and economic agenda for what would become the United States. Given the dominance of Protestantism among these people, it is not surprising that at the heart of this agenda lay what has been characterized by Weber as *ascetic Protestantism*, the core values of which are: personal discipline and responsibility; individualism; hard work; efficiency and rationality; accumulation; and profit. It is not difficult to see how these values have persisted as a central part of the American culture and psyche. Nor is it difficult to see how this value system enabled the institutionalization of slavery—a practice which accounted for the forced migration of thousands of Africans. In a country where land was plentiful, entrepreneurs came to rely on slave labor to ensure their profits. Consequently, by the time slavery was legally abolished in 1808, half a million slaves had been imported; many continued to be forcibly and illegally imported throughout the remainder of the century.

The period between the 1840s and 1870s was a period of expansion in economic and geographic terms. Irish and German immigrants were attracted to the northern United States by the promise of employment in emerging industries such as textile and iron works. This was especially appealing to the Irish—mostly indentured laborers—forced from their homeland by the economic crisis engendered by the potato famine and by English oppression. As indentured servants, they would receive money for their passage to the United States, and pay it off by working for their sponsor for a specified period of time, after which they could leave to seek their "fortunes."

The westward expansion of the United States had dramatic implications for immigration trends. Irish laborers were joined, and often replaced, by cheap Asian laborers from China and Japan. Between 1848 and 1882, more than 200,000 male Chinese workers were imported, largely for employment in the railroads and mines.

By the end of this era, however, Chinese immigration was largely halted by the Chinese Exclusion Act of 1882.

With the end of the Mexican–American War, U.S. demographics once again shifted. The annexation of the Southwest (Arizona, New Mexico, etc.) meant that, without physically moving, many Spanish-speaking Mexicans suddenly became U.S. immigrants.

The period following the Civil War—1880s to 1920s—was characterized by a dramatic economic and demographic explosion. Employment in agriculture shrank, while employment in manufacturing doubled. Racism and discrimination kept many black laborers tied to southern agriculture. The resultant labor shortage meant that northern industrial employers turned to immigrant labor. By 1910, 6 of 10 such workers were foreign born (Feagin and Feagin, 1996). The vast majority of the 21 million immigrants drawn to the United States by these promises of employment were drawn from the impoverished regions of southern and eastern Europe. Thus, this era saw the beginning of mass migration of Italians, Poles, Russians, and Eastern European Jews.

The 1930s and 1940s were relatively quiet in terms of immigration. It was not until the 1950s—perhaps owing to the apparent affluence of the United States—that immigration levels began to climb gradually. Throughout the decades of the 1950s and 1960s, Europeans and Canadians continued to dominate. However, by the 1970s, the trend reversed itself, due in large part to changes in immigration policy. The 1965 Immigration Act eliminated discriminatory country-of-origin quotas. For the first time in U.S. history, white European immigrants were the minority (Aguirre and Turner, 1997), representing less than 15% of all newcomers. Instead, Asians and Latin Americans (especially Mexicans) led the queue. As a result of sweeping changes in immigration policy, the number of foreign-born people in the United States has increased dramatically since the 1960s. Indeed, currently, the United States is at a peak in terms of the number of foreign-born residents: 33.5 million foreign-born—or 11.7% of the population—live in the United States (U.S. Census Bureau, 2003). Approximately 53.3% of these hail from Latin America (including Central America, South America, and the Caribbean), 25.0% from Asia, and 13.7% from Europe—a dramatic departure from earlier patterns (Larsen, 2004). According to the Department of Homeland Security (DHS), 705,827 people legally immigrated to the United States in 2003, mainly from Mexico (115,864), India (50,379), the Philippines (45,397), China (40,659), El Salvador (28,296), the Dominican Republic (26,205), and Vietnam (22,133).

Interestingly, however, these numbers represent a large decrease in immigrant admissions, down over 30% from 1,063,732 in 2002. In large part, this can be attributed to heightened security precautions introduced after the September 11, 2001, terrorist attacks. The terrorist attacks on 9/11 transformed the United States in many ways, including how we view and deal with immigrants. In the aftermath of the terrorist attacks, the U.S. government passed several laws restricting the civil rights of non-U.S. citizens, justifying the acts because many of the terrorists were not U.S. citizens. Soon after these legal changes, immigration law became ground zero in the "war on terror" (Engle, 2004), unfortunately negatively affecting many innocent immigrants along the way.

The recent changes in the immigration law have historical precedent. As far back as the Alien and Sedition Act of 1798, the United States had rejected entry to individuals on the basis of ideology and national security (Motomura, 2006). Because of the Sedition Act, non-U.S. citizens can still be detained, arrested, and even deported with little constitutional protection. U.S law enforcement agents have applied the act several times in U.S. history. For instance, during the first Red Scare in the early 1920s, the FBI used the Sedition Act to round up and arrest over 10,000 people suspected of being Communists and anarchists, using subscription lists to radical magazines as evidence of anti-government involvement (Churchill and Vander Wall, 2002).

Recent immigration laws are only the latest incarnation of the long-standing link between immigration and threats to national security. Immigration legislation, including the USA PATRIOT Act, the creation of the Department of Homeland Security, and the Secure Fence Act of 2006, takes an enforcement approach to immigration and mostly ignore economic factors. To accomplish this task, governmental bodies that regulate immigration were dramatically restructured in an attempt to secure the border (Johnson and Trujillo, 2007). For instance, Congress dissolved the Immigration and Naturalization Service (INS) and reconstituted it as the Immigration and Customs Enforcement (ICE), now housed as a part of the Homeland Security Department.

The most significant effect of the changes since the terrorist attacks involves an increase in racial profiling of Arab-Americans and Muslims. Historically, non-U.S. citizens have been the most vulnerable to civil rights deprivations, largely because the law permits more intense governmental conduct with minimal protection of the rights of non-citizens (Akram and Johnson, 2002). Recently, the U.S. government required the special registration of some Arab-Americans and Muslim non-citizens. In addition, the FBI also arrested, detained, and interrogated large numbers of Arab and Muslim individuals and selectively deported some of them (Johnson and Trujillo, 2007). Secret immigration hearings, closed to public scrutiny, became common in cases involving alleged terrorists (Aldana, 2004). In the end, the aggregate effect of these policies was felt mostly by the Arab and Muslim communities, leaving them, like in other historical instances, vulnerable to law enforcement abuse.

To understand the connection between immigration and national security, one must examine the complex link of "otherness" as it intertwines with race, national origin, religion, and political ideology. As has occurred in the past with anarchists and Communists, the intrusion on the civil rights of non-U.S. citizens has the potential not only to harm innocent immigrants, but also to have long-term adverse effects on the civil rights of U.S. citizens. Much of this restrictive policing of our national boundaries has been grounded in deep suspicion and often mistreatment of newcomers. Each cohort of "new immigrants" was perceived as the alien and foreign "Other." They have been regarded as outside the boundaries of the imagined community of the United States. Successive groups of immigrants were thought to represent distinct and threatening "races."

ANTI-IMMIGRANT SENTIMENTS

Having established themselves as the "nativist" core of the United States, Anglo Protestants were loath to welcome the cultural influence of other immigrants. While grateful for the cheap labor provided by subsequent immigrants, the English

American "founders" nonetheless saw themselves as the only true Americans. Unless and until the "foreigners" subordinated themselves to the ethnic ideology of Anglo Protestantism, they would remain outsiders, with the corresponding lack of power. They would be reminded of their inferiority by the actions of organized and unorganized mobs of nativists—anti-immigrant leagues, Ku Klux Klan, even political parties like the Know-Nothings (Bailey, 1991; Feagin and Feagin, 1996).

The ghosts of the 1920s have returned to haunt us in the contemporary era. Now, as then, there is a widespread fear that unbridled immigration will destroy the moral, economic, and (mono)cultural fiber of the United States. We see resurrected a political discourse which seeks also to construct immigrants as dangerous "Others" within. In fact, opponents are fond of using the explicitly exclusionary term "alien" rather than "immigrant," presumably to highlight the marginal status of these people. This reflects the historical ambivalence toward immigrants in a nation of immigrants, a notion reinforced by the former governor of Colorado and his co-author:

> Immigration policy was once an asset to this country, helping to make us strong. But its current uncontrolled state will seriously harm this country and its institutions. (Lamm and Imhoff, 1985:49)

Now, the United States is faced by an "immigration crisis." As is often the case, the public looks to its political leaders for a cue on how to interpret the real and perceived impact of the dramatic demographic and cultural changes associated with immigration. The most vocal of discourses tend not to paint a favorable portrait. Unlike the cases of the earlier waves of immigration, the current arrivals are not predominantly European, are not even predominantly white. On the contrary, they are overwhelmingly Asians, and Hispanics from South and Central America. On the basis of race alone, these immigrants are not as readily assimilable as their predecessors.

Culturally, non-white, non-European immigrants are constructed as major contributors to the breakdown of United States' morality, unity, and stability. An integral element of the perceived danger involves the invocation of the theme of "immigrant criminality." Immigrants are presented as the "partners in crime" to the black native-born male. California governor Pete Wilson drew out this implication in a speech at a Los Angeles Town Hall: "As we struggle to keep dangerous criminals off our streets, we find that 14% of California's prison population are illegal immigrants—enough to fill eight state prisons to capacity" (April 25, 1994). *Has it not been ever thus?* Shaw and McKay, and their colleagues of the Chicago school noted in the first half of the century the tendency of politicians to assign delinquent labels to immigrants, as if this were part of their genetic makeup, or part of their cultural ethos. The same stigma is attached to immigrants in the latter half of the century.

The association between immigrants and criminality is often supplemented by messages implying that they are also the root of the nation's economic woes. Immigrants—especially Third World immigrants—come to this country for two reasons: to sack the welfare system and to take the jobs of Americans. The former belief underlies Wilson's Proposition 187, which would have excluded illegal immigrants and their children from most state social services, and recent proposals to exclude even legal immigrants from Social Security payments. Presumably, immigrants are getting rich off the United States' welfare system; it is catapulting them into the middle class, over the heads of long-suffering native-born Americans. It is, however, unclear what computations place welfare recipients in a middle-income bracket. Moreover, immigrants are in a double bind. On the one hand, they are berated for their presumed exploitation and plundering of the social safety net. Yet, on the other hand, should they turn instead to legitimate employment—as the vast majority do—they are then reviled for stealing "American" jobs.

The media have been especially complicit in the demonization of immigrants. This has long been the case; however, today it appears that the role of media in structuring immigration discourse and public attitudes has significantly expanded. Through the use of technological developments and various media, contested definitions of undocumented immigration are readily accessible and widely distributed. Not only do newspapers and television news continue to provide extensive coverage of immigration concerns, but they are also represented in popular culture through such sources as books, movies, and television. Websites and blogs also provide forums for individuals and special interest groups, who tend to address the problem in the narrowest of terms, terms that best reflect their values, beliefs, and interests.

What is even more striking is that supposedly objective news stations (and some not so objective) actually employ "personalities" such as Glenn Beck (CNN Headline News) and Bill O' Reilly (FOX News), who host talk shows that are politically slanted and that ultimately play a major role in framing the immigration debate. These individuals can only be termed "personalities" as the term "newsperson" does not technically apply. "Newsperson" denotes a certain level of objectivity that is plainly absent in these cases. Instead, these individuals wear their social and political opposition to undocumented immigration as a badge of honor. In fact, it appears that they have taken on undocumented immigration as a personal crusade. Bill O'Reilly even goes so far as to bestow on himself the title of "culture warrior" (O'Reilly, 2006). These personalities and others cast undocumented immigration almost exclusively in negative terms, emphasizing and describing the perceived threats that are posed by increasing unauthorized immigration.

Mainstream news is also at times complicit in presenting sensationalized and negative images of undocumented immigration. We have all seen news reports that show unauthorized immigrants streaming over the border in the dead of night as the Border Patrol looks on helplessly. Porous borders are thus shown to be open floodgates, if you are to believe these stories. The images are dramatic in effect and instill fear and invoke outrage. They also, however, lack context. What is often missing from these stories are explanations as to why these people feel compelled to risk their lives crossing miles and miles of unforgiving desert terrain in deadly heat to come to this country. The stories ignore the dire personal, social, and economic circumstances that force these people to leave their own country, and they ignore the pulls and enticements that bring them to the doorstep of the United States. In other words, media portrayals often ignore, and at times implicitly deny, the humanness of those who risk their lives for a chance to support themselves and their families.

Another way media influence perceptions of undocumented immigration is through crime news stories that explicitly mention the "illegal" status of those who commit crimes. Recently, a local police officer in Phoenix was shot and killed by an undocumented immigrant. An *Arizona Republic* newspaper article on September 19, 2007, noted that "the gunman, an illegal immigrant who had been deported last year, fled after shooting." This in fact became one of the focal points of stories about the incident, at times even overshadowing the tragedy of the death. The result has been an even greater firestorm against immigration. While the murder of a police officer is always dreadful and should to be treated as such, these news stories are presented in such a way that they fail to provide a realistic view of the actual problem. Rarely, if ever, are stories like these accompanied by the obvious fact that most police officers who are killed in the line of duty are killed by legal residents, and it is indeed a rather rare occurrence when an undocumented immigrant kills a police officer.

Addressing the undocumented status of those involved in criminal activity undermines the reality that most immigrants who come to the United States lead law-abiding lives. While there has been a scarcity of good research examining the link between immigration and crime, what has been done tends to suggest that the relationship between these two phenomena is either fairly small or non-existent (see, e.g., Aguirre, Saenz, and James, 1997; Butcher and Piehl, 1998a, b; Hagan and Palloni, 1998; Martinez, 2006). Some researchers have even gone as far as to suggest that Latinos have a stabilizing effect in most communities (Martinez, 2006). In fact, many Latinos report crime, serve on neighborhood watches and are a source of informal social control in their neighborhoods, thus assisting rather than hindering law enforcement. Media sources often omit these realities of undocumented immigrants in their stories.

Whether framed in economic, cultural, or criminal terms, the underlying message of the anti-immigration forces is that war must be declared on the invading force of immigrants. To frame a problem in such terms plants the seeds of hostility and violence in the broader culture—for they are the "enemies" of the American way of life. Presumably, they present a threat that can only be contained by extreme means:

> Immigrant bashing is a popular activity in assigning blame for the nation's economic problems. When stagnation is evident in the national economy and unemployment exceeds seven percent, a pervasive fear that one's job is on the line often emerges. Anxiety triggers frustration and blame; resentment towards immigrants, documented and undocumented, becomes an ugly side of racism, nativism, and xenophobia. (Ochoa, 1995:227)

A backlash against immigrants is also reflected in public sentiments. Gallup's annual poll on immigration issues found that, in 2005, 46% of Americans said they wanted the level of immigration into the country decreased (Gallup, 2005). Granted, this is down from 65% a decade earlier (Gallup, 1993). Nonetheless, it still represents a substantial and worrying proportion of the population. Moreover, just as 9/11 affected government policy, it also affected popular sentiment. Prior to the attacks, in June 2001, a similar proportion of Americans felt that immigration should be kept at its present level (42%) or decreased (41%). One month after the attacks, a majority (58%) said immigration should be decreased (Gallup, 2005). Unpacking this position, we find rationales which speak to perceived threats associated with immigrants. Responses to the following question continue to demonstrate negative attitudes toward immigrants and the "threats" they represent: "For each of the following areas, please say whether immigrants to the United States are making the situation in the country better or worse, or not having much effect." The proportions attributing blame for immigrants making problems worse were as follows:

- The economy in general—46%
- Social and moral values—37%
- Job opportunities for you and your family—34%
- Taxes—55%
- The crime situation—58% (Gallup, 2007).

The report asserts that these results are much stronger than they had been in previous years.

IMMIGRANTS AS OFFENDERS

Illegal Aliens

Contrary to historical and contemporary perceptions of immigrant criminality, immigrants tend not to be overrepresented in crime statistics. Undocumented immigrants are the obvious exception to this observation—"illegals," as they have come to be labeled. Undocumented immigrants are, by definition, engaging in criminal behavior. They have either entered the country illegally (without inspection) or have overstayed their visa subsequent to legal entry. Between 60 and 75% of the more than 10 million undocumented immigrants entered illegally and without inspection. The other 25 to 40% entered legally and subsequently overstayed visas or otherwise violated the terms of their admission (Capps and Fix, 2005). There are about 10.3 million unauthorized migrants estimated to be living in the United States as of March 2004, 57% of whom were from Mexico; 25% from other parts of Latin America; 9% from Asia; 6% from Europe and Canada; and 4% from Africa and other regions (Passel, 2005).

Immigration and Customs Enforcement (ICE)—formerly the Immigration and Naturalization Service (INS)—is responsible for the apprehension and expulsion of illegal aliens. In an average year, the agency expels one million undocumented immigrants, the majority of whom tend to be Mexicans. Only a small proportion of those found to be in the country illegally are *forcibly deported*. Consistently, upwards of 90% take the option of *voluntary return with safeguards*. While the former is barred from re-entering the United States for five years, the latter can re-enter legally at any time.

The potential consequences of a deported alien re-entering the United States at a later date can be very serious. Entry is a criminal offence, punishable by up to two years imprisonment. Entry by a deported individual with a drug offense or felony conviction is punishable by up to 10 and 20 years respectively. The latter groups are in fact considered not just illegal aliens, but criminal aliens.

Criminal Aliens

It is important to note, in light of the earlier discussion of the demonization of immigrants, that "The fact that many of these immigrants enter the country through unauthorized channels or overstay their visas often is framed as an assault against the 'rule of law,' thereby reinforcing the impression that immigration and criminality are linked. This association has flourished in a post-9/11 climate of fear and ignorance where terrorism and undocumented immigration often are mentioned in the same breath" (Rumbaut and Ewing, 2007). However, this denies several important realities. First, criminal aliens must be distinguished from illegal aliens. The former are non-citizens who have been convicted of such offenses as felonies, drug trafficking, firearms offenses, or offenses endangering national security. These people may be legally in the United States, as resident aliens or on visas. However, by virtue of their conviction for law-breaking behavior, they are automatically deportable as well as subject to penalties ranging from probation to long-term incarceration—after which they may still be deported. Moreover, Miller and Moore (1997:318) argue that most non-citizens in federal prisons are not immigrants, but international criminals who were in the country temporarily. Consequently, the available data on non-citizens in the criminal justice system must be considered with that caveat in mind.

Rumbaut and Ewing (2007) cite an array of sources—including census and criminal justice statistics—that show that immigrants are consistently *underrepresented* in the nation's jails and prisons, including Mexicans, Salvadorans, and Guatemalans who represent the largest proportions of undocumented migrants. To summarize, they assert that:

> Among men age 18–39 (who comprise the vast majority of the prison population), the 3.5 percent incarceration rate of the native-born in 2000 was 5 times higher than the 0.7 percent incarceration rate of the foreign-born. The foreign-born incarceration rate in 2000 was nearly two-and-a-half times less than the 1.7 percent rate for native-born non-Hispanic white men and almost 17 times less than the 11.6 percent rate for native-born black men. (Rumbaut and Ewing, 2007:1)

Non-citizens are overwhelmingly charged with immigration and drug-related offenses. Together, these categories accounted for 69% of all convictions. Of all federally sentenced immigration offenders, the vast majority (66.5%) were convicted for illegal entry or re-entry (Bureau of Justice Statistics, 1996). The remainder were convicted of offenses related to smuggling non-citizens, or handling fraudulent entry and passport documents.

Non-citizens—immigrants among them—have found themselves caught in the double bind of the war on drugs and anti-immigrant sentiment and policy. The outcome of this has been a dramatic sweep of non-citizen drug offenders. Consequently, 85% of all non-citizen federal inmates and 45% of all non-citizen state inmates were convicted of drug offenses. However, these were not the "hardened traffickers" of popular imagery. On the contrary, the majority of those incarcerated for drug offenses tend to be users, and small-scale dealers (Dunn, 1996).

In contrast, few non-citizens appear to be involved in violent offenses, especially at the federal level. While 35.2% of all non-citizens in state prisons in 1991 were convicted of violent offenses, only 1.9% of those in federal prisons were convicted of the same (Bureau of Justice Statistics, 1996). Again, one must regard these figures with some care, since violent crime rates tend to be more closely associated with non-resident aliens, and with international organized crime.

IMMIGRANTS AS VICTIMS

In spite of the above-mentioned data suggesting that immigrants are (a) less criminal than their native-born counterparts and (b) less violent, the popular perception of immigrants as threatening creates an environment in which violence against immigrants flourishes. Hostility toward those perceived as "foreign" is apparent in acts across the nation ranging from vandalism and graffiti to brutal assaults. Inspired by political and media constructions of immigrants as the root of all problems, native-born Americans express their opinions in hateful words and deeds. "Immigrant bashing" has become a part of the daily reality of those who have reached these shores in search of the promised freedom and opportunity.

Unfortunately, there are no concrete data on anti-immigrant violence. Violence against a Korean shop owner, for example, is classified and recorded as anti-Asian violence. However, the connection between the perpetrator's tendency to equate ethnicity with immigrant status is apparent in the verbal assaults that often accompany physical assaults. When East Indians, or Haitians, are told to "go back where you belong," the assumption is clear: regardless of whether they are first, second, or third generation, those who are "different" are perpetual foreigners who do not belong here. It is likely, therefore, that a significant proportion of the 355 anti-Asian and 516 anti-Hispanic hate crimes recorded by the FBI in 1995 (Federal Bureau of Investigation, 1996) were motivated by anti-immigrant sentiments. Perhaps even some of the 2,988 anti-black hate crimes were motivated by the perception that the victims were Nigerian, or Haitian, or South African, for example.

The perceived conflation of race/ethnicity and immigrant status is apparent in the case of the thousands of Hmong refugees who had been resettled in Philadelphia, PA, in the late 1970s. By 1985, fewer than 700 remained, a factor many have attributed to the ongoing harassment and intimidation of the refugees. A witness reported to a Human Relations hearing that:

> It is not uncommon for complete strangers to come up to me and say, "Are you Chinese?" We are all identified as Chinese . . . It is not uncommon for a refugee to be accosted with a statement like, "Chinese go home" . . . In addition to the beating of a Hmong from Canada in West Philadelphia, . . . there were many instances of debris being thrown through windows of apartments and houses occupied by refugees. (U.S. Commission on Civil Rights, 1992:48–49)

These examples are not atypical of the victimization of those deemed to be "foreign." They reflect the simmering hostility toward those held responsible for economic and social ills alike.

Not surprisingly, there are regional variations in the intensity and frequency of immigrant bashing. It tends to be most prevalent in those areas which host a disproportionate share of newly arrived immigrants—the Northeast (especially New York and New Jersey) and the Southwest (especially Arizona, California, and Texas). Consequently, anti-immigrant hate crime is relatively frequent in these areas. In particular, California, Arizona, and Texas see their share of border violence, wherein legal and illegal immigrants are victimized by vigilantes and by Border Patrol agents alike. In the late 1980s, the Arizona Border Patrol was "aided" by a paramilitary group calling itself Civilian Military Assistance (CMA). CMA patrolled the border with assault weapons and night-time binoculars in an effort to apprehend undocumented immigrants. The KKK continues to periodically burn crosses along the border in an attempt to frighten both legal and illegal immigrants (Nuñez, 1992). At a camp for homeless migrant workers in Alpine California, a Hispanic man was beaten by six men with baseball bats who later bragged about "kicking Mexican ass" (Southern Poverty Law Center, 1997:223). Nuñez (1992) documents numerous cases of such anti-immigrant bias along the U.S.–Mexico border, ranging from verbal taunts to rock throwing to shots fired.

There is little the victims can do to defend themselves. Whether legal or illegal, they often fear and mistrust Border Patrol authorities. The threat of secondary victimization is a very real one. Border Patrol and INS agents are not without blame. A report issued by the American Friends Service Committee of Los Angeles documented 55 incidents of brutality (a mere fraction of what is suspected) and misconduct by INS (now ICE) agents, one of which ended in death. Of these, 10 of the complainants were U.S. citizens, and 27 were legal residents or visitors (Southern Poverty Law Center, 1997).

Undocumented immigrants are at a heightened risk of victimization and revictimization because of their particular fears of reporting abuses by civilians and state agents. They have far more to lose by drawing attention to themselves. A 1979 Task Force finding remains true today: there exists an "extra-legal society whose members are unable to have wrongs redressed through legitimate channels without risking discovery and subsequent deportation" (Interagency Task Force on Immigration Policy, 1979:363–364). Moreover, the people to whom one might report a crime are often the offenders. ICE and Border Patrol agents have a job to do: stop illegal border crossings. However, buoyed by a climate of anti-immigrant hostility, officials can be overzealous in their policing of the border. Excessive use of force and unwarranted abuses do occur. An America's Watch report documents several such cases, including that of Francisco Ruiz and his pregnant wife Evelyn. When Ruiz attempted to protect his wife from an attack by a Border Patrol agent (which included him pressing his foot on her abdomen), he was shot once in the stomach and once in the buttock (Nuñez, 1992:1574–1575).

The border violence experienced by Mexican immigrants in particular is an extension of the broader sense—noted above—that the United States is in the midst of an "immigration crisis," that the nation has lost control of the flow of disruptive newcomers. All too often, reports of misconduct are thus met with indifference, if not support. The construction of immigrants as "alien" and as a menace ensures that anti-immigrant violence will persist unless the ideology and action are confronted directly. In short, immigrants require the protections afforded by representation of their interests in and by the criminal justice system.

IMMIGRANTS AS SERVICE PROVIDERS IN THE CRIMINAL JUSTICE SYSTEM

Data on immigrants as service providers within the criminal justice system are as meager as those on victimization. Again, immigrant status is collapsed within racial and ethnic categories. Given the paucity of racial and ethnic minorities as employees in the criminal justice system, it is plausible to assume that immigrants are underrepresented. Keep in mind the earlier discussion of the distribution of the "new immigrants"—predominantly Asians, Latin Americans, and Africans. These people of color are not highly visible as criminal justice practitioners (Cashmore, 2002; Flowers, 1990; Shusta, 1995). It is especially troubling that the Border Patrol—with its enforcement emphasis on the U.S.–Mexico border—has a relatively low proportion of Latino officers. The border is the site of some of the most frequent and brutal victimization of legal and illegal residents. Enhanced minority hiring would establish a more empathetic environment. Nuñez (1992) also recommends that the internal review process of the INS (now ICE) and Border Patrol be replaced with an independent civilian review board as a means of establishing accountability.

To some extent, there are legitimate reasons for the slow absorption of immigrants into the criminal justice system. Non–native-born individuals lack the familiarity with U.S. culture, customs, and legal order that would facilitate immediate entry. Moreover, they are often excluded by reason of language barriers. However, once they have acclimated to the New World, they would bring numerous advantages to the criminal justice system. Immigrant personnel would act as both cultural and linguistic bridges between immigrants and their native-born counterparts, between the community and the criminal justice system.

Other means of making the criminal justice accountable and accessible to the immigrant community include the related initiatives of cultural awareness training, language training, and the availability of bilingual officers and/or translators. Long Beach, CA, provides a model, in that its police department addresses the needs of the community's 17,000 Khmer speakers and several thousand Spanish speakers with two-person patrols consisting of Spanish and Khmer speaking officers. Additionally, all officers are required to attend a 40-hour cultural awareness training program.

Immigrant social and cultural organizations are also indispensable mechanisms by which to ease the transition for newcomers (e.g., Cambodian Association of America; Japanese American Social Service, Inc.). Such programs represent the interests of immigrants through community organizing, social functions, and the provision of services and service links to social and medical agencies. Communities with particularly large immigrant populations have established settlement centers and organizations. The Haitian Refugee Center, for example, provides counseling and guidance on post-traumatic stress, employment and employment skills, and housing. Perhaps more important in light of the anti-Haitian activities of the INS, the Center also protects Haitian immigrants from wrongful expulsion and deportation (Nuñez, 1992).

In response to the harassment and violence often suffered by immigrants, many anti-violence and civil rights groups have emerged in recent years. Some, like the Coalition Against Asian Violence, and the California Border Violence Delegation Project, serve regionally and ethnically specific interests by monitoring and publicizing violence against them. Others, like the American Friends Service Committee's Immigration Law Enforcement Monitoring Project have a broader mandate to address violence experienced by all immigrants regardless of country of origin.

It is unfortunate that the United States still requires the presence of such watchdogs. However, this is a nation grounded in a legacy of racist and anti-immigrant sentiment and practice, which will not disappear on their own. The civil rights organizations and activists which represent immigrants will continue to play a dominant role in enhancing the perception, place, and power of all newcomers, whatever the color of their face or sound of their voice.

References

Aguirre, Alberto, and Jonathan Turner. 1997. *American Ethnicity*. Boston, MA: McGraw-Hill.

Aguirre, B. E., Rogelio Saenz, and Brian Sinclair James. 1997. Marielitos Ten Years Later: The Scarface Legacy. *Social Science Quarterly* 78: 487–507.

Akram, Susan Musarrat, and Kevin Johnson. 2002. Race, Civil Rights, and Immigration Law After September 11, 2001: The Targeting of Arabs and Muslims. *New York University Annual Survey of American Law* 58 (3): 295–355.

Aldana, Raquel. 2004. The September 11 Immigration Detentions and Unconstitutional Executive Legislation. *Southern Illinois Law Journal* 29 (5): 5–41.

Bailey, Frankie. 1991. Law, Justice and "Americans:" An Historical Overview. In *Race and Criminal Justice*, ed. Michael Lynch and Britt Patterson, 10–21. Albany, NY: Harrow and Heston.

Bureau of Justice Statistics. 1996. *Non-Citizens in the Federal Criminal Justice System, 1984–94*. NCJ-160934. Washington DC: Bureau of Justice Statistics

Butcher, Kristin, and Anne Morrison Piehl. 1998a. Cross-City Evidence on the Relationship Between Immigration and Crime. *Journal of Policy Analysis and Management* 17: 457–493.

Butcher, Kristin, and Anne Morrison Piehl. 1998b. Recent Immigrants: Unexpected Implications for Crime and Incarceration. *Industrial and Labor Relations Review* 51 (4): 654–679.

Capps, Randolph, and Michael Fix. 2005. *Myths and Reality*. Washington, DC: Urban Institute.

Cashmore, Ellis. 2002. Behind the Window Dressing: Ethnic Minority Police Perspectives on Cultural Diversity. *Journal of Ethnic and Migration Studies* 28 (2): 327–341.

Churchill, Ward, and J. Vander Wall. 2002. *Agents of Repression: The FBI's Secret Wars Against the Black Panther Party and the American Indian Movement*. Cambridge, MA: South End Press.

Dunn, Timothy. 1996. *The Militarization of the U.S. Mexico Border, 1978–1992*. Austin, TX: Center or Mexican American Studies Press.

Engle, Karen. 2004. Constructing Good Aliens and Good Citizens: Legitimizing the War on Terror(ism). *University of Colorado Law Review* 75: 59–114.

Feagin, Joe, and Clairece Booher Feagin. 1996. *Racial and Ethnic Relations*. Upper Saddle River, NJ: Prentice-Hall.

Federal Bureau of Investigation. 1996. *Hate Crime Statistics, 1995*. Washington, DC: Federal Bureau of Investigation. http://www.fbi.gov/ucr/hatecm.htm.

Flowers, Barri. 1990. *Minorities and Criminality*. New York, NY: Praeger.

Gallup. 1993. Americans Feel Threatened by New Immigrants. *Gallup Poll Monthly* (July): 2–6.

Gallup. 2005. American Public Opinion About Immigration. http://www.gallup.com/poll/14785/Immigration.aspx.

Gallup. 2007. Americans Have Become More Negative on Impact of Immigrants. http://www.gallup.com/poll/28132/Americans-Become-More-Negative-Impact-Immigrants.aspx.

Hagan, John, and Alberto Palloni. 1998. Immigration and crime in the United States. In *The Immigration Debate*, ed. J. P. Smith and B. Edmonston, 367–387.Washington, DC: National Academy Press.

Interagency Task Force on Immigration Policy. 1979. *Staff Report*. Washington, DC: Interagency Task Force on Immigration Policy, Departments of Justice, Labor, and State.

Johnson, Kevin and Bernard Trujillo. 2007. Immigration Reform, National Security After September 11, and the Future of North American Integration. Research Paper No. 101, Legal Studies Research Paper Series, University of California Davis.

Lamm, Richard, and Gary Imhoff. 1985. *The Immigration Time Bomb.* New York, NY: Truman Tally Books.

Larsen, Luke J. 2004. *The Foreign-Born Population in the United States: 2003.* Current Population Reports 20–551. Washington, DC: U.S. Census Bureau.

Martinez, Ramiro. 2006. Coming to America: The Impact of the New Immigration on Crime. In *Immigration and Crime: Race Ethnicity and Violence*, ed. R. Martinez, Jr. and A. Valenzuela, Jr., 1–19. New York: New York University Press.

Miller, John, and Stephen Moore. 1997. The Index of Leading Immigration Indicators. In *Immigration: Debating the Issue*, ed. N. Capaldi, 306–322. Amherst, NY: Prometheus.

Motomura, Hiroshi. 2006. *Americans in Waiting: The Lost Story of Immigration and Citizenship in the United States.* London: Oxford University Press.

Nuñez, Michael. 1992. Violence at Our Border: Rights and Status of Immigrant Victims of Hate Crimes and Violence Along the Border Between the United States and Mexico. *Hastings Law Journal* 43: 1573–1605.

Ochoa, Albert. 1995. Language Policy and Social Implications for Addressing the Bicultural Experience in the U.S. In *Culture and Difference: Critical Perspectives on the Bicultural Experience in the United States*, ed. Antonia Dander, 227–253. Westport, CT: Bergin and Garey.

O'Reilly, Bill. 2006. *Culture Warrior.* New York, NY: Random House.

Passel, Jeff. 2005. *Unauthorized Migrants: Numbers and Characteristics.* Washington, DC: Pew Hispanic Center.

Rothenberg, Paula. 1997. Introduction, PT II. In *Race, Class and Gender in the United States*, ed. Paula Rothenberg, 110–114. New York, NY: St. Martin's Press.

Rumbaut, Rubén, and Walter A. Ewing. 2007. *The Myth of Immigrant Criminality and the Paradox of Assimilation: Incarceration Rates Among Native and Foreign-Born Men.* Washington, DC: American Immigration Law Foundation.

Shusta, Robert. 1995. *Multicultural Law Enforcement: Strategies for Peacekeeping in a Diverse Society.* Englewood Cliffs, NJ: Prentice Hall.

Southern Poverty Law Center. 1997. Anti-Immigrant Violence in Virginia. In *Experiencing Race, Class and Gender in the United States*, ed. Virginia Cyrus, 223–228. Mountain View, CA: Mayfield.

U.S. Census Bureau. 2003. *Current Population Survey.* Washington, DC: U.S. Census Bureau.

U.S. Commission on Civil Rights. 1992. *Civil Rights Issues Facing Asian Americans.* Washington, DC: Commission on Civil Rights.

Wilson, Pete. 1994. Securing Our Nation's Borders. *Vital Speeches* 60 (17): 534–536.

CHAPTER 8

The Significance of Race

African Americans and Criminal Justice

Brian J. Smith

During the first decade of the twenty-first century, the implications of race for understanding crime and criminal justice are all around us. In September 2007, thousands of people marched in Jena, Louisiana, to protest the criminal charges lodged against a group of African American youth known as the "Jena 6" (some of whom were charged with attempted murder). These young men allegedly beat a white youth during a racially charged confrontation that had its origins in the hanging of nooses from a tree at the local high school. Black youth at the school had sat under the tree, apparently designated as "for whites," and, soon after, the nooses were hung. In October 2007, an all-white jury acquitted eight former guards in the death of a boot camp inmate, a teenage African American; the case had resulted in the closing of all of Florida's boot camps a few years earlier. During the trial, guards claimed they were following proper procedure when they kicked and subdued the inmate, and defense attorneys argued that a prior medical condition killed the young man. A state senator reacting to the verdict stated, "I'm surprised they didn't have nooses outside the courthouse . . . [t]his is the Florida of yesterday" (Nelson, 2007). In 2005, a white former Texas police officer, Tom Coleman, was convicted for perjury related to an undercover drug sting operation that had resulted in 44 arrests—37 of those arrested were black (Blaney, 2005). Relying solely on the word of Coleman, who provided no evidence to the court, the Tulia justice system convicted the defendants, and sentenced most of them to prison. All living defendants were pardoned, and the group received a $5 million settlement. The case also resulted in the disbanding of the regional task force, and the creation of the "Tulia Law," which requires corroborating evidence in undercover sting operations (Blakeslee, 2005, CBS News, 2004a, 2004b).

Finally, a case from the late 1990s also illustrates how race, crime, and criminal justice are intertwined. On an early summer evening in 1998, three young men were driving around the town of Jasper, Texas, when one of them spotted James Byrd walking along the side of the road. One of the men knew Byrd from the local parole office, so they gave him a ride. The three men savagely beat Byrd, and then chained him to the back of their pickup truck. They proceeded to drag him for more than two miles, dismembering and killing him (Hohler, 1998; King, 2002). As would be expected, the public and political leaders were outraged by this brutal crime. Although some called for harmony between blacks and whites, black political groups marched in Jasper and suggested that local blacks arm themselves for self-protection. Today, we consider this lynching to be a heinous crime committed by immoral individuals; yet, 200 years ago, James Byrd's body parts could have been legally and publicly displayed to deter against slave rebellion. Even 100 years ago, this lynching would have been legally accepted in Jasper and would have received very little public attention. The Jena 6, the Florida boot camp case, Tom Coleman's drug sting, and James Byrd's dragging and murder show us the enduring significance of race, and specifically, of being African American in the United States. Racial differences produce tensions, conflict, inequalities, and violence in the United States. Consequently, racial identity is very important; in the United States, "race matters" (West, 1993).

Historically in the United States, social institutions have often treated African Americans unfairly. In the twenty-first century, African Americans' racial identity can still cause them to be targets of institutional and/or individual discrimination. Of course, there has been much progress and significant institutional inclusion of African Americans. African Americans enjoy legal rights that were non-existent just 40 or 50 years ago. The African American middle-class is larger than it has ever been. Tom Coleman was convicted and James Byrd's killers were harshly punished (King, 2002). However, in spite of this progress, African Americans, in aggregate, remain significantly disadvantaged in the twenty-first century. They are still more likely to suffer from inequalities which are shaped by structural constraints, including the following: childhood and adult poverty, unemployment, inadequate health care, residence in communities with high-crime rates, lack of educational achievement, unequal legal treatment, and a lack of economic and educational opportunity. African Americans are also more likely to be in prison or jail, and to be victims of personal and property crimes.

This chapter has the following purposes: (1) to provide a brief legal historical overview regarding African Americans; (2) to present the current criminal justice status of African Americans as victims and offenders; (3) to discuss the types of legal and criminal justice discrimination that affect African Americans currently; (4) to highlight a few contemporary criminal justice issues which are especially troublesome; and (5) to present the current status of African Americans as justice practitioners. Law's power has been used to exclude African Americans from meaningful participation in social life, and it has also been utilized in attempts to better their social status. The fact that African Americans as a group continue to be relatively disadvantaged in today's society indicates that they have not yet attained full social and legal inclusion in the United States.

LEGAL HISTORICAL CONTEXT: SLAVERY, BLACK CODES, AND JIM CROW

Goldberg (1995:284) writes that "[r]easonable people generally now agree that it is wrong for both persons and social institutions to discriminate against others . . . on grounds of their race." Historically, African Americans have suffered greatly from systematic, institutional, and individual discrimination. From their initial bonds of slavery to their exclusion from and segregation within various spheres of social life, the United States has often treated African Americans in an extremely unequal and unjust manner. This section provides the historical context that is necessary for understanding the contemporary criminal justice status of African Americans.

Widespread belief in the natural inferiority of blacks (i.e., racist ideology) helped underpin discriminatory policies and actions (Bailey, 1991; Flowers, 1988; Russell, 1998). From 1619 to 1865, slaves were subject to states' "slave codes," which declared blacks' inferiority and upheld their exclusion from American life. The codes banned slaves from enjoying the following rights or freedoms: speech, privacy, association, education, employment, voting, holding political office, and owning property (Turner, Singleton, and Musick, 1984). Slave codes enabled plantation owners to police and control their slaves, and owners often punished in cruel and inhumane ways. If a slave was discovered outside of plantation boundaries, he/she could be killed for refusing to answer questions. A dismembered slave's body parts could be publicly displayed, and codes made it illegal for whites to "actively oppose" the institution of slavery (Russell, 1998). Plantation owners could also punish slaves by denying them fulfillment of basic human needs such as social contact and food (Schwarz, 1988).

In response to the post–Civil War legal emancipation of African Americans, many states passed "black codes" and "Jim Crow laws" that helped maintain the social and institutional discrimination of the pre–Civil War era. These laws specifically targeted African Americans, restricting their freedoms and preventing their inclusion into white society. Politically, the codes denied blacks the right to vote or public assembly (Jones, 1998; Russell, 1998). Economically, the codes did allow freed slaves to enter into contracts but restricted them to menial and inferior employment positions. In apparent contradiction with the Fourteenth Amendment, the Supreme Court ruled in *Plessy* v. *Ferguson* (1896) that "separate but equal" institutions for blacks and whites were constitutional.

Jim Crow statutes created a legally segregated society across the United States—an "American apartheid" (Bailey, 1991); thus, simply "being black" remained a crime during this era (Russell, 1998). Blacks were not allowed to associate with whites in public places such as golf courses, parks, and restaurants. They were not allowed to attend many of the best public schools and universities. Like the earlier slave codes, black codes and Jim Crow statutes allowed blacks to be punished for certain "social actions," such as talking with friends on the street corner or making eye contact with whites (Russell, 1998). Neighborhoods and housing developments enforced covenants that did not allow African American residents in white neighborhoods (Turner, Singleton, and Musick, 1984). Many blacks were forced to live in distressed inner-city neighborhoods that had inferior schools (Jones, 1998). In large part through legal institutional discrimination, blacks remained politically and economically excluded during the post–Civil War era (Jones, 1998).

Economic institutions utilized black codes and Jim Crow laws to discriminate, segregate, and exclude blacks through the mid-1900s. Laws called for harsher punishments based on race, and generally did not punish whites for most crimes committed against blacks. The death penalty continued to be practiced in a discriminatory way through the mid-1900s (Bohm, 1991; Gabbidon and Greene, 2005; Walker, Spohn, and DeLone, 2007). The historical phenomenon of lynching during the early part of the twentieth century provides dramatic evidence of institutional *and* individual discrimination against blacks. Police were often present at lynchings, and courts generally did not prosecute whites who lynched blacks (Russell, 1998).

AFRICAN AMERICANS, CRIME, AND THE CRIMINAL JUSTICE SYSTEM

Regarding African Americans, how extensive are the current disparities in the criminal justice system? What types of discrimination affect this group's experiences with the criminal justice system? Are system processes characterized by direct discrimination, or are individuals arrested, charged, and/or convicted based upon their past actions? Are African Americans overrepresented in our prisons because they commit more crime, or because the system treats them unfairly?

To a certain extent, the United States has made positive strides in its treatment of African Americans. As noted earlier, African Americans are generally treated more justly by social institutions than they have been historically; often they are treated equally and protected by law. Furthermore, the post–civil rights era has seen a dramatic rise in the number of middle-class African Americans. Yet, they continue to be overrepresented at the bottom of our social class stratification system; in short, African Americans are more likely to suffer from numerous economic inequalities. Consider the following data from 2003 to 2004: 24.4% of African Americans were living below the poverty line, compared with 10.5% of whites; the median family income for African Americans was $30,134, compared to $46,697 for whites; and, 60% of African American children were living in poverty. During 2005, the African American unemployment rate was twice that of whites (9.6% versus 4.2%). In 2000, the median family net worth (assets such as homes, cars) for whites was ten times greater than that of African Americans— $79,400 to $7,500 (Walker, Spohn, and DeLone, 2007). Furthermore, poverty is linked with other social disadvantages, including inadequate housing and health care, illiteracy, shorter life expectancy, higher infant mortality rates, and less educational and economic opportunity (Jones, 1998; Reiman, 2007; Russell, 1998; Walker, Spohn, and DeLone, 2007). The fact that African Americans are more likely to occupy the bottom rungs of the U.S. social class ladder provides the social framework for understanding (1) their increased likelihood of criminal victimization, (2) their overrepresentation as offenders in the criminal justice system, and (3) their experiences within the system.

Victimization

National victimization data have consistently demonstrated that African Americans are more likely to be victims of crime than other racial/ethnic groups. In 2005, blacks were six times more likely than whites to be homicide victims. Although blacks represent only about 13% of the total U.S. population, they accounted for 46.9% of homicide victims between 1976 and 2005, and 94% of black victims were killed by blacks (Bureau of Justice Statistics, 2005). The National Crime Victimization Survey (NCVS) shows that in 2005, blacks were three times more likely than whites to be victims of sexual assault, and approximately twice as likely to be victims of robbery, aggravated assault, and personal theft (Bureau of Justice Statistics, 2005). In 2003, the NCVS changed its race categories, enabling people to choose "more than one race" for themselves; this obviously complicates the determination of African American victimization rates. Overall violent victimization rates (per 1,000 people) for 2005 were 20.1 for whites, 20.7 for blacks, and 83.6 for "two or more races." Regarding hate crimes that are racially motivated, African Americans, along with Hispanics, are the most likely victims; in 2005, African American hate crime victims reported that the offender was white in over 85% of cases (Walker, Spohn, and DeLone, 2007). Finally, an important type of victimization that is not included in traditional crime measures is environmental crimes/pollution. Poor, minority individuals are much more likely to live in communities where they are subjected to harmful air and water pollution, as well as exposure to dangerous levels of lead (Reiman, 2007).

Disparities in Crime Involvement

The disparities are alarming, overwhelming. They speak to a seriously disadvantaged group. During his lifetime, an African American male has a one in three chance of going to prison; in comparison, a white male has a one in seventeen chance (Travis, 2005). In 2005, African Americans were seven times more likely to commit homicide. According to the 2000 census, African Americans represented 12.7% of the U.S. population; yet, during 2002 they accounted for 38% of arrests for violent crimes. In addition, compare the population percentage (12.7) with the following percentages for 2004–2005, when African Americans represented: 39% of jail inmates, 40% of state and federal prison inmates, 41% of parolees, 30% of probationers, and 42% of death row inmates (Bureau of Justice Statistics, 2006a,b; 2007a; Walker, Spohn, and DeLone, 2007). Thus, given their numbers in the general population, African Americans are overrepresented in our criminal justice system— there are significant disparities. How can we understand these facts, this "virtual gulag of racial incarceration" (Patterson, 2007)?

Most scholars argue that African Americans commit a disproportionate amount of crime, especially the types of crime that result in prison sentences (Cole, 1999; Kennedy, 1997; Patterson, 2007; Tonry, 1995; Walker, Spohn, and DeLone, 2007). There is large degree of consensus among researchers that African Americans' overinvolvement in crime is the primary reason why they are so overrepresented in police statistics, jails, prisons, and on probation and parole caseloads. Researchers often find that when legal factors (seriousness of the crime, prior record) are taken into consideration, these factors explain much of the racial disparity in the criminal justice system—at the arrest, pretrial, and sentencing stages (Cole, 1999; Kennedy, 1997; Tonry, 1995, 2004; Walker, Spohn, and DeLone, 2007). Of course, such involvement in crime must be understood within the context of the social forces (e.g., unemployment rates, education levels, community programs, neighborhood, and family dynamics) which shape people's lives, criminal involvement, and legal records. Structural inequalities in the United States, and their effects on families and other social institutions, provide the framework for understanding African Americans' overinvolvement in crime. Furthermore, crime involvement certainly does not tell the whole story of African Americans' overrepresentation in our criminal justice system. Generally, scholars agree that the system is character-ized, in various ways, by discriminatory practices which play a role in the creation of racial disparities (Barak, Flavin, and Leighton, 2007; Cole, 1999; Gabbidon and Greene, 2005; Kennedy, 1997; Walker, Spohn, and DeLone, 2007).

Discrimination

Institutional discrimination, discriminatory practices, and unbridled discretion at various stages of the criminal justice system have a significant impact on African Americans. First, the overall institutional focus of our legal and criminal justice system functions to create racial disparities. The harms of the wealthy and powerful, if they are defined as crimes at all, are often processed through civil courts—where, most often, monetary fines are paid. Even when the harms of the powerful are criminalized, the punishments for such harms are usually much less compared to the punishments for "street crimes." The harms which are disproportionately committed by the lower classes (to the extent one considers them harms) are generally codified as "crimes" and focused on by the system. The fact that the police, and the overall system, focus on lower class harm/"street crime" (e.g., robbery, drug dealing, car theft) rather than wealthy harm/white-collar crime (e.g., pollution, employee safety, embezzlement, bank fraud)—results in a disproportionate number of African Americans getting caught up in the criminal justice system (Barak, Flavin, and Leighton, 2007; Cole, 1999; Gabbidon and Greene, 2005; Reiman, 2007). Street crimes are more likely to be committed by those at the bottom of the social class system, and African Americans are more likely to occupy those bottom rungs. Furthermore, the "get tough" on crime policies of the 1980s and 1990s produced dramatic increases in our prison population. In 2005, the United States had the highest incarceration rate in the world (491 per 100,000, compared with a rate of 139 in 1980). Approximately, 319,000 people were in prison in the United States in 1980; by 2005, that number had increased to about 1,446,000 (Bureau of Justice Statistics, 2007b). Since the system was already focused on those lower-class individuals engaging in street crime, such "get-tough" policies exacerbated existing racial disparities in the system (Petersilia, 2003; Tonry, 1995, 2004; Travis, 2005; Western, 2006).

Second, specific institutional policies which are officially "race-neutral" can create racially disparate outcomes. Several examples illustrate this issue. First is the "war on drugs," which has had a devastating impact on African Americans. Researchers have documented how this war has been fought primarily in low-income, minority communities, and note that African Americans are not more frequent drug users than other racial/ethnic groups in society (Tonry, 1995; Walker, Spohn, and DeLone, 2007). Federal and state drug statutes often have an unfair effect on young African American drug offenders. Federal statutes prescribe a five-year mandatory minimum sentence for 5 grams of crack cocaine; the same amount of powder cocaine calls for a one-year mandatory minimum sentence. In fact, one must possess 500 grams of powder cocaine in order to fall under the five-year federal mandatory minimum sentence. This 100–1 ratio continues to be debated, but was still in place as of 2007 (Barak, Flavin, and Leighton, 2007; Miller, 1996; Tonry, 1995, 2004; Walker, Spohn, and DeLone, 2007). African Americans (and Latinos) are much more likely to be processed through the system for crack cocaine offenses, and thus suffer greatly from this institutional policy.

Other examples of institutional discrimination occur at the bail and arrest stages. Research has found that "community ties" are often important for determining how much, if any, a bail amount should be for an accused offender. Since African Americans are less likely to have significant community ties (e.g., employment, being a homeowner), they are indirectly discriminated against at this stage in some jurisdictions (Walker, Spohn, and DeLone, 2007). Research has demonstrated that, depending on the circumstances, police officers are more likely to arrest a person if they have a hostile demeanor. In addition, we know that young, urban, minority males are more likely than other demographic groups to have hostile attitudes toward the police. Thus, when demeanor is a "race neutral" factor in the decision to arrest, African Americans will be overrepresented in arrest statistics (Walker, Spohn, and DeLone, 2007).

Third, is the issue of *direct racial discrimination*—the unequal treatment of an individual based upon their racial/ethnic group identity—during criminal justice system processing. To what extent and how does race matter in criminal justice system processing? The idea that U.S. criminal justice system processes are *either* fair *or* unfair is much too simplistic and ignores the complex and varied nature of social organizations and system processing. Rather, regarding fairness and discrimination, the best way to understand our contemporary criminal justice system practices is by utilizing the concept of *contextual discrimination* (Cole, 1999; Gabbidon and Greene, 2005; Kennedy, 1997; Walker, Spohn, and DeLone, 2007). Again, legal factors appear to explain most racial/ethnic disparities, but certainly not all. Research suggests that in some jurisdictions, at certain processing stages, and for certain types of crimes, our criminal justice system continues to be characterized by direct discrimination against African Americans (Barak, Flavin, and Leighton, 2007; Gabbidon and Greene, 2005; Walker, Spohn, and DeLone, 2007). In other words, prosecutors may be directly discriminatory in Chicago, but not in New York; or police may discriminate in arrests decisions for misdemeanors, but not for serious felonies; or judges may discriminate when sentencing young minority men for drug offenses, but not for robbery offenses. In regard to policing, researchers have documented direct discrimination at the both the prearrest and arrest stages (Barak, Flavin, and Leighton, 2007; Cole, 1999; Gabbidon and Greene, 2005; Walker, Spohn, and DeLone, 2007). Consider the name for an apparent crime on Maryland's interstates—"Driving While Black" (Barovick, 1998; Cole, 1999). Between 1995 and 1997, only 17% of drivers on I-95 were black, yet they represented 70% of drivers stopped by the police (Barovick, 1998). Research illustrates that such racial patterns in stops cannot be explained by driving patterns—that is, the fact that some racial groups are "bad" drivers (Walker, Spohn, and DeLone, 2007). These disproportionate percentages are partly the result of police "profiles" of drug couriers; part of the profile appears to include being black. Finally, research documents contextual discrimination at the sentencing stage of the system. For example, research has found evidence of discrimination for the crime of sexual assault where the offender is African American and the victim is white, in federal drug cases, and in "borderline" (relatively minor) felony cases (Gabbidon and Greene, 2005; Walker, Spohn, and DeLone, 2007). Often times, the race effect is enhanced when combined with other extralegal factors—so, for example, young, unemployed, African American males may face particularly harsh sentencing for drug crimes in certain jurisdictions (Barak, Flavin, and Leighton, 2007; Gabbidon and Greene, 2005; Walker, Spohn, and DeLone, 2007).

Highlighted Issues: Peremptory Challenge, Death Penalty, Mass Incarceration

This section highlights a few contemporary criminal justice issues that are especially troublesome. First, is the *peremptory challenge*. Peremptory challenges are used by prosecutors and defense attorneys during the creation of the trial jury. Both the prosecution and the defense are provided with a certain number of challenges, which they can use to strike, without explanation, an individual from the jury pool (and thus eliminate her/him from possibly sitting on the trial jury). Generally, scholars agree that race/ethnicity is a factor in the peremptory challenge process, and that something needs to be done to fix the problem (Cole, 1999; Gabbidon and Greene, 2005; Kennedy, 1997; Walker, Spohn, and DeLone, 2007). In 2005, the U.S. Supreme Court overturned the murder conviction of a black man, Thomas Miller-El, with the majority opinion stating that the selection of the jury for his trial was "infected with racial discrimination" (Greenhouse, 2005). The prosecution had used its peremptory challenges to eliminate 10 of 11 potential black jurors for Miller-El's trial. Justice Breyer stated that peremptory challenges "seem increasingly anomalous in our judicial system" and that "the use of race- and gender-based stereotypes in the jury-selection process seems better organized and more systematized than ever before" (Greenhouse, 2005). It is important to remember that the jury trial represents an individual's ultimate trump card against government power, effectively saying to the government "you have to prove to my peers" that I committed the crime. Thus, even though the vast majority of cases are plea-bargained, one cannot overestimate the importance of having a fair jury selection process in place.

Second, the research evidence regarding the importance of the victim's race/ethnicity in death penalty cases is very strong and consistent. Baldus and his colleagues' (1990) seminal study illustrated how killers of whites were more likely to be charged with a capital offense, and ultimately sentenced to death in Georgia; this likelihood was enhanced when the offender was African American. Baldus, Woodworth, and Pulaski (1990) found the race of victim effect to be important in "mid-range" cases—the type of cases that could "go either way—life or death"—where prosecutors and juries have to make a choice. Mid-range cases might have a few aggravating factors present, but are not especially heinous (i.e., they do not involve torture or multiple victims). Although African Americans are overrepresented on death row (42% of such inmates in 2005), contemporary studies find an inconsistent race of offender effect; however, research continues to document a strong, consistent race of victim effect in death penalty cases (Barak, Flavin, and Leighton, 2007; Cole, 1999; Gabbidon and Greene, 2005; Walker, Spohn, and DeLone, 2007). In 1976, the death penalty was effectively reinstated by the Supreme Court; from 1976 through the fall of 2007, 79% of those executed had killed a white person (Death Penalty Information Center, 2007). Quite simply, if a person (allegedly) murders a white person, he/she is more likely to be charged with a capital offense and a jury is more likely to vote for a death sentence; this finding is consistent across different states and areas of the country (Walker, Spohn, and DeLone, 2007). Furthermore, there is an issue of institutional discrimination regarding the death penalty. Given that the vast majority of African Americans in capital cases are poor, they are often represented by lawyers whose resources are extremely limited, and, who may be rather inexperienced in trying death penalty cases (Cole, 1999; Reiman, 2007). Several states have stopped performing executions due to concerns about unfair practices.

Finally, the reader should consider the following. Our rates of incarceration have exploded since the 1970s due to the "get tough on crime" movement, and the racial disparities in our criminal justice system are worse than they have ever been. Linked with this explosion and worsening of disparities is the fact some groups did not benefit from the economic growth of the 1990s. Specifically, African Americans and especially African American males were "left behind," and many African American families, communities, and neighborhoods have been decimated by mass incarceration (Clear, 2002; Travis, 2005; Western, 2006; Western, Pettit, and Guetzkow, 2002). The "get-tough" movement included numerous "side effects" to becoming a felon. African American males have been politically disenfranchised in numerous ways, such as losing the right to vote, and losing eligibility for housing, education funding, and assistance programs; these collateral consequences of mass incarceration have further disadvantaged large numbers of African Americans, their families, and their children (Mauer and Chesney-Lind, 2002; Travis, 2005). Communities are faced with large numbers of felons cycling in and out of prison, with few skills and little hope for the future. To what extent does it make sense to understand this mass incarceration and worsening of disparities as the latest means by which the state exercises control over disadvantaged segments of the population? To what extent has mass incarceration functioned (in part) as a replacement for past means of exclusion and social control (e.g., slavery, black codes, Jim Crow statutes)? It is certainly true that many benefited in the post–civil rights era; however, many have been left behind, and our criminal justice system has played a central role.

PRACTITIONERS

The number of African Americans working in the criminal justice system has increased dramatically since the civil rights era. In 1960, African Americans represented 3.6% of police officers in the United States; in 2003, they represented 11.7%. Furthermore, African Americans have attained the top police position in numerous cities, including Atlanta, New Orleans, Chicago, and New York City. Compared with their percentage of the general population, African Americans are well represented as workers in correctional facilities. The number of African American judges in the United States had reached over 500 by 1989 (Walker, Spohn, and DeLone, 2007). From 1981 through early 2006, African Americans represented 12.8% of presidential appointees to the U.S. Court of Appeals (Barak, Flavin, and Leighton, 2007). Although African Americans are better represented than they have ever been as system practitioners, significant disparities still exist in important system positions. Furthermore, the lack of African American legislators (at both the federal and state level) is certainly important to consider, given that legislatures create laws and punishments in our society.

CONCLUSION

The story of African Americans, crime, and criminal justice is one of real progress, but also one of inequality, disparities, and discrimination. Historical legacies, institutional policies, and social inequalities which shape life choices and pathways drive the overrepresentation of African Americans in our police, court, and correctional statistics. Discriminatory practices are also a contributing factor in the criminal justice system's disparities. The get-tough movement and the civil and social exclusions that came with it have exacerbated these disparities and wreaked havoc on African American communities. Although there has been significant and meaningful progress regarding African Americans and criminal justice in the United States, it is also evident that much more needs to be done. On a system level, addressing problematic areas, such as the peremptory challenge and the death penalty, is paramount. Continuing to research, publicize, and confront discriminatory practices is necessary. Politicians and researchers are now recognizing the financial cost and overall ineffectiveness of the mass incarceration policy of the past 30 years. Numerous authors (e.g., Reiman, 2007; Tonry, 1995; Travis, 2005) suggest that the criminal justice system should, at the very least, not cause more harm than it prevents. Using prison less, and working with those inmates who are released in order to prevent their return to prison, is extremely important.

Often, people cannot discuss racial differences and inequalities without having the communication process deteriorate into hostility and ineffectiveness. It is hoped that this chapter presents a framework for both understanding the contemporary criminal justice discriminations that African Americans continue to face and exploring practical means of changing these practices. The power of the law should be harnessed and utilized to achieve a more just society for all. African Americans are more likely to suffer from a childhood of poverty, an inferior education, an increased likelihood of being under the control of the criminal justice system, and being a victim of crime. Such statuses do not equate with equal opportunity. African Americans began their time here as slaves, and some now have decent opportunities, good employment, and live relatively safe and free lives. Yet, African Americans as a group continue to be burdened by socioeconomic inequalities, institutional policies, and discriminatory criminal justice system practices. These burdens create their overrepresentation in our criminal justice system, and have a detrimental impact on their life experiences. Addressing these inequalities, policies, and practices is necessary to create a more just society, and, a more just criminal justice system.

References

Bailey, Frankie. Y. 1991. Law, Justice, and "Americans": An Historical Overview. In *Race and criminal justice,* ed. M. Lynch and E. B. Patterson, 10–21. New York: Harrow and Heston.

Baldus, David C., George Woodworth, and Charles Pulaski. 1990. *Equal Justice and the Death Penalty: A Legal and Empirical Analysis.* Boston: Northeastern University Press.

Barak, Gregg, Jeanne Flavin, and Paul Leighton. 2007. *Class, Race, Gender, Crime: The Social Realities of Justice in America,* 2nd edn. Lanham, MD: Rowman & Littlefield.

Barovick, H. 1998. DWB: Driving While Black. *Time* 151 (23): 35.

Blakeslee, N. 2005. *Tulia: Race, Cocaine, and Corruption in a Small Texas Town.* New York: Public Affairs.

Blaney, B. 2005. Ex-agent Convicted in Tulia Drug Case. CBS News.

Bohm, R. 1991. Race and the Death Penalty in the United States. In *Race and Criminal Justice,* ed. M.J. Lynch and E.B. Patterson, 71–85. New York: Harrow and Heston.

Bureau of Justice Statistics. 2005. Criminal Victimization. Washington, DC: U.S. Department of Justice.

Bureau of Justice Statistics. (2006a). Capital Punishment, 2005. Washington, DC: U.S. Department of Justice.

Bureau of Justice Statistics. (2006b). Homicide Trends in the U.S. Washington, DC: U.S. Department of Justice.

Bureau of Justice Statistics. (2007a). Prison and Jail Inmates at Midyear 2006. Washington, DC: U.S. Department of Justice.

Bureau of Justice Statistics. (2007b). Prisoners in 2005. Washington, DC: U.S. Department of Justice.

CBS News. 2004a. Settlement for Tulia's Victims. March 11. http://www.cbsnews.com/stories/2004/03/11/national/main605225.shtml?source = search_story.

CBS News. 2004b. Targeted in Tulia, TX? June 30. http://www.cbsnews.com/stories/2004/06/30/60minutes/main626853.shtml?source = search_story.

Clear, T. 2002. The Problem with "Addition by Subtraction": The Prison-Crime Relationship in Low-Income Communities. In *Invisible Punishment: The Collateral Consequences of Mass Imprisonment,* ed. Marc Mauer and Meda Chesney-Lind, 181–193. New York: The New Press.

Cole, David. 1999. *No Equal Justice: Race and Class in the American Criminal Justice System.* New York: The New Press.

Death Penalty Information Center. 2007. www.deathpenaltyinfo.org.

Flowers, R. 1988. *Minorities and criminality.* New York: Greenwood Press.

Gabbidon, Shaun L., and Helen Taylor Greene. 2005. *Race and Crime.* Thousand Oaks, CA: Sage Publications.

Goldberg, David T. 1995. *Ethical Theory and Social Issues.* Orlando, FL: Harcourt Brace.

Greenhouse, L. 2005. Supreme Court Rules for Texan on Death Row. *The New York Times,* June 14.

Hohler, B. 1998. Terror in a Texas Town. *Boston Globe,* June 14, p.A3.

Jones, Jacqueline. 1998. *American Work: Four Centuries of Black and White Labor.* New York: W.W. Norton.

Kennedy, Randall. 1997. *Race, Crime, and the Law.* New York: Vintage Books.

King, Joyce. 2002. *Hate Crime: The Story of a Dragging in Jasper, Texas.* New York: Pantheon Books.

Mauer, Marc, and Meda Chesney-Lind (Ed). 2002. *Invisible Punishment: The Collateral Consequences of Mass Imprisonment.* New York: The New Press.

Miller, Jerome G. 1996. *Search and Destroy: African-American Males in the Criminal Justice System.* Cambridge, UK: Cambridge University.

Nelson, M. 2007. Guards Acquitted in Boot Camp Death. Miami: Associated Press.

Patterson, O. 2007. Jena, O.J., and the Jailing of Black America. *New York Times,* September 30, Op-ed.

Petersilia, Joan. 2003. *When Prisoners Come Home: Parole and Prisoner Reentry.* New York: Oxford University Press

Plessy v. *Ferguson.* 1896. 163 U.S. 537 (1896).

Reiman, Jeffrey. 2007. *The Rich Get Richer and the Poor Get Prison,* 8th edn. Boston: Allyn & Bacon.

Russell, K. 1998. *The Color of Crime.* New York: New York University Press.

Schwarz, Philip J. 1988. *Twice Condemned: Slaves and the Criminal Laws of Virginia, 1705–1865.* Baton Rouge, LA: Louisiana State University Press.

Tonry, Michael. 1995. *Malign Neglect: Race, Crime, and Punishment in America.* New York: Oxford University Press.

Tonry, Michael. 2004. *Thinking About Crime: Sense and Sensibility in American Penal Culture.* New York: Oxford University Press.

Travis, J. 2005. *But They All Come Back: Facing the Challenge of Prisoner Reentry.* Washington, DC: The Urban Institute Press.

Turner, J. H., R. Singleton, and D. Musick. 1984. *Oppression: A Socio-History of Black-White Relations in America.* Chicago: Nelson-Hall.

Walker, Samuel, Cassia Spohn, and Miriam DeLone. 2007. *The Color of Justice: Race, Ethnicity, and Crime in America,* 4th edn. Belmont, CA: Wadsworth.

West, Cornel. 1993. *Race Matters.* Boston: Beacon Press.

Western, Bruce. 2006. *Punishment and Inequality in America.* New York: The Russell Sage Foundation.

Western, B., B. Pettit, and J. Guetzkow. 2002. Black economic progress in the Era of mass imprisonment. In *Invisible Punishment: The Collateral Consequences of Mass Imprisonment,* ed. Marc Mauer and Meda Chesney-Lind, 165–180. New York: The New Press.

CHAPTER 9

Unwelcome Citizens

Latinos and the Criminal Justice System

Luis A. Fernandez

Alexander Alvarez

The commonly held perception that, "every Texas Ranger has some Mexican blood. He has it on his boots," (Murguia, 1975) illustrates well the adversarial and sometimes violent relationship that many Mexican Americans in particular, and Latinos in general, experience with the criminal justice system. Frequently reported stories of blatant abuse and harassment by law enforcement agents only reinforce the perception that, in this society, past and present discriminatory practices are often the norm where Latinos are concerned. It is clear that discrimination against Latinos exists both within the criminal justice system and in the larger population (Aguirre and Turner, 1995). Studies in various states continue to show that judges impose harsher sentences on Latinos and African Americans than they do on whites, even if the offense and prior record are comparable (Demuth and Steffensmeier, 2004). For example, Latinos are 18% more likely to be incarcerated in non-drug cases than are whites. In contrast, Latinos are less likely than whites to get reduced sentences when pleading guilty, hiring a private attorney, or providing evidence or testimony for another case (Harrington and Spohn, 2007).

In addition, Latinos are often incorrectly characterized as foreigners and immigrants (Mata, 1998), a depiction that ignores the fact that many Mexican Americans, for example, never immigrated here, but became U.S. citizens when the border changed. This representation also ignores the reality that Puerto Ricans became U.S. citizens as a direct result of military conquest when the United States defeated Spain in the Spanish–American War. Similarly, a misinformed panic about the "alien invasion" of illegal immigrants from Mexico is a topic of urgent concern for some who perceive a threat to the "American way of life," and frequently apply their xenophobia to all Latinos in the United States (see Chapters 7 and 17). However, one never hears of the threat of illegal immigration from Canada, which is also a source of illegal immigrants.

Subject to dehumanizing popular stereotypes in the entertainment media, Latinos are often negatively typecast by police officers and other officials of the criminal justice system (Portillos, 1998). Common images of Latinos as greasers, drug dealers, gang members, and other assorted criminals reinforce the notion that Latino populations are dangerous and need to be continuously monitored and controlled. Unfortunately, criminal law agents sometimes adopt these stereotypes, leading to the criminalization of the Latino population. Looking at empirical data, researchers conclude, "that the specific social and historical context facing Hispanic Americans will exacerbate perceptions of their cultural dissimilarity and the 'threat' they pose" (Steffensmeier and Demuth, 2001:170).

In short, the Latino experience in the United States has frequently been punctuated by conflict, misunderstanding, racism, and violence. It is, however, a history that in recent years has emerged into our national consciousness. The belated recognition that this country is a multicultural society has exploded onto the political and social scene as issues such as multilingual education, affirmative action, and racism provide fodder for debate and discourse in communities across the nation. This awareness has sparked attention to the impact of race and ethnicity in the criminal justice arena and the role various minority groups play as actors in that domain. One such group is Latinos.

LATINO DEMOGRAPHICS

The term "Latino" serves as a versatile category that includes various groups of people in the United States, who have arrived or have ancestry from different Latin American and Spanish origins. Other terms in use to self-identify may include Latino/a, Hispanic, *hispano*, Latin American, "Spanish," or part of "la raza."

Regardless of the terminology, Latino populations have had an impact on the American criminal justice system in numerous ways as perpetrators, victims, and practitioners, and that influence is likely to grow in the coming years. Latino populations comprise approximately 14% of the U.S. populace, or roughly 43 million people (U.S. Census Bureau, 2006). Not surprisingly, these numbers are expected to rise dramatically, due in part to the high levels of legal and illegal immigration coupled with high birth rates. In fact, the Latino population increased by 50% from 1995 to 2005. And in 2007, Latinos became the largest single minority group in the United States, surpassing African Americans.

There are several other significant issues that must be addressed when studying Latino populations. Even though Latinos are typically referred to as a minority group, they can more accurately be described as being composed of many diverse groups, each with its own unique history, culture, and experience. Mexican Americans comprise the largest single Latino population (59%), with Puerto Ricans (10%) second, and Cubans (4%) third. The rest of the Latino population (27%) comes from various countries in Central and South America (U.S. Census Bureau, 2000). Although these populations share a common language, they are typically quite distinct in their cultural traditions, heritage, history, and backgrounds. And, in fact, some recent immigrants speak Indian languages such as, Nahuatl in addition to or instead of Spanish. As Himilce Novas writes, "Perhaps no other ethnic group in the United States is as diverse in its culture, physical appearance, and traditions as the Hispanics" (1994:2). Indeed, there is even a great deal of variation within specific Latino populations. Mexican Americans, for example, may be of pure Spanish origin, Indian, or mestizo. Contrary to popular representation, the category of class also complicates the Latino category, since some Latinos are wealthy and educated, while others are not.

Sometimes, however, it is useful to aggregate Latino groups because it allows scholars to search for patterns of discrimination. Without the term *Latino*, we might never know if discrimination practices are diminishing or increasing. Although several terms have been used to describe Latinos (such as people of Spanish origin, and Hispanic), we use the term *Latino*. As Hayes-Bautista and Chapa argue, "Latino is the best label to describe Hispanics since it preserves national origin of the referents as a significant characteristic, it is culturally and racially neutral, and may be the least objectionable of all possible ethnic labels" (1987:21–22). In addition, it is important to note that when we use the term *African American*, we are referring to non-Latino African Americans. The terms *Anglo* and *white* should be perceived as referring to whites not of Latino origin. In addition to the issue of identification, we must also recognize that the present experience of Latino groups is firmly rooted in the events and ideologies of the past.

HISTORY

Even though the history of Latinos in the Americas goes back further than practically any other group with the exception of indigenous peoples, their relationship with the Anglo culture has been a difficult and contentious one. The first Spanish colony in the continental United States was established in 1598 at Santa Fe, now in the state of New Mexico (Shorris, 1992), and it was not long before similar Mexican settlements were established in what are now California, Arizona, and Texas. Similarly, Spanish settlements were founded in Florida and in various locations along the southeastern seaboard (Steele, 1994). The Spanish presence in North America, especially in the southwest and southeast, therefore predates the Anglo presence on much of the continent. However, even though their pedigree in North America was long and distinguished, Latinos were often the losers when they came into contact with Anglos. For example, after Mexico lost the Mexican–American War in 1847 and was coerced into signing the Treaty of Guadalupe Hidalgo a year later, Mexico lost approximately 50% of its sovereign territory as Texas, New Mexico, California, Arizona, Nevada, Utah, and half of Colorado were delivered over to the United States (Novas, 1994). The 80,000 Mexicans in this vast territory became citizens of the United States overnight.

Within a short period of time, these new citizens were made second-class citizens, being deprived of their land, property, wealth, and in some cases, their lives. The law and agents of criminal justice system, such as the Texas and Arizona Rangers, were often the mechanisms by which this was accomplished (Acuña, 2000). As Mary Romero writes, "Maintaining the interest of cattle barons in Texas, the Texas Rangers treated Mexicans living along the border as cattle thieves and bandits when they attempted to reclaim stolen property from cattle barons. Similarly, the Arizona Rangers protected capitalist interests by protecting strikebreakers against Mexican Miners" (2006:449).

Shorris (1992:2) writes, "Ironically, it was through the use of the new democratic practices of the United States that the once dominant population group was excluded from having a voice in the government. Anglo legislators passed tax laws and land-use laws designed to wrest the huge ranches away from the rich Californians and to take the modest homesites of the poor." Deprived of their economic resource base, Mexican Americans were consigned to the economic underclass of this society where they have labored for most of this country's history. This would not be the last time that Mexican Americans were exploited and discriminated against. The exploitation of the Braceros work programs, the violence of the Zoot suit riots of 1943, and the more recent demonization and stereotyping of illegal immigrants all indicate as much.

In regards to the issue of immigration, Mexican Americans are generally portrayed as the only illegal-immigrant group. In her research, Romero (2006) documents how law enforcement apply immigration law unevenly, resulting in the criminalization of the Mexican American worker. For instance, historically the INS rarely raided the fields during harvest time, waiting for periods of economic recession to conduct mass immigration raids.

Similarly, local police have also applied the law unevenly. Aguirre and Turner state that "Studies of police tactics in small communities have shown that Mexican Americans are victims of prejudiced attitudes, indiscriminate searches and detentions, and high arrest–conviction rates" (1995:133). Evidence also indicates that Mexican Americans have frequently been the victims of racist-motivated police violence, ritualized ceremonies of degradation, as well as numerous other examples of discriminatory treatment (Garza, 1995; LaFree, 1995; Padilla, 1992; Rodriquez, 1993; U.S. Commission on Civil Rights, 1970).

The history of Puerto Ricans in the United States is also a story replete with examples of economic, social, and legal discrimination. After the United States defeated Spain in the Spanish–American War, Puerto Rico became a U.S. protectorate and, subsequently, in 1917, its people were granted U.S. citizenship, which allowed for unrestricted migration and travel from the island to the mainland. Although American businesses have certainly profited from their association with Puerto Rico, the same cannot be said for its inhabitants who have traditionally suffered from high rates of poverty and unemployment (Bourgois, 1996; Rodriguez, 1991). Throughout the twentieth century, large numbers of Puerto Ricans migrated to the mainland United States in search of better economic opportunities. In most cases, they have merely traded rural poverty on the island for urban poverty in the slums and barrios of New York City and other large eastern cities. Of this deprivation, Bourgois writes,

Few other ethnic groups, except perhaps Native American Indians, fared more poorly in official statistics than the 896,753 Puerto Ricans who lived in New York City at the time of the 1990 census. They have the highest welfare dependency and household poverty rates, as well as the lowest labor force participation rates, of any other ethnic group in the city. In fact, in 1989 their poverty rate (38 percent) was double that of New York City's (19 percent). One statistical survey showed their family poverty rate in the late 1980s to be 500 percent higher than New York City's average (1996:53).

In short, Puerto Ricans are the most economically disadvantaged Latino group in the United States (Myers, Cintron, and Scarborough, 2000). Their experiences with the criminal justice system, similar to those of Mexican Americans, have also been marked by sometimes blatant discrimination. One study, for example, found that Puerto Ricans are more likely to be institutionalized than to receive probation and receive longer sentences than do whites for the same offenses (Sissons, 1979). Given the stereotypes that portray Puerto Ricans as, "lazy, submissive, and immoral, with propensities for crime and gang violence" (Aguirre and Turner, 1995:139), the inequities they suffer at the hands of the criminal justice system are hardly surprising.

In marked contrast to both Mexican Americans and Puerto Ricans, the position of much of the Cuban American community in the United States is a relatively privileged and powerful one. There are several specific reasons for this rather peculiar position (peculiar when compared to other Latino groups).

First, Cuban immigrants to this country did not really arrive in any large numbers until the 1950s, as large numbers of middle- and upper-class Cubans sought refuge from Fidel Castro's new society. They, therefore, escaped many of the earliest excesses and images directed against longer-established Latino populations that have colored subsequent relationships with those groups. Many of the dominant negative stereotypes of Mexican Americans, for example, are derived from old animosities embedded in the historic landscape, and Cuban Americans have largely escaped these sorts of traditional negative images. Second, these Cubans were relatively well educated and were largely from the middle and upper tiers of the Cuban economic ladder. The Cuban American community thus arrived with the necessary economic resources needed not only to survive, but also to succeed. This economic clout, when combined with the Cuban American political conservatism and antipathy toward communism, gave this population access to political and social circles not common to most Latino communities (Hess, Markson, and Stein, 1998).

This is not to say, however, that Cuban Americans have not suffered from some of the same racism so endemic to most Latino/Anglo relations. This is especially true for one subgroup of Cubans known as the Marielitos. In 1980, Fidel Castro emptied his prisons of political prisoners and predatory criminals, and the mental hospitals of their patients, and "encouraged" them to emigrate to the United States. Thus was born the Mariel boatlift, named after the Cuban port from which they fled. These latest arrivals were usually "darker skinned, poorer, and often unemployable" (Aguirre and Turner, 1995:143). Whereas only a relatively small number of Marielitos were actually criminals, they were constantly portrayed as dangerous deviants and defectives (Hamm, 1995). These new Cuban Americans helped change the way Cuban Americans were perceived and treated. Whereas the older, whiter, and wealthier Cuban Americans are relatively isolated from contact with the criminal justice system, the Marielitos have not enjoyed the same privileged position and consequently have had more conflict with law enforcement agencies and other criminal justice organizations.

To summarize, then, the experience of Latinos in the United States is a varied one that reflects the diversity of Latino populations in this country. One persistent element for the various Latino populations is the role that discrimination has played in their relationship with the criminal justice system.

PERPETRATORS

As perpetrators of crime, Latino populations continue to comprise a relatively little-studied group. What work there is, however, indicates that Latino groups are at a greater risk of perpetration than are non-Latino whites. Generally speaking, although African Americans tend to have the highest perpetration rates for various types of crime and whites the lowest, Latinos often have intermediate rates between the two. For example, the research on homicide in Latino communities in different states and cities generally reveals that the Latino homicide rates are usually above those of whites but below those of African Americans (Becker *et al.*, 1990; Martinez, 2002; Mercy, 1987; Smith, Mercy, and Rosenberg, 1986). However, contrary to popular belief, some scholars argue that "The presence of Latino homicide is not as high as expected relative to that of other impoverished ethnic groups" (Martinez, 2002:4). Interestingly enough, within the Latino population, it is Puerto Ricans who experience the highest homicide rates (Rodriguez, 1991). This may well be a result of the fact that Puerto Ricans suffer from the highest poverty rates and lowest educational attainment of any Latino group.

Latinos are also overrepresented in the prison population at the local, state, and federal levels. For instance, Latinos make up 19% of those individuals jailed in county facilities. Similarly, 17% of those individuals in state prisons are Latino. The life chances of a Latino ending up in prison are 10%, while only 3.5% for Anglos (Bureau of Justice Statistics, 2006a).

Coramae Richey Mann reports that during the mid-1980s, when Latinos comprised roughly 6.5% of the population, they constituted almost 13% of all persons arrested (Mann, 1993). In 1986, this amounted to approximately 1,172,609 Latinos (Flowers, 1990)—an arrest rate double their population size. These numbers, it is important to point out, vary widely by region of the country. Not surprisingly, the highest arrest rates come from those regions of the country such as the southwest that have large Latino populations.

Although Latinos are overrepresented in the official arrest statistics relative to their size in the population, it is noteworthy that this exaggerated representation is only partially due to perpetration. As illustrated earlier, at every stage of the criminal justice process, Latinos may be treated more harshly and punitively than are whites. The discretion available to law enforcement officers and court officials is frequently used against Latinos, and their overrepresentation in arrest and incarceration statistics reflects this reality.

In terms of the types of crimes for which they are arrested, the evidence indicates that in 1986, the ten most common offenses for which Latinos were arrested were DUI, drunkenness, larceny–theft, drug violations, other assaults, disorderly conduct, burglary, liquor law violations, aggravated assault, and weapons violations

(Mann, 1993:42). According to Coramae Richey Mann's analysis, these ten offenses account for more than two-thirds of all offenses for which Latinos are arrested. Most of these, it should be noted, are not index offenses. Rather, five of the ten arrest offenses appear to be drug and alcohol-related. This certainly does not appear to vindicate the popular stereotypes that portray all Latinos as violent gang members and criminals.

Theoretical attempts to explain Latino patterns of criminality tend to focus either on structural issues of poverty and discrimination or, alternatively, on cultural roles and identity within Latino communities. Many of the structural arguments are guided by the notion that various forms of inequality, including economic and political disparities, influence the perpetration of crime. It is important to note, therefore, that Latino populations are often ranked among the lowest rungs of this society's economy. In 2004, for example, the median family net worth for Latinos was approximately $8,000, far below that of whites ($88,000) (*USA Today*, 2004). A similar pattern is revealed when the median family income is examined. In 2006, the per capita income for Latinos was $15,421, a figure slightly lower than that for African Americans ($17,902), but much lower than that for whites ($27,821) (U.S. Census Bureau, 2007).

These aggregates, however, conceal the fact that poverty varies tremendously between Latino groups. For example, although only 16% of Cuban families lived below the poverty level in 1995, 36% of Puerto Rican families and 28% of Mexican American families were also impoverished in the 1990s (del Pinal and Singer, 1997). Similar patterns emerge when educational attainment and unemployment figures are reviewed. We have already discussed the ways in which Latinos have been discriminated against in the criminal justice system, but it is important to note that they are sometimes treated unequally in other contexts as well, such as choice of residency (Massey and Denton, 1987; Santiago and Wilder, 1991). This practice produces increased levels of social, spatial, and economic isolation of Latino communities and, therefore, exacerbates the effects of poverty and other social ills.

Other researchers point to social disorganization within Latino communities (Block, 1985; Valdez and Nourjah, 1987) and difficulties in cultural assimilation and adjustment (Bondavalli and Bondavalli, 1981) as possible explanations for Latino criminality. In short, many Latinos continue to exist at the bottom of this society, economically, politically, and socially, and it is these kinds of conditions that have been linked to criminality in the social science literature (Blau and Blau, 1982; Blau and Golden, 1986; Blau and Schwartz, 1984; Crutchfield, 1989; Harer and Steffensmeier, 1992; Sampson, 1986). It is said that poverty breeds crime, as members of impoverished communities commit crime for either economic advantage (e.g., theft-related crimes), escape (e.g., drug-related crimes), or out of rage, anger, and frustration (e.g., violent crimes). Given the economic state of many Latino communities, these arguments go a long way toward explaining many of the crime patterns exhibited by Latino groups.

Many cultural theories of Latino crime revolve around the related concepts of *machismo* and the subculture of violence thesis. The notion of machismo relates to a specific definition of masculinity, in which physical aggression, virility, pride, strength, and courage are all necessary qualities for Latino males (Marín and

Marín, 1991; Shorris, 1992; Vigil, 1998). In essence, then, some have suggested that the cultural premiums placed on these male qualities lend themselves to aggression and violence, and involvement in gangs (Erlanger, 1979; Flowers, 1990; Mann, 1993). The subculture of violence thesis, however, suggests that certain regions and/or groups have adopted values that are conducive to the use of violence in order to resolve conflict (Wolfgang and Ferracuti, 1967). Commonly used to explain the violence in African American communities, this argument suggests that Latino cultural values support and encourage the use of violence in everyday conflictual situations because it is one way of asserting power in groups that are relatively powerless (Erlanger, 1979).

The difficulty with these cultural arguments is that they do not recognize the very real diversity of culture among Latino populations. It is difficult to understand how one cultural theory is applicable to culturally diverse populations. Nevertheless, it remains a popular way of explaining Latino criminality. It is important to note that many of these cultural explanations of crime have been criticized as victim-blaming strategies and as having racist overtones for suggesting a cultural inferiority among Latino groups. In other words, these arguments implicitly posit dysfunctional or deviance-producing qualities to the cultures of various minority groups, rather than making allowance for the fact that much of the criminality within Latino communities is also seen as deviant by many members of that group. In addition, these cultural arguments ignore the role of the criminal justice system in producing criminal identities. That is, crime is as much a political manifestation as it is a behavioral one. When law enforcement officials target Latino communities for heightened and more punitive attention, they effectively criminalize that population and help to perpetuate the stigmatized identity of the targeted group. In short, these cultural arguments often manifest many of the same discriminatory attitudes so prevalent in this society at large.

VICTIMS

Victimization of violent crime has significantly decreased for all the U.S. population since 1993. However, the available evidence indicates that Latinos are still at a higher risk of victimization for both property and violent offenses than are non-Latinos. In 2005, for example, the Latino rate of violent victimization was 25 per 1,000, whereas the rate for non-Latinos was 20.6 (Bureau of Justice Statistics, 2006b). For the crime of robbery, Latinos are twice as likely to be victimized as non-Latinos. Specifically, the Latino robbery victimization rate in 2005 was 4 per 1,000, compared to a rate of 2.4 per 1,000 for non-Latinos (Bureau of Justice Statistics, 2006b). For the crimes of burglary, household larceny, and motor vehicle theft, Latino households invariably experience higher rates than non-Latino households (Bureau of Justice Statistics, 2006b). Finally, Latinos also have a higher chance of being victims of gang violence than do non-Latinos (Bureau of Justice Statistics, 2005a).

Recent data also suggest that Latinos continue to be victimized by hate crimes targeted against them specifically because of their ethnicity. Although this is not a new type of victimization for Latinos, its reporting certainly is new. In 2005, there were 522 reported incidents of this type of crime that victimized a total of 722 Latinos (Bureau of Justice Statistics, 2005b). Whereas this number is relatively small compared to hate crimes against African Americans (2,630 reported incidents in 2005), this number is certainly underreported. Latinos are much less likely to report victimizations to official sources than are non-Latinos (Bureau of Justice Statistics, 2006b). This marked tendency toward underreporting is largely due to the widespread perception among Latinos that law enforcement is the enemy and unfairly targets and harasses Latinos simply because of their ethnic identity. As the Latino populations continue to grow in the United States and assume ever more visible roles in the shaping of this society, it is likely that hate crimes targeting them will also grow more prevalent.

Patterns of discrimination are present within policing as well. In 2005, the U.S. Department of Justice conducted a study that showed that while Latino and non-Latino drivers were stopped at the same rate by police officers, Latino drivers were searched 11.4% of the time, compared with 3.5% for white drivers (Glater, 2007). Interestingly, the increase in Latino searches failed to yield an increase in arrests or discovery of criminal behavior.

PRACTITIONERS

In recent years, Latinos have made strong strides toward greater occupational representation in the criminal justice system. For example, in 2002, approximately 17% of federal law enforcement officers were Latino, an increase of 10% from 1991 (Bureau of Justice Statistics, 2003). A similar pattern of growth holds for the number of Latino police officers hired. The percentage of Latino officers in the United States grew from 9.2% in 1995 to 14.1% in 2000 (Walker and Katz, 2008). This is a tremendous improvement, and as Latino involvement in law enforcement increases, it can be hoped that many of the worst excesses of the past years will decrease.

There have also been similar improvements in other areas of the criminal justice system as an examination of the characteristics of presidential appointees to U.S. District Court judgeships reveals. Under President Nixon, 1.1% were Latinos, and under President Ford, 1.9% were Latinos. President Clinton selected Latinos 6.5% of the time, while George W. Bush did so for 10% of his nominations (Herman, 2007). Slowly, the representation of Latinos in the criminal justice system appears to be increasing, this time not merely as clients of the system, but as practitioners.

Having criminal justice agents and personnel drawn from the communities they serve, and sensitive to the cultures, ethnic identities, and languages of the various populations and minority groups can only serve to help reduce the conflict, misunderstanding, and outright discrimination that has so often been a part of the Latino history in this country. The Latino population in the United States is here to stay, and the voices of its people are heard increasingly in all arenas of social, economic, and political life. This society must recognize that this is a positive and beneficial reality, not something to be fought against. When the United States embraces this multiculturalism that is so much a fact of modern American life, then perhaps this society can truly begin to live up to its ideals and promises of justice and equality.

References

Acuña, Rodolfo. 2000. *Occupied America*. New York, NY: Longman.

Aguirre, Jr., Adalberto, and Jonathan H. Turner. 1995. *American Ethnicity: The Dynamics and Consequences of Discrimination*. New York, NY: McGraw-Hill, Inc.

Becker, T. M., J. M. Samet, C. L. Wiggins, and C. R. Key. 1990. Violent Death in the West: Suicide and Homicide in New Mexico, 1958–1987. *Suicide and Life Threatening Behavior* 20: 324–334.

Blau, Judith R., and Peter M. Blau. 1982. The Cost of Inequality: Metropolitan Structure and Violent Crime. *American Sociological Review* 47: 114–129.

Blau, Peter M., and Reid M. Golden. 1986. Metropolitan Structure and Criminal Violence. *Sociological Quarterly* 27: 15–26.

Blau, Peter M., and Joseph E. Schwartz. 1984. *Crosscutting Social Circles*. San Diego, CA: Academic Press.

Block, Richard. 1985. Race/Ethnicity and Patterns of Chicago Homicide 1965 to 1981. *Crime and Delinquency* 31: 104–116.

Bondavalli, Bonnie J., and Bruno Bondavalli. 1981. Spanish-Speaking People and the North American Criminal Justice System. In *Race, Crime, and Criminal Justice*, ed. R. L. McNeely and Carl E. Pope, 49–69. Beverly Hills, CA: Sage Publications.

Bourgois, Philippe. 1996. *Selling Crack in El Barrio*. New York, NY: Cambridge University Press.

Bureau of Justice Statistics. 2003. *Federal Law Enforcement Officers, 2002*. Washington, DC: U.S. Department of Justice.

Bureau of Justice Statistics. (2005a). *Crime Data Brief: Violence by Gang Members, 1993–2003*. Washington, DC: U.S. Department of Justice.

Bureau of Justice Statistics. (2005b). *Hate Crime Report: 2005*. Washington, DC: U.S. Department of Justice.

Bureau of Justice Statistics. (2006a). *Criminal Offenders Statistics*. Washington, DC: U.S. Department of Justice.

Bureau of Justice Statistics. (2006b). *Criminal Victimization in the United States, 2005 Statistical Tables*. NCJ-215244. Washington, DC: U.S. Department of Justice.

Crutchfield, Robert D. 1989. Labor Stratification and Violent Crime. *Social Forces* 68: 489–512.

del Pinal, J., and A. Singer. 1997. Generations of Diversity: Latinos in the United States. *Population Bulletin*. 52 (3). Washington, DC: Population Reference Bureau, Inc.

Demuth, Stephen, and Darrell Steffensmeier. 2004. Ethnic Effects Outcomes in Large Urban Courts: Comparison among White, Black an Hispanic Defendants. *Social Science Quarterly* 85 (4): 994–1011.

Erlanger, Howard. 1979. Estrangement, Machismo, and Gang Violence. *Social Science Quarterly* 60 (2): 235–248.

Flowers, R. B. 1990. *Minorities and Criminality*. New York, NY: Praeger.

Garza, H. 1995. Administration of Justice: Chicanos in Monterey County. In *Latinos in the United States. Vol. 3. Criminal Justice and Latino Communities*, ed. A. S. Lopez. New York, NY: Garland.

Glater, Jonathan. 2007. Race Gap: Crime vs. Punishment. *New York Times* Week in Review section: 3.

Hamm, Mark S. 1995. *The Abandoned Ones: The Imprisonment and Uprising of the Mariel Boat People*. Boston, MA: Northeastern University Press.

Harer, Miles D., and Darrell Steffensmeier. 1992. The Differing Effects of Economic Inequality on Black and White Rates of Violence. *Social Forces* 70:1035–1054.

Harrington, Michael P., and Cassia Spohn. 2007. Defining Sentence Type: Further Evidence against Use of the Total Incarceration Variable. *Journal of Research in Crime & Delinquency* 44 (1): 36–63.

Hayes-Bautista, D. E., and J. Chapa. 1987. Latino Terminology: Conceptual Bases for Standardized Terminology. *American Journal of Public Health* 77: 61–68.

Herman, Ken. 2007. Bush Has Appointed More Hispanic Federal Judges than Past Presidents. *Cox News Service*, Monday, September 24, 2007.

Hess, Beth B., Elizabeth W. Markson, and Peter J. Stein. 1998. Racial and Ethnic Minorities: An Overview. In *Race, Class, and Gender in the United States: An Integrated Study*, ed. Paula S. Rothenberg, 4th edn., 258–270. New York, NY: St. Martin's Press.

LaFree, Gary D. 1995. Official Reactions to Hispanic Defendants in the Southwest. In *Latinos in the United States. Vol. 3. Criminal Justice and Latino Communities*, ed. A. S. Lopez. New York, NY: Garland.

Mann, C. R. (1993). *Unequal justice: A Question of Color.* Bloomington, IN: Indiana University Press.

Marín, G., and B. VanOss Marín. 1991. *Research with Hispanic Populations.* Newbury Park, CA: Sage Publications.

Martinez, Ramiro. 2002. *Latino Homocide: Immigration, Violence, and Community.* London: Routledge.

Massey, Douglas S., and Nancy A. Denton. 1987. Trends in the Residential Segregation of Blacks, Hispanics, and Asians: 1970–1980. *American Sociological Review* 52: 802–825.

Mata, Jr., Alberto G. 1998. Immigrant Bashing and Nativist Political Movements. In *Images of Color: Images of Crime*, ed. Coramae Richey Mann and Marjorie S. Zatz, 145–155. Los Angeles, CA: Roxbury Publishing.

Mercy, J. A. 1987. Assaultive Injury Among Hispanics: A Public Health Problem. In *Research Conference on Violence and Homicide in Hispanic Communities*, ed. J. Kraus, S. Sorenson, and P. Juarez, 1–12. Office of Minority Health, U.S. Department of Health and Human Services: UCLA Publication Services.

Murguia, E. 1975. *Assimilation, Colonialism, and the Mexican American People.* Austin, TX: The University of Texas at Austin, Center for Mexican American Studies, Monograph Series No. 1.

Myers, Laura B., Myrna Cintron, and Kathryn E. Scarborough. 2000. Latinos: The Conceptualization of Race. In *Multicultural Perspectives in Criminal Justice*, ed. James Hendricks and Bryan Byers, 2nd edn., 151–180. Springfield, IL: Charles C. Thomas.

Novas, H. 1994. *Everything You Need to Know About Latino History.* New York, NY: Plume Books.

Padilla, Felix. 1992. *The Gang as an American Enterprise.* Rutgers, NJ: Rutgers University Press.

Portillos, Edwardo L. 1998. Latinos, Gangs, and Drugs. In *Images of Color: Images of Crime*, ed. Coramae Richey Mann and Marjorie S. Zatz, 156–166. Los Angeles, CA: Roxbury Publishing.

Rodriguez, Clara E. 1991. *Puerto Ricans: Born in the U.S.A.* Boulder, CO: Westview Press.

Rodriquez, Luis J. 1993. *Always Running, La Vida Loca: Gang Days in L.A.* New York, NY: Touchstone.

Romero, Mary. 2006. Racial Profiling and Immigration Law Enforcement: Rounding Up Usual Suspects in the Latino Community. *Critical Sociology* 32 (2): 448–473.

Sampson, Robert J. 1986. Effects of Inequality, Heterogeneity, and Urbanization on Intergroup Victimization. *Social Science Quarterly* 67: 751–766.

Santiago, Anne M., and Margaret G. Wilder. 1991. Residential Segregation and Links to Minority Poverty: The Case of Latinos in the United States. *Social Problems* 38: 492–515.

Shorris, E. 1992. *Latinos: A Biography of the People.* New York, NY: W. W. Norton and Company.

Sissons, Peter. 1979. *The Hispanic Experience of Criminal Justice.* New York, NY: Hispanic Research Center at Fordham University.

Smith, J. C., J. A. Mercy, and M. L. Rosenberg. 1986. Suicide and Homicide among Hispanics in the Southwest. *Public Health Reports* 101: 265–270.

Steele, Ian K. 1994. *Warpaths: Invasions of North America.* New York, NY: Oxford University Press.

Steffensmeier, Darrell, and Stephen Demouth. 2001. Ethnicity and Judges' Sentencing Decisions: Hispanic-Black-White Comparisons. *Criminology* 39 (1): 145–178.

USA Today. 2004. Study Says Gap Widened for Blacks, Hispanics After Recession. October 18 file:///Users/luis/Desktop/Wealth% 20gap%20with%20latinos.htm (accessed October 1, 2007).

U.S. Census Bureau. 2000. Hispanic or Latino by Type: 2000. http://factfinder.census.gov/servlet/QTTable?_bm=y&-qr_name=DEC_2000_SF1_U_QTP9&-geo_id=01000US&-ds_name=DEC_2000_SF1_U&-_lang=en&-format=&-CONTEXT=qt (accessed on September 24, 2007).

U.S. Census Bureau. 2006. Press Release: Nation's Population One-Third Minority. May 10, http://www.census.gov/Press-Release/www/releases/archives/population/006808.html (accessed on October 1, 2007).

U.S. Census Bureau. 2007. *Income, Poverty, and Health Insurance Coverage in the United States: 2006.* Report no. P60–233. Washington, DC: U.S. Government Printing Office.

U.S. Commission on Civil Rights. 1970. *Mexican Americans and the Administration of Justice in the Southwest.* Washington, DC: Government Printing Office.

Valdez, R. Burciaga, and Parivash Nourjah. 1987. Homicide in Southern California, 1966–1985: An Examination Based on Vital Statistics Data. In *Research Conference on Violence and Homicide in Hispanic Communities,* ed. Jess Kraus, Susan Sorenson, and Paul Juarez, 31–65. Office of Minority Health, U.S. Department of Health and Human Services: UCLA Publication Services.

Vigil, James Diego. 1998. *From Indians to Chicanos: The Dynamics of Mexican-American Culture.* Prospect Heights, IL: Waveland Press.

Walker, Samuel, and Charles M. Katz. 2008. *The Police in America: An Introduction.* London: McGraw-Hill.

Wolfgang, Marvin E., and Franco Ferracuti. 1967. *The Subculture of Violence: Towards an Integrated Theory in Criminology.* London: Tavistock.

CHAPTER 10

Perpetual Outsiders

Criminal Justice and the Asian American Experience

Barbara Perry

A century and a half after their first arrival on the shores of the United States, Americans of Asian descent are still perceived as "foreigners." Whether part of the "old" or "new" immigration, whether fifth or first generation, Asian Americans continue to be constructed as the "Other." As this chapter reveals, this perpetual outsider status has been maintained through legal and extralegal mechanisms such as exclusionary immigration policies, rhetorical images of Asians, and anti-Asian violence.

MIGRATION HISTORY

The 1840s and 1850s marked the beginning of Asian immigration to the United States, starting with the arrival of Chinese in Hawaii and on the mainland West Coast. Initially, laborers found work on the sugar plantations and in the gold mines, and later supplied much of the manual labor for the building of the western leg of the transcontinental railway. By the turn of the twentieth century, the same employment opportunities began to draw increasing numbers of immigrants from other parts of Asia, including Japan, the Philippines, Korea, and India.

However, successive waves of Asian immigration tended to create corresponding waves of anti-Asian sentiment. Labor leaders, temperance activists, and agricultural interests pressed the government to react to the perceived threats that Asians were thought to represent to employment (e.g., wage deflation), morality (e.g., opium use), and hygiene (e.g., prostitution). This agitation was met with increasingly restrictive immigration and naturalization policies that slowed Asian immigration to a trickle throughout the first half of the twentieth century.

The liberalization of immigration policy following World War II brought with it a new wave of Asian immigration. Whereas Asian Americans represented less than one half of 1% of the U.S. population in 1940, by 1990 they made up nearly 3%, or 7 million, and by 2005, the Asian American population had grown dramatically to 14.4 million, or 5% (U.S. Census Bureau, 2007). However, Asian Americans are not a homogeneous community. On the contrary, they represent a very diverse population, with regionally and culturally specific language, dialects, traditions, and beliefs. Moreover, each cultural group was drawn (or pushed) to the United States by different motives. Most early immigrants—whether Chinese, Japanese, or Filipino, for example—sought employment as unskilled labor. By the 1960s, this trend began to reverse, as many Chinese and Japanese, in particular, migrated under policies designed to attract skilled laborers and professionals. Those seeking enhanced employment opportunities were later joined by Southeast Asians fleeing the political upheavals in that part of the world. During and after the Korean War (1956–1965), many of those impressed by their view of Americans' affluence, together with political dissidents, fled to the United States. During the 1970s, nearly 200,000 Vietnamese emigrated to the United States—many of whom were admitted with refugee status. More recent immigration of Asians, including that of Asian Indians, has been motivated by educational and professional opportunities. Very often, Asians who come to this country to pursue a university education will decide to stay and embark on a career in this country.

CONTEMPORARY DEMOGRAPHICS

The diverse and uneven patterns of migration associated with Asian Americans have resulted in a dramatically heterogeneous Asian "community," representing dozens of Asian identities, ranging from Chinese to Filipino to Laotian to Taiwanese. Those of Chinese and Filipino descent dominate the Asian population, followed by Asian Indians, Koreans, and Vietnamese.

Given the differences between these groups, it is not surprising that their experiences have been quite different in the United States. While most Asian Americans have tended to concentrate in the West, there is some geographical dispersion. This is especially the case for Asian Indians and Pakistanis, who are scattered throughout the country, with only a small concentration (approximately one-third settle in the Northwest). Asian Americans do not fare equally well in socioeconomic terms. Specifically, Koreans and Vietnamese consistently lag behind Chinese, Japanese, and Asian Indians on most indicators of socioeconomic status. While Asians as a whole tend to have among the highest median income of any racialized group in the United States ($61,094), this differs greatly by group. Asian Indians, for example, earned a median income of $73,575 in 2005, whereas Vietnamese Americans earned only $50,925 (U.S. Census Bureau, 2007). Thus, the often-touted belief that Asians are the "successful" minority thus masks the dramatic differences between groups. While summary statistics do suggest higher education, higher income, and higher occupational status for Asians, what such generalizations fail to reveal are the factors that underlie the trends:

- concentration of Asians in geographical areas with a high cost of living
- high proportion of multiple incomes within the household
- low per capita incomes

- with educational levels held constant, Asian Americans earn about the same or less than their white counterparts
- many Asian immigrants, especially Hong Kong Chinese and Asian Indians, relocate here with resources and credentials already established (Ancheta, 2006; U.S. Commission on Civil Rights, 1992:18).

In other words, discrimination in employment, income, and education continues to affect Americans of Asian descent in ways that are concealed by the cultural emphasis on the "model minority" myth.

IMAGING ASIAN AMERICANS

More so, perhaps, than any other ethnic or racial minority group in the United States, Asian Americans are held up as the model minority—they work hard, they save and invest their earnings, they succeed in achieving the American dream. By dint of hard labor, and "inherent" abilities in math and sciences, Asians are perceived as the epitome of the "good" immigrant, that is, the model by which all other groups are measured, to which all other groups should aspire.

This seemingly glowing endorsement of Asian Americans is not without its pitfalls. First, as noted above, it occludes the dramatic differences between and within the diversity of the Asian population. It denies the reality of those who live in poverty, who do not receive advanced degrees, and who do not attain a middle class standard of living. Moreover, it renders invisible the related reality of discrimination faced by many segments of the Asian American population: the persistence of the glass ceiling, and discriminatory admission policies in colleges and universities, for example. Consequently, the model minority myth minimizes the tendency—and apparent need—to provide services and resources specific to the problems faced by Asian Americans. As the United States Commission on Civil Rights (1992:20) concluded, "despite the problems Asian Americans encounter, the success stereotype appears to have led policy makers to ignore those truly in need."

This stereotype also has dramatic implications for interethnic relationships, to the extent that it represents a wedge, pitting minority against minority. It discredits other minority groups by reinforcing the ideology of meritocracy, that is, that *anyone* regardless of race, creed, or color can succeed in the United States. In other words, "people earn (or don't earn) what they deserve" (Nakayama, 1998:184). This plays a valuable ideological role in defending economic and political structures from the claims of discrimination levied by the civil rights movement. As such, it also creates friction between Asian Americans and other disadvantaged minority groups. In particular, African Americans and Hispanic Americans are made to feel inadequate for not having succeeded in the same way as have Asian Americans. This has been most apparent recently in Los Angeles' Chinatown, which shouldered much of the destruction and violence of the L.A. riots in 1992. During the riots, 300 Korean businesses were looted and burned; in all, 40% of the businesses lost were Asian owned (Cho, 1993).

Of course, interethnic hostilities engendered by the model minority myth emerge in the broader context of anti-Asian sentiment and stereotypes, not all of which are as "positive" as this one. Subordinate groups are not immune to the power of dominant ideologies and images. They too are part of the audience, having listened to, observed, and lived within the structures of inequality:

> We must remember that racial minorities, having been socialized in a society that sees them as inferior to whites, are likely to believe in the inferiority of racial groups other than their own. (McClain and Stewart, 1995:149)

There is an impressive and disturbing slate of stereotypical constructs available by which to reinforce the inferiority of Asian Americans. Propagated through the media political rhetoric, and public debate, these images portray Asians—regardless of national origin—in very unsympathetic, often exclusionary terms. As noted earlier, Asian Americans are seen as perpetual *foreigners,* whose loyalty remains with their "homeland," and not with the United States. There is the persistent question, "Where did you learn to speak English?" Consequently, anti-Asian sentiments fluctuate with the relationship between the United States and the East. When the Japanese auto industry expanded its activity in the United States, for example, regions dependent on U.S. auto-making (e.g., Detroit) witnessed increased hostility. It was in this context, for example, that Vincent Chin was beaten to death with a baseball bat, while his attackers shouted that it was "because of you . . . we're out of work" (United States Commission on Civil Rights, n.d.:43).

Just as Asian economies are presumed to represent a threat to U.S. dominance, so too are Asian Americans—as individuals—seen as unfair competitors within U.S. borders. Like other immigrants, they have come to this country and taken away "our" jobs, "our" businesses. In fact, Asians often create wealth and employment by investing savings in the U.S. economy and by creating small businesses. Unfortunately, even the latter is often interpreted in negative terms, as Asian business people and Asians in general are depicted as *deceitful and devious.* In their business dealings, they are not to be trusted; they are said to inflate their prices and minimize their service.

Finally, Asians occupy an ambiguous ideological space with respect to sexuality. The "exotic" Chinese male laborer of the nineteenth century, for example, was feared to be sex-starved, predatory, and lascivious. Thus he was seen as a threat to white women. However, Espiritu (1997) points out the fact that the image of Asian males as sexually rapacious is generally overshadowed by the opposite extreme: the image of Asian men as undersexed or effeminate. Espiritu (1997) traces this tendency historically to the anti-Asian exclusionary immigration policies of the turn of the twentieth century. By restricting the entry of women, such policies created all-male Asian enclaves, which subsequently "reversed the construction of Asian masculinity from 'hypersexed' to 'asexual' and even 'homosexual'" (1997:90). The perceived emasculation of Asian men continues to be reflected in the model minority stereotype, with its presumption of passivity and subordination.

INSTITUTIONALIZED DISCRIMINATION AGAINST ASIAN AMERICANS

The negative images by which Asian American identity is constructed in the United States have consistently legitimated discriminatory treatment, while the model minority myth has rendered it invisible. Evidence of discrimination is apparent on many levels and in many different intersecting institutions.

Immigration and Citizenship

It was not until 1965 that the borders of the United States reopened to welcome immigration of people of Asian descent. Up until that time, successive immigration policy reforms limited and outright denied new immigration and citizenship to those claiming Asian ancestry. Responding largely to public sentiment and political rhetoric that portrayed Asians as unfair labor competition and opium-smoking fiends, the U.S. Congress passed the Chinese Exclusion Act of 1882. That act accomplished two things: It suspended Chinese immigration for ten years and it prohibited resident Chinese from attaining U.S. citizenship. The act was regularly renewed. It was finally repealed in 1943.

Japanese immigrants faced similar restrictions after the turn of the century. Under the 1907 Gentlemen's Agreement between Japan and the United States, admission of skilled and unskilled laborers (and their wives and children) was halted. In 1917, the Immigration Act barred all immigrants from most parts of Asia. The 1924 National Origins Act went even further, to bar admission of Japanese wives, even those whose husbands were U.S. citizens, and to prohibit immigration of aliens ineligible to attain U.S. citizenship. Given the 1922 Supreme Court decision that those of Japanese descent could not become naturalized, the 1924 act effectively halted Japanese immigration.

Japanese Internment

The anti-Japanese sentiments that underlaid the immigration reforms of the 1920s intensified during World War II. Executive Order 9066, signed by President Roosevelt in 1942, initiated the forced evacuation of persons of Japanese descent from the West Coast. Those moved to the "relocation camps" were often given little advance notice. Moreover, they were allowed to take with them only what they could carry. This meant that most were forced to sell their property and other belongings at outrageously low prices. That negative stereotypes underlaid this mistreatment is evident from public statements of the day. For example, California Congressman Rankin declared,

> Once a Jap, always a Jap! You can't any more regenerate a Jap than you can reverse the laws of nature. I'm for taking every Japanese and putting him in a concentration camp. (cited in United States Commission on Civil Rights, 1992:10)

Educational Discrimination

In light of the dramatic recent influx of Asian immigrants, primary and secondary schools are confronted with the special problems of first- and second-generation Asian students, many of whom are ill-prepared for the educational experience in this country. Teachers and students unprepared for the diversity introduced by Asian students often create an unfriendly atmosphere which maintains the "difference" and outsider status of immigrant youth. While the data are sketchy and inconclusive, it seems as if there is a connection between this lukewarm reception and the success of the students:

> When students feel like outsiders in the school environment, do not have a sense of belonging, have few friends involved in school, and are not integrated into the social or academic life of school, they become likely candidates for academic failure. (United States Commission on Civil Rights, 1992:70)

Problems of a different sort emerge for Asian Americans with aspirations of higher education. In spite of the broad belief in Asian educational success, there is evidence that they are subject to both negative sentiments and treatment at these institutions. Chiu (cited in Aguirre and Turner, 1998:190) notes the reconstruction of university acronyms which highlight this animosity:

> MIT becomes "Made in Taiwan," UCLA becomes "University of Caucasians Living among Asians," and U.C. Irvine (UCI) becomes "University of Chinese Immigrants."

Inquiries at a number of post-secondary institutions have uncovered damning evidence of discrimination in recruitment and admissions in particular. For example, the Brown University Corporation Committee on Minority Affairs (1984:4) reported that

> It was clearly stated by all admission staff to whom we spoke that Asian American applicants receive comparatively low non-academic ratings. These unjustified low ratings are due to the cultural biases and stereotypes which prevail in the admission office.

Economic Discrimination

The experiences of educational and legal discrimination are reinforced in economic forums, which once again contradicts the success stereotype of Asian Americans. Owing largely to the fears of Asian economic competition, and "unscrupulous business practices," many Asian Americans face the glass ceiling. Although highly represented in white-collar occupations, Asian Americans often find that their mobility within these organizations is curtailed. Aguirre and Turner (1998:185) quote an Asian white-collar worker's perceptions of his limited opportunities:

> I suspect that the minds of many corporate managers and the senior staff members who have direct control . . . are still in the 1960s. As a consequence, for most of them we Asians are a suspect class, and we usually have to prove that we are better in order to be equal.

Research consistently illustrates the validity of these perceptions. There is ample evidence to suggest that management, especially its upper tiers, is off-limits to Asian

American professionals (Aguirre and Turner, 1998; Ancheta, 2006). Perhaps not surprisingly, income discrimination often follows similar patterns, wherein equally qualified Asian American employees earn less than their non-Asian, especially white, counterparts.

ASIAN AMERICANS AS OFFENDERS

As noted above, the ironic opposite pole of the model minority stereotype is that of the mysterious, devious, fearsome Asian. Media, politicians, and social commentators too often confuse this stereotype with the reality of Asian criminal activity. If we were to believe the words of Senator Sam Nunn, we might make the mistake of accepting the sensational media images of Asian gangsters: "Chinese organized crime . . . is in many ways as mysterious, if not more so, than its portrayal in movies such as *Year of the Dragon*" (cited in Laidler, 1998:170). According to such portrayals, all Asians are martial arts experts; all are stealthy and silent; all are violent gang members; all are connected by a network of organized crime. These images consistently mark Asians as "different," as the Other, thereby reinforcing their "foreign" and alien nature. It also makes them something to be feared and, therefore, avoided.

What little is known about Asian criminality refutes these images of Asian violence and stealth. On the contrary, the offenses for which Asian Americans are most likely to be arrested are public order offenses. Asian Americans are far less likely than any other ethnic group to be involved in homicide, for example (Lee and Martinez, 2006). The contemporary patterns of criminality that emerge are very much in line with the historical evolution of Asian criminality, and with discrimination against Chinese and Japanese immigrants in particular. Earlier restrictions on Asian immigration—especially with respect to women—often meant that Asian immigrant laborers were confined to all-male communities. Anti-miscegenation laws around the turn of the twentieth century only exaggerated this tendency. Consequently,

> Living in a world of men, Asian laborers sought a sexual outlet and intimacy from prostitutes . . . Most Chinese male sojourners viewed prostitutes as providers of a necessary service to their largely bachelor community. (Espiritu, 1997:31)

By 1870, over 75% of the nearly 3,000 Chinese women workers in the United States identified themselves as prostitutes. In 1900, most Japanese immigrant women were also prostitutes. With the easing of immigration restrictions later in the century, there was a transition from the importation of prostitutes to the importation of "picture brides."

Both practices, however, were "big business"—not so much for the women themselves as the men who profited from their labors:

> . . . the procurers and importers who brought women to the United States; the brothel owners who controlled the labor of the prostitutes; the

high-binders, policemen and immigration officials who were paid to protect the business; and the white Chinatown property owners who charged these brothels exorbitant rents. (Espiritu, 1997:31)

Although initially controlled by individual men (and some women), prostitution ultimately fell under the control of emerging Asian "secret societies" and Chinese *tongs* in particular. These organizations were originally created to meet the needs for community and representation of the isolated Asian male immigrants in the context of a hostile social climate. However, many evolved into criminal organizations, or developed links with Chinese triads. Consequently, the tongs came to dominate prostitution, along with gambling, drugs, and other vice crimes. So, in addition to providing sexual outlets, they also created other opportunities for recreation and escapist behavior.

With respect to the criminal involvement of Asians in public order offenses, Mann (1993:133) observes that "minority people commit the crimes that are created for them." In other words, particular behaviors come to be criminalized as a means of regulating specific communities. For example, turn of the century opium legislation was clearly an effort to curtail the economic power of Asians. Mann (1993) offers other examples, drawn from Portland Oregon's ordinances: prohibiting the use of poles across the shoulders as a means of carrying heavy loads (a Chinese practice); and the "Chinese Theater Ordinance," which prohibited the playing of any instrument other than a guitar in any theater after midnight.

As a result of this discriminatory application of the criminal law, Asians were among the most heavily incarcerated groups on the West Coast. However, in the contemporary era, Asian Americans are consistently underrepresented in the crime statistics, unlike other communities of color. In 1993, for example, Asian Americans represented approximately 3% of the population, but only 1% of those arrested. Moreover, they were most likely to be arrested for public order offenses— prostitution or gambling—rather than violent offenses.

The vice crimes for which Asians—especially Japanese, Chinese, and Vietnamese—are most likely to be arrested are lucrative sources of revenue for organized crime groups: Chinese tongs and triads and Japanese yakuza, for example. There is a consensus among scholars and law enforcement agencies that Asian organized crime is growing at a more rapid rate than those of any other cultural group (Flowers, 1990; Ho, 1998; Mann, 1993; Marshall, 1997). Consequently, these groups are assuming a growing share of illegal markets. It is the effort to protect these market shares that is responsible for the recent increases in violent crime associated with Asian Americans.

Sometimes connected to and sometimes independent of Asian organized crime are the growing numbers of Asian youth gangs. Flowers (1990) and Mann (1993) both report that Chinatowns across the United States have recently witnessed dramatic and violent increases in Asian gang membership. Although triads and yakuza tend to be involved in racketeering, smuggling, and so on, Asian youth gangs are more likely to be involved in localized extortion and robbery, as well as internecine conflicts. The older, more formalized groups tend to include both immigrants and U.S.-born Asians, while the youth gangs are dominated by recent immigrants, leading Parillo (1985:251) to conclude,

> The growing problem of youthful militancy and delinquency appears to reflect the marginal status of those in the younger generation who experience frustration and adjustment problems in America. Recent arrivals from Hong Kong are unfamiliar with the language and culture, they are either unemployed or in the lowliest of jobs, and they live in overcrowded, slum-like quarters with no recreational facilities. Gang behavior serves as an alternative and a way of filling status and identity needs.

ASIAN AMERICANS AS VICTIMS OF CRIME

Many of the same sentiments that perpetuate anti-Asian discrimination and sensational images of Asian crime also underlie anti-Asian victimization. Consider, for example, the implications of the aforementioned image of Asian men as "sexual eunuchs." While such a passive picture of Asian men does not engender much in the way of hostility or antagonism, it does, nonetheless, present an opportunity for engaging in hate crime as a means of policing the relative sexual identities of perpetrator and victim. *Because* of their reputation for passivity, Asian men are seen to be easy victims on which to practice domination; *because* of their reputation as a model minority, Asian men are seen to be legitimate victims; *because* of their reputation as sexual eunuchs, Asian men are not "real men," and, thus, represent a weak link in the chain of masculine domination; *because* of their racial difference and all that entails, Asian men must also be refused access to white women, lest they threaten the purity of the race.

Moreover, the legacy of discriminatory legislation and activity finds a violent supplement in victimization motivated by anti-Asian bias. The current environment of intolerance—highlighted by California's Proposition 187, and the nationwide impetus for immigration reform—has meant that immigrants are increasingly held up as scapegoats, thereby encouraging and legitimating violent acts perpetrated against these "invading foreigners." Might there not be a link between the following scenarios?

> New York City Councilwoman Julia Harrison referred to the growing Asian American population in Queens as "an invasion not an assimilation." Moreover, she laid the blame for such widespread problems as crime and high real estate prices at the feet of Asian Americans. For her, the changing face of her community was "very upsetting, very discombobulating". (National Asian Pacific American Legal Consortium (NAPALC), 1996:14)
>
> New York City has one of the highest and fastest growing rates of anti-Asian violence in the country. One example of such violence includes the attack by three white youths on a Chinese American man. The assault was prefaced by their exclamation that "I don't want you Chinks thinking you own the world". (NAPALC, 1996:14)

Anti-Asian violence accounts for a relatively small proportion of all racially motivated hate crime. However, it does represent a growing proportion. Many sources suggest that it constitutes the most dramatically and rapidly growing type of racial violence (FBI, 1997; NAPALC, 1996, 2002; United States Commission on Civil Rights, 1992, n.d.). Until 2002, the most comprehensive source of data on violence against Asian Americans was the Asian American Justice Center (formerly the National Asian Pacific American Legal Consortium) yearly audit. The range of their data sources was broad and varied: telephone and intake sessions, newspaper reports, community-based organizations, churches, human rights commissions, bar associations, and government agencies. Their annual audits represented veritable treasure troves of information, providing summary counts, synopses of cases, information on legal action taken by the organization, analyses of regional and national trends, and extensive policy recommendations.

Unfortunately, the organization ceased such reporting after the 2002 audit. Nonetheless, we can glean some trends from that final report. Owing to the variation in reporting methods and agencies, the NAPALC data are not to be taken as accurate in terms of absolute numbers. However, the trends and analyses offered in the audits are nonetheless informative and indicative of underlying patterns. Interestingly, the final 2002 audit indicates, for the first time, a dramatic decrease in anti-Asian violence from 2001 to 2002. However, the authors of the report are hesitant to celebrate these findings. They suggest that the decrease may be attributable to factors other than a real decrease in violence. Among the alternative explanations they offer are a decrease in investigative resources within police departments, and failure to reporting because of fears of "falling into the wide dragnet put out by the Department of Justice under the name of anti-terrorism measures" (NAPALC, 2002:2).

Even in the face of declining rates of violence against Asian Americans, there is concern about the intensity of the violence. The 2002 NAPALC report observed that

> "Hate crimes that occurred immediately after September 11th demonstrated a high degree of physical violence, with perpetrators using baseball bats, metal poles, and guns as weapons while attacking their victims. In 2002, this violent trend continues, as the most commonly reported hate crime offense against APAs known to NAPALC and its affiliates is assault and/or battery (29%), followed by vandalism (27%), harassment (21%), and threats (16%). Violent acts included two murders in Brooklyn, New York and a hate rape in Kansas". (NAPALC, 2002:3)

As an example, consider the drowning death of a 62-year-old Vietnamese fisherman in Chicago in September of 2007. A white male, an alleged member of a skinhead group, was charged with his murder. The death followed an earlier incident in the same place on the same day, and another parallel incident in which an Asian American man was pushed into the harbor (Japanese American Citizens' League, 2007). While the death itself is disturbing, so, too, is the fact that it appeared to be part of a broader trend.

It is interesting to note that a substantial number of suspected offenders involved in violence against Asian Americans are African American or Hispanic. In 1995, these two groups accounted for nearly 45% of offenders (NAPALC, 1996). The inter-ethnic hostilities noted earlier in this chapter also manifest themselves in inter-ethnic violence, wherever other minority groups feel further alienated and marginalized by "newcomers" who appear to have surpassed them in their pursuit of the American

Dream. For example, in Washington, DC, between 1984 and 1995, nine Korean-owned businesses within a three-block area in a predominantly black neighborhood were firebombed. While police failed to investigate these as racially motivated, Koreans in the neighborhood had little doubt as to their motivation, given the intensity of black hostility toward Korean shop-owners.

The NAPALC (1996) audit of anti-Asian incidents provides ample evidence of the relationship between anti-Asian themes and violence. Consider just a few illustrative examples.

Asians as foreigners:

> An East Indian woman was approached by her white neighbors and told "You Hindu bitches, why did you have to move into here?" The victim also found a flag, used in religious ceremonies, broken in her yard.

Asians as economic competitors:

> A Chinese American man was assaulted in a supermarket parking lot. A white male stabbed him four times, resulting in multiple injuries, including a punctured lung. The assailant justified his actions when he confessed that he sought to kill an Asian person because "they got all the good jobs."

These few examples are not atypical. Asians—regardless of the longevity of their ties to the United States—are frequent victims of violence ranging from offensive bumper stickers, to verbal harassment, to assault, to murder. Moreover, it is only recently that the problems faced by Asian Americans have been acknowledged and finally addressed by advocacy groups and state agencies alike.

ASIAN AMERICANS AS SERVICE PROVIDERS

Increasingly, the particular needs of Asian communities, victims, and offenders are being recognized in the context of criminal and social justice concerns. This task is complicated by the distrust of criminal justice agents on the part of many Asians. One of the contributing factors here is the traditional reliance on private resolution of conflicts, which excludes police involvement. In addition, there is often a great fear of authority figures, especially among recent immigrants from autocratic or war-torn countries. We must also recognize the very real fear, on the part of victims, of retaliation in the event that they point accusing fingers at their offenders.

Some efforts have been made by law enforcement agencies to overcome the barriers between Asian communities and police departments. Cultural awareness training has been implemented as a means of improving police officers' understanding and treatment of Asian Americans. Interpreters have been hired where numbers warrant. Community policing initiatives have been implemented as a means of integrating police and public. One of the greatest disappointments in police–Asian relations has been in the area of representation in police departments. Stokes and Scott's (1996) review of hiring practices found that in spite of affirmative action initiatives, Asian Americans are dramatically underrepresented among police officers, even in communities where Asians make up a substantial proportion of the population. Most cities with 1% Asian population had negligible representation on police forces. Even San Francisco and Oakland, California, with 29% and 15% Asian populations respectively, had a very low proportion of Asian officers. By 2000, Asians still accounted for only 2.8% of all full-time sworn officers in large cities, a minimal increase from their 2% representation a decade earlier (Bureau of Justice Statistics, 2002).

Some police departments across the country are making admirable efforts to enhance the accessibility and civility of their personnel. San Diego and Oakland, California, for example, have established Asian Advisory Committees which act as liaisons between the police department and the Asian communities. The Committee brings concerns to the police departments and mobilizes community support for the police force. San Diego and Los Angeles have introduced Civilian Community Service Officers who work out of storefront offices in the Asian communities. Their role is to act as a buffer between the two communities, by taking reports, attending community events, offering crime prevention and counseling programs, and other similar community-oriented services. While such efforts represent valuable innovations, they demand long-term commitment to ensure that they do not become merely token initiatives meant to quell public complaint.

As supplements—or more often alternatives—to criminal justice agencies, Asian communities across the nation have begun to establish their own advocacy and action groups, intended to represent and protect Asian interests. This is a dramatic step, given the historical failure of Asian Americans to protest or speak out against their plight. Perhaps buoyed by the gains of other civil rights movements, and by the findings of recent civil rights commissions' reports, Asian Americans have begun to mobilize their growing numerical strength into political and social power. In addition to Pan-Asian umbrella organizations like the Asian American Justice Center (formerly the NAPALC) and employment, resettlement, and workers' organizations, Asians have established several legal centers geared toward assisting and advocating for the community. American Citizens for Justice was originally founded in 1983 in protest of the lenient sentences given to Vincent Chin's murderers. It continues to fight for the civil rights of all Americans, and especially Asian Americans, by engaging in legal consultations, the monitoring of anti-Asian violence, and the provision of educational services. The Asian American Legal Defense and Education Fund is similarly committed to promoting the civil rights of Asian Americans. It has established an Anti-Asian Violence Project, which litigates and provides counseling for victims of hate crimes and police brutality. The Asian Immigrant Women Advocates (AIWA) recognizes and addresses the particular problems of immigrant women who are often exploited and subjugated by both their originating culture and that of the United States. AIWA seeks to empower these women by providing job training and counseling, as well as education on their rights in their new home.

One could go on endlessly. There are literally hundreds of local, regional, and national organizations committed to enhancing the place and power of Asian Americans in the United States. Given the historical and systemic nature of violence and discrimination against this community, they are correct in recognizing that meaningful and lasting change requires activity on the part of the many Asian communities—singly and collectively.

References

Aguirre, Adalberto, and Jonathan Turner. 1998. *American Ethnicity*, 2nd edn. Boston, MA: McGraw-Hill.

Ancheta, Angelo. 2006. *Race, Rights, and the Asian American Experience*. New Brunswick, NJ: Rutgers University Press.

Brown University Corporation Committee on Minority Affairs. 1984. *Report to the Corporation Committee on Minority Affairs from Its Subcommittee on Asian Americans*. Providence RI: Brown University.

Bureau of Justice Statistics. 2002. *Police Departments in Large Cities, 1990–2000, Special Report*. NCJ 175703. Washington, DC: U.S. Department of Justice.

Cho, Sumi. 1993. Korean Americans vs. African Americans: Conflict and Construction. In *Reading Rodney King, Reading Urban Uprisings*, ed. Robert Gooding-Williams, 196–211. New York, NY: Routledge.

Espiritu, Yen Le. 1997. *Asian American Women and Men*. Thousand Oaks, CA: Sage Publications.

Federal Bureau of Investigation. 1997. *Hate Crime Statistics, 1996*. Washington, DC: U.S. Department of Justice.

Flowers, Ronald Barri. 1990. *Minorities and Criminality*. New York, NY: Praeger.

Ho, Taiping. 1998. Vice Crimes and Asian Americans. In *Images of Color, Images of Crime*, ed. Coramae Richey Mann and Marjorie Zatz, 195–204. Los Angeles, CA: Roxbury.

Japanese American Citizens' League. 2007. Anti-Hate Program. http://www.jacl.org/antihate/ahresponses.html.

Laidler, Karen Joe. 1998. Senator Sir, Meet Susie Wong and the Inscrutable Fu Manchu. In *Images of Color, Images of Crime*, ed. Coramae Richey Mann and Marjorie Zatz, 169–178. Los Angeles, CA: Roxbury.

Lee, Matthew, and Ramiro Martinez. 2006. Immigration and Asian Homicide Patterns in Urban and Suburban San Diego. In *Immigration and Crime: Race, Ethnicity and Violence*, ed. Ramiro Martinez and Abel Valenzuela, 90–116. New York: New York University Press.

Mann, Coramae Richey. 1993. *Unequal Justice*. Bloomington, IN: Indiana University Press.

Marshall, Ineke Haen. 1997. Minorities, Crime and Criminal Justice in the United States. In *Minorities, Migrants and Crime*, ed. Ineke Haen Marshall, 1–35. Thousand Oaks, CA: Sage Publications.

McClain, Paula, and Joseph Stuart. 1995. *Can We All Get Along? Racial and Ethnic Minorities in American Politics*. Boulder, CO: Westview Press.

Nakayama, T. 1998. Framing Asian Americans. In *Images of Color, Images of Crime*, ed. Coramae Richey Mann and Marjorie Zatz, 179–187. Los Angeles: Roxbury.

National Asian Pacific American Legal Consortium. 1996. *Audit of Violence Against Asian Pacific Americans*. San Francisco CA: NAPALC.

National Asian Pacific American Legal Consortium. 2002. *Audit of Violence Against Asian Pacific Americans*. San Francisco CA: NAPALC.

Parillo, Vincent. 1985. *Strangers to These Shores: Race and Ethnic Relations in the U.S.* New York, NY: John Riley.

Stokes, Larry, and James Scott. 1996. Affirmative Action and Selected Minority Groups in Law Enforcement. *Journal of Criminal Justice* 24 (1): 29–38.

U.S. Census Bureau. 2007. Press Release: Asian/Pacific Heritage Month. http://www.census.gov/Press-Release/www/releases/archives/facts_for_features_special_editions/009714.html.

U.S. Commission on Civil Rights. 1992. *Civil Rights Issues Facing Asian Americans*. Washington, DC: U.S. Government Printing Office.

U.S. Commission on Civil Rights. n.d. *Recent Actions Against Citizens and Residents of Asian Descent*. Washington, DC: U.S. Government Printing Office.

CHAPTER 11

Women's Difference in the Criminal Justice System

Constructions of Victims, Offenders, and Workers

Karla B. Hackstaff

Paula K. Rector

In 2001, after a jury deliberated just 15 minutes, Regina McKnight became the first woman in the U.S. history to receive a homicide conviction for a late-term fetus. After the fetus was stillborn, the murder by child abuse was attributed to Regina's use of crack cocaine. She was sentenced to 12 years in prison (Rector, 2002). The majority of the prosecutions and convictions of pregnant women for child abuse across the nation have been women who are poor and of color, particularly black women who used crack cocaine (Beckett, 1995:601; Logan, 1997; Roberts, 1997). Regina McKnight fits this profile. Given that drug usage rates for black women parallel the rates of drug usage by white women, these differential enforcement patterns are striking. Had Regina been a white and middle-class addict, would she have been prosecuted at all? If race and class are crucial determinations for Regina's prosecution, what about her sex? Does pregnancy—a biological distinction—mark women as essentially "different" from men and therefore subject to distinct regulations for drug delivery via their umbilical cord?

Pregnancy seems to be a "natural" sex difference to many of us, yet socially constructed structures and meanings thoroughly infuse such an experience. For example, medical research on fetal harm targets women's and not men's behaviors.

Gustavsson and MacEachron (1997:674) state that "the exclusion of men from studies on the influence of drugs on the fetus lends credence to the notion that research serves the purposes of power elites who want to police women and control their behavior." Daniels (1997:602) observes that "maternally mediated fetal risks are assumed to be certain and known," while research on paternal risks are "qualified and limited." The limited research has revealed, however, that men's drug use during procreation can have negative effects on sperm morphology and fetal outcomes. In sum, medical systems—along with legal structures and social service organizations—determine who is targeted for what kinds of prosecutions. Indeed, women's experiences suggest that the categories of offender and victim are intertwined. Could Regina's status as an offender follow from being a victim?

Regina McKnight's case and the prosecutions of pregnant drug users reveal the typical "dilemma of difference" facing women (Jaggar, 1994; Messerschmidt, 1997; Minow, 1984). On the one hand, to emphasize "difference" from men can lead to perceptions of leniency and ironically legitimize harsher treatment by the criminal justice system, such as homicide charges for problematic behaviors during pregnancy. On the other hand, to emphasize similarity to men has often meant succumbing to a male standard. In regard to the McKnight case, if men face punitive sentencing for drug violations, so too should women. Yet, women's experience of the criminal justice system *has* been different; they have been defined as different and subject to laws not of their own making.

This chapter focuses on women as victims, offenders, and workers and suggests that the concept of "difference" has been a tool used by those in power to marginalize women as well as a tool used by women to resist and to regain power—though the differences *between* women often impact the tools and strategies used to resist, as well as their success in doing so. Whether difference from men has been emphasized or de-emphasized, women have found it difficult to break free of male standards as victims, makers, and/or breakers of the law.

HOW HISTORY PERVADES WOMEN'S "DIFFERENT" EXPERIENCES WITHIN THE CRIMINAL JUSTICE SYSTEM

History reveals that the process of criminalization is permeated with the power dynamics of differentiating social groups through processes of social construction. Regina's individual story is intimately tied to her gendered, classed, and raced social location. Intersectional theory reveals how these constructed differences have affected each and every one of us historically, and contributed to our current experience. Insofar as the McKnight case appears to be rooted in biological difference—instead of socially constructed—it echoes how the U.S. justice system has historically rationalized inequality. An extensive history shows how women's biology has been used to construct women as "natural" rather than "cultural," irrational rather than rational, childlike rather than adult-like, sexually passive rather than aggressive, caregivers rather than warriors, and as morally superior based on childbearing capacities. These constructions of women have been invariably based upon a portrait of "ladies" or the white, middle-class woman's experience. Biological theories of sexual and racial deficiency have been used as tools of difference to legitimize the oppression of men of color and all women.

White men have used this tool to exclude women from the making and enforcing of law, to deny women jobs, to criminalize women, and to justify their victimization. Conditions today reflect this gendered history.

During the Colonial era, women were legally defined as less than full persons and thereby excluded from both legal protection and prosecution. Until the turn of the twentieth century, women were not allowed to vote, sue, serve on juries, control their own wages, or enter into contracts; they did not have legal rights to their children, their ability to own property was limited, and they were dependent upon the legal identities of their fathers if unmarried, or husbands if married, rather than their own (Pollock, 1995:8). White women's legal status as "nonpersons" was primarily circumscribed by the legal constructions of heterosexual marriage. Fathers or husbands served as women's legal representatives because women were not viewed as persons who could "intend" in general, or in matters of crime (Sokoloff and Price, 1995a:24). White women of the middle class were afforded some protection, opportunity, and a chivalrous, though condescending exemption from prosecution or severe sentences that African American women under slavery and American Indian women under conquest, and poor and working-class women were not (Dill, 1988:416; Sokoloff and Price, 1995a:24).

The growth of industrialization from the eighteenth to nineteenth centuries brought with it a white, middle-class, family ideal—the ideology of separate spheres—that polarized men's and women's activities. As men increasingly "went out" to do paid labor for wages, women were associated with the unpaid labor in the home—feeding, clothing, caring for family members and thereby sustaining the labor force. Mothers became constructed as different due to their superior moral capacities, and these capacities were conceived as rooted in biology. As motherhood was glorified, white women could make claims about their special womanly qualities. Women used the tool of difference, that is, their claims to superior morality, to advance the abolitionist, suffrage, and temperance movements, and ultimately, to expand their own legal personhood. Women secured rights to child custody and property ownership in the nineteenth century and the vote early in the twentieth century. Yet, women's advances still differ by race and class. Although African American women similarly valued motherly qualities, they have always had to contend with the larger society's devaluation of black motherhood (Collins, 2000; Roberts, 1997). Indeed, such historical devaluation underlies the McKnight precedent. Social control over McKnight's reproduction as a black and poor woman echoes privileged white men's near total control of African women's reproduction during the era of enslavement. While control over reproduction has emerged in new guises, McKnight's case is more deeply understood if we see the links from enforced reproduction during enslavement, through the underhanded medical sterilization of poor women of color in the twentieth century, to criminalization of pregnant women into the twenty-first century.

A second Women's Movement in the 1970s, the Court's recognition of women as "persons" in the case of *Reed* v. *Reed* in 1971 (Sokoloff and Price, 1995a:23), and new legislative action have advanced women's rights, yet women have not escaped the dilemma of difference. Women continue to experience less power to construct behaviors as crimes, determine who is a criminal, and define the relation between the two.

CRIMES AGAINST WOMEN

Women's and men's victimization have one thing in common: they are mostly victimized by men. What makes crimes against women different from those against men? Women are most often victimized through crimes against their persons, in their homes, and in their personal lives. The majority of men's nonfatal violent victimizations are committed by strangers; while the majority of women's nonfatal victimizations are committed by someone the woman knows (Barak, Flavin, and Leighton, 2001:161). In addition, one-third of all women homicide victims are murdered by intimate partners, compared to 5% of men (Barak, Flavin, and Leighton, 2001). Behaviors such as domestic violence and sexual assault have resisted definition as crimes. The legacy of separate spheres, wherein men are conceived as having prerogatives as household heads and the home is conceived of as private and inviolable, has made it difficult for many people—especially men—to recognize that the home is not simply a "haven," but also a site of crime. Women have rallied every political and legal resource to redefine such harmful behaviors as crimes. Indeed, words like "battered woman," "wife abuse," and "marital rape" were not even known concepts just 40 years ago, and incest was perceived to be pathological and rare.

Both girls and boys are subject to neglect and abuse by mothers who remain primary caretakers of children—though men's role in child abuse is surprisingly high given that they are not as likely to be primary caregivers (U.S. Department of Health and Human Services, 2005). Men are overwhelmingly the perpetrators of sexual assault of both girls and boys (Belknap, 2001). While boys and girls both experience child sexual abuse, 70% of child sexual assault victims are girls (Belknap, 2001). Sexually abused girls are in a double bind: they are victimized by the very people who are their protectors. Incest is a key link to and condition of eventual offending by females, and foreshadows women's victimization by intimates in adulthood.

Research shows that both wives and husbands commit violent acts—they kick, hit, and throw objects at their partners (Straus, Gelles, and Steinmetz, 1980). Yet, research also shows that men initiate the violence, whereas women act in self-defense and are overwhelmingly among the injured (Belknap and Potter, 2006). Dobash and Dobash report, "from police and court records, national crime surveys and historical documentation all confirm the asymmetrical pattern of male violence directed at female partners" (1992:269). "In a given year, anywhere from 10 to 25 percent of women are beaten by a male intimate, and a quarter to a half of all women will experience violence at the hands of a male intimate in their lifetime" (Kurz, 1995:52). While both men and women murder their intimate partners, the number of men murdered by women has *decreased* by 68% between 1976 and 2000, while the murder of women by men has remained stable (Belknap, 2001). According to the Bureau of Justice Statistics (2005), 63.5% of female homicide victims were killed by an intimate partner, compared to 36.5% of males killed by an intimate partner.

Russell (1990:90) has shown that more women are raped than beaten by their husbands. In a study of 2,588 rape cases, 38% were committed by husbands and between 70 and 80% of the victims of wife rape reported being raped more than once (Websdale and Chesney-Lind, 2004:309). Rape is the brutal use of difference to dominate and control others. Until 1977, when Oregon became the first state to repeal marital exemptions in its rape statute, rape was legally impossible in marriage. This marital exclusion reflected the historical perception of women as nonpersons, as property to whom husbands had a right, and rape as an offense against the woman's husband or father, rather than the woman herself. Spousal rape is a crime in all 50 states. However, some state statutes allow for less punitive sentencing for spousal rape. For example, until 2006 in Arizona, the perpetrator could receive probation for the crime of rape if married to the victim. The Arizona law was changed after the heroic efforts of a victim whose husband brutally raped her and only received probation (Bommersbach, 2005). For a woman raped by her partner, who must fear for her safety even while asleep in her bed, her home is not a haven.

Perhaps the most frequently asked question when it comes to wife abuse is, why don't women leave? This question overlooks the fact that *most women do leave* and it reveals a social resistance to constructing "the husband" as an "offender." Given who is harming, we should ask, why aren't men compelled to leave? Wondering why women don't leave reveals a stubborn unwillingness to see how women's different economic, legal, and social status makes departing difficult. Women who leave must make "choices" within a limited structure of options. Not only does leaving increase her risk of attack (Browne, 1995:230), but she must secure alternative income, housing, social supports, and schools for her children. These difficulties can be particularly acute for poor and rural women (Websdale, 1998).

Women of color face additional obstacles to protection. Having witnessed brutality and racism by police, trust in police is rare and battered women of color are more likely to turn to health care systems (Ritchie and Kanuha, 1993). Language barriers, sustaining the honor of their communities, and awareness of the disproportionate criminalization of men of color are all additional obstacles for women of color who seek to escape domestic violence (Rasche, 1988; Ritchie and Kanuha, 1993). Victims of intimate violence who are women of color or immigrant women often run the risk of their culture being blamed for men's violence and their victimization if they choose to report it (Dasgupta, 2004). All of these obstacles to "leaving" suggest that it is extraordinary when women escape abuse and forge a new life for themselves.

Of course, women are also victimized outside the context of marriage. Women of color experience the highest rates of rape; black females are more at risk than white females and Native American females experience the highest rates (Belknap, 2001). Furthermore, women with disabilities experience very high rates and are at an increased risk for sexual assault victimization (Belknap, 2001). Most research indicates that about one-quarter of women will experience a rape in their lifetime (Scully, 1995:199); such prevalence suggests that it is not simply an act committed by a "pathological" fringe group (Johnson cited in Scully, 1995). The idea that rapists are different from other men overlooks the numbers of men who would like to rape. Research that asked college men if they would rape if they could be assured they would not be caught revealed that anywhere from 28 to 37% reported they would rape, and another 30% would use force (Briere and Malamuth, 1983; Tieger, 1981; cited in Scully, 1995:207).

A stubborn belief is that men are different from women because they are sexually aggressive by nature; indeed, sociobiologists try to substantiate this belief (Hubbard, 1995). Yet, attributing rapist behaviors to biology absolves rapists of responsibility and prevents a social analysis of men's sense of powerlessness. This essentialist notion of manhood is complemented by the construction of women as sexually passive and aroused by the use of force. Such a construction of women suggests that no means yes, that women ultimately desire rape, and that women act to provoke rape; this, in turn, holds women accountable and "blames the victim" (Belknap, 2001; Karmen, 1995; Scully, 1995). It is no wonder that the majority of rapes go unreported; women know they will have to account for their behavior and deportment to significant others, the police, and in the courts (Konradi, 1996). A sex worker or prostitute rarely reports rape knowing that others presume she not only "asked for it," but "got paid for it."

Although the prevailing image of stranger rape influences women's daily lives, research repeatedly shows that most rape in the U.S. occurs in the context of personal relationships (Herman, 1979; Scully, 1995). The National Crime Victimization Survey statistics indicate that approximately 60% of all rapes are acquaintance rapes—that is, sexual intercourse coerced by someone the victim knows (Renzetti and Curran, 2003:282). Rape and sexual assault are among the least reported crimes. It is estimated that among all rapes, less than 50% end in arrest and among these only 22% result in conviction (Renzetti and Curran, 2003:280).

Sentencing is generally lenient, but this depends upon the race of the perpetrator as well as the victim. Indeed, the issue of rape provides yet another example of how women's and men's relational experiences vary by race and reflect historical legacies. Historically, black men have faced death because of accusations of raping white women; such accusations became an excuse for lynching during the Jim Crow era. When perpetrators are black men and victims are white women, black men can expect the harshest treatment of all (LaFree, 1980; cited in Renzetti and Curran, 1995:343). In contrast, white men raping black women in recent decades receive the most leniency; and, historically the law has not always defined the rape of black women by white men as criminal at all—reflecting the devaluation of black women. Crenshaw (2000) explains how rape laws have been grounded in controlling and protecting white women's sexuality, whose purity could be restored; in contrast, given projections about promiscuity, there has been no attempt to protect black women's sexuality.

Finally, another myth is that rape is a sexual rather than a fundamentally violent act. Clearly, sexuality cannot be extricated from rape. Yet, the use of rape in wars to subdue conquered populations across cultures, the use of rape to control black slaves' behavior and procreation in U.S. history, and the use of rape by men against men in prisons reveal that the goal is dominance. Such histories reveal rape for what it is: an act of concerted violence for purposes of social control and not a result of losing sexual control. The history of violence against women is substantial, yet women are also quite capable of being violent.

CONSTRUCTING CRIMINALITY: THE WOMAN AS "CRIMINAL"

Although constructions of "difference" have impeded criminalizing behaviors that harm or victimize women, in recent years the construction of women as criminals has gained momentum and resulted in an explosion of imprisoned women (Chesney-Lind, 1995:106). Although women still only constitute 7% of the total prison population, their rates of imprisonment have grown immensely: in 1970, there were 5,635 women in prison, but by 2005, there were 107,518 women in prison (Bureau of Justice Statistics, 2005). Furthermore, since 1995 the annual rate of growth of women inmates is 4.6% compared to the annual rate of 3% for men (Bureau of Justice Statistics, 2005;4). Chesney-Lind and Pollock (1995) have deemed this trend "equality with a vengeance," meaning that in aiming to treat women the "same" as men, we have lost sight of constructed differences. Both "sameness" and "difference" have been tools for constructing women's criminality. Still, what are all these women doing?

Violent crimes may seem to represent increased "criminality" among women, but violent crimes like murder are not representative of the *growth* in women's incarceration. Like men, most women who are arrested and imprisoned have primarily committed property and drug-related crimes. Women are more likely than men to be jailed or imprisoned for drug offenses. Of sentenced offenders in 2005, 29.1% of women were sentenced for drug offenses compared to 19.3% of men (Bureau of Justice Statistics, 2005:9). Women are also more likely to be in prison for property offenses. Thirty percent of female prisoners are serving time for property offenses compared to 20% of men (Bureau of Justice Statistics, 2005:9).

According to a Bureau of Justice Statistics (1999) special report on women offenders, the majority of women inmates were serving time for their first offense and half of the women inmates were under the influence of drugs or alcohol when they committed the offense. In addition, most incarcerated women are overwhelmingly young, economically marginalized, single mothers with a high school diploma or GED. The overrepresentation of women of color in prison is most striking. Black women are twice as likely as Hispanic women and over three times more likely to be in prison than white women (Bureau of Justice Statistics, 2005). Latinas and African American women make up 60% of the prison population and Native American women are ten times more likely to be imprisoned than white women (Sudbury, 2003). Further, Latinas make up one in three women held in federal custody (Bureau of Justice Statistics, 1999).

While Regina McKnight's conviction for homicide of her late-term fetus makes her case unique, in every other way she represents the growth in women's incarceration. At the time of conviction, she was only 24, an economically marginalized woman of color, who was an unmarried mother; finally, she is part of the ballooning prosecutions that are drug related. Women who use drugs are viewed as selfish, pleasing themselves instead of making others their priority (Szalavitz, 1999). "Female addicts are seen as doubly deviant" because of their behavior and this is why "our response to addicted women tends to be more punitive than our admittedly harsh treatment of male addicts" (Szalavitz, 1999:43). Regina's motherhood is crucial to highlight because, as several scholars document, the leniency of sentences for women (and not men) depends upon whether they fulfill gender "roles" of caring for children, husbands, or family in general—and, as we've seen, African American motherhood has been excessively scrutinized (Belknap, 2001; Rector, 2002; Roberts, 1991, 1999). Rector (2002) reports on an illuminating contradiction in McKnight's case that represents this devaluation of black motherhood. McKnight's attorney argued to the court that she was being punished for continuing her pregnancy: ". . . Regina could have had an illegal abortion. And the most this state could prosecute her is two years. But because she decided to go forward with this, she now faces life in prison" (Rector, 2002). Although she did not receive life, but rather 12 years, her case should elicit some unease about how justice proceeds.

How is criminality constructed through social, legal, and institutional processes? At every step of the criminal justice system, behaviors and groups go through differentiating processes. Self-report surveys, for example, show that white girls are fully as "delinquent" as nonwhite girls, but are not similarly represented in detention rates (Chesney-Lind and Shelden, 1998:27). Among adults, more whites report drug use than African Americans but whites are less likely to be arrested (Mann, 1995:120). More African American women are arrested for prostitution than whites—perhaps reflecting street workers' visibility and vulnerability to arrest (Mann, 1995:119). Some studies show that whereas the proportion of white women moving through the criminal justice process appears to decrease at each step—from their proportion in the population, to their proportion booked, to their proportion returned to jail, to their proportion receiving sentences—the proportion of African American women increases (Mann, 1995). The "seriousness" of the offense does not explain this disparity (Mann, 1995:125). Thus, racism and poverty are structured into the process of criminalization from arrest to sentencing (Wonders, 1996). While the rate of incarceration for women has increased, the rate is astronomically higher for women of color. For example, the rate of incarceration for black women increased 571% from 1980 to 2002 (Young and Adams-Fuller, 2006). The tool of difference simultaneously subordinates the disadvantaged by race, class, and gender, locating poor women of color at the most vulnerable of social intersections.

Despite economic gains for some women since the 1970s, the impoverishment of women continues to grow. Women still predominate in jobs distinguished by low pay, low job security, and few benefits or promotional opportunities. Working full-time and year-around, women still make only about 81% of what men earn—with women of color and older women making even less (U.S. Department of Labor, 2006). Also, women increasingly live in female-headed households, supporting children without access to a male wage, and without the support of a society that could provide social assistance with child care, job training, health care, and drug addiction.

At least half of incarcerated women share a history of disadvantage as girls (Chesney-Lind, 1995:110). About one-half of all girls who encounter the juvenile justice system are arrested for larceny-theft or status offenses such as running away (Chesney-Lind and Shelden, 1998:10). Status offenses are "crimes" applied only to juveniles, including curfew regulations, running away, truancy, and incorrigibility, and girls have been and continue to be subject to these offenses disproportionately. For example, in 1991 "girls made up 61 percent of young people appearing in juvenile courts charged with running away from home, and they are about half (41 percent) of all youths charged with a status offense; by contrast, girls made up only 19 percent of those in juvenile court for criminal offenses" (Chesney-Lind and Shelden, 1998:3). Although girls and boys run away from home in equal numbers, girls appear to be held more accountable for that behavior than boys—by parents, police, and society generally.

Historically, status offenses have served to control girls' sexuality. Yet it is not the girls' sexuality that needs controlling. Two-thirds to three-quarters of girls who end up in juvenile detention facilities or runaway shelters have been sexually abused (Chesney-Lind and Shelden, 1998:3). The girl who tries to escape this victimization by running away from home becomes arrested for "status offenses" and thereby criminalized (Arnold, 1995; Chesney-Lind and Shelden, 1998). These girls are caught between victimization in families and victimization by the criminal justice system. The robust connection between being a victim and an offender is transparent here. This double bind has led some girls to construct new "families" in gangs. Girls in gangs resist society's devaluation of their class and racial identities as do home boys given the racist education and a dearth of legitimate economic opportunities, yet the girl gangsta must regularly contend with sexualization by home boys as well as by white, middle-class, mostly male, legal authorities. Ironically, many heterosexual girls use the tool of difference, their sexuality, as a means to power and economic survival, even though they have been sexually abused in their families. If more criminal justice workers were women, might they be more sensitive to the double bind facing young girls or women?

WOMEN WORKING AT THE BORDERS OF CRIME AND JUSTICE

Over the last two decades, women have become visible as workers in the criminal justice system. For the first time in our history, women are represented on the U.S. Supreme Court, thereby participating in shaping law. The appointments of Sandra Day O'Connor in 1981 and of Ruth Bader Ginsburg in 1993 to the U.S. Supreme Court have been crucial symbolic developments. Women have traveled an enormous legal distance since the nineteenth century, when women could not enter into contracts or vote, let alone become judges (Pollock, 1995). By the beginning of the twenty-first century, women have secured these rights and young girls have models through which they can imagine their presence on the Supreme Court.

The court represents a pinnacle of power in the criminal justice system, but the number of women workers has grown throughout the system. Women's entry into legal work, corrections, and policing is notable because these professions have all been dominated by men and are considered "masculine" professions. In spite of the growth, female underrepresentation continues. Like most professional occupations that came to be constituted by men since the nineteenth century, a male-based structure underlies law, policing, and corrections in the criminal justice system. Women who enact the aggressive, tough, rational, strong, or violent elements of these various occupations are seen and treated as "different." Thus women face a double bind; they must negotiate the dilemma of difference whether they mirror or repudiate the masculine traits associated with the job.

MacKinnon (1987) has argued that women should use the tool of difference to create laws and policies based on women's experiences of injuries or harm. For example, sexual harassment law was the first law made by and for women that criminalizes behaviors which women experience as harmful. However, other legal scholars have argued that the conservative nature of the law—such as the accumulated history of case law—will impede change in the legal apparatus regardless of the number of women who are in, use, or challenge the criminal justice system (Smart, 1989). Yet, if women cannot rely upon the tool of difference, can they rely upon "sameness," which is likely to be based upon a male-standard? To examine the dilemma of difference for workers, we will begin by looking at the legal profession.

Women in Law

Increases in women law students suggest women's equal participation is on the horizon. For example, the number of female law students has reached parity with the number of male law students in the last decade or so (Pollock and Ramirez, 1995:82).

In 2002 women accounted for 49% of first-year law students (Siemsen, 2006). Despite their numbers and solid academic records, the career trajectories of female lawyers suggest women will not change the legal profession in the immediate future. Currently women constitute only 29% of practicing attorneys (Siemsen, 2006). Women's choices are made within a structure of opportunity that channels their specialties, professional relationships, perceptions of their competence, and influences their strategies for contending with "gendered organizational logic" (Acker, 1990). Female attorneys cluster in different occupational locations and describe different experiences in the practice of law than men do (Anleau, 1995; Pollock, 1995). In private practice, corporate firms, and in government, women "choose" arenas of legal practice that minimize obstacles based upon a male standard—as they seek flexible hours to attend to their competing domestic responsibilities and lower rates of sexual harassment (Martin and Jurik, 1996:120). Yet, these same positions also result in lower pay and prestige, fewer promotions, as well as less power in the profession overall (Pollock, 1995:26).

Does the presence of women attorneys in the courtroom make a "difference"? Research comparing women's and men's interpretation of the law has yielded inconsistent results so far (Pollock and Ramirez, 1995:92). Practicing female attorneys still report biased treatment by a mostly male judiciary (Martin and Jurik, 1996:220). For example, judges do not necessarily treat behaviors the same when performed by men and women. A combative style in the courtroom may be interpreted as appropriately aggressive if a man, but too shrill or aggressive if a woman; a soft-spoken, non-combative style may be interpreted as a negotiating skill if a man, but as an incapacity for aggression if a woman (Martin and Jurik, 1996:124). Interpretations of the same behavior are changed when we look through the lens of difference—both gender and race—and can change how people perform their job.

Women in Policing and Corrections

Occupations like law enforcement and corrections stand in contrast to the white-collar legal professions. They are treated together here because traditionally they have been blue-collar occupations, and have only recently gained a semi-professional status through increased training and educational criteria—in part to advance more humane practices (Martin and Jurik, 1996:160). In contrast to attorneys where workers are "about one-quarter female but only about one percent black female" (Sokoloff and Price, 1995b:327), in policing and corrections racial-ethnic women experience greater representation. Women account for 12.7% of all sworn officers, with 4.8% being women of color (National Center for Women and Policing, 2001). However, women of color are severely underrepresented in supervisory positions. In agencies with 100 or more officers, women of color hold only 1.6% of top command positions and 87.9% of these agencies reported having no women of color in top command positions (National Center for Women and Policing, 2001). Women of color's greater representation in policing and corrections is related to the financial and educational hurdles associated with legal careers as well as the higher wages and job security of these occupations compared to traditional female jobs like clerical work or waiting tables.

Until the 1960s, women working in policing were treated in terms of "difference"—receiving special assignments, titles, and lower pay than male officers (Pollock, 1995:27).

Women took a variety of actions to be treated the "same": they sued for equal pay, challenged a male-standard of physical height and weight requirements and sued for the right to take promotional exams (Pollock, 1995). Also, in 1973, the Crime Control Act "made it illegal to discriminate against women if the agency or organization received Law Enforcement Assistance Administration funds" (Pollock, 1995:27).

Sexual harassment and discrimination in police work is less blatant and systematic today due to these legal advances, yet female police officers continue to face hostility, resistance, and sexual harassment from male colleagues and supervisors (National Center for Women and Policing, 2001). In contrast to the female lawyer whose authority might be undermined in the courtroom by sexist remarks, the female police officer can face threats to her life as well as her authority if other officers fail to back her up at the scene of a violent crime. Research has found that white women are more likely to be protected than black women by fellow male officers who are predominantly white (Barak, Flavin, and Leighton, 2001). A woman of color cannot always tell if hostility by co-workers or the public is related to her sex, her race, or both at once since these structures of dis/advantage intersect. Racialized sexual harassment may keep some women of color from entering or remaining in a field that is dominated by white males (Barak, Flavin, and Leighton, 2001). Women encounter hostility in male-dominated occupations when unwanted and/or perceived as a threat.

One perceived threat for men is that women introduce an alternative organizational culture through a different approach to conflict. Some women draw upon their negotiating skills as a tool of "difference" to diffuse inmate conflict. Moreover, some female corrections workers have been shown to prefer "treatment" over "custodial" approaches to offenders. Similarly in police work, the efforts to hire and treat women the "same" as male officers were also accompanied by an increased emphasis upon interpersonal skills in police work to improve community relations (Jurik, 1985). These new emphases seem to revalue "different" traits conventionally associated with women, yet they have also met with resistance. Women officers have fewer citizen complaints, are less likely to use excessive force, and tend to be better at defusing potentially dangerous situations (Harrington and Lonsway, 2004). However, policies, training, and evaluations still do not emphasize the interpersonal skills that might benefit women (Harrington and Lonsway, 2004).

Even as more women enter policing and corrections, they appear to confront a "glass ceiling" when it comes to promotions. A record number of 30 women were elected as sheriffs in 2002, yet only a few women have served as police chiefs in large cities and most female chiefs served on university police departments (Schulz, 2004). Policies, practices, and assumptions that sustain gendered organizations continue to privilege the upward mobility of men, particularly white men. Gratch (1995:69) reports that in policing, "Women are assigned more often to nonpatrol areas; few are in mid-level management positions; and almost none are in command positions." Evaluations also affect promotions. Although women and men have equal performance evaluations in policing, a male standard for promotion endures (Martin, 1995). Evaluations are based upon a male standard to the degree that they emphasize aspects of the work which men value; currently, the dangerous aspects of policing are emphasized in evaluations and promotions. Thus, for example, Chicago's Police Department stresses the number of arrests, rather than public service and crime prevention, when assessing quantity of work (Martin and Jurik, 1996:86). It is telling that only 2.6% of police duty time is spent in crimes against persons and 14.82% in crimes against property; in contrast, 50.19% of police work time is spent in administrative duties (Gratch, 1995:67). In short, promotions are often based upon performance in less than a quarter of the overall job.

Women account for 40% of correctional officers (Stohr, 2006). However, women's experience in corrections is similar to that in policing. Britton (1997) analyzed the effect of policies upon women and men corrections officers in women's and men's prisons. Britton found that prison training and evaluations were predicated on the worker being male, that the skills perceived as unique to men were more valued, and that male workers were disproportionately benefited by policies and practices—though not all men had equal access to higher rewards (1997:813). Officer training assumed a "male officer" in a "men's prison", which does not include coping with sexual harassment or the different conditions in smaller women's prisons. Training appeared to be gender-neutral, yet it was gendered in its content and consequences: "the rewards of gender-neutral training essentially accrue to male officers who will for the most part be employed in men's prisons" (Britton, 1997:807).

Britton also found that many assignments presumed a need for men. Men's stereotypical "strength" was perceived to be crucial not only in men's prisons, but also in women's prisons! Ironically, the physical strength of female prisoners was emphasized, even as female correctional officers' physical strength was discounted. This reveals how men can use the tool of difference in contradictory ways to disadvantage women workers. Further, while the rhetoric in training films emphasized the prison as a site of "unimaginable violence," when asked to describe the job of correctional officer, workers depicted the job as more of a mental job than a physical one (Britton, 1997:803–804).

This section has focused upon the more privileged and male-dominated occupations in the criminal justice system. Women's numbers in all these occupations have grown, yet they remain in the minority and the verdict is still out whether women will change these occupations or these occupations will change women.

CONCLUSION: WOMEN FOR JUSTICE

Aristotle perceived that "justice consists not only in treating like cases alike but also in treating different cases differently" (Jaggar, 1994:19). For women, both approaches have yielded justice in various contexts and eras. Arguments for justice that focus either on women's difference or sameness are doomed. To stress "difference" succumbs to reinforcing stereotypes whether by race or sex, while to stress sameness invariably relies upon established standards, such as a hegemonic masculinity or prevailing racial projects. As Collins (2000) has argued, we must resist thinking in terms of "either/or" and embrace "both/and" thinking in order to adapt to the vagaries of social context and flex with intersectional realities.

When we opened this chapter, we asked whether Regina McKnight is only an offender or a victim too. When we look at her life, we discover that she sought treatment for her drug addiction to be a responsible mother. Needless to say she didn't find it. In South Carolina, where McKnight was convicted, there were only two treatment centers that accepted pregnant women and they were full when McKnight sought treatment

(Rector, 2002). Drug treatment programs are scarce for women and even scarcer for pregnant women (Humphries *et al.*, 1995)—and few treatment facilities accept pregnant and poor women. Indeed, it took going to jail to access the treatment she wanted as a pregnant woman. Now, while she is categorized as an offender for the murder of her fetus, one can see that she is also the victim of a society unwilling to offer support services to the impoverished. Drug treatment that addresses the economic, psychological, and social reasons for women's drug use would be a much more efficient use of tax dollars than building additional prisons, and, in Regina's case, paying for her 12 years in prison. In this way, Regina is *both* an offender *and* a victim; this relationship is especially transparent to those who work with imprisoned women (Ferraro, 2006). Ferraro (2006) found that women who kill their intimate partners were usually victims too and that those who work with offenders perceive, assume, and know this deep connection between offender and victim; spreading this knowledge to society at large might force us to address the absence of services when women are victimized but before women are criminalized. Beyond decriminalizing drug abuse, custody without treatment does not make sense, knowing, as we do, that drug users relapse into drug use and criminal means for economic survival. Further, we know that women who cannot find help when they are abused, as girls or women, can become criminalized in their efforts to save themselves or their children.

Incarcerated women have increasingly been treated the same as incarcerated men. This approach has yielded educational and vocational programs that had been offered previously to male, but not to female inmates (Merlo, 1995:253). It is clear that women and men similarly need education and training if they are to create alternative ways of making a living after imprisonment. Yet, as Chesney-Lind and Pollock (1995) point out, the circumstances of female offenders are also different. First, women's health care includes gynecological needs. Second, most incarcerated women have been the primary caretakers of children. If mothers are expected to build a life after imprisonment, they need facilities and policies that enable them to sustain relations with children, particularly if they are nonviolent offenders. Third, unlike male offenders, women tend to be less violent and less of a threat to the community. Attention to these issues is essential because Chesney-Lind and Pollock also observe that "[t]he geometric increase in female offenders suggests we may be witnessing equality—yet we also may be witnessing 'equality with a vengeance'" (Chesney-Lind and Pollock, 1995).

In the case of female victims, it has been crucial to recognize how women's victimization is different from men's: they are more often harmed in the context of personal relationships. To not only criminalize, but to enforce laws against men who rape, beat, harass, stalk, or commit incest with female victims, is to not only recognize women's different experience, but also to recognize that harm is harm whether committed by a husband or a stranger. The Women's Movement has used the tool of difference in public education, policy formation, and in the initial development of rape crisis centers and shelters for abused women and their children. The increase of victim/witness, rape crisis, and battered women shelters over the last few decades has brought recognition and remedy to crimes against women. By emphasizing women's different needs, these developments have empowered women. Such programs speak to women's rejection of passive victimization and their ability to actively secure resources to turn victims into survivors—in spite of the power differentials in society at large.

Still, there are limits to temporary shelters and counseling supports. Women require training, education, jobs, health care, homes, and support for child care responsibilities to become survivors. Further, judges, police, and prosecutors have also needed education to take crimes against women seriously. The Violence Against Women Act of 1994 (VAWA) made federal funds for state and local governments contingent upon a "stronger commitment to arresting and prosecuting offenders"; it made it a federal crime to cross states lines to intimidate a partner or in violation of a protection order; it incorporated a civil rights remedy so women can sue and receive compensatory damages if the crime is motivated by gender; and it made funding and protections available to rural and immigrant women (Hirshman, 1994:46; Pollock, 1995:24; Websdale, 1998). In 2000 and 2005 VAWA was reauthorized (VAWA, 2005 Fact Sheet). In 2005, new support for women of Native American communities and communities of color, and immigrant women were developed, which were essential given previous neglect; furthermore, programs focusing on youth and the prevention of violence was an initiative that acknowledged the link or "both/and" relationship between being an offender and being a victim.

Services for men who commit acts of violence are equally important. Some efforts to prevent violence by men have arisen across the country from Emerge in Cambridge, Massachusetts, to the Oakland Men's Project (OMP) in California. The OMP, formed in 1979, aims to "eradicate male violence, racism, and homophobia" (Allen and Kivel, 1993:50; Kivel, 1999). Such projects do not simply aim to cure individual men of violence, but rather to educate men "how power, inequality, and the ability to do violence to others are structured into social relationships in this country" (Allen and Kivel, 1993:52). Cross-cultural research suggests that "rape-prone" societies, like the United States, are characterized by women's devaluation and a lower social and economic status relative to the men of their group (Scully, 1995:204–205). Thus, our remedies for crimes against women should not simply focus on blaming the offender, rather than the victim; as Karmen (1995) argues, we need to focus on the social structures that construct such individuals. Furthermore, gender and racial diversity across all occupations in the criminal justice system could help implement the insights offered by intersection theory.

Gendered organizational logic continues to shape the culture and the structure of occupations that are either prototypically male or female (Acker, 1990). There are several ways to change the conservative bias of gendered occupations. One way is to increase women's presence in male-dominated occupations—a solution that reflects the aim of affirmative action policies, which assume that women are just like men if only they are given the opportunity. Another approach is to change the remuneration in female-dominated occupations through "comparable worth" policies; these would revalue female jobs and move beyond a male standard of valuation and embrace women's difference. Still another approach would be to extend career ladders; clerical and service workers could move through "bridge" positions into administrative positions if the criminal justice system were to promote it (Reskin and Padavic, 2002:112).

The law remains an essential tool for social change. For example, while acknowledging the limits of sexual harassment law, Stambaugh (1997) has argued that women are empowered through their efforts to harness a law made by and for women. Whether women avail themselves of the tool of difference or sameness will depend upon the circumstances in which they find themselves. Sometimes it will be more just to recognize gender differences and other times more just to insist upon sameness. Above all, future criminal justice workers, educated in feminist criminology, should encourage new theoretical questions about and research on constructions of gender, race, and class. Such efforts could help to expose the interrelationships between victim, offender, and justice worker categories and ultimately reconstruct the dilemma of difference.

ACKNOWLEDGMENT

We thank Marianne Nielsen and Lynn Jones for their editorial assistance. Also, this version still reflects assistance from Phoebe Morgan, Barbara Perry, Marianne Nielsen, Neil Websdale, and Hollie Vargas on an earlier version of this chapter.

References

Acker, Joan. 1990. Hierarchies, Jobs, Bodies: A Theory of Gendered Organizations. *Gender and Society* 4 (2): 139–158.

Allen, Robert, and Paul Kivel. 1993. Men Changing Men. *Ms. Magazine,* September/October, 50–53.

Anleau, Sharyn L. Roach. 1995. Women in Law: Theory, Research, and Practice. In *The Criminal Justice System and Women: Offenders, Victims, and Workers,* ed. Barbara Raffel Price and Natalie J. Sokoloff, 2nd edn., 358–371. New York, NY: McGraw-Hill.

Arnold, Regina. 1995. Processes of Victimization and Criminalization of Black Women. In *The Criminal Justice System and Women: Offenders, Victims, and Workers,* ed. Barbara Raffel Price and Natalie J. Sokoloff, 2nd edn., 136–146. New York, NY: McGraw-Hill.

Barak, Gregg, Jeanne Flavin, and Paul Leighton. 2001. *Class, Race, Gender, and Crime: Social Realities of Justice in America.* Los Angeles, CA: Roxbury.

Beckett, Katherine. 1995. Fetal Rights and "Crack Moms": Pregnant Women in the War on Drugs. *Contemporary Drug Problems* 22 (4): 587–612.

Belknap, Joanne. 2001. *The Invisible Woman: Gender, Crime, and Justice.* Belmont, CA: Wadsworth.

Belknap, Joanne, and Hillary Potter. 2006. Intimate Partner Abuse. In *Rethinking Gender, Crime, and Justice,* ed. Claire Renzetti, Lynne Goodstein, and Susan Miller, 168–184. Los Angeles, CA: Roxbury Publishing.

Bommersbach, Jana. 2005. Rape is Rape. *Phoenix Magazine,* September.

Britton, Dana M. 1997. Gendered Organizational Logic: Policy and Practice in Men's and Women's Prisons. *Gender and Society* 11 (6): 796–818.

Browne, Angela. 1995. Fear and the Perception of Alternatives: Asking 'Why Battered Women Don't Leave' is the Wrong Question. In *The Criminal Justice System and Women: Offenders, Victims, and Workers,* ed. Barbara Raffel Price and Natalie J. Sokoloff, 2nd edn., 228–245. New York, NY: McGraw-Hill.

Bureau of Justice Statistics. 1999. *Women Offenders.* NCJ-175688. Washington, DC: U.S. Department of Justice, December

Bureau of Justice Statistics. 2005. *Prisoners in 2005.* NCJ-215092. Washington, DC: U.S. Department of Justice, January 2006

Chesney-Lind, Meda. 1995. "Rethinking Women's Imprisonment: A Critical Examination of Trends in Female Incarceration." In *The Criminal Justice System and Women: Offenders, Victims, and Workers,* ed. Barbara Raffel Price and Natalie J. Sokoloff, 2nd edn., 106–117. New York, NY: McGraw-Hill.

Chesney-Lind, Meda, and Jocelyn M. Pollock. 1995. Women's Prisons: Equality with a Vengeance. In *Women, Law, and Social*

Control, ed. Alida V. Merlo and Jocelyn M. Pollock, 155–176. Boston, MA: Allyn and Bacon.

Chesney-Lind, Meda, and Randall B. Shelden. 1998. *Girls, Delinquency, and Juvenile Justice*, 2nd edn. Belmont, CA: West/Wadsworth.

Collins, Patricia Hill. 2000. *Black Feminist Thought*, 2nd edn. New York: Routledge.

Crenshaw, Kimberle. 2000. Demarginalizing the Intersection of Race and Sex: A Black Feminist Critique of Antidiscrimination Doctrine, Feminist Theory and Antiracist Politics. In *The Black Feminist Reader*, ed. Joy James and T. Denean Sharpley-Whiting, 208–238. Malden, MA: Blackwell Publishers.

Daniels, Cynthia. 1997. Between Fathers and Mothers: The Social Construction of Male Reproduction and the Politics of Fetal Harm. *Journal of Women in Culture and Society* 22 (3): 579–616.

Dasgupta, Shamita D. 2004. Women's Realities: Defining Violence Against Women by Immigration, Race and Class. In *The Criminal Justice System and Women: Offenders, Victims, and Workers*, ed. Barbara Raffel Price and Natalie J. Sokoloff, 3rd edn., 361–374. New York, NY: McGraw-Hill.

Dill, Bonnie Thornton. 1988. Our Mothers' Grief: Racial Ethnic Women and the Maintenance of Families *Journal of Family History* 13 (4): 415–431.

Dobash, R. Emerson, and Russell P. Dobash. 1992. *Women, Violence and Social Change*. New York: Routledge.

Ferraro, Kathleen J. 2006. *Neither Angels nor Demons: Women, Crime, and Victimization*. Boston: Northeastern University Press.

Gratch, Linda. 1995. Sexual Harassment Among Police Officers: Crisis and Change in the Normative Structure. In *Women, Law, and Social Control*, ed. Alida V. Merlo and Jocelyn M. Pollock, 55–78. Boston, MA: Allyn and Bacon.

Gustavsson, Nora S., and Ann E. MacEachron. 1997. Criminalizing Women's Behavior. *Journal of Drug Issues* 27 (3): 673–688.

Harrington, Penny, and Kimberly Lonsway. 2004. Current Barriers and Future Promise for Women in Policing. In *The Criminal Justice System and Women: Offenders, Victims, and Workers*, ed. Barbara Raffel Price and Natalie J. Sokoloff, 3rd edn., 495–510. New York, NY: McGraw-Hill.

Herman, Dianne. 1979. The Rape Culture. In *Women: A Feminist Perspective*, ed. Jo Freeman, 2nd edn., 41–63. Palo Alto, CA: Mayfield Publishing Company.

Hirshman, Linda. 1994. Making Safety a Civil Right. *Ms. Magazine*. September/October, 44–47.

Hubbard, Ruth. 1995. Sexism and Sociobiology: For Our Own Good and the Good of the Species. In *Profitable Promises: Essays on Women, Science and Health*, 103–121. Monroe, Maine: Common Courage Press.

Humphries, Drew, John Dawson, Valerie Cronin, Phyllis Keating, Chris Wisniewski, Jennine Eichfeld. 1995. Mothers and Children, Drugs and Crack: Reactions to Maternal Drug Dependency. In *The Criminal Justice System and Women: Offenders, Victims, and Workers*, ed. Barbara Raffel Price and Natalie J. Sokoloff, 3rd edn., 167–179. New York, NY: McGraw-Hill.

Jaggar, Alison M. 1994. Sexual Difference and Sexual Equality. In *Living with Contradictions: Controversies in Feminist Social Ethics*, ed. Alison Jaggar, 18–27. Boulder: Westview Press.

Jurik, Nancy C. 1985. An Officer and a Lady: Organizational Barriers to Women Working as Correctional officers in Men's Prisons. *Social Problems* 32 (4): 375–387.

Karmen, Andrew. 1995. Women Victims of Crime. In *The Criminal Justice System and Women: Offenders, Victims, and Workers*, ed. Barbara Raffel Price and Natalie J. Sokoloff, 3rd edn., 181–196. New York, NY: McGraw-Hill.

Kivel, Paul. 1999. *Boys Will Be Men: Raising Our Sons for Courage, Caring and Community*. Gabriola Island, BC, Canada: New Society Publishers.

Konradi, Amanda. 1996. Preparing to Testify: Rape Survivors Negotiating the Criminal Justice Process. *Gender and Society* 10 (4): 404–432.

Kurz, Demie. 1995. *For Richer, For Poorer: Mothers Confront Divorce*. New York: Routledge.

Logan, Enid. 1997. The Wrong Race, Committing Crime, Doing Drugs, and Maladjusted for Motherhood: The Nations Fury over Crack Babies. *Social Justice* 26 (1): 115–140.

MacKinnon, Catharine. 1987. Sexual Harassment: Its First Decade in Court. In *The Criminal Justice System and Women: Offenders, Victims, and Workers*, ed. Barbara Raffel Price and Natalie J. Sokoloff, 3rd edn., 297–311. New York, NY: McGraw-Hill.

Mann, Coramae Richey. 1995. Women of Color and the Criminal Justice System. In *The Criminal Justice System and Women: Offenders, Victims, and Workers*, ed. Barbara Raffel Price and Natalie J. Sokoloff, 3rd edn., 118–135. New York, NY: McGraw-Hill.

Martin, Susan. 1995. The Interactive Effects of Race and Sex on Women Police Officers. In *The Criminal Justice System and Women: Offenders, Victims, and Workers*, ed. Barbara Raffel Price and Natalie J. Sokoloff, 3rd edn., 383–396. New York, NY: McGraw-Hill.

Martin, Susan Ehrlich, and Nancy C. Jurik. 1996. *Doing Justice, Doing Gender: Women in Law and Criminal Justice Occupations*. Thousand Oaks, CA: Sage Publications.

Merlo, Alida V. 1995. Female Criminality in the 1990s. In *Women, Law, and Social Control*, ed. Alida V. Merlo and Jocelyn M. Pollock, 241–264. Boston, MA: Allyn and Bacon.

Messerschmidt, James.1997. *Crime as Structured Action: Gender, Race, Class, and Crime in the Making*. Thousand Oaks, CA: Sage Publications.

Minow, Martha. 1984. Learning to Live with the Dilemma of Difference: Bilingual and Special Education. *Law and Contemporary Problems* 48 (2): 157–211.

National Center for Women and Policing, a Division of the Feminist Majority Foundation. 2001. *Equality Denied: The Status of Women in Policing 2001*. Los Angeles, CA: Feminist Majority Foundation.

Pollock, Jocelyn M. 1995. Gender, Justice, and Social Control: A Historical Perspective. In *Women, Law, and Social Control*, ed. Alida V. Merlo and Jocelyn M. Pollock, 3–35. Boston, MA: Allyn and Bacon.

Pollock, Jocelyn, and Barbara Ramirez. 1995. Women in the Legal Profession. In *Women, Law, and Social Control*, ed. Alida V. Merlo and Jocelyn M. Pollock, 79–96. Boston, MA: Allyn and Bacon.

Rasche, Christine. 1988. Minority Women and Domestic Violence: The Unique Dilemmas of Battered Women of Color. In *The Criminal Justice System and Women: Offenders, Victims, and Workers*, ed. Barbara Raffel Price and Natalie J. Sokoloff, 3rd edn., 246–261. New York, NY: McGraw-Hill.

Rector, Paula. 2002. Enforcing and Maintaining Identities Through the Criminalization of Pregnancy: The Regina McKnight Case. Master's Thesis. Department of Criminal Justice, Northern Arizona University.

Renzetti, Claire, and Daniel Curran. 1995. *Women, Men and Society*, 3rd edn. Boston, MA: Allyn and Bacon.

Renzetti, Claire and Daniel Curran. 2003. *Women, Men and Society*, 5th edn. Boston, MA: Allyn and Bacon.

Reskin, Barbara, and Irene Padavic. 2002. *Women and Men at Work*. Thousand Oaks, CA: Pine Forge Press.

Ritchie, Beth E., and Valli Kanuha. 1993. Battered Women of Color in Public Health Care Systems: Racism, Sexism, and Violence. In *Through the Prism of Difference: Readings in Sex and Gender*, ed. Maxine Baca Zinn, Pierrette Hondagneu-Sotelo, and Michael A. Messner, 121–129. Boston: Allyn and Bacon.

Roberts, Dorothy E. 1991. Punishing Drug Addicts Who Have Babies: Women of Color, Equality, and The Right Of Privacy. *Harvard Law Review* 104 (7): 1419–1481.

Roberts, Dorothy E. 1997. Unshackling Black Motherhood. *Michigan Law Review* 94 (4): 938–965.

Roberts, Dorothy E. 1999. Mothers Who Fail to Protect Their Children: Accounting for Public and Private Responsibility. In *Mother Troubles Rethinking Contemporary Maternal Dilemmas*, ed. Julia Hanisberg and Sara Ruddick, 50–58. Boston, MA: Beacon Press

Russell, Diana. 1990. *Rape in Marriage*. Bloomington, IN: Indiana University Press.

Schulz, Dorothy M. 2004. Invisible No More: A Social History of Women in U.S. Policing. In *The Criminal Justice System and Women: Offenders, Victims, and Workers*, ed. Barbara Raffel Price and Natalie J. Sokoloff, 3rd edn., 483–494. New York, NY: McGraw-Hill.

Scully, Diana. 1995. Rape is the Problem. In *The Criminal Justice System and Women: Offenders, Victims, and Workers*, ed. Barbara

Raffel Price and Natalie J. Sokoloff, 3rd edn., 197–215. New York, NY: McGraw-Hill.

Siemsen, Cynthia. 2006. Women Criminal Lawyers. In *Rethinking Gender, Crime, and Justice*, ed. Claire Renzetti, Lynne Godstein, and Susan Miller, 228–239. Los Angeles, CA: Roxbury.

Smart, Carol. 1989. *Feminism and the Power of Law*. London: Routledge.

Sokoloff, Natalie J., and Barbara Raffel Price. (1995a). The Criminal Law and Women. In *The Criminal Justice System and Women: Offenders, Victims, and Workers*, ed. Barbara Raffel Price and Natalie J. Sokoloff, 3rd edn., 11–29. New York, NY: McGraw-Hill.

Sokoloff, Natalie J., and Barbara Raffel Price, 1995b. Women Workers in the Criminal Justice System. In *The Criminal Justice System and Women: Offenders, Victims, and Workers*, ed. Barbara Raffel Price and Natalie J. Sokoloff, 3rd edn., 321–331. New York, NY: McGraw-Hill.

Stambaugh, Phoebe Morgan. 1997. The Power of Law and the Sexual Harassment Complaints of Women. *National Women's Studies Association Journal* 9 (2): 23–42.

Stohr, Mary K. 2006. Yes, I've Paid the Price, but Look How Much I Gained. In *Rethinking Gender Crime and Justice*, ed. Claire Renzetti, Lyne Goodstein, and Susan Miller, 262–277. Los Angeles, CA: Roxbury Publishing Co.

Straus, Murray, Richard Gelles, Suzanne Steinmetz, 1980. The Marriage License as a Hitting License. In *Family in Transition*, ed. Arlene Skolnick and Jerome Skolnick, 8th edn., 202–215. New York: HarperCollins.

Sudbury, Julie. 2003. Women of Color, Globalization, and the Politics of Incarceration. In *The Criminal Justice System and Women: Offenders, Prisoners Victims, Workers*, ed. Barbara Raffel and Natalie J. Sokoloff, 3rd edn. New York: McGraw-Hill.

Szalavitz, Maria. 1999. "War on Drugs, War on Women." *On The Issues* 8 (1): 42–47.

U.S. Department of Health and Human Services. 2005. Child Maltreatment, 2005. Washington, DC: U.S. Department of Health and Human Services.

U.S. Department of Labor. 2006. Highlights of Women's Earnings 2005. Washington, DC: U.S. Department of Labor, September, 1995.

Violence Against Women Act. 2005 Fact Sheet. http://www.ovw.usdoj.gov/regulations.htm Retrieved April 25, 2008.

Websdale, Neil. 1998. *Rural Woman Battering and the Justice System*. Thousand Oaks: Sage Publications.

Websdale, Neil, and Meda Chesney-Lind. 2004. Doing Violence to Women: Research Synthesis on the Victimization of Women. In *The Criminal Justice System and Women: Offenders, Victims, and Workers*, ed. Barbara Raffel Price and Natalie J. Sokoloff, 3rd edn., 303–332. New York, NY: McGraw-Hill.

Wonders, Nancy. 1996. Determinate Sentencing: A Feminist and Postmodern Story. *Justice Quarterly* 13 (4): 611–648.

Young, Vernetta, and Terri Adams-Fulle. 2006. Women, Race/Ethnicity, and Criminal Justice Processing. In *Rethinking Gender, Crime, and Justice*, ed. Claire Renzetti, Lynne Godstein, and Susan Miller, 185–199. Los Angeles, CA: Roxbury.

CHAPTER 12

Gay Men, Lesbians, and Criminal Justice

Barbara Perry

For centuries, gay men and lesbians in the United States have been stigmatized as sinners and perverts, diseased in mind and body. As a result, they have historically been silenced at best and brutally beaten to death at worst. It is only since the late 1970s that gay men and lesbians in the United States have begun to break out of these constraining images and to empower themselves socially and politically. This has often been accomplished in spite of, rather than because of, the criminal justice system. Law enforcement agents, judges, and most other actors within the justice system have long been resistant to accept homosexuality as legitimate. Consequently, the criminal justice system has offered little in the way of protection or redress. As this chapter will illustrate, the criminal justice system represents at best an ambiguous site for gay and lesbian struggles.

INVESTIGATING HOMOSEXUALITY

The stigmatization of homosexuality is not historically or cross-culturally universal. Biery (1990:10) suggests that what we now refer to as homosexuality really "began in the nineteenth century when the word was used for the first time." However, "a label does not give birth to something. Same-sex affection and eroticism have existed since the beginning of recorded history—and probably long before that."

Same-sex relationships have flourished in cultures as diverse as Ancient Greece, Medieval England, and contemporary Polynesia. Moreover, the social and moral assessment of such behavior varies dramatically by time, place, and culture. More so than most cultural groups in the United States, Native Americans have long held flexible, fluid views of sexuality. Behavior is more likely to be evaluated according to the appropriateness of the context, rather than the behavior itself. Thus, there is no rigid proscription against homosexuality. On the contrary, many Native traditions refer to the "Two Spirited" as ones who are valued because of their inherent combination of both the male and female spirits (Tafoya, 1997:8).

Some Asian cultures share some of this tolerant outlook on sexual diversity. Historically, same-sex relationships have permeated the upper echelons of Japanese society, including the wealthy urban classes, Buddhist clergy, and the military. In fact, *nanshoku* ("male colors") or *shudo* ("way of companions") was so intimately connected to the warrior society that it was often referred to as the "past-time" of the Samurai. However, while this tradition was readily accepted for centuries, it seems to have become latent since the turn of the century, a phenomenon Miller (1995) attributes to the Westernization of Japan—a process that included a transition in sexual morality.

Nonetheless, there remains a significant distinction between Asian and Western reactions to homosexuality. Miller (1995) and Greene (1997) both assert that Asian resistance is grounded not in homophobia, nor in heterosexism, but in pressure to marry. Asian American men and women are held accountable to family rather than gender expectations. Homosexuality is thus a punishable threat to the family line and name. This may be especially important for Asians living in the United States, where the Western culture generally poses a threat to the continuation of the traditional Asian family line and values.

Family also provides a context for anti-gay sentiment between Latinos and Latinas, yet in a different- and generally more intense—manner (Greene, 1997). In Latino American communities, the family has primacy. Associated with this are narrowly defined gender roles. Masculinity is rigidly enacted through the patriarchal family roles of provider and protector, while femininity is associated with passivity and virtue. Homosexual men, on the other hand, are regarded as effete, and both incapable and unwilling to assume these roles, whereas lesbians are perceived to threaten male dominance and control. Consequently, both gay men and lesbians are labeled as traitors to the family as well as to the culture itself. Moraga (1996:299) argues that the rigidity of Latino conceptions of masculinity and femininity is greater than virtually those of any other culture in the United States.

However, this homophobia is not without its contradictions. Often, homosexual behavior is less threatening than the explicit assumption of a homosexual identity (Greene, 1997). Moreover, drawing on anthropological evidence, Almaguer (1995) asserts that the Chicano understanding of homosexuality revolves around sexual acts rather than sexual preferences *per se*. For men, a distinction is drawn between *activo* and *pasivo*, with stigmatization and ridicule reserved for the *pasivo*. The latter is deemed to be enacting a passive, subservient, and feminine identity, very much out of line with the favored *activo*, who is by definition active, aggressive, and masculine. The *activo* may in fact gain status through his dominance of the weaker recipient, who is judged to be a feminized man: biologically male, but not really a man (Almaguer, 1995).

The dynamics of Latino intolerance for homosexual men, in particular, take on a special significance in the United States. Here, traditional resources for enacting masculinity are limited by structures of inequality—racism and classism—which inhibit the Latino male's ability to express his manhood through the familial roles of provider and protector. Elevated rates of unemployment, underemployment, and impoverishment have meant that many of Mexican, Puerto Rican, or Cuban heritage, for example, continue to find that their ability to support a family is dramatically undermined (Feagin and Feagin, 1996). This predisposes them to judge harshly those who choose not to struggle beside them to preserve the family, and concomitantly, the culture.

If this holds true for Latino males, it is perhaps doubly true for African American men whose capacity to enact masculinity has been even more thoroughly circumscribed. Greene (1997) postulates that homophobia among African Americans may be more pronounced because it is multiply determined by sexism, Christian religiosity (especially Southern Baptist), and external and internalized racism. By virtue of their long experiences within a white Christian society, African Americans have also internalized the norms and values associated with white patriarchal notions of sexuality; yet by virtue of their class and race subordination, poor black male youths, in particular, do not have access to the resources by which they might "appropriately" enact acceptable gender-specific behavior.

Regardless of the varied conceptions of homosexuality across cultures, the dominant U.S. view has been shaped by the social and moral agenda of the Euro-Christian majority. Drawing on the English common law, the Colonial state determined that "what was sinful in the eyes of the church was illegal in the eyes of the state" (Biery, 1990:10). So it was that "sodomy" and "buggery" came to be seen as immoral acts and "crimes against nature."

While there are still proponents of the "homosexuality as sin" perspective, this religiously grounded view has been supplemented by the more "scientific" view of same-sex relations as disease. This interpretation "which also sees homosexuality as wrong and deviant, maintains that sexual acts are symptoms of a sickness. In contrast to the sin conception, the sickness view sees the desire to engage in homosexual activity inhering in the individual's identity"(Editors of the *Harvard Law Review*, 1990:4). It was this designation of "deviant" that facilitated the persistence of the criminalization and pathologizing of same-sex relations. Consequently, gay men and women were harassed, persecuted, and disempowered for their difference, and they continued to be marked as the sexual Other.

While it was science that labeled homosexuality as an illness, it was also science that began to break down the notion that homosexual behavior was abnormal. In 1948, Dr. Alfred Kinsey published the groundbreaking book *Sexual Behavior in the Human Male*. It was Kinsey's work which revealed that same-sex relationships and behaviors were far more common than had previously been imagined. His work suggested that more than one-third of all adult males had engaged in homosexual activity at least once, and that 10 to 12% of the general population saw themselves as homosexual.

Kinsey's research was one among many factors that enabled an emerging gay and lesbian movement to systematically challenge the dominant negative perceptions of same-sex relations. The cause was furthered by the broader momentum of the civil rights and women's rights movements of the 1960s. Gay activists came to share in the demand for a revolutionary vision of U.S. democracy. While the gay rights movement has been very effective in establishing civil and legal rights, gay men and lesbians continue to struggle against the persistence of stigmatizing stereotypes, legal persecution, and violent victimization.

ANTI-GAY MYTHOLOGY

Contemporary imagery and stereotypes surrounding gay men and women often resurrect the historical construction of homosexuality as sin and illness. Former Oklahoma City Representative Graves openly stated his repulsion of gays. He claimed that he, like the "majority" of people, knows that "Gays are the reason for the AIDS plague." He added that "It is not the city's place to subsidize immorality. The next thing you know, why, we'll have paedophiles in day care" (NGLTF, 1994:31–34). More recently, gay men and lesbians were among those chastised by the evangelist Jerry Falwell as contributing to the terrorist attacks of September 11, 2001.

Graves' statement contains references to the three most egregious sins for which gays are held accountable: the spread of AIDS, ungodliness, and pedophilia. Similar sentiments abound in this culture. It is still possible, for example, to find evidence of publicly expressed views which mirror the generations-old words of Justice Blackstone, who set precedents for British and American interpretations of sodomy. In the early 1800s, and still in the opening years of the twenty-first century, there are public figures who would describe sodomy as "the infamous crime against nature," "a crime not fit to be named" (Blackstone, 1811:215). A 1973 Arkansas district court decision reiterated Blackstone's sentiments in much more graphic terms: "It will be unnecessary for us to set out the sordid testimony about the (alleged homosexual) act, which appeared so revolting to one of the two deputies sheriff . . . that he vomited thrice during the evening" (cited in Goldyn, 1981:34).

This was reinforced in 1993 when an Ohio Supreme Court judge—in a case of a gay man's parole violation—railed against the "evils" and "immorality" of homosexuality (NGLTF, 1994:34). The following was a standard response by Dallas District Court judge Jack Hampton, whose views on homosexuality were no secret:

> I don't care for queers cruising the streets picking up teen-age boys . . .
> I've got a teen-age boy . . . Those two guys wouldn't have been killed if
> they hadn't been cruising the streets picking up teen-age boys. (cited in
> Bissinger, 1995:82)

That such openly anti-gay slurs are not simply artifacts of an archaic past is evident in recent court decisions. In February 2002, Alabama former state Chief Justice Roy Moore denied a lesbian mother custody of her child based on the state's sodomy law, stating, "common law designates homosexuality as an inherent evil, and if a person openly engages in such a practice, that fact alone would render him or her an unfit parent" since it would have a "a destructive and seriously detrimental effect" on the child. He claimed that homosexuality is "abhorrent, immoral, detestable, a crime against nature." Finally, he stated that the government has the power "to prohibit conduct with physical penalties, such as confinement and even execution." George County, CA, judge Connie Glen Wilkerson similarly supported institutionalization of gays and lesbians in a March 2002 decision: "In my opinion, gays and lesbians should be put in some type of a mental institution."

An immutable stigma is applied to gay identity, which is perceived as a moral and physical threat to the public's well-being. By engaging in "unnatural" sexual behavior, gays are said to thwart God's law; they promote a "deviant lifestyle" to the young and pliable; they carry disease and degeneracy like rats carry the plague. Homosexuals of both sexes are perceived to be predatory and menacing. The unspoken threat is that they are gender traitors: gay men, because they have broken ranks with dominant males; lesbians, because they have rejected their wifely roles. Carefully arranged gender boundaries are uncomfortably blurred by homosexuality.

Given such pervasive negative sentiments, especially on the part of government officials, it is perhaps not surprising the gay men and lesbians still suffer considerable legal discrimination.

GAY MEN AND LESBIANS AS OFFENDERS

To an alarming extent, gay men and lesbians remain outside the law. Restrictions on their sexuality, relationships, and civil rights mean that gay men and women typically have not enjoyed the same freedoms as their heterosexual counterparts. This interventionist stance is in contrast to the practices of many other Western democratic nations. Canada's former prime minister Pierre Trudeau once claimed that the state "has no place in the bedrooms of the nation." Additionally, compare the national backlash to Hawaii's legalization of same-sex marriages to the normalization of such relationships in the Netherlands, or more recently, in Canada.

In 1992, Herek summarized the marginal legal status of gay men and lesbians at the time:

> Except in four states . . . and several dozen municipalities, discrimination on the basis of sexual orientation is not prohibited in employment, housing, or services. Gay relationships generally have no legal status, and lesbian and gay male parents often lose legal custody of their children when their homosexuality becomes knows . . . Nearly one half of the states outlaw private consenting homosexual acts and their right to do so was upheld by the U.S. Supreme Court in 1996. (1992:91)

Disturbingly little has changed in the 15 years since that statement. Only 20 states and the District of Columbia have initiated legislation barring discrimination on the basis of sexual orientation/identity. Only 11 states recognize any form of same-sex marriage or "civil unions." In contrast, most of the remaining states have in fact passed decidedly anti-gay marriage measures, including outright bans on same-sex marriage. This is very much in line with the federal Defense of Marriage Act, which said that no state is required to honor same-sex marriages performed in another state. The Act also sought to restrict how marriage may be defined or interpreted under federal law to "a legal union between one man and one woman as husband and wife." Finally, few states protect the absolute rights of gay men or lesbians to become foster parents or to adopt children—even those of their same-sex partner. Indeed, a handful of states ban such actions completely (NGLTF, online).

The one bright spot in terms of legal advances in gay rights would have to be the 2003 Supreme Court decision overturning states' sodomy legislation. Prior to this case, *Bowers v. Hardwick* was the most significant contemporary statement of the status and rights of gays (Editors of the *Harvard Law Review*, 1990; Leiser, 1997; Mohr, 1988). In that case, the court upheld the constitutionality of Georgia's sodomy statute. In his majority opinion, Chief Justice Warren Burger concluded that "To uphold that the act of homosexual sodomy is somehow protected as a fundamental right would be to cast aside millennia of moral teaching." With these words, he denied the legal right to private, consensual same-sex sodomy. Moreover, he reaffirmed the moral prescriptions against homosexuality as defined by Christian canons.

Until 1961, all states outlawed homosexual sodomy—and most classed it as a felony. Twenty states continued to criminalize same-sex sexual relations until the end of the twentieth century, referring to them variously as "sodomy," "unnatural intercourse," "deviate sexual conduct," "sexual misconduct," "unnatural and lascivious acts," and "crimes against nature." Significantly, such restrictions were struck down federally in 2003 by the Supreme Court in the case of *Lawrence* v. *Texas*. In that case, the Court voted 6 to 3 that a Texas sodomy law banning anal and oral sex *if performed by two same-sex persons* was unconstitutional. Speaking for the majority, Justice Anthony Kennedy said that gays were "entitled to respect for their private lives. The state cannot demean their existence or control their destiny by making their private sexual conduct a crime." Even one of the dissenters, Justice Clarence Thomas, referred to the Texas legislation as "uncommonly silly." He further stated that "Punishing someone for expressing his sexual preference through noncommercial consensual conduct with another adult does not appear to be a worthy way to expend valuable law enforcement resources." While the case specifically involved a Texas statute, the broader effect was to render invalid the remaining sodomy statutes in 13 other states.

While prosecutions under these various statutes were rare, their presence nonetheless has historically had a dramatic impact on gay men and lesbians. Symbolically, this legislation, and the terminology used, both marginalizes and stigmatizes a whole community. They send the message that same-sex activity is "unnatural," "deviant," and not to be tolerated. At the practical level, these laws are "frequently invoked to justify other types of discrimination against lesbians and gay men on the ground that they are presumed to violate these statutes" (Editors of the *Harvard Law Review,* 1990:11). So, for example, the "criminality" of gay men or lesbians has been used to refuse parental rights, or the right to adopt, or the right to marry. The legally ambiguous status of gay men and women can even be invoked as a means of denying them freedom from discrimination in employment and job benefits (e.g., domestic partner benefits).

As noted earlier, sodomy statutes were rarely enforced. In 1990, for example, 150 lesbians and gay men were arrested under such legislation; fewer still were eventually charged or convicted (Singer and Deschamps, 1994). Much more likely to be enforced are sexual solicitation laws (Editors of *Harvard Law Review,* 1990; Mohr, 1988). The Editors of the *Harvard Law Review* (1990) imply that solicitation laws are more zealously employed against gay men, in particular, than against heterosexual men or women, and often constitute entrapment. Police officers may haunt gay bars or cruise gay parks, specifically seeking suspects who by word or deed appear to be soliciting illegal, but nonetheless non-commercial, consensual same-sex sexual activity.

The regulation of public sex has become particularly pronounced in the current era, thanks largely to the emergence of AIDS as a public health issue. While AIDS is not only a gay disease, gay men are certainly an at-risk group, and are publicly perceived to be the predominant carriers. Consequently, New York City, for example, has become the site of a crusade against commercial sex establishments (e.g., bathhouses) and public sex of all kinds—with the result that such locations and behaviors are becoming heavily policed under both the criminal and public health laws. Consequently, "regulatory laws collapse public sex with unsafe sex, promiscuity with the spread of HIV, and legality with public health" (Dangerous Bedfellows, 1996:17).

Ultimately, the persistent criminalization of homosexual behavior leaves gay men and lesbians vulnerable to public and private persecution. This is especially evident in the contemporary patterns of violence against gay men and lesbians.

ANTI-GAY VICTIMIZATION

What are ya', a fag? Come on sissy, fight me. Don't touch me, ya' homo!

Such are the epithets teenagers thoughtlessly hurl against friends and foes alike in their less enlightened adolescent years. Yet, for many, the underlying message—that homosexuality is an inherently undesirable identity—remains, and may in fact reemerge in much more violent ways. It is important to note at the outset that violence against homosexuals is not a new problem (Bensinger, 1992). Historically, it has been a legally sanctioned policy, as in the Medieval Europe or the colonial United States, where sodomy was punishable by various forms of mutilation, or even death. Homosexuals were imprisoned and exterminated alongside German Jews in Nazi death camps. Some American "liberators," noting the pink triangles worn by gay men in the camps, returned the "deviants" to their prisons in sympathy with the Nazis' intentions (Herek and Berrill, 1992:1).

This community continues to suffer as victims of violence, harassment, and hatred. It is difficult, however, to determine the extent of change in hate and bias crimes directed against gays and lesbians. In spite of the federal Hate Crime Statistics Act of 1990, systematic nationwide data on which to base such judgments do not exist. Data from the National Gay and Lesbian Task Force (NGLTF), National Coalition of Anti-Violence Projects (NCAVP, formerly the New York City Gay and Lesbian Anti-Violence Project), and police department bias units across the country all documented dramatic increases over the last two decades of the twentieth century (Berrill, 1993; Jenness, 1995). However, it is not at all clear whether this reflects a "real" increase in such violence or a greater willingness to report victimization.

Nonetheless, together, data from the Uniform Crime Report, from NGLTF reports, and from other regional and national victimization surveys paint a disturbing picture of widespread violence against gay men and women. Victimization surveys, for example, consistently find upwards of 60%—often as high as 80 or 90%—of subjects experiencing verbal abuse, and physical abuse is as high as 30%. Moreover, rates of victimization and the proportion of victimizations involving assaultive offences, are dramatically higher than for the general population (Berrill, 1992, 1993; Kuehnle and Sullivan, 2001).

Attacks against homosexuals tend to be among the most brutal acts of hatred. They often involve severe beatings, torture, mutilation, castration, and even sexual assault. They are also very likely to result in death (Comstock, 1991; Levin and McDevitt, 1993). This feature of violence against gays may account for its emergence as a recognizable social problem, worthy of public attention. Jenness's (1995) examination of gay and lesbian anti-violence projects seems to support this contention, in that many of the groups were initiated in response to particularly dramatic cases.

What accounts for the persistence of violence against gays? Perhaps a consideration of the common traits shared by its perpetrators provides some insight. Consistently, the data show that they are "predominantly ordinary young men" (Comstock, 1991:2; Hamm, 1994). In particular, they are young white men or adolescents, often from working-class or middle-class backgrounds (Berk, Boyd, and Hamner, 1992; Berrill, 1992; Hamm, 1994). Anti-gay violence, then, may serve to define, regulate, and express sexuality, masculine sexuality in particular. Acts of violence perpetrated against gays serve to reaffirm gendered hierarchies by asserting the superiority and strength of the perpetrators, while sanctioning those seen to violate the standard gender and sexual boundaries.

Violence against lesbians appears to be less pervasive than violence against gay men. To be sure, they are often victims of homophobic violence, but at a much lower rate than gay males (Berrill, 1992; Comstock, 1991; National Gay and Lesbian Task Force, 1992, 1993, 1994). Berrill (1992:28) identifies several pragmatic reasons why lesbians may appear to be at lower risk of victimization: the fact that men, in general, are at a greater risk of violence; the higher visibility of gay men as opposed to gay women; the earlier recognition and outing of gay men; gay women's greater tendency to alter behavior, and therefore vulnerability to assault; and the difficulty in distinguishing anti-woman violence from anti-lesbian violence.

von Schulthess's (1992; see also Thomson and Mason, 2001) study of anti-lesbian violence in San Francisco reveals close links between anti-woman and anti-lesbian violence. In fact, she argues that anti-lesbian violence is an extension of misogynistic sentiment generally. Thus the two are difficult to untangle. Nonetheless, once identified as gay, lesbians are subject to similar social censure. Pharr (1988:181) reminds us that "To be a lesbian is to be *perceived* as someone who has stepped out of line, who has moved out of sexual/economic dependence on a male, who is woman identified." Yet it may also be the case that the gender hierarchy demands somewhat greater conformity of men than of women (Connell, 1987). That is, challenges to masculinity are more likely to elicit negative social sanctions than are similar challenges to femininity. "(N)o pressure is set up to negate or subordinate other forms of femininity in the way hegemonic masculinity must negate other masculinities" (Connell, 1987:187). Gay men, on the other hand, threaten the very fiber of the gender hierarchy. Their violations touch the basic assumptions on which the hierarchy is predicated: that of the primacy of the heterosexual male.

Nationwide, anti-gay ballot initiatives, especially during the 1990s, played on all of the fears and stereotypes mentioned earlier—of sexual predators, of disease carriers, of destroyers of families—in their calls for the denial of civil protections for gays. Oregon, Maine, Arizona, and Florida are among those states which have been the sites of bitter political campaigns oriented around the prevention or repeal of what Far Right representatives have inaccurately termed "special rights" for gay men and lesbians. The anti-gay rhetoric at the heart of these explicitly political campaigns has fanned the flames of homophobia:

> Far Right operatives created an atmosphere of loathing and contempt for lesbian, gay and bisexual people by poisoning communities with rhetoric and misinformation that vilify and demonize lesbians, gay men and bisexuals as sexual predators and undeserving of basic human rights and protections against discrimination . . . (They) portrayed gay people as degenerate, un-American, privileged, sexually perverse and subhuman. (NGLTF, 1994:16–17)

The first of such campaigns was perhaps the most vicious in its assaults on gays. The 1992 Oregon measure explicitly defined homosexuality as "abnormal, wrong, unnatural, and perverse" (Moritz, 1995:57). Moreover, its very title, "Minority Status and Child Protection Act," openly equates homosexuality with pedophilia. During Colorado's campaign in the same year, Pastor Pete Peters—on the basis of his Scriptural interpretation—called for the death penalty for gays. Concerned Maine Families, the primary sponsor of the Maine anti-gay initiative, explicitly vilified homosexuals as pedophiles and as the transmitters of AIDS.

There is ample evidence that some citizens took these threats seriously. The NGLTF (1994) documented a frightening increase in violence against gays corresponding to Colorado's November 1992 initiative. Similarly, Maine's Attorney General logged elevated numbers of attacks on homosexuals in that state, leading up to the November 1995 vote (Maine Attorney General Office, Personal communication, February 1996). Interestingly, the opposite appears to hold true as well. When such initiatives and their surrounding vitriol are absent, hate crime also declines. The 2007 report on *Anti-Lesbian, Gay, Bisexual, And Transgender Violence in 2006* from the National Coalition of Anti-Violence Projects (NCAVP) observed that "the relative and ongoing lull in anti-LGBT rhetoric from the political and cultural arenas had a profound effect on violence against LGBT people in both 2005 and 2006" (NCAVP, 2007:2). Consequently, 2006 saw the first decrease in reported incidents of hate crime against gay and lesbian people in some time.

In part, then, the elevated rates of violence against gays in recent years may be a reaction to their increasing visibility and activism. Similarly, the emergence and spread of AIDS—originally called GRIDS (Gay Related Immune Deficiency Syndrome)—has drawn negative attention toward the community. The association of AIDS and HIV with gay men provides yet another justification—not cause—for already existing homophobia. Just as gay activism elicits a violent response, so too does the presence of AIDS. Berrill (1992:38) cites the Presidential Commission on the Human Immunodeficiency Virus Epidemic in support of this contention:

> Increasing violence against those perceived to carry HIV, so called hate crimes, are a serious problem. The commission has heard reports in which gay men in particular have been victims of violent acts that are indicative of a society that is not yet reacting rationally to the epidemic.

National Gay and Lesbian Task Force Reports (NGLTF, 1994, 1995) as well as NCAVP annual reports support the link between anti-gay violence and HIV. Their data reveal that violence against people with AIDS or HIV is increasingly widespread. Individual victims are often assaulted and taunted with such labels as "AIDS faggot" or "plague-carrying faggot." AIDS service providers are also often victimized, as in the case of a Burlington, VT, organization whose building was burned down.

As is the case with other minority victims of crime, gay victims are reluctant to report their experiences to police. In particular, they are reluctant to come forward because of their fear of secondary victimization, which occurs when "others respond negatively to a crime survivor because of his or her sexual orientation" (Berrill and Herek, 1992:289). If the victims are not yet out as gay, they may fear disclosure to friends, family, co-workers, or employers. Given the paucity of anti-discrimination laws protecting gay men and lesbians, this disclosure could very well lead to loss of job, housing, or child custody. It could result in violence as well. Moreover, gay victims may legitimately fear violence at the hands of police. Distrust of law enforcement agents is another factor which gays often share with other minority groups, given the history of police intolerance for gay men and lesbians (Leinen, 1993). Gay men and lesbians are mindful of police harassment, extortion, and beatings of gay victims. Evidence suggests that such fears are warranted. For example, the 2007 report of the NCAVP found that "victims described law enforcement response as 'courteous' 49% of the time, 'indifferent' 34% of the time, verbally abusive 11% of the time, and physically abusive 6% of the time" (NCAVP, 2007:13). This reflects a very high ratio of abusive behavior on the part of police.

Gay victims of crime may also fear the courtroom experience. Judicial statements noted above—about the "unnaturalness" of homosexuality—remind victims that they may not receive a sympathetic hearing. Moreover, recent years have seen increasing use of the homosexual panic defense, whereby perpetrators of violence posit their fear of a homosexual advance as a mitigating circumstance in the assault. It is, oddly, presented as a form of self-defense. Symbolically, such a defense reaffirms the broader cultural stereotype of gay men and women as sexual predators (Berrill and Herek, 1992). You may recall the homicide of a young gay male who had appeared on a nationally televised talk show to proclaim his "crush" on the straight male. The latter claimed to have murdered out of shame and embarrassment at having been identified as the object of a gay man's affection.

Neither primary nor secondary victimization of gay men and women will be eliminated in the absence of concentrated efforts to counter the homophobia and heterosexism that motivate such violence. We turn now to a consideration of criminal justice interventions that may play a role in enhancing the status and role of gay men and lesbians, and which serve the needs of this community.

SERVICE PROVISION

As long as the sexuality of gay men and women continues to be criminalized and stigmatized, they will be beyond the protection of the criminal justice system. Consequently, the primary mechanism for eliminating legal and, indirectly, illegal victimization of gay people will be to decriminalize sodomy, same-sex solicitation, and same-sex sexual activities. However, this will not occur in a vacuum, but within the context of broader initiatives intended to ensure the realization of the civil and legal rights of all gay men and women.

It may appear paradoxical to expect change of this kind to occur on the "front-lines," that is, within police organizations. Police departments remain militaristic organizations, whose officers are expected to symbolize the essence of aggression and "manliness." Gay men, in particular, are erroneously assumed to be the antithesis of this—weak and effeminate. Resistance grounded in this perceived contradiction is exaggerated by the corollary fact that "police also tend to see themselves as upholders of society's social and moral order and to view homosexuals as a serious threat to that order" (Leinen, 1993:xi). Consequently, gay men and women who do decide to join the force face a serious dilemma: remain closeted and thus lead a double life; or come out and risk harassment, or restricted promotions (Burkhe, 1996; Leinen, 1993).

In spite of all this, increasing numbers of gay men and women are opting for careers in law enforcement. In fact, some cities with especially large and visible gay communities—New York City and San Francisco, for example—have begun to actively recruit gay and lesbian officers (Burkhe, 1996; Leinen, 1993). As the numbers of openly gay officers increase, support organizations are also emerging in the law enforcement community. Among these are such gay police fraternal organizations as the Society of Law Officers (SOLO) in San Diego, the Golden State Peace Officers Association based in Los Angeles, the Lesbian and Gay Police Association in Chicago, and the nation-wide Gay Officers Action League (GOAL).

It is not just personnel within the criminal justice system who benefit from service organizations. Victims and alleged offenders also warrant special attention. As an outgrowth of the emergence of a viable gay rights movement, recent years have seen the parallel development of gay rights organizations (Jenness, 1997). As Wertheimer (1992:229) proclaims,

> . . . the lesbian and gay community has taken upon itself the tasks of identifying and defining the problem of violence against its members, providing appropriate services to individuals in need, and working to heal the injuries that violence can create in the larger community.

Such bodies serve two primary roles, relevant to the current context: lobbying for the elimination of discriminatory laws and practice (e.g., ACLU Lesbian and Gay Rights Project, Lambda Legal Defense and Education Fund); and monitoring and responding to anti-gay violence (e.g., New York City Gay and Lesbian Anti-Violence Project). Consequently, they are important actors, working in the interests of both criminalized and victimized gays.

Virtually every community with an identifiable gay presence—even college campuses—hosts a gay and lesbian coalition of some kind. Jenness (1995) catalogs a number of these organizations, and the role they have played in constructing violence against gays and lesbians as a social problem. However, the most active and visible of such organizations at the national level is the National Gay and Lesbian Task Force. Since 1973, NGLTF has been actively gathering data on the extent, nature, and dynamics of hate crime. Moreover, the organization acts as a clearinghouse for information on anti-gay violence. As the NGLTF Mission Statement asserts, this body addresses the full range of anti-gay initiatives outlined in this chapter:

> Since its inception, NGLTF has been at the forefront of every major initiative for lesbian, gay, bisexual and transgender rights . . . NGLTF is the front line activist organization in the national gay and lesbian movement. As such, it serves as the national resource center for grassroots lesbian, gay, bisexual and transgender organizations that are facing a variety of battles at the state and local level—such as combating anti-gay violence, battling Radical Right anti-gay legislative and ballot measures, advocating an end to job discrimination, working to repeal sodomy laws, demanding an effective governmental response to HIV and reform of the health care system and much more. (NGLTF)

As history attests, the grassroots and national activities of gay-rights organizations will be crucial to the continuing recognition of gay men and lesbians as a vital part of the broader community. In light of widespread misunderstandings and misperceptions of what it is to be gay, this cultural group must overcome similar barriers to those faced by racial and ethnic minorities throughout the history of the United States. That will require ongoing and persistent mobilization for changes in attitude and policy alike.

References

Almaguer, Tomás. 1995. Chicano Men: A Cartography of Homosexual Identity and Behavior. In *Men's Lives*, ed. Michael Kimmel and Michael Messner, 418–431. Boston, MA: Allyn and Bacon.

Bensinger, Gad. 1992. Hate Crime: A New/Old Problem. *International Journal of Comparative and Applied Criminal Justice* 16: 115–123.

Berk, Richard, Elizabeth Boyd, and Karl Hamner. 1992. Thinking More Clearly About Hate-Motivated Crimes. In *Hate Crimes: Confronting Violence Against Lesbians and Gay Men*, ed. Gregory Herek and Kevin Berrill, 123–143. Newbury Park, CA: Sage Publications.

Berrill, Kevin. 1992. Anti-Gay Violence and Victimization in the United States: An Overview. In *Hate Crimes: Confronting Violence Against Lesbians and Gay Men*, ed. Gregory Herek and Kevin Berrill, 19–45. Newbury Park, CA: Sage Publications.

Berrill, Kevin. 1993. Anti-Gay Violence: Causes, Consequences and Responses. In *Bias Crime: American Law Enforcement and Legal Responses*, ed. Robert Kelly, 151–164. Chicago: Office of International Criminal Justice.

Berrill, Kevin, and Gregory Herek. 1992. Primary and Secondary Victimization in Anti-Gay Hate Crimes: Official Responses and Public Policy. In *Hate Crimes: Confronting Violence Against Lesbians and Gay Men*, ed. Gregory Herek and Kevin Berrill, 289–305. Newbury Park, CA: Sage Publications.

Biery, Roger. 1990. *Understanding Homosexuality*. Austin, TX: Edward-William Publishing.

Bissinger, H. G. 1995. The Killing Trial. *Vanity Fair*, (February): 84–88; 142–145.

Blackstone, William. 1811. *Commentaries on the Laws of England*, Vol. 4. London: William Reed.

Burkhe, Robin. 1996. *A Matter of Justice: Lesbians and Gay Men in Law Enforcement*. New York, NY: Routledge.

Comstock, Gary. 1991. *Violence Against Lesbians and Gay Men*. New York, NY: Columbia University Press.

Connell, Robert. 1987. *Gender and Power*. Stanford, CA: Stanford University Press.

Dangerous Bedfellows. 1996. Introduction. In *Policing Public Sex*, ed. Ephen Glenn Colter, Wayne Hoffman, Eva Pendleton, Alison Redick, and David Serlin. Boston, MA: South End Press.

Editors of the *Harvard Law Review*. 1990. *Sexual Orientation and the Law*. Cambridge, MA: Harvard University Press.

Feagin, Joe, and Clarice Booher Feagin. 1996. *Racial and Ethnic Relations*. Upper Saddle River, NJ: Prentice-Hall.

Goldyn, Lawrence. 1981. Gratuitous Language in Appellate Cases Involving Gay People: Queer-baiting From the Bench. *Political Behavior* 3 (1): 31–48.

Greene, Beverly. 1997. Ethnic Minority Lesbians and Gay Men: Mental Health and Treatment Issues. In *Ethnic and Cultural Diversity Among Lesbians and Gay Men*, ed. Beverly Greene, 216–239. Thousand Oaks, CA: Sage Publications.

Hamm, Mark. 1994. *American Skinheads*. Westport, CT: Praeger.

Herek, Gregory. 1992. The Social Context of Hate Crimes: Notes on Cultural Heterosexism. In *Hate Crimes: Confronting Violence Against Lesbians and Gay Men*, ed. Gregory Herek and Kevin Berrill, 89–104. Newbury Park, CA: Sage Publications.

Herek, Gregory, and Kevin Berrill. 1992. Introduction. In *Hate Crimes: Confronting Violence Against Lesbians and Gay Men*, ed. Gregory Herek and Kevin Berrill, 1–10. Newbury Park, CA: Sage Publications.

Jenness, Valerie. 1995. Social Movement Growth, Domain Expansion, and Framing Processes: The Gay/Lesbian Movement and Violence Against Gays and Lesbians as a Social Problem. *Social Problems* 42 (1): 145–170.

Jenness, Valerie. 1997. *Hate Crime: New Social Movements and the Politics of Violence*. New York, NY: Aldine de Gruyter.

Kuehnle, Kristen, and Anne Sullivan. 2001. Patterns of Anti-Gay Violence. *Journal of Interpersonal Violence* 16 (9): 928–943.

Leinen, Stephen. 1993. *Gay Cops*. New Brunswick, NJ: Rutgers University Press.

Leiser, Burton. 1997. Homosexuality and the Unnaturalness Argument. In *Sex, Morality and the Law*, ed. Lori Gruen and George Panichas, 44–51. New York, NY: Routledge.

Levin, Jack, and J. McDevitt. 1993. *Hate Crimes: The Rising Tide of Bigotry and Bloodshed*. New York, NY: Plenum Press.

Miller, Neil. 1995. *Out of the Past: Gay and Lesbian History from 1969 to the Present*. New York, NY: Vintage Press.

Mohr, Richard. 1988. *Gays/Justice*. New York, NY: Columbia University Press.

Moraga, Cherrie. 1996. Queer Aztlán: The Reformation of Chicano Tribe. In *The Material Queer*, ed. Donald Morton, 297–304. Boulder, CO: Westview Press.

Moritz, Marguerite J. 1995. The Gay Agenda: Marketing Hate Speech to Mainstream Media. In *Hate Speech*, ed. Rita Kirk Whillock and David Slayden, 55–79. Thousand Oaks, CA: Sage Publications.

NCAVP. 2007. Anti-Lesbian, Gay, Bisexual and Transgender Violence in 2006. New York: NCAVP.

NGLTForce. www.thetaskforce.org.

NGLTF. 1992. Anti-Gay/Lesbian Violence, Victimization and Defamation in 1991. Washington, DC: NGLTF Policy Institute.

NGLTF. 1993. Anti-Gay/Lesbian Violence, Victimization and Defamation in 1992. Washington, DC: NGLTF Policy Institute.

NGLTF. 1994. Anti-Gay/Lesbian Violence, Victimization and Defamation in 1993. Washington, DC: NGLTF Policy Institute.

NGLTF. 1995. Anti-Gay/Lesbian Violence, Victimization and Defamation in 1994. Washington, DC: NGLTF Policy Institute.

Pharr, Suzanne. 1988. *Homophobia: A Weapon of Sexism*. Inverness, CA: Chardon Press.

Singer, Bennett, and David Deschamps. 1994. *Gay and Lesbian Stats*. New York, NY: The New Press.

Tafoya, Terry. 1997. Native Gay and Lesbian Issues: Two Spirited. In *Ethnic and Cultural Diversity Among Lesbians and Gay Men*, ed. Beverly Greene, 1–10. Thousand Oaks, CA: Sage Publications.

Thomson, Stephen, and Gail Mason. 2001. Engendering Homophobia: Violence, Sexuality and Gender Conformity. *Journal of Sociology* 37 (3): 257–273.

von Schulthess, Beatrice. 1992. Violence in the Streets: Anti-Lesbian Assault and Harassment in San Francisco. In *Hate Crimes: Confronting Violence Against Lesbians and Gay Men*, ed. Gregory Herek and Kevin Berrill, 65–75. Newbury Park, CA: Sage Publications.

Wertheimer, David. 1992. Treatment and Service Intervention for Lesbian and Gay Male Crime Victims. In *Hate Crimes: Confronting Violence Against Lesbians and Gay Men*, ed. Gregory Herek and Kevin Berrill, 227–240. Newbury Park, CA: Sage Publications.

CHAPTER 13

Old Enough and Knowing Better
Aging and Criminal Justice

Carole Mandino

The criminal profession has its share of the elderly. Just as everyone ages in their profession, so do criminals. Many times, crime is all they know how to do for a living. Oftentimes, older people may be at the center of a crime organization, having worked their way up from doing crime to ordering crime. Local newspapers and national news reports oftentimes showcase senior criminal activity, perhaps as the occurrences are rare and catch a reporter's or editor's attention. Aging inmates, whether they be people sentenced to crimes for long periods of time, living out their days in prison, or those recently sent to prison, cost state and federal governments more than younger inmates due to their failing health and chronic diseases.

Because of the portrayal of the elderly as being frail and easily deceived, they have become prime targets of crime. Many elderly live alone and may suffer from loneliness, making them targets for phone frauds and other types of fraud. Today is much different from the era in which today's elderly grew up. Perhaps due to loneliness and isolation, or perhaps due to the elderly having more trust, they may be easy targets to cons. New con games and access to personal information through the Internet offer criminals more ways to scam the elderly. Beyond scams, the elderly also suffer abuse from others. Many frail or vulnerable elderly are physically unable to protect themselves from such abuse. Many are abused by people they know, while others are abused by personnel who are supposed to be providing them care. The physical abuse some elderly experience can be more severe depending on their medical condition. Furthermore, neglect is a serious abuse if the elderly person is unable to care for themselves. Psychological and financial abuse or exploitation may also have very devastating results to elderly victims.

In this chapter, discussion will center on elderly criminals, aging prisoners, elder abuse, and crime committed against the elderly.

WHO ARE THE ELDERLY?

An unprecedented shift in the demographics of the United States is occurring. As a result of medical advancement, the lowering of the infant mortality rate, decreasing birth rates and the baby boomers advancing in age, a larger portion of the population is classified as older adults (aged 60+). Average age in the United States in 1990 was 32.7 years. By the year 2050, it is predicted that the average age of the population will be 50 years. According to the Administration on Aging (AoA, 2006), those aged 65 and older numbered 36.8 million in 2005, or about one of every eight people (12.4% of the population) in the United States (Administration on Aging Fact Sheet). It is projected by the U.S. Census Bureau that from 2000 to 2050 there will be a projected increase of 147% of those aged 65 and over. Women outlive men; in the plus 65 age category, 58% are women, and 42% men (AoA, 2006). More women aged 65 and older are widowed than there are women married and living with their spouse. Only 4.5% of the elderly live in skilled nursing facilities (AoA, 2006); 81% own their own homes (U.S. Census Bureau, 2007). The median net worth of households with one member aged 65 or over is approximately $108,000.

As can be seen by the preceding figures, the population of the United States is growing older and crimes committed against and by the elderly may also increase.

ELDERLY CRIMINALS

Impossible as it may seem, the "nice" old man or woman down the street could be a criminal. Criminologists used to laugh at the thought of elderly criminals. In fact, it was gerontologists, or those who study aging, who brought out the issue of elderly offenders (Chaneles and Burnett, 1989).

While crime has historically been thought of as more of a youth-oriented issue from the stand point of criminals having to be strong, strength isn't the only characteristic needed to be a criminal. Just as with every other age group, one cannot tell a criminal by their looks or daily behavior. Arrest records are mostly dominated by those aged 16–24, and most offenders tend to quit committing crimes in their early to mid-thirties (Newman *et al.*, 1984). Younger adults are ten times more likely than the elderly to commit crimes (Barrow, 1996). Those aged 55 and older commit only 0.7% of violent crimes, such as murder or manslaughter, and just over 1.3% of rapes. They also commit fewer than 7% of crimes involving robbery, burglary, motor vehicle theft, and arson (Feldmeyer and Steffensmeier, 2007). Nonetheless, elderly criminals may be the heads of organized crime and can commit high payoff crimes. In *The Sting*, the character played by Paul Newman was a prototype of several real-life older criminals, one of which was Joseph Weil, last arrested when he was 72 years old.

Feldmeyer and Steffensmeier (2007) conducted a study that reviewed crimes committed by the elderly from 1980 to 2004. Results concluded that the elderly have the second lowest rates of arrests for crimes; only those aged 12 and under showed a smaller arrest rate. The elderly made up only 4% of those arrested for crimes in overall categories, with arrests being mostly for minor offenses such as alcohol law violations and disorderly offenses. While news reports and articles are written about elderly criminals, neither the rate of crimes committed by the elderly nor the seriousness of their crimes has increased. Feldmeyer and Steffensmeier (2007:317) state, ". . . the relative criminal involvement of the elderly is about the same now as 25 years ago; however, where noticeable change has occurred, the trend is a decline in proportionate criminal involvement of the elderly and a widening of the age gap in crime." They attribute this to the biological effects of aging, such as the decline in physical strength. Yet, not all crimes take physical strength, especially when committed against vulnerable people. They also believe that material attainment is not as important to elders as it is to younger generations. One conclusion Feldmeyer and Steffensmeier (2007) draw is that as the age of the population of the nation increases, there is likely to be less crime. How likely will this scenario ring true?

The elderly do make up a percentage of those arrested for driving under the influence (DUI), shoplifters, homicide offenders, sex offenders, and those arrested for elder abuse. Arrest rates for simple assault and drug violations have increased from 1980 to 2004 for those aged 55 and older (Feldmeyer and Steffensmeier, 2007). Let's take a quick look at each of the areas mentioned here.

Elderly and DUI

The majority of arrests of older adults are for DUI. Males with long-term substance abuse problems and histories of alcohol-related crimes are the most likely to be offenders in this category. Age-related theories, such as disengagement theory, suggest that because of social isolation, widowhood, illness, and the effects of limited incomes, many older adults may turn to substance abuse for their problems. However, most substance abuse offenders are those with long-term abuse problems that did not start in old age. Older adults make up only about 5% of DUI arrests (Newman *et al.*, 1984). However, arrest rates for those aged 55 and older shrank from being 195.9 per 100,000 elders in 1980 to 118.2 per 100,000 in 2004. Even though arrest rates have dropped for DUI, it is still the highest-rated offense committed by those aged 55 and over. Furthermore, arrests for drug violations increased from 7.9 per 100,000 elders in 1980 to 37 per 100,000 elders in 2004 (Feldmeyer and Steffensmeier, 2007). This increase may be linked to the elderly selling prescription drug medication to addicts (Elder Law Prof Blog, 2005).

Elderly and Shoplifting

Larceny dominates the field of those aged 55 and older who commit crimes. Shoplifting fits under the general category of larceny. Although shoplifting may be thought of by some as a crime committed by more females than males, "with increasing age there is no difference between the proportion of men and the proportion of women among the elderly shoplifting population" (Newman *et al.*, 1984). Interestingly, shoplifting is a crime that seems to increase with age. Shoplifting amongst the elderly is not always in proportion to income as would be largely thought. More of those who are middle-income earners tend to be shoplifters than those who are lower-income earners. Items shoplifted are not for sustenance of life but considered more to be extra items such as clothing and cosmetics. Increases in shoplifting in the elderly may be due to the ease with which it can be completed—it doesn't take strength or physical agility, it may only take opportunity. Brogden and Nijhar (2000:130) state, "It may be that such relatively petty activities are due to the gradual retirement of career criminals as they descend from more serious to less serious crimes, a result of ageing."

It is also often thought that the elderly have memory loss and forget to pay for the item they shoplift. However, in 48% of incidences reported, more than one item was taken, negating forgetfulness. When asked, 75% of the elderly respondents knew they were guilty of shoplifting.

Elderly and Homicide

The elderly commit fewer and different types of homicides than younger offenders. In fact, homicide rates for elder offenders have declined from 1980 to 2004 (Feldmeyer and Steffensmeier, 2007; Rothman *et al.*, 2000). Sex and race are factors that must be taken into account when looking at elderly offenders. Elderly white females account for approximately one-tenth of 1% of all elderly committed homicides, while African American males are the highest offenders in this age category (Newman *et al.*, 1984; Rothman *et al.*, 2000). One must remember that the elderly commit less than 1% of all homicides in the country. Often, these homicides are a form of euthanasia, committed when a spouse is suffering from prolonged illness or incapacitation. Another factor that may affect elder homicide rates are the biological changes that take place in aging or changes that occur as part of a disease or consequences/side affects of prescription medication. They may have low tolerance and produce aggression. Still other factors affecting elderly homicide offenses may be social factors such as isolation, disengagement, financial stress, vulnerability, dependency, and so on (Rothman *et al.*, 2000).

Most homicide offenses by elderly offenders are committed against family members, disproportionately compared to other age groups; most offenses occur in residences by means of firearms. Studies found that most elderly homicide offenders committed the crime while in an altercation with the victim and while under the influence of alcohol. Only 9% committed suicide after committing homicide (Rothman *et al.*, 2000).

Elderly and Sex Offenses

"Dirty old man" is an ageist phrase often associated with the elderly. It is believed that sex offenses involving children are a common crime with older adults, usually by first-time offenders (Newman *et al.*, 1984). Grandparent figures tend to be trusted by young children who may be unable to defend themselves.

Elderly sex offenders usually engage in more passive sexual activity and rarely use force against their victims. Offenses are commonly committed in the home of the victims as the offenders may be friends of the victim's parents. Occasionally, offenses also occur within day care facilities, which can be either in a large commercial setting or within a private home. Only about 1% of elderly sex offenders serve any prison time for their crime.

More often than not, elderly persons convicted for the first time are usually sexual offenders. Jonathon Turley, Professor of Law at George Washington University Law School and the founder of the Project for Older Prisoners (POPS), states that "child molestation is unique in that while other types of crime fall away as people age, child molestation remains a certain constant" (Bowers, 1996). Of those arrested for rape, the elderly comprise about 5%, and for other sex offenses (exposure, decency), the elderly represent 10% (Rothman *et al.*, 2000). There are a disproportionately large amount of older sex offenders who occupy our prisons and are on probation; about one-third of prisoners aged 55 and older are serving sentences for sex offenses, while as many as 53% of probationers aged 55 and older are on probation for sex offenses (Rothman *et al.*, 2000; Wahidin *et al.*, 2006).

THE INCARCERATED ELDERLY

The population of today's prisons is changing. With tougher sentencing mandates, more time is being spent behind bars. Longer sentences beget an aging prison population. Many prisoners are middle aged, while some are in their 60s and 70s. Between 1996 to 2000 the elderly population in prison changed. In 1996 approximately 3% of the prison population was age 55 and older, while in 2000 that figure rose to 7% of the prison population. (Mergenhagen, 1996; Rothman *et al.*, 2000). The number of prisoners who are aged 55 or older rose from 9,000 in 1986 to over 30,000 in 1996. Loosely defined, older prisoners are those 50 and older.

Most women aged 50 and older are incarcerated for offenses such as violence against others and drug-related offenses. Men are more commonly incarcerated for violence against others, sexual offenses, or drug offenses. Demographics show that the majority of older prisoners are white males, followed closely by African, Latin, and Native Americans (Rothman *et al.*, 2000).

Older prisoners are more costly to care for, estimated to cost more than $2 billion per year. Older inmates, as with older non-prisoners, suffer from chronic diseases and diseases associated with age such as Alzheimer's disease and cardiovascular-related diseases. Older prisoners may have more than one medical condition and may require between 7 and 10 prescription medications for their conditions (Rothman *et al.*, 2000). Individually, inmates aged 55 and over cost approximately $69,000 to imprison (Coalition for Federal Sentencing, 1998). In the future, states may need to set up geriatric care units within prison facilities as the option of sending elderly prisoners into conventional nursing homes does not always work. There are only a limited number of beds and not all nursing homes are willing to take in prison inmates.

Although more research is needed regarding the causes of recidivism, the likelihood of committing new offenses is reduced as a person ages. However, not everyone fits this mold, and those who are convicted for crimes committed when they are older are less likely to be reformed. Each case needs to be viewed individually.

Colorado's Territorial Prison developed a hospice program for terminally ill inmates. More than 12 inmates went through the hospice program, although not all were elderly. As the infirmary at Territorial cannot maintain life-support systems, inmates needing such are sent to nearby private hospitals. In 1996, the Utah Legislation required the Utah Department of Corrections to develop a plan to provide for medical care and mental health, grief, and family support for the incarcerated frail elderly and the terminally ill, keeping in mind the economic practicality of imprisoning the elderly (Baird, 1996). With the elderly, who as a whole are not likely to reoffend, is it wise to spend extra dollars to keep them incarcerated? As Jonathon Turley points out, "the simple fact is that our prison population is graying and prisons make perfectly horrible nursing homes" (Bowers, 1996).

CRIMES COMMITTED AGAINST THE ELDERLY

Elder Abuse

What exactly constitutes elder abuse? Physical abuse includes the intentional use of physical force, or infliction of pain or injury including beating, pushing, choking, burning, restraining, sexual abuse or assault, slapping, hitting, forced feeding, and physical neglect. Physical abuse may cause bruises, broken bones, bed sores, internal bleeding, complications to existing conditions, and pain.

Psychological or mental abuse is conduct that causes mental anguish. Abuses can include verbal assaults, threats, intimidation, humiliation, and isolation. Results from psychological or mental abuse may include confusion or disorientation, embarrassment, shame, loss of self–respect, and/or loss of dignity. Psychological abuse is about control.

The failure of the caregiver to provide the basics of life constitutes *neglect.* The denial of food, shelter, or necessary health or dental care may be included as neglect. Neglect may be intentional, such as withholding food, or unintentional, simply not being able to provide food or shelter. Neglect is the most common form of abuse (Barrow, 1996).

Self-abuse or *neglect,* while not a crime, is the elderly person's failure to give proper care, either intentionally or unintentionally, to themselves. Results could be lack of proper clothing or shelter, weight loss, or improper health or dental care. When investigating neglect, authorities may need to be cautious in determining whether the person committed self-neglect or whether neglect was committed against the individual. An elderly person deserted by their custodian or caregiver is a crime of abandonment (National Center on Elder Abuse, 2007).

Illegally or improperly misusing or mismanaging funds, property, or other resources of another resulting in the personal gain of either a financial advisor, caretaker, or family member or a con artist comprises *financial exploitation* or *abuse.* Financial exploitation can result in the loss of independence for a senior if they have lost their home or their financial freedom.

Personal freedom includes the right to personal space and to freedom of movement. Restraining someone to their bed or to only a closet or room may violate their personal freedom. Elderly persons, like all others, should be able to feel safe in the home in which they live.

Physical and/or mental abuse affects over 1 million elderly each year. However, it is thought that approximately only one in six cases of elder abuse is reported. Those who are being abused may not be able to report the abuse or may be embarrassed to report the abuse. The most likely abusers are family members or caretakers. Within the family structure, the most likely to commit abuse are sons (21%), daughters (17%), followed by spouses, and other family members (e.g., grandchildren, siblings) and caretakers (LaRue, 1992). Females are the most likely victims to be abused.

Stress is one factor contributing to a family member committing abuse against an older family member. Stress may be due to the loss of income or may be due to taking care of an incapacitated elder. Resistance may be lower when there is financial strain, thus increasing the odds of abuse (Wolf, 1996). Stress can also contribute to emotions being out of control and can be expressed by violence or intimidation or withdrawal of love, support, or communication. A family history of violence or revenge for violence that occurred by the elder to the caretaker in the past may also contribute to physical or mental abuse. (The cycle of violence theory has not been confirmed in elder abuse cases; see Wolf, 1996). Other factors which may contribute to physical and/or mental abuse may include strained family ties, addiction to alcohol or drugs, and/or psychiatric illnesses. While not making it right, the strain of taking care of an elder person compounded with the isolation this may bring may be another cause of the abuse. Those abused may be reluctant to report the abuse due to shame, dignity, the fear of being placed in a nursing home or fear of retaliation from the abuser, or may feel some of the blame for the abuse. It is estimated that elder abuse is reported only in 1 in 14 incidences (National Center on Elder Abuse, 2007).

Mandatory reporting doesn't always solve the problem of elder abuse. Help may be administered through professional counseling for the family or through providing respite care for the main caretakers. Having knowledge of their rights helps the abused know when things are wrong (LaRue, 1992). Police must be sensitive to elder abuse and need to be aware that arresting the abuser may mean placing the victim in a nursing home (Plotkin, 1996). In many cases, Adult Protective Services (APS) workers may be the best at assessing what course of action to follow and may be best equipped to respond to the victim's needs.

Abuse also happens within nursing institutions, private group homes, and other long-term care facilities. Abuse is not always easy to detect and usually occurs when family members or other staff are not present. Abuse in institutions may include such things as unsanitary conditions, dental or medical neglect, overmedication or oversedation, the use of psychotropic drugs to quiet patients, physical mistreatment or abuse, utilization of physical restraints, the lack of proper nutrition or stimulation, and sexual abuse.

Workers in such institutions may be overworked and underpaid. Most states require background checks on workers in such facilities; however, if reports of abuse weren't filed, background checks will not pick up this information. Job demands may be demeaning, such as emptying bed pans, turning and bathing patients, or feeding patients. Many times, the abuse may not be intentional, such as improper feeding techniques, but happens nonetheless. If patients are not properly cared for or are neglected, bed sores may develop and become problematic. Also called pressure sores, if not treated properly or within a certain time frame, they can require surgery, cause irreversible damage, or become life threatening.

Patients cannot always eat as quickly as a caregiver would like or may not be able to feed themselves. If caregivers do not spend the proper time feeding the patient and neglect the patients need to be fed, drastic weight loss may occur, which may be life threatening. Severe dehydration can also be problematic and a form of neglect or abuse if the patient is not supplied with water or the means to obtain such. Oftentimes because patients may be incontinent, workers do not want to give them water as they may have to change them more often if the patient is fully hydrated (Harter and Nichols, 1997).

Many times, it is very hard to press charges against care facilities. It is difficult to prove intent and sometimes the witnesses (the patients) have already died or are unable to be reliable witnesses as they may be too afraid or confused. Death certificates identify only the major cause of death and rarely list dehydration or bed sores as causes (Harter and Nichols, 1997).

Workers and care homes are not the only ones to blame. Many times, families abandon their incapacitated elders after putting them in institutions. Time constraints and the inability to communicate with the elderly are poor excuses used by family members who abandon their elderly members.

Neglect is still the largest form of abuse, from private homes to care homes, with 58.5% of all cases falling in this category. Physical abuse accounts for 15.7% of reported cases, followed by financial exploitation (12.3%), psychological, emotional, or mental abuse (7.3%), and other forms of abuse (6.2%) (Harter and Nichols, 1997).

Prevention of elder abuse is on the rise. There are many agencies and organizations that can help the abused and the abuser. Prevention programs are more prevalent, with background checks being mandatory in most states. Training for staff and caretakers is also given more frequently. However, the number of elderly is expected to rise tremendously in the future, with those in the 85-and-older age category showing the largest percentage of growth. With the increase in the number of women in the workforce and with many families with two wage earners this may lead to many more elderly being institutionalized or receiving care from someone coming into their home, which could lead to more elder abuse (LaRue, 1992).

OTHER CRIMES COMMITTED AGAINST THE ELDERLY

Many elderly have a great fear of crime, so much so that one would believe that crime affects the elderly more so than the young. However, the elderly are less likely to be victims of crime than those who are younger. Violent crimes such as rape, robbery, and assault affect those who are younger more frequently than those who are older. Purse snatching occurs more frequently to older victims. While 33 million elderly persons make up the population of the United States, only about 2% of them fall victim to crime (Bureau of Justice Statistics, 1994). Older adults have more than a trillion dollars in assets and many scam artists are aware that the elderly, as a group, have money (West, 1998).

As with all age groups, the elderly cannot be thought of as homogeneous. Some fear crime more than others. Those elderly with the highest fear of crime are females, followed by those who have low income. African Americans, city dwellers, those who are physically challenged, and those who are socially isolated follow (McCoy, 1996).

Victimization of elderly persons is more frequent near where the older victim resides. Older adults tend to stay closer to home when shopping and tend to stay at home in the evenings. They also tend to avoid dangerous places. However, because the elderly are more vulnerable and they may bear more bodily injury, they tend to take more precautions against crime (McCoy, 1996). They may be more likely to purchase security systems and be more likely to install bars on their windows and doors.

The elderly are often portrayed as victims of crime and as being a highly vulnerable population. Society usually assigns the role of victim to "women, children, and the elderly" (Bichler-Robertson, 1997). Younger offenders may see the elderly as defenseless and unable to protect themselves, thus, targeting the elderly as victims. The media is also likely to report attacks on the elderly. Some elderly live in high crime neighborhoods such as "city" or "project" housing and are vulnerable to young offenders. Robbing an elderly person is often referred to as a "crib job" because it's said to be like taking candy from a baby (Barrow, 1996). When confronted by crime, the elderly are more likely to give a burglar what they want as they may be fearful of their lives. However, some elderly crime victims do fight back successfully. Not all elderly are vulnerable, and with the changing demographics and the aging of the "baby boomers," more elderly are stronger and take measures to protect themselves against crime.

As with all victims, crime can destroy self-esteem and emotional well-being. With the elderly, crime can also take away independence if family members believe they may be vulnerable or if they have been robbed and the family are afraid it will happen again.

While the elderly comprise only 13% of the total population, they comprise 30% of those who are victims of fraud (Barrow, 1996). There are many different types of fraud schemes committed against the elderly. They can range from companies who send prize notices in the mail to those who call after seeing obituaries in the newspaper.

Those in grief may be very vulnerable to scam artists. Scam artists prey on survivors, many times presenting "false" bills of items the dead had ordered "special" for the survivor prior to death, or they may sell unnecessary or unneeded items to survivors. There have been news reports about states suing magazine companies making false prize claims. Some elderly persons have flown across country to claim prizes only to find they have not won. These companies make money preying on the elderly and other victims. Elderly persons living alone may be more vulnerable to telephone solicitors. They may be lonely and in need of hearing a "friendly" voice or may be too polite to interrupt, allowing the solicitor to give their pitch.

The elderly may be conned into thinking they are doing a good deed by helping others. Some well-known schemes include the "bank auditor," "the pigeon drop," and "the concerned citizen" or "repair person."

There are many other fraud schemes committed against the elderly. Among them may be the following: social, land, home equity, mail order, telephone, credit card, and neighborhood frauds. These frauds against the elderly may go unreported as the victim does not want to lose self-esteem, dignity, or their independence. Those who do report crimes of this nature may suffer from embarrassment and many times do not want family members to know. The crime becomes more than just robbery of money—it is a crime of robbery of self-value and worth.

As the population continues to age, it will affect all aspects of criminal justice. There will be more abuse and neglect of the elderly, more elderly who are scammed, more elderly involved in crime, and more elderly prisoners or prisoners growing old while incarcerated. Those working in the field of criminal justice may want to prepare themselves for this change by taking course work or seminars in aging.

References

Administration on Aging (AoA). 2006. *Did You Know?* [On-line]. http://aoa.gov/press/did_you_know/2006/may/may.asp.

Baird, B. 1996. Old Folks in Prison: A Not So Wonderful Life for the Growing Population of Incarcerated Elderly. *Private Eye Weekly*, December 26, 1996.

Barrow, G. M. 1996. *Aging, the Individual and Society*, 6th edn., Minneapolis/St. Paul, MN: West Publishing Company.

Bichler-Robertson, G. 1997. Review of the book *Violence in Canada: Sociopolitical Perspectives. Social Pathology* 3 (3): 245.

Bowers, K. 1996. Stealing Time [On-line Publication]. *Denver Westword.com*. http:// www. westword.com/1996–08–01/news/stealing-time/

Brogden, Mike, and Preeti Nijar. 2000. *Crime, Abuse and the Elderly*. Devon, EX: Willan Publishing.

Bureau of Justice Statistics. 1994. *Elderly Crime Victims: National Crime Victimization Survey* [On-line]. http://www.ojp.usdoj.gov/bjs/abstract/ecv.htm.

Chaneles, Sol, and Cathleen Burnett. 1989. *Older Offenders: Current Trends.* New York: The Haworth Press.

Coalition for Federal Sentencing. 1998. *Elderly Prisoner Initiative* [On-line]. http://www.sentencing.org/elder.html.

Elder Law Prof Blog. 2005. Elderly Criminals Sell Pain Pills to Buy Food [On-line]. http://lawprofessors.typepad.com/elder_law/2005/12/elderly_crimina.html.

Feldmeyer, B., and D. Steffensmeier. 2007. Elder Crime: Patterns and Current Trends, 1980–2004. *Research on Aging.* [On-line]. http://roa.sagepub.com/cgi/contnet/abstract/29/4/297.

Harter, V., and J. Nichols. 1997. Homes Without Hope, Preying on the Elderly. Special Report. *The Arizona Republic,* reprint EC5–24, June 8–12.

LaRue, G. A. 1992. *Gero-Ethics: A New Vision of Growing Old in America.* Buffalo, NY: Prometheus Books.

McCoy, H. V. 1996. Lifestyles of the Old and Not So Fearful: Life Situation and Older Person's Fear of Crime. *Journal of Criminal Justice* 24 (3): 191–205.

Mergenhagen, P. 1996. *The Prison Population Bomb* [On-line Publication]. http://findarticles.com/p/articles/mi_m4021/is_/ai_17966621.

Newman, E. S., D. J. Newman, M. L. Gewirtz, et al. 1984. *Elderly Criminals.* Cambridge, MA: Oelgeschlager, Gunn & Hain, Publishers, Inc.

Plotkin, M. R. 1996. Improving the Police Response to Domestic Elder Abuse Victims. *Aging Magazine,* n 367, 28.

Rothman, M. B., B. D. Dunlop, P. Entzel, *et al.* 2000. *Elders, Crime, and the Criminal Justice System.* New York, NY: Springer Publishing Company, Inc.

U.S. Census Bureau. 2007. Facts for Features. http://www.census.gov/Press-Release/www/releases/archives/facts_for_features_special_editions/004210.html.

Wahidin, A., M. Cain, *et al.* 2006. *Ageing, Crime and Society.* Portland, OR: Willan Publishing.

West, M. 1998. March 16. Investigators Join Forces to Expose Elder Killings. *The Arizona Republic,* A8, B3.

Wolf, R. S. 1996. Elder Abuse and Family Violence: Testimony Presented Before the U.S. Senate Special Committee on Aging. *Journal of Elder Abuse & Neglect* 8 (1): 81.

CHAPTER 14

Youth Crime and Justice in a Changing Society

Rebecca Maniglia

Five African American teenagers were initially charged as adults for assaulting a white teenager after a series of racially charged exchanges at a Louisiana high school in December of 2006 (CNN, November 2007). In August of 2007, police arrested two adults as well as a 15- and a 16-year-old in the execution-style killings of three college students in New Jersey (CNN, August 2007). In October of 2007, a 14-year-old walked into his high school in Cleveland, Ohio, and shot four students before turning the gun on himself (CNN, October 2007). That same day, police arrested another 14-year-old for allegedly planning a Columbine-like attack on his high school; so named for the 1999 school shootings by two Colorado teenagers who killed 12 of their classmates and one teacher before committing suicide (CNN, October 2007). Unfortunately, stories such as these of teenagers involved in series crime have become an all too familiar part of nightly newscasts and newspaper coverage in recent years, often obscuring the truth about kids and crime. The true picture of juvenile crime is far more complicated than these examples indicate, as are the contemporary challenges faced by the system designed to respond to them.

HISTORY OF THE JUVENILE JUSTICE MOVEMENT

In the United States, recent decades have redefined the nature of parenting, providing parents with books, toys, and musical resources all designed to provide babies and young children with the best opportunity for personal growth and intellectual development. Childhood has become a time for focused parental effort, a time for play and protection, and for innocence and care. Yet, even in the United States the idea of a distinctive period of innocence and protection known as childhood has not always been an accepted notion. Before the nineteenth century, children were often seen as an additional labor force, necessary for an agricultural society where familial relations centered on responsibilities for the economic stability of the family. As the country became more urbanized and industrial, children continued to be recognized as a potential labor force, staffing factories for pennies a day. At the same time, new waves of immigration led to extreme poverty and overcrowded living conditions for many children, as well as new concern for their well-being (Sanborn and Salerno, 2005). It is out of this not so innocent picture of childhood that the historical juvenile court emerged.

In the 1800s, Quakers concerned both with protecting children from the harsh conditions in which many lived and with controlling their unsupervised behavior advocated for a system of justice that would account for the unique state of childhood. The result was the creation of Houses of Refugee, an institutional answer to child poverty and delinquency focused as much on restoring morality as on meeting the needs of the children it served (Regoli, Hewitt, and Delisi, 2008; Sanborn and Salerno, 2005). Later reformers, known as the Child Savers, sought to find alternative, community-oriented solutions for the growing number of neglected, homeless, and delinquent youth. Out of these efforts, the first juvenile court was developed in 1989 in Cook County, Illinois (Regoli, Hewitt, and Delisi, 2008).

Initially developed under the principle of *parens patriae*, the juvenile court was designed to intervene in the lives of youth in much the same way a parent might, providing a stable environment, loving care, and concern, and both educational opportunities and meaningful activities. To this end, the juvenile justice system deliberately distinguished itself from the criminal justice system in critical ways (see Table 14.1). Youth were adjudicated delinquent rather than convicted of crimes, with the resulting intervention of the court being focused on rehabilitation rather than punishment. Delinquent juveniles were understood primarily to be in need of re-parenting; thus, the court and resulting treatment stepped in where parental or familial connections had failed, saving the child from a certain life of crime (Regoli, Hewitt, and Delisi, 2008). From the beginning, youth could also be arrested for what would come to be known as status offenses or those acts that are offenses only because of age (i.e., underage drinking, truancy, and incorrigibility). While this broad definition of and justification for

TABLE 14.1 Differences Between Criminal and Juvenile Justice Systems

Juvenile Justice System	Adult Criminal Justice System
• Juvenile records confidential	• Adults record public information
• Juvenile held pre-hearing in detention	• Adult held pre-trial in jail
• Juvenile is adjudicated delinquent	• Adult is convicted of a crime
• Juvenile has disposition hearing	• Adult has criminal sentencing
• Juvenile is committed to a training school or secure juvenile institution	• Adult is incarcerated in adult prison
• Juvenile can be held under indeterminate sentencing until age of majority (18–21 depending on the state)	• Adult is sentenced determinately and can be released for good behavior
• Released juveniles are subject to aftercare efforts	• Released adults are subject to parole

intervention continued to result in youth being declared delinquent for moral as well as criminal failures, it did provide more community-based "treatment" which focused on both moral and skill development (Sanborn and Salerno, 2005).

In the years since the development of the juvenile justice system, the exclusive focus on youth rehabilitation has been repeatedly contested even as contemporary society argues over the basic notion of adolescence. Developmental theories have long established adolescence as a period of particular importance. In these years between childhood and adulthood, youth must develop their own identities, differentiate from their caregivers, and overcome their own impulsive tendencies. For many, although not most, the juvenile justice system plays a role in that development, attempting to fill the gaps left by poverty, violent neighborhoods, absent families, and inadequate education environments (Siegel, Welsh, and Senna, 2006). Yet, there continues to be debate concerning the ability of youth to form *mens rea* or the intent necessary to knowingly commit a crime as well as controversy concerning how the juvenile justice system should respond to this fluid question.

JUVENILES AS OFFENDERS

Despite the attention juvenile crime receives, adults commit the majority of crime in the United States, with juveniles consistently representing only a small portion of the overall crime rate. For instance, in 2005, juveniles (those under age 18) represented only one of every 11 arrests for homicide (about 9%) and one in every 10 arrests for drug abuse (Snyder, 2005). The highest proportion of juvenile crime was for robbery, where youth represented about 25% of all arrests as opposed to 15% of arrests for forcible rape, and 14% for aggravated assault (Snyder, 2005). Even given the smaller numbers, however, juvenile crime has always demanded public attention because it violates societal notions that continue to connect childhood or adolescence with innocence. When an adult kills a child, society frequently reacts with disgust or anger, but when a child lashes out violently at another child, reactions seem to betray surprise and perhaps even a fear that something may be wrong in society at large.

Yet, even though it continues to elicit strong public reaction, since a spike in the mid-1980s to mid-1990s, statistics actually indicate that juvenile violent crime has been declining steadily, with 2002 juvenile homicide rates the lowest since 1984 (Snyder and Sickmund, 2006). While in 56% of these homicides the juvenile acted alone, it should also be noted that an adult was also involved in 39% of them (Snyder and Sickmund, 2006). Similarly, arrest rates for aggravated assaults dropped 20% from 1996 to 2005, and dropped 5% just from 2001 to 2005 (Snyder, 2005). However, even with rates of violent crime dropping in recent years, the effects of the 1980s–1990s spike are still felt in the juvenile justice system as a whole.

The juvenile homicide rate hit an all-time high from the mid-1980s to the mid-1990s, resulting in a nationwide call for juvenile justice reform to address the emergence of what became known as a "super-predator" (McCollum, 1996:9). It even brought calls to disband the juvenile system entirely in favor of the tougher, more highly regulated criminal justice system (Butts and Mears, 2001). While that has yet to happen, in the years since 1992, every state but Nebraska has responded by modifying existing waiver laws to make it easier for youth to be waived into adult courts (Snyder and Sickmund, 2006). While some states still leave waiver to the discretion of the prosecutor, many have mandatory waiver laws for youth committing certain kinds of violent offenses. Further, 29 states have passed legislation removing certain criminal offenses entirely from the jurisdiction of the juvenile court (Snyder and Sickmund, 2006). It is true that many states have authorized juvenile court blended sentencing, allowing youth to receive both a juvenile and an adult sentence (often suspending the adult sentence as long as the juvenile does not re-offend) or criminal court blended sentencing allowing the youth waived to be tried and convicted in criminal court but to serve their sentence in juvenile treatment facilities (Snyder and Sickmund, 2006). However, even with these safety-gap measures, the result of weakening waiver laws has been more juveniles in the adult criminal justice system than ever before. Similarly, the rash of school-related shootings in the late 1990s and early 2000s has resulted in many schools adopting no-tolerance policies that in some cases have led to an increased law enforcement presence in urban high schools (Stinchcomb, Bazemore, Riestenberg, 2006). Notwithstanding these reactions to juvenile violent crime, it remains true that most delinquency is non-violent. For example, in 2005, property crimes index offenses made up about 20% of all juvenile arrests, while violent crime index offenses represented only almost 5%. In comparison, drug abuse arrests made up 8.9% of juvenile arrests and disorderly conduct, 9.4%, while curfew and running away represented 6.5 and 5.1% respectively (Snyder, 2005). In other words, more youth were arrested for running away from home than were arrested for all violent crime index offenses (murder, rape, robbery, and aggravated assault).

JUVENILES AS VICTIMS

While the juvenile justice system was designed to intervene in delinquent behavior, society has always recognized the general link between victimization and delinquency (Regoli, Hewitt, and Delisi, 2008). It remains true that children and adolescents are at risk of victimization both by other children/adolescents and by adults. In fact, in 2002, homicide was the fourth leading cause of death for youth ages 1–11. Statistics for that same year show that 10% of all murders in the United States involved a juvenile victim, about a third of which were female, and 47% of which were African American. For juvenile homicide victims ages 12–17, offenders were most likely to be acquaintances and to use a handgun, while children under age 6 are most likely to have been killed by family members (Snyder and Sickmund, 2006).

Aside from homicide rates, however, youth ages 12–17 are more than two times as likely as adults to be victims of nonfatal violent offenses such as rape, sexual assault, robbery, aggravated assault, and simple assault. More than half of these violent victimizations for youth ages 12–14 took place in school, with immediately after school representing the time of highest risk for youth. Males are more likely than females to be victims, and those youth in urban areas are at higher risk than rural youth (Snyder and Sickmund, 2006).

Adolescence is also a period of great risk from personal victimization, with almost as many youth falling victim to suicide as to homicide. While juvenile males are four times more likely to successfully commit suicide than girls; white juveniles are at greater risk than African American or Hispanic youth. Native American youth commit suicide at the highest rate, however—nearly double that of white juveniles (Snyder and Sickmund, 2006).

SPECIAL POPULATIONS AND EMERGING ISSUES

JUVENILE FEMALE OFFENDERS.   Juvenile female offenders have garnered the attention of state juvenile justice systems in recent years largely because of their offending patterns. While arrests of girls have been declining since 1995, they still remain higher than they have been historically (Schaffner, 2006). In fact from 1994 to 2003, arrest rates for girls either increased more or decreased less than arrest rates for boys. Similarly, the percentage of juvenile crime committed by girls has risen from 20% in 1980 to 29% in 2003 (Snyder and Sickmund, 2006).

Of particular concern are the numbers of girls involved with more violent offenses such as aggravated and simple assaults. For instance, girls accounted for 18% of juvenile arrests for violent index crimes in 2005 (up from 10% in 1980) but for 32% of aggravated assaults (up from 21% in 1980) and 24% of simple assaults (up from 15% in 1980) (Snyder, 2005; Snyder and Sickmund, 2006). Historically, girls have not been involved in violent offenses at such high rates, leading to much debate in the field about whether the increase reflects changes in girls offending (Schaffner, 2006) or differences in the systemic processing of girls (Chesney-Lind and Irwin, 2007), particularly the impact of new mandatory arrest policies for domestic violence cases. Of aggravated assault arrests for girls in 2003, 33% were against family members as opposed to 18% for boys (Snyder and Sickmund, 2006).

The increase in female offending has also led to changes in treatment and juvenile justice policy. In 1992, the Juvenile Justice and Delinquency Prevention Act was reauthorized, requiring states to analyze their state systems for gender bias. Since the early 1990s, states have begun to address these inequities by designing specialized female responsive interventions for girls (Schaffner, 2006). This is due, in part, to recent research that confirms sexual victimization as a meaningful risk factor for female delinquency (American Bar Association and National Bar Association, 2001; Belknap and Holsinger, 2006) coupled with victimization rates as high as 70% in the juvenile female offender population (Schaffner, 2006).

MENTAL HEALTH.   In recent years, there has been growing concern that the juvenile justice system is ill-equipped to deal with the growing number of offenders who have identified mental health issues. Recent prevalence studies indicate that as many of 60–70% of juveniles referred to the juvenile court nationwide have at least one recognizable mental health diagnosis (Grisso, 2007) and as many as 20% may have serious mental health issues (Pullmann *et al.*, 2006). Despite these high rates, many juvenile justice systems are unable to offer the intensive mental health treatment necessary to address these conditions. In fact, some studies show that not quite 50% of juvenile justice agencies have any services available to address youth mental health concerns beyond the initial assessment screening (Pullmann *et al.*, 2006).

JUVENILE GANGS.   Juvenile gang involvement peaked in the mid-1990s, showing a steady decline since then, particularly in towns smaller than 50,000. Yet, despite the declines, gang involvement remains an important predictor of juvenile criminality and juvenile victimization from crime. While only about one percent of all youth ages 10–17 were involved in gang activity in 2002, those juveniles from poor, urban communities with large minority populations were more at risk of successful gang recruitment as were those with poor school performance or friends and family members in gangs. Of all reported juvenile members, 94% were male, 49% Hispanic, and 37% African American (Snyder and Sickmund, 2006).

MINORITY OVERREPRESENTATION.   The overrepresentation of minorities in juvenile justice has been of concern since the 1990s, with all minority groups overrepresented at both arrest and incarceration. Overrepresentation means, in essence, that given their percentage in the population at large, too many Hispanic, African American, and Native American youth have been arrested or are currently under the care of the juvenile justice system.

For example, while African American juveniles represented only about 16% of the juvenile population for the years 1980–2002, they accounted for 47% of homicide victims, and African American youth are four times more likely to be victims of a homicide than white youth (Snyder and Sickmund, 2006). Similarly, African American juveniles are also more likely to be arrested as juvenile offenders. According to Uniform Crime Report (UCR) data, in 2003, African American juveniles represented 63% of the juvenile arrests for robbery, 48% of the juvenile arrests for murder, 40% of the juvenile arrests for motor vehicle theft, and 38% of the juvenile arrests for aggravated assault (Snyder and Sickmund, 2006). Interestingly, however, there is virtually no difference between the rates of African Americans and whites involved in minor delinquency (Agnew, 2005).

There continues to be debate among researchers as to the cause of such overrepresentation, with some asserting that it simply represents the higher number of black youth involved in serious crime or at least the higher number of serious offenders among those African American youth involved in crime (Agnew, 2005). Others assert that the issue is more directly related to the active policing of urban, minority neighborhoods, or even to racist policies in juvenile justice processing (Snyder, Puzzanchera, and Adams, 2007).

LGBT (LESBIAN, GAY, BISEXUAL, AND TRANSGENDER) ISSUES.   Recent years have brought a greater concern for the unique issues of LGBT youth both as juvenile victims and offenders. Studies show that LGBT youth are at least three times more likely to commit suicide than non-LBGT youth and that homelessness for LGBT youth is at epidemic rates, with 20–40% of homeless youth being LGBT (Ray, 2006). Similarly, it has been estimated that nearly 42% of those LGBT youth in out-of-home placements (i.e., foster care, group homes) are there because of being kicked out or removed from their original homes due to issues related to their sexual identity or sexual orientation (Wilbur, Ryan, and Marksamer, 2006). LGBT youth are also more likely to be the victims of violence because of their sexual orientation, including physical attacks and harassment at school (Feinstein *et al.*, 2001; Human Rights Watch, 2001).

Recently, the Child Welfare League of America created Best Practice Guidelines for those providing services to LGBT youth offenders. The first document of its kind, it addresses issues such as the identification of practices that victimize LGBT youth (i.e. being subjected to negative staff attitudes or inconsistent enforcement of policies) and specialized issues related to the classification and housing of LGBT youth, particular those with transgender issues (Wilbur *et al.*, 2006).

JUVENILES AS SERVICE PROVIDERS

The nature of juvenile justice and of adolescence has always necessitated that most intervention efforts be created and run by adult workers. Yet, contemporary juvenile justice systems have attempted to use the power of peers to reconceptualize juvenile justice intervention, in essence allowing youth to serve as both service providers and clients. Historically, these have concerned peer involvement in the actual treatment environment. For instance, in the 1970s, youth were encouraged to participate in the development of a positive peer culture, holding one another accountable in residential treatment settings through behavioral intervention (Vorrath and Bendtro, 1985). While these programs have come under criticism, especially as they relate to specialized populations (Maniglia and Albrecht, 2006), they remain in place in various forms in many states, although not usually in their original form. In their place, some contemporary juvenile justice programs utilize youth as peer counselors or as members of youth leadership boards.

Many of the newer efforts to include youth as system practitioners function as alternatives to traditional juvenile court involvement, sometimes even embracing emerging justice strategies such as restorative justice. These approaches attempt to redefine crime to be understood as a violation of relationships, both between individuals and between an offender and the larger community. This re-conceptualization means that intervention efforts attempt to restore those relationships by identifying and repairing root causes of behavior and providing the necessary peer support to make such change possible (Bazemore and Schiff, 2004; Van Ness and Strong, 1997). Perhaps, the best known of these efforts is the Teen Court model.

Teen courts were developed initially to reduce the number of first offender cases that were being heard in juvenile court by offering an alternative (Forgays, Demilio, and Schuster, 2004). Instead of going to juvenile court, youth agree to have their cases "heard" by a jury of their peers who work with the offender to create an appropriate sentence or consequence. While adults participate as support personnel in the process, peer jurors are responsible for the actual running of the court hearing as well as for the design of the ultimate sentence (Butts, Buck, and Coggeshall, 2002). While jurors receive specialized training, the basic intent of the program is to capture the power of the peer group and use it to create opportunities for change in individual young offenders. Once offenders complete their sentence, they are sometimes even invited to join the teen court as jury members (Butts, Buck, and Coggeshall, 2002).

Current estimates indicate there may be as many as 800 teen courts currently operating in the United States, handling literally thousands of juvenile cases each year. While there are not many studies on the overall effectiveness of teen courts, they do appear to be more effective than traditional juvenile justice intervention in terms of reducing recidivism. Further, they appear to offer a number of other benefits such as reduced costs and increases in student volunteerism (Butts, Buck, and Coggeshall, 2002). For instance, some studies of teen courts have found that jury members experienced increased levels of self-efficacy and knowledge of the law and legal processing (Forgays, Demilio, and Schuster, 2004).

Beyond formalized Teen Courts, which can still be somewhat adversarial in nature (Butts, Buck, and Coggeshall, 2002), juvenile justice systems and even schools have adopted programs such as peer mediation or peer juries that utilize peer influence but usually in ways even more connected with the classic concepts of restorative justice mentioned above. For instance, in peer mediation, specially trained youth mediate conflicts between other youth, working with the key players to find solutions before conflicts escalate. The mediator does not operate as judge or jury, but instead encourages dialogue between youth, guiding discussions to ensure that both sides are heard and to create mutually accepted plans of intervention. Similarly, peer juries bring together groups of pro-social youth who agree to assist their peers with behavior problems at school or behavior brought to the attention of the court. As with peer mediation, the emphasis is on empathy development, active listening, and finally, collective problem solving. The goal is that struggling youth find ongoing support systems within this "peer jury" enabling them to give voice to and find solutions for the root causes of their delinquency (Riestenberg, 2001).

References

Agnew, Robert. 2005. *Juvenile Delinquency: Causes and Control,* 2nd edn. Los Angeles: Roxbury Publishing Company.

American Bar Association and National Bar Association. 2001. *Justice by Gender.* New York: American Bar Association and National Bar Association.

Bazemore, Gordon, and Schiff, Mara. 2004. *Juvenile Justice Reform and Restorative Justice: Building Theory and Policy from Practice.* Cullompton, Devon, UK: Willan Publishing.

Belknap, Joanne, and Holsinger, Kristi. 2006. The Gendered Nature of Risk Factors for Delinquency. *Feminist Criminology* 1 (1): 48–71.

Butts, Jeffrey, and Daniel Mears. 2001. Reviving Juvenile Justice in a Get Tough Era. *Youth and Society* 33: 169–198.

Butts, Jeffrey, Janeen Buck, and Mark B. Coggeshall. 2002. *Impact of Teen Court on Young Offenders: Research Report.* Washington, DC: Urban Institute.

Chesney-Lind, Meda, and Irwin, Katherine. 2007. *Beyond Bad Girls: Gender, Violence and Hype.* New York: Routledge.

CNN. November 7, 2007. Charges Against Jeno 6 Defendant Reduced.

CNN. October, 2007. Police Chief: Teen Shoots Four, Kills Self at Cleveland High School.

CNN. August, 2007. Two Arrested in Schoolyard Slayings.

Feinstein, Randi, Andrew Greenblatt, Lauren Hass, Sally Kohn, and Julianne Rana. 2001. *And Justice for All?: A Report on LGBT Youth in New York's Juvenile Justice System.* New York: Lesbian and Gay Youth Project.

Forgays, Deborah Kirby, Lisa Demilio, and Kim Schuster. 2004. Teen Court: What Jurors Can Tell Us About the Process. *Juvenile and Family Court Journal* (Winter): 25–33.

Grisso, T. 2007. Progress and Perils in the Juvenile Justice and Mental Health Movement. *The Journal of the American Academy of Psychiatry and the Law* 35:158–167.

Human Rights Watch. 2001. *Hated in the Hallways.* New York: Human Rights Watch.

Maniglia, Rebecca, and Linda Albrecht. 2006. Female responsive Services and Positive Peer Culture: Thoughts for Consideration. *Women, Crime and Criminal Justice* 7 (2): 17–32.

McCollum, Bill. 1996. Hearings on the Juvenile Justice and Delinquency Prevention Act. House Committee on Economic and Educational Opportunities, Subcommittee on Early Childhood, Youth and Families. Serial No. 104–68. 104th Congress.

Pullmann, M. D., N. Koroloff, E. Veach-White, R. Gaylor, and D. Sieler. 2006. Juvenile Offenders With Mental Health Needs: Reducing Recidivism Using Wraparound. *Crime & Delinquency* 52 (3): 375–397.

Ray, Nicholas. 2006. *LGBT Youth: An Epidemic of Homelessness.* New York: National Gay and Lesbian Task Force Policy Institute and the National Coalition for the Homeless.

Regoli, Robert M., John D. Hewitt, and Matt Delisi. 2008. *Delinquency in Society.* New York: McGraw Hill Higher Education.

Riestenberg, Nancy. 2001. *In-School Behavior Intervention Grants: A Three Year Evaluation of Alternative approaches to Suspensions and Expulsions: Monograph.* Roseville, Minnesota: Minnesota Department of Children, Families, and Learning.

Sanborn, Jr., Joseph B., and Anthony W. Salerno. 2005. *The Juvenile Justice System.* Los Angeles: Roxbury Publishing Company.

Schaffner, Laurie. 2006. *Girls in Trouble with the Law.* New York: Rutgers.

Siegel, Larry J., Brandon C. Welsh, and Joseph J. Senna. 2006. *Juvenile Delinquency.* Belmont, CA: Wadsworth Publishing.

Snyder, Howard. 2005. *Juvenile Arrests 2005.* Washington: Office of Juvenile Justice and Delinquency Prevention.

Snyder, Howard, and Melissa Sickmund. 2006. *Juvenile Offenders and Victims: 2006 National Report.* Washington, DC: Office of Juvenile Justice and Delinquency Prevention.

Snyder, H., C. Puzzanchera, and B. Adams. 2007. *National Disproportionate Minority Contact Databook.* Washington, DC: National Center for Juvenile Justice for the Office of Juvenile Justice and Delinquency Prevention.

Stinchcomb, J., G. Bazemore, N. Riestenberg. 2006. Beyond Zero Tolerance: Restoring Justice in Secondary Schools. *Youth Violence and Juvenile Justice: An Interdisciplinary Journal* 4 (2): 123–147.

Van Ness, D., and K. H. Strong. 1997. *Restoring Justice.* Cincinnati, OH: Anderson Publishing.

Vorrath, Harry, and Larry Bendtro. 1985. *Positive Peer Culture,* 2nd edn. Hawthorne, New York: Aldrine Transaction Publishing.

Wilbur, Shannon, Caitlin Ryan, and Jody Marksamer. 2006. *Serving LGBT Youth in Out-of-Home Care: Best Practices Guidelines.* Washington, DC: Child Welfare League of America.

CHAPTER 15

The Invisible Minority
Individuals with Disability

Cynthia Baroody-Hart

Meghan G. McDowell

This book attempts to address diversity in the criminal justice system by attending to the differences and similarities among individuals of various groups defined by the social science disciplines as "minority groups." What gets defined as majority and defined as minority is a social construct. Historically, a focus on differences and similarities has sought to deal with the question of what is "normal"—in terms of individual characteristics, capabilities, values, behaviors, and interactions with others. In talking of minority/majority relations, minority gets defined in terms of power differentials, not the size of the groups in question.

The process of definition entails the development of a "we/they" dichotomy— "we" are the same; "they" are different. "We" understand others who are similar to us, not those who are different from us. Similarity is familiar, normal, and comfortable; difference is not! Many of the groups discussed in this text are groups of individuals with common characteristics that are seen as different. Additionally, while there is diversity across groups, there is also much diversity within these groups. We are all both different and similar to others. In order to do justice in the operation of the criminal justice system, it is necessary to find commonality with those who are defined as different among those working in and who are processed by the justice system. An understanding of the diversity within the justice system will facilitate the operation of the system. Seeing these differences among us as commonality begins with an understanding of the historical experiences of these groups.

DISABILITY

This chapter addresses individuals with disability who work in and are clients of the criminal justice system. For the purpose of this chapter, people who are visually impaired, hearing or speech impaired, developmentally/learning disabled, and those who face physical and mental challenges are defined as individuals with disability. Individuals with disability participate in all aspects of the criminal justice system: they are judges, lawyers, law enforcement officers, offenders, victims, dispatchers, and counselors among other things.

The subject matter of this chapter is incredibly broad; it encompasses a very diverse group of individuals reflecting many types of impairments, as well as the many roles that are included in the operation of the criminal justice system. The merging of these two broad areas into one will undoubtedly be incomplete; however, it is crucial for students of criminal justice to be sensitive to the issue of individuals with disability as equal participants within criminal justice.

With respect to people with disability, society focuses on a defining status or "master status" that serves to define the individual by their disability. A master status (Goffman, 1959) is a pivotal position in society, one that is permanent and defining in interaction. For example, one's gender is most notably a master status that is a pivotal identity and dictates social interaction. It is the first thing someone recognizes about an individual. A person will interact with, attribute different characteristics to, and make different assumptions about an individual based on that status. Disability is most definitely a master status. One's inability to hear, to walk, to learn, or to see is extended to every other ability. The folly of this perception is easily dispelled by mentioning the accomplishments of a few extraordinary individuals with disability who are more than able. Ironically, Beethoven was hearing-impaired, and Einstein was learning disabled. There are many more examples: Stevie Wonder, Ray Charles, Steven Hawkins, and President Franklin Delano Roosevelt, to name a few. It should not be necessary to point to individuals who have made such extraordinary contributions in order to recognize the abilities of individuals with disability.

People attribute many characteristics to individuals with disability. If you are unable to walk, people may talk loudly as if you were unable to hear, or slowly as if you were unable to understand. Historically, individuals with disability have been seen as non-entities, having no role in "mainstream" society. There is a paternalism in interacting with individuals with disability, in that they come to be defined as unable to think for themselves or be involved in self-determination (Scotch, 1989). In essence, they are perceived to be unworthy of equal treatment. Even our language defines individuals with disability as not valid (invalid). The lack of a meaningful role necessitates that disabled individuals accommodate to society, rather than that society should accommodate to the individual.

Paternalism is also reflected in social interactions. The person without disability (if there is such a thing) always knows best, and the individual with disability is, of course, deemed not capable of making their own decisions. People "help" assuming they know what will help without asking. This paternalism, along with "prejudicial attitudes and exclusionary practices are far greater barriers to social participation for many disabled people than are [their] physical or mental impairments" (Scotch, 1989:380).

On the basis of these perceptions and attitudes, individuals with disability have been discriminated against. People with disability have been "invisible"—hidden out of sight "for their own good" or so as not to offend others (Thomas, 1990). Yet, by hiding them from sight, the non-disabled person fails to understand the reality that they can become a person with disability at any time. Although a racist person need not consider ever becoming a member of the group they dislike, those with negative attitudes toward persons with disability cannot be so certain. Unlike most groups presented here, individuals with disability have not been recognized as "minority" in terms of power differential, even though they most clearly meet that definition (Scotch, 1989; Shakespeare, 1993; Theirs, 1994; Young, 1998). The community of individuals with disability is a diverse community who share, as do all of us, similarities and differences. Individuals with disability have all of the social, cultural, and religious identities that accompany other statuses associated with the individual (Backman, 1994). To be disabled and black, disabled and Asian, disabled and Latino/a, and so on, carries different "baggage" for the individual.

Discriminatory laws, termed the "ugly laws," have excluded individuals with disability from participation in society. These laws encoded a variety of prohibitions against specific activities: restrictions on immigration to the United States on the basis of disability, presentation of self in public, regulations against marriage, and forced sterilization.

To reiterate, the community of individuals with disability is a diverse community that shares, as do all of us, similarities and differences. According to Scotch (1989) and Young, (1998) the diversity and the isolation within the disabled community has prevented a sense of collective identity, slowing the development of the disability movement as a social movement. The disability movement will ultimately lead to equal treatment and self-determination. Young (1998) traces the disability movement through five stages from stigmatization to political/legal action, seeing it as analogous to other social movements such as the civil rights, women's, Native American, and gay rights movements. Self-determination is the most crucial issue: the ability of an individual to have control over one's own life. To successfully traverse this stage requires the willingness of others to "lose" the paternalistic approach so common in peoples' dealings with individuals with disability and to fully and equally include these individuals within the community. In addition, it is necessary for individuals with disability to collectively identify their own and others' common status problems. This call to collective social action is embodied in the disability rights movement, which has existed in Europe and the United States since the 1970s.

The disability rights movement has engaged in political and legal action using tactics similar to the civil rights and women's movements. This political and legal activism is gradually helping to change the lives of people with disability. The necessary changes for full and equal participation are twofold: to change the physical and structural barriers in the environment, and to change negative social attitudes regarding individuals with disability. The historical antecedents of the disability rights movement are: (1) Civil Rights Act of 1964 (2) the Rehabilitation Act of 1973 and, most notably, and (3) the Americans with Disability Act (ADA) of 1990. Although it is not possible to legislate attitude, the ADA legislates equal access for all to counter the functional discrimination against individuals with disability that has existed historically.

As a society, we have only recently begun to deal with the issue of access for people with disability. The ADA has influenced various social institutions, businesses, public social services such as public works, and transportation to provide access to people with disability that most of us take for granted. However, certain social institutions are resistant, if not antagonistic to this change. The literature is replete with articles debating whether the law is an annoyance or an accommodation, characterizing ADA as a "nightmare," a "quagmire," a "burden," and a "threat."

The Supreme Court has issued a series of rulings since 1990 intended to clarify provisions of the ADA. While some of the Supreme Court decisions have protected the rights of disabled individuals (see, e.g., *Olmstead* v. *L.C.*, *Sutton* v. *United Airlines*, and *Cleveland* v. *Policy Management Systems Corporation*), many of the decisions, as the National Council on Disability (NCD) noted in 2002, "have dramatically changed the way ADA is interpreted, in most cases, contrary to what Congress intended." In one particularly devastating decision, *Board of Trustees of the University of Alabama* v. *Garrett*, 531 U.S. 356 (2001), the Supreme Court ruled that state employees could no longer sue their employer for monetary damages for violations of Title 1 of the ADA, which "prohibits employment discrimination against people with disability" (National Council on Disability, 2002). With few exceptions, the Supreme Court has consistently sided with employers and not workers with disabilities, prompting Professor Robert Burgdorf, Jr., to comment, "Twelve years ago, as I drafted the original version of the Americans with Disabilities Act, I never dreamed that this landmark civil rights law would become so widely misunderstood and my words so badly misinterpreted, particularly by the body meant to protect the very rights guaranteed by the law" (The Center for an Accessible Society, 2007).

The ADA was designed to make the environment more accessible for individuals with disability. We all adjust our environments to facilitate the requirements of life and work. The disability rights movement has ". . . espoused the philosophy that it is the limitations of the inaccessible environment, not the handicap itself, that makes a disability limiting" (Theirs, 1994:21).

DISABILITY AND CRIMINAL JUSTICE

The American Association of People with Disabilities (2007) estimates that 56 million people have some form of disability, or, put differently, one out of every five Americans is either moderately or severely disabled in this country. These individuals are more likely to be poor and undereducated, consequently having fewer opportunities than others in society. Disabled individuals may work within or use the services of the police, the courts, and correctional agencies. Security and safety issues, which may be in conflict with access issues, are examples of two areas of concern in these environments. Indeed, as Toth (2008:175) argues, "the population of disabled employees, victims, offenders, and inmates may very well incur intensified experiences of discrimination as they pass through the criminal justice system." The following sections examine the "multiple marginalization factors" that are commonly experienced by disabled individuals within the criminal justice system.

INDIVIDUALS WITH DISABILITIES AS VICTIMS IN THE CRIMINAL JUSTICE SYSTEM

Individuals with disability are often assumed to be "victims" in many contexts. There is an element of truth to this idea in that some individuals with disability are particularly vulnerable to victimization because of their actual or perceived inability of "fight or flight." With respect to conventional crime, individuals with disability are "easy targets." The National Organization for Victim Assistance (2007) reports on their website that individuals with disabilities are "invisible victims," whose victimizations often go unreported, and those crimes that are investigated rarely result in prosecution. Individuals with developmental disabilities are at particularly high risk for physical and sexual abuse. For example, some studies have suggested that anywhere from 68 to 83% of women with developmental disabilities are sexually assaulted in their lifetime; children with any disability are twice as likely to be victimized than their non-disabled peers; and individuals with severe mental disabilities are victims of violent crime at a rate *more than eleven times* that of the general population (Tyiska, 2001).

Moreover, victimization—and revictimization—is often at the hands of family members, caregivers, and organizations that are designed to serve the disabled community. Tyiska (2001) reports that nearly half (48.1%) of the perpetrators of sexual assault against people with disability gained access to their victims through disability agencies. In light of these facts, the reticence of individuals with disability to report their victimization is understandable due to fear of retaliation, as well as the dependence of many individuals on their victimizers. Furthermore, accessibility to many criminal justice agencies is often limited by both attitudinal and physical barriers, making it difficult for disabled victims to utilize the criminal justice services available to them.

The following anecdote illustrates the complex interplay between victimization, revictimization, and reporting:

> An elderly woman who was unable to walk was cared for at home by family members. Her grandson, a drug user, frequently stole money from her when her Social Security Disability Income check arrived. The woman would tuck her money under her to hide it from her grandson. Once, in a state of anger when he could not find her money, he flipped her over and she fell out of the bed onto the floor. She sustained several bruises but was not seen by a doctor. She did not report the abuse or the theft to the police out of fear that her family would no longer want to care for her. (Office for Victims of Crime, 1998)

Such events are often the trigger for increased suffering on the part of the victim. The physical harm was evident in the bruising. What may not be so evident is the emotional damage done. Victimization and revictimization in particular may enhance one's sense of vulnerability, fear, and distrust, while reaffirming one's experience of stigmatization, isolation, and lowered self-esteem. Crimes against individuals with disability are defined as hate crimes. In 1994, Congress amended the Hate Crimes Statistics Act to include "bias against persons with disabilities" (Federal Bureau of Investigation, 2006a). The 2006 *Hate Crimes Statistics Report* recorded 94 hate crime incidents against individuals with disability (Federal Bureau of Investigation, 2006b).

INDIVIDUALS WITH DISABILITIES AS OFFENDERS IN THE CRIMINAL JUSTICE SYSTEM

While it is common to assume that people with disability are likely victims, it is less common to assume that they are likely offenders. The paternalistic perceptions noted earlier often mean that society believes people with disability to be "incapable" of engaging in criminal behavior. However, activists in the disability rights movement, for example, have seen their share of arrests for civil disobedience just as did women and people of color. People with disability also engage in the more mundane conventional crimes such as shoplifting and larceny, as well as more serious violent offences such as homicide and assault (Kardasz, 1995; Miller and Hess, 1998). The latter offenses are often associated with people experiencing mental disorders which leave them violent and aggressive if untreated.

Individuals with disability in the criminal justice system are considered "special category offenders" and are disproportionately represented among the incarcerated population. Although no reliable data exists on the number of disabled individuals in prison, She and Stapleton (2006:2), using survey data from the Department of Justice, estimate that 37% of jail inmates, 31% of state prison inmates, and 23% of federal prison inmates self-identify as having some form of disability. The rates of mental and learning disabilities are "spectacularly high" among the jail and state prison populations. In 2003, the Bureau of Justice Statistics reported that approximately 300,000 people with mental illnesses were incarcerated in the United States (Pustilnik, 2005). The extraordinarily high rate of incarceration for individuals with mental illness has prompted Pustilnik (2005:226) to argue that jails and prisons across the country are becoming "confinement centers" for individuals with mental illness, "many of whom have committed only a public order infraction or no offense at all." Overall, the rate of disability among the working-age incarcerated population is two to three times higher then the non-institutionalized working-age population (She and Stapleton, 2006).

Once incarcerated, the barriers faced by individuals with disability are immense. These individuals face dangerous obstacles when seeking access to basic needs within state and federal jails, prisons, and juvenile facilities. Many horrific cases of blocked access and lack of accommodation have occurred because disabled prisoners are "almost wholly dependent on the physical conditions and services of their facilities" (Greifinger, 2006:2). Furthermore, disabled offenders often face heightened levels of abuse, neglect, and discrimination at the hands of guards and other inmates. For example, Russell and Stewart, (2001:11) documented the practice of correctional officers confiscating from inmates with disabilities "whatever will be more acutely missed: wheelchairs, walkers, crutches, braces, hearing aids, glasses, catheters, egg crates, and medication. Prisoners who require personal care or assistance—for example, quadriplegic inmates who need help with eating, dressing, and bathing—are simply ignored; they go without meals and are forced to urinate on themselves in the absence of bathroom assistance."

Ostensibly, the discrimination and abuse of disabled prisoners detailed above constitutes a violation of the Supreme Court decision in *Pennsylvania Department of Corrections* v. *Yeskey* (1998). In *Yeskey*, the Supreme Court ruled that ADA protections extend to state prison inmates and that prisons must provide "reasonable accommodation" for disabled inmates housed in state facilities. However, because offenders with disabilities are often seen as least eligible for any type of accommodation by the criminal justice system, following the *Yeskey* decision many states passed legislation exempting disabled prisoners from protection against discrimination (Greifinger, 2006). In response to some states' failure to comply with the *Yeskey* decision, the Supreme Court heard the case of Tony Goodman, a paraplegic inmate housed in a state facility in Georgia. Goodman argued that he had been confined for

23 to 24 hours a day in a cell too small to turn his wheelchair around. Furthermore, he had been denied access to basic needs such as sanitation, medical care, and program participation (Greifinder, 2006). Eventually, Goodman seriously injured himself when trying to move from his wheelchair to the toilet, and in 1999, he filed a discrimination suit against the state of Georgia. In *United States* v. *Georgia* (2006), the Supreme Court ruled in favor of Goodman, arguing that Congress has the authority, over states, to apply provisions of the ADA to state prisons.

However, despite rulings by the Supreme Court that support the rights of disabled inmates to "reasonable accommodation" in state prisons, legislators are hesitant to allot extra funding for "luxury items" such as structural modifications and the implementation of special services for these inmates that are necessary in order to meet the basic requirements of "reasonable accommodation." Correctional officials justify the "denial of services or aides to disabled inmates by suggesting that prison conditions are part of the penalty for a criminal offense and are intended to be restrictive and even harsh" (Toth, 2008:165). The prison population has reached unprecedented levels in this country, due in large part to the "War on Drugs" and the mass incarceration of the poor, people of color, and individuals with mental illness (Walker, Spohn, and DeLone, 2004). Thus, as the prison population continues to rise (and age) in this country, so, too, will the number of disabled offenders, potentially bringing the issues of disability and reasonable accommodation in the criminal justice system to a "crisis level."

INDIVIDUALS WITH DISABILITIES AS EMPLOYEES IN THE CRIMINAL JUSTICE SYSTEM

The same types of accommodations made for visitors and the general public must be made for employees. Ramps and wide door ways for mobility impaired people, as well as telecommunications devices for speech and hearing impaired individuals, are examples of such accommodations. In addition to these accommodations, special equipment such as high technology telephones (TTY), speech synthesized computers, and modified training manuals and work schedules may be required. It may be necessary to change the way certain procedures are done to accommodate an employee with a disability. Any services provided for employees without disability must also be provided for employees with disability. In an adaptation to the workplace, innovation is the key.

For a vast number of individuals, having a disability does not fundamentally change who they are, their knowledge, or their job skills. If an individual is qualified for a position, they cannot—ethically or legally—be denied that position on the basis of a disability. To reiterate, employees with disability participate in all aspects of the criminal justice system: they are judges, lawyers, law enforcement officers, dispatchers, and counselors. Based on an analysis of data from the 2005 American Community Survey, William Erickson, a research specialist with Cornell University's Rehabilitation Research and Training Center on Disability Demographics and Statistics, reported that 6.7% of correctional officers and/or jailers are disabled, 3.3% of police officers are disabled, and 3.5% of all judges, magistrates, and other judicial employees self-identified as having some form of disability (these percentages are likely underestimates since these are self-identified). Disabled professionals often encounter the same discriminatory physical and social barriers that are faced by victims and offenders. These professionals are often denied the opportunity to attend conferences or workshops and then maligned for not keeping up with their respective fields. In this instance, due in part to the misinterpretation of the ADA by the Supreme Court, there is little legal remedy available to disabled professionals because this form of workplace discrimination falls under a "gray area" of the law.

Activists for the disabled community have highlighted the persistent lack of employment opportunities. The 2004 NOD/Harris Survey reported that only 35% of people with disability between the ages of 18 and 64 were employed, compared to a 75% employment rate for individuals without disability. In 2007, John R. Vaughn, the chairperson of the National Council on Disability, remarked, "For Americans with disabilities, no less than for all other citizens, the opportunity to earn a living and be self-supporting is a universally held goal. Yet in perhaps no area of public policy has the expectations gap so stubbornly resisted our efforts to achieve equality." It is easier to change environments than attitudes. Perceptions of disability and individuals with disabilities make a difference; negative attitudes toward co-workers and clients with disability are problematic and discriminatory. In other words, "Society hasn't yet made the jump where it's OK for a person [with disability] to be your boss or your brother-in-law" (Theirs, 1994:23). It is time now, in the twenty-first century, for our society to make that jump—to create an inclusive, empowering community for everyone.

THE FUTURE OF DISABILITY RIGHTS

Since the inception of the ADA in 1990, many of the physical barriers preventing equal access for disabled individuals have been addressed, and now disabled individuals, through the ADA, have a form of legal recourse to protest discrimination. On a global scale, in response to the estimated 600 million people (or 10% of the world's population) who live with some form of disability, the United Nations General Assembly is in the process of adopting a convention that expressly protects the human rights of disabled individuals (Stein, 2007). However, employees, victims, and offenders with disability in the criminal justice system continue to face serious social and attitudinal barriers that prevent their full inclusion and access to the rights, privileges, and dignity afforded to non-disabled individuals.

References

American Association of People With Disability. http://www.aapd-dc.org/index.php (accessed November 28, 2007).

Americans with Disabilities Act of 1990. Public Law 101–336 101st Cong., 2nd sess. (26 July 1990).

Backman, E., 1994. Is the Movement Racist? *Mainstream* (May): 24–31.

Board of Trustees of the University of Alabama v. *Garrett*, 531 U.S. 356 (2001).

Burgdorf, Robert L. Jr. 2007. A Misunderstood Law. The Center for an Accessible Society.

http://www.accessiblesociety.org /topics/ada/misunderstood.htm (accessed November 20, 2007).

Cleveland v. Policy Management Systems Corporation. 526 U.S. 795 (1999).

Federal Bureau of Investigation. 2006a. *About Hate Crimes Statistics, 2006.* http://www.fbi.gov/ucr/hc2006/abouthcs.htm (accessed January 5, 2008).

Federal Bureau of Investigation. 2006b. *Incidents and Offenses.* http://www.fbi.gov/ucr/hc2006/incidents.html (accessed January 5, 2008).

Goffman, E. 1959. *The Presentation of Self in Everyday Life*. Garden City, NY: Anchor/Doubleday.

Greifinger, Robert B. 2006. Disabled Prisoners and "Reasonable Accommodation". *Criminal Justice Ethics* 25 (1): 2, 53.

Kardasz, Frank. 1995. Apprehending Mental Patients. *Law and Order* (November): 91–92.

Miller, Linda, and Kären Hess. 1998. *The Police in the Community: Strategies for the 21st Century*. Belmont, CA, West/Wadsworth.

National Council on Disability. 2002. *Supreme Court Decisions Interpreting the Americans with Disability Act*. http://www.ncd.gov/newsroom/publications/2002/supremecourt_ada.htm (accessed November 1, 2007).

National Organization for Victim Assistance. 2007. *Working With Victims of Crime With Disabilities*. http://www.trynova.org/victiminfo/ovc-disabilities/ (accessed November 20, 2007).

Office for Victims of Crime. 1998. *Working with Victims of Crime with Disabilities* (September).

Olmstead v. *L.C.* (98–536) 527 U.S. 581 (1999).

Pennsylvania Department of Corrections v. *Yeskey* (141 L.Ed. 2d 215, 118 S. Cp. 1952) 1998.

Pustilnik, Amanda C. 2005. Prisons of the Mind: Social Value and Economic Inefficiency in the Criminal Justice Response to Mental Illness. *The Journal of Criminal Law & Criminology* 96 (1): 217–265.

Russell, Marta, and Jean Stewart. 2001. Disablement, Prison, and Historical Segregation. *The Monthly Review* 53 (3) http://www.monthlyreview.org/0701russell.htm (accessed November 15, 2007).

Scotch, R. K. 1989. Politics and Policy in the History of the Disability Rights Movement. *The Milbank Quarterly* 67 (Suppl. 2, Pt. 2): 380–400.

Shakespeare, T. 1993. Disabled People's Self-organisation: a new social movement? *Disability, Handicap and Society* 8 (3): 249–263.

She, Peiyun, and David C. Stapleton. 2006. A Review of Disability Data for the Institutional Population. Cornell University Rehabilitation Research and Training Center on Disability Demographics and Statistics http://digitalcommons.ilr.cornell.edu/edicollect/1205/ (accessed November 1, 2007).

Stein, Michael Ashley. 2007. Disability Human Rights. *California Law Review* 95 (1): 75–121.

Sutton v. *United Airlines*, 527 U.S. 471 (1999).

Theirs, N. 1994. Beyond Pity: Americans' Perceptions of Citizens with Disabilities. *OT Week* (April 1994): 20–24.

Thomas, S. 1990. The Disability Rights Movement to Stop Protecting Y'all from Me. *The Guild Practitioner* 25: 33–41.

Toth, Reid C. 2008. The Disabled and Physically Challenged in the Criminal Justice System. In *In the Margins: Special Populations and American Justice*, ed. Reid C. Toth, Gordon A. Crews and Catherine E. Burton, 145–175. Upper Saddle River, NJ: Pearson Prentice Hall.

Tyiska, Cheryl Guidry. 2001. *Working with Victims of Crime with Disabilities*. Washington, DC: Office for Victims of Crime, U.S. Department of Justice. http://www.trynova.org/victiminfo/ovc-disabilities/ (accessed November 10, 2007).

United States v. *Georgia* (04–1203) 546 U.S. 151 (2006).

Walker, Samuel, Cassia Spohn, and Miriam DeLone. 2004. *The Color of Justice: Race, Ethnicity, and Crime in America*. Belmont, CA: Thompson/Wadsworth.

Young, J. 1998. *The Genealogy of a Social Movement: Disability Rights in Comparative Perspective*. Paper presented at the meeting of the Western Social Science Association, Denver, CO.

CHAPTER 16

In Whose God We Trust?

Religious Difference, Persecution, and Criminal Justice

Barbara Perry

Phoebe Morgan

From the time European settlers landed on the shores of what is now the United States, there has been a close connection between the "immigrant experience" and religion. For many ethnic groups arriving in this new land, religion has provided the basis for continued (albeit often short-lived) solidarity and sense of community. It has often served as the glue which would reinforce group identity. At the same time, religion has been a frequent source of divisiveness between groups, where religious beliefs and practices have defined worshipers as "different."

The "normative standard" against which religious communities have been measured has historically been British Protestantism, which includes denominations such as Anglicans, Presbyterians, Baptists, and Quakers. After the American Revolution, successive waves of non-Protestant immigrants broke this religious monopoly. Eastern European Jews, Irish, German, and Mexican Catholics, and diverse religions of the East have contributed to the contemporary religious pluralism of the United States. Nonetheless, Protestantism was so deeply embedded prior to the Revolution that its dominance and influence on cultural values remained intact. Puritanism, in particular, provided the model upon which much of the U.S. political and legal structures were based.

The impact of early religious beliefs on all aspects of civil society—including the criminal justice system—was pervasive and long-lasting. Friedman (1993:32) maintains that

> It would be hard to over-emphasize the influence of religion in shaping the criminal codes, in framing the modes of enforcement, and, generally, in creating a distinctive legal culture. The criminal justice system was in many ways another arm of religious orthodoxy.

Consequently, under colonial rule, there was little if any distinction between sin and crime. The laws of God were also the laws of humankind; offences against humans were offences against God. The Laws and Liberties of Massachusetts, for example, specified capital offences and included scriptural references justifying the inclusion of both the crime and its attendant punishment. The criminal codes and court dockets throughout the colonies were replete with proscriptions and punishments for what we now think of as "moral" offences: blasphemy, violating the Sabbath, misbehaving in church, consorting with the Devil, or fornicating. In 1758, Abel Wood of Plymouth was tried for "irreverently behaving himself by chalking the back of one Hezekiah Purrington in church, playing and recreating himself in the *time of publick worship*." Another young man was tried for "lewd and unseemly behavior" for kissing his wife on the Sabbath—upon his return from three years at sea (cited in Friedman, 1993:33).

By the end of the eighteenth century, religious orthodoxy had largely lost its hold on the criminal justice system. Increasing diversity and secularization were accompanied by the rationalization and bureaucratization of the legal system. Nonetheless, remnants of the country's religious past and its legacy of religious intolerance remained intact within the criminal justice system for some time: the exclusion of religious minorities from citizenship; the courts' religious oath; and criminalization of religious practices, for example. As we shall see throughout this chapter, religious difference has often provided the foundation for discriminatory rhetoric, policy, and action.

RELIGIOUS PERSECUTION

It is ironic that a country resettled by people seeking freedom from religious persecution has had such an extensive history of religious bigotry and violence. It is equally ironic that while the First Amendment guarantees religious freedom, some religious minorities have been met with considerable legal and extra-legal intolerance. It remains the case, in spite of our popular mythology, that the United States is not a melting pot of religious "tolerance and harmony." On the contrary, "all of the ancient European hatreds based on nation and religion reappeared on this side of the Atlantic. Cities became boiling cauldrons of suspicion and hatred" (Walker, 1998:44). From Puritan persecutions of "heathens" and "heretics," to contemporary acts of anti-Muslim violence, religious difference has inspired periodic waves of hostility culminating in violent rhetoric and action.

Native Americans

The first to suffer the impact of European religious bigotry in the United States were, of course, Native Americans. In the absence of such European religious trappings as churches, shrines, or chalices, Columbus and his followers assumed Native Americans to be without religion, and thus in need of "salvation." Stannard (1992:200) characterizes Columbus as a typical European religious fanatic, who saw it as his divine duty to eliminate "difference" through the conversion, conquest, or execution of non-Christians. He was

> . . . a man with sufficient intolerance and contempt for all who did not look like or believe as he did, that he thought nothing of enslaving or killing such people simply because they were not like him . . . As such, the fact that he launched a campaign of horrific violence against the Natives of Hispaniola is not something that should surprise anyone.

Subsequent evangelists to the Americas took up Columbus' mission to "civilize" the Natives by Christianizing them. It was those who steadfastly resisted conversion—individually and collectively—who would suffer the violence of Christian intolerance.

It was the imagery of Natives as "savages" and "wild men" that allowed their persecution. Drawing on the emerging notions of social Darwinism, Europeans in the Americas constructed Native Americans as "less than human." Some went so far as to characterize them as consorts of the Devil. Rather than acknowledge the validity and richness of Native religions, Europeans characterized them as heathens to be saved or eradicated. All too often, the latter was the case. In the Spanish Southwest, for example, Pueblo peoples risked beatings, or even death, if they dared to practice traditional rituals (Mihesuah, 1996). The decline in the population of Natives in the United States from 2.5 million in 1600 to approximately 200,000 in 1990 can be attributed at least in part to genocidal practices which resulted in decimated, sometimes lost tribes. While violence against Native Americans persists today, it is less likely to be motivated by religious difference than by broader ethnic differences.

Anti-Semitism

Like Native Americans, Jewish Americans have age-old histories of persecution in this country. Moreover, they are probably among the most vulnerable to contemporary victimization, individually and collectively. Jews have been attacked and even massacred for holding their beliefs since the days of the Roman occupation of Israel. In the modern era, anti-Semitism reached its tragic zenith with the holocaust in Nazi Germany. In fact, it was Nazi persecution which motivated the great migration of European Jews to the United States in the early part of the twentieth century. While these immigrants and their descendants have enjoyed relative freedom and prosperity in the United States, they have also experienced persistent anti-Semitic sentiment and violence.

American Jews occupy an ambiguous and often difficult position in the United States. On the one hand, they are among the "white ethnics" to which Gould refers in Chapter 3. On the other hand, they are also perceived as a "people apart." By virtue of skin color, they are relatively privileged; by virtue of their religion, they are subordinate. There is one particularly tenacious element of "white anti-Semitism" which seems indissoluble:

> . . . that is the general American belief that the Christian faith is superior to all others, that Jews stubbornly refuse to accept the truthfulness of Christianity, and that until they do,. . . as a group they can never be given the respect that Christians receive. (Dinnerstein, 1994:xii)

From this perspective, Jews are "unworthy" because of the fallibility of their beliefs. They are not the "chosen ones," after all. Moreover, Jews have long been associated with horrific practices and rituals, befitting the vulgar beliefs of Judaism: child sacrifices and drinking the blood of Christians, for example. Their perceived most grievous sin, of course, was the murder of Christ. Consequently, the perceived economic success of Jews as a group is deemed to be undeserved. Instead, they are thought to have achieved their success through deceit and conspiracy.

Informed by these misperceptions of Jews, anti-Semitic violence has been relatively persistent throughout the history of Jews in the United States. An overview of recent audits of anti-Semitic activity reveals an especially disturbing trend: since 1991, anti-Semitic violence has been increasingly more likely to involve personal rather than property crimes. Historically, this has been a group victimized by crimes against property, such as synagogue or cemetery desecrations. However, the tide has turned in recent years. Additionally, the decline in the number of anti-Semitic incidents beginning in the late nineties has corresponded to an increase in the intensity of the violence associated with the incidents. The 2006 Audit of Anti-Semitic Incidents, for example, found that anti-Semitic activity declined by 12% from 2005 to 2006; however, "the decline came in a year marked by several violent attacks, including the shooting at the Greater Seattle Jewish Federation in July by an Islamic extremist, in which staffer Pamela Waechter was killed and three others seriously wounded" (Anti-Defamation League, 2006).

THE SPECIAL CASE OF AMERICAN MUSLIMS: GUILT BY ASSOCIATION

As the Muslim American community has become more visible and the politics of religion in the Middle East more salient, there has occurred a corresponding shift in focus of religiously motivated violence toward Muslim-American communities. Most notably, religious fundamentalists and Zionists have become openly hostile to Islam and those who practice it. Among them is a misperception that, as a religion, Islam is primitive and therefore the antithesis of all that is modern and good (Sabbagh, 1990:27). Exacerbating this is the growing tendency to collapse all Muslims with Arabs and to paint all with the same tainted brush. Stereotypes of the "crazed," "religiously fanatical" Arab/Muslim abound.

Due in part to their post-9/11 increased awareness of Islamic fundamentalism, a growing number of Americans who are not religious fundamentalists have also come to assume that Islam condones violence. Consequently, Muslims of all sects and moderation are increasingly treated as though they are proponents of terrorism or as terrorists themselves.

A series of historic events that include the 2001 attack on the World Trade Center by Islamic revolutionaries, the ensuing U.S. invasions of two predominately Muslim countries (Afghanistan and Iraq), and President George Bush's vilification of two other Muslim countries (Iran and Syria) as "evil" have reinforced this tendency to conflate all things Islamic with terror and evil. For example, when survey respondents were asked, "when you hear the word *Muslim*, what comes to mind?" 32% used negative terms, many of which alluded to images of war, guns, and violence. In addition, a stunningly one-fourth of the respondents believed that Muslims teach their children to hate (CAIR, 2006a).

The result has been a significant increase in blatant and often violent forms of religious persecution and discrimination of not only Muslims, but also of those associated with them, as well as those who appear to be Muslim but who are not. In 1996, for example, The Center for American-Islamic Relations (CAIR, 2007) received only 80 civil rights complaints. But since September 2001, the number of complaints has increased exponentially, with 366 complaints filed in 2001 and 2,476 logged in 2006. Beneath these complaints lie three types of unfounded or erroneous assumptions of guilt by association.

ASSUMED TERRORISTS. As she opened her beauty salon, Zohreh Assemi was viciously assaulted and robbed, her establishment was vandalized, and she was left with a towel stuffed in her mouth. Like many Iranian Americans, she came to the United States to escape Ayatollah Khomeini's terrorist regime. In recounting her experience to a *Newsday* reporter, she claimed the anti-Muslim slurs painted on her salon's mirrors hurt more than the physical abuse. Having been a victim of terrorism, she explained, "the worst thing they can do is call me is a terrorist" (Maloney, 2007).

Assemi's story, while extreme, illustrates a disturbing pattern of hostility justified by an erroneous suspicion that those who openly practice Islam must be terrorists, friends or family of terrorists, or sympathetic to the cause of Islamic terrorism. For example, while in transit from a religious conference, six imams were deplaned, handcuffed, and questioned by law enforcement because their observance of evening prayers was deemed suspicious by a US Airways passenger. When asked to account for the mistaken identity, a US Airways spokesperson stated, "we're sorry the imams had a difficult time, but we do think the crews have to make these calls and in this case they made the right one" (Miller, 2006).

ASSUMED UN-AMERICAN. Even when Muslims are not assumed to be terrorists, hostility toward them has been justified by the assumption that the practice of Islam is simply un-American. Thirty-two percent of participants in a 2006 *Newsweek* poll believed that fellow Muslim citizens are less loyal to the United States (Ghazali, 2007). When Keith Ellison, the first Muslim American elected to Congress, chose to take his oath on the Koran rather than the Bible, high profile blogger Dennis Prager argued he should not be allowed to do so "not because of any American hostility to the Koran, but because the act undermines American civilization . . . If you are incapable of serving your country on that book, you shouldn't serve in Congress" (Prager, 2006). Apparently, Prager's distrust of Muslim loyalty is more mainstream than extreme, as a shocking 44% of participants in a Cornell University national opinion survey believed the curtailment of the civil liberties of Muslims to be a necessity for national security (Friedlander, 2004).

MISTAKEN IDENTITIES. Widespread ignorance about Islam and Muslims undergirds much of the misplaced suspicion that lies behind Islamophobia. Like Dennis Prager, more than two-thirds of Christian Americans are unaware that Muslims worship the god of Abraham (CAIR, 2006b). According to the same report, even fewer Americans appreciate ethnic and denominational diversity of the Islamic World. Despite the facts that the majority of Muslims in America are South Asian in origin and not all Arab Americans are Muslim, too often Americans assume that if you are Arabic, you must be Muslim and if you are Muslim, you must be either a terrorist or an un-American sympathizer.

As a result, merely speaking Arabic in public can provoke unfounded suspicion. An American Airlines flight from San Diego to Chicago was forced to return to its gate and all passengers deplaned because a passenger defined six Arabic-speaking men as suspicious. They were neither Muslims nor terrorists but were in fact U.S. military subcontractors on their way to train Marines. In requesting an apology from the airline, their attorney explained, "you can't just assume that everyone who speaks Arabic has a bomb strapped to [his] chest" (Colson, 2007).

Similarly, slightly more than half (52%) of the civil rights complaints made to the Council on American–Islamic Relations in 2006 were regarding mistreatment based upon mistaken identity. According to the Sikh Coalition (http://www.sikhcoalition.org), simply because they wear turbans, the American Sikh community has suffered a significant spike in anti-Muslim hate crimes since 9/11. Two days after the 9/11 attacks, Balbir Singh Sodhi was murdered in a drive-by retaliatory shooting, and more recently, Iqbal Singh was stabbed while standing on a street corner because his assailant wanted to "kill a Taliban."

GOVERNMENT ABUSE. Unlike most other religious minorities in the United States, the primary complaint among persecuted Muslims is neither hate crimes, nor workplace discrimination, but rather abuse of authority by government officials. A majority of Muslim Americans believe the USA Patriot Act encourages surveillance and detention for purposes of intimidation rather than for crime investigation and intelligence gathering (CAIR, 2007). Imam Malik Majahid claims a quarter (25%) of Muslim American households have, in fact, been visited by the FBI and 35% of the Council on American-Islamic Relations civil rights complaints are regarding unexplained detention and deportation (CAIR, 2007).

Safana Jawad's daughter filed a civil rights complaint with CAIR because her mother, a British citizen, was deplaned, jailed, strip searched, held in a maximum security cell for two days, and then deported without charge or explanation (Raman, 2006). Jawad had been on her way to see her newborn granddaughter. Similarly, Brandon Mayfield, a Muslim convert, was held as a material witness in the Madrid Bombings for 14 days in a secret location under a fake name without access to family or legal council (Eggen, 2007). His family learned of his detention while watching the television news. Finally, Syrian-Cuban immigrant Ahmed Sheikh-Khalil's application for citizenship was all but signed four years ago, but, despite repeated complaints, he has yet to receive a legitimate reason for the delay (Politove, 2007). Disproportionate name checks among Muslim applicants have caused similar delays in the issuance of visas and green cards (Chin, 2007). As a result, "thousands of men with suspicious names have changed them, making Mohammed 'Moe,' and Osama 'Sam'" (Elliott, 2006).

What these otherwise diverse religious minorities share is a failure to measure up to the WASP core that has shaped the values of the United States. They have been persecuted, driven away, even murdered for the "sins" of holding different religious beliefs, engaging in different religious practices, and steadfastly refusing to succumb to the Puritan impulse. This intolerance has emerged in a nation thought to be a haven for those escaping victimization elsewhere (Pipes and Duran, 2002).

Religious minorities, then, have been identifiable victims of personal and property crimes. The preceding was a cursory glance at but a few such cases. We might also explore the experiences of the Amish, the Rastafarians, and other marginal groups for evidence of religious persecution. Time and space preclude more extensive examination. Instead, we turn now to look at the other side of the equation. Minority and majority religious beliefs have motivated other types of criminal (sometimes legal) offending, not only against other religious groups, but against others who might be practicing "intolerable" behavior.

VIOLENCE MOTIVATED BY RELIGIOUS BELIEF

Religion has always played some role in defining difference in the United States. In the language of deviance theorists, religion is a mechanism of boundary maintenance by which behaviors are defined as acceptable or unacceptable, moral or immoral, appropriate or inappropriate. Those who transcend those boundaries are constructed as the "Other"—often dangerous, always notably different. Religious communities are especially apt at this, since they generally subscribe to a rigid doctrine which explicitly defines these boundaries: the Ten Commandments is one such typology of proscriptions.

Where proselytizing and other forms of "persuasion" have not convinced the "deviants" to change their ways, violence justified by scripture has frequently taken its place. Both religious and secular communities have felt the effects of (usually) Christians' attempts to police the boundaries of acceptable, moral, and "Christian" conduct in the United States. Again the examples are legion. We have chosen but a small sample to illustrate the theme here.

Puritans and the "City Upon the Hill"

It was with a sense of their historical mission that the first Puritans arrived on the shores of what would become the United States. It was also this mission which would shape their relationships with everyone they encountered here. In particular, the Puritan preoccupation with piety and sin set the stage for rigid intolerance of religious difference, but also of non-conforming behavior in general. Haught (1990) goes so far as to characterize the Puritan colony as a "religious police state" driven by an obsessive aversion to "doctrinal deviation." In other words, "there was a high degree of consensus over proper behavior. The central norm was obedience to authority: first to God, then to clergy, and finally to the male head of the household" (Walker, 1998:15–16). It is in this context that we can make sense of the violence perpetrated by Puritans against Quakers, and later, against witches.

The colonial Quakers were ahead of their time. Their democratic vision threatened the contrary vision of an ordered world. Boorstin (1992) identifies three particular traits that set the Quakers in dangerous opposition to Puritanism. First, their belief in equality clearly contradicted the Puritan hierarchy which privileged God, clergy, and men, especially white men. Second, their informality of dress, language, and comportment was directly opposite to the Puritan traditions of formality in all spheres. And third, the Quaker tradition of tolerance flew in the face of Puritan demands for conformity. This difference was especially evident in their perceptions of Native Americans. Where Puritans saw them as consorts of the Devil, Quakers were in awe of their democratic and spiritual nature. At root, then, Puritan hostility toward Quakers can be attributed to the latter's rejection of earthly formality and authority.

This hostility would take on a viciously punitive face. The first two Quakers to arrive in Massachusetts in 1656—two women from the Barbados—were forcibly expelled almost before they disembarked from their ship. Before their expulsion, they were "jailed, stripped and searched for signs of witchcraft, their books publicly burned" (Newton and Newton, 1991:13). The "heretics" would henceforth be subject to brutal punishments. Floggings, mutilations, imprisonment, and hangings awaited the undaunted Quaker martyrs. In 1657, two Quaker men were arrested and immediately received 30 lashes with a knotted whip, subsequently starved in a bare prison cell for three days, imprisoned for nine winter weeks, during which they received weekly lashings, and then finally banished by ship to the Barbados. By 1661, at least four Quakers were executed for their beliefs.

Similar treatment awaited suspected witches. In fact, the threats represented by Quakers and witches seemed indistinguishable to Puritans. Both were heretics—consider the fate of the first two Quakers who had been checked for "signs of witchcraft." Witches—women in particular—presented similar challenges to the authority of God, clergy, and men:

> . . . the war against witches was also a war against women: or at least against disorderly, troublesome deviant women . . . Those who rebelled against order "were the very embodiment of evil." The "subordination of women" was part of the natural order; the witch symbolized or embodied a kind of double rebellion—of women against men, and women against Godly society. (Friedman, 1993:46–47)

Erickson (1966:154) has traced the origins of the witch hunts to widespread anxiety about the shifting cultural and political climate of the Massachusetts colony, or a perceived "shift of religious focus—society, we would say, confronting a relocation of boundaries." More broadly, Butler (1990:70) points to "three decades of disputing over ministers, churches, taxes and roads that . . . uprooted almost any notion of community, secular or religious." The era of rigid religious homogeneity and conformity was coming to an end. The witch hunts, then, were a last effort to maintain the vision which had inspired the settlers of the earlier part of the 1600s.

Ultimately, between May and September of 1692, 21 people (mostly women) and several domestic animals would die in the midst of the witchcraft hysteria. Most were hanged; many suffered mutilation and confessional torture before their death.

Anti-Gay Violence

While the seventeenth century witch hunts were short-lived and narrowly confined to Massachusetts, a contemporary parallel continues to rage. The modern equivalent is anti-gay violence, which also arises largely out of religious beliefs. Scriptural interpretations have also informed hostility and violence against gay men and lesbians. Leviticus is held to be the authoritative Biblical decree outlawing homosexuality. It is there that we find the often cited passages thought to prohibit homosexuality as sin:

You shall not lie with a male as with a woman; it is an abomination (Leviticus 18:22).

If a man lies with a male as with a woman, both of them have committed an abomination; they shall be put to death, their blood is upon them (Leviticus 20:13). Comstock (1991) and Biery (1990) contest the literal reading of these passages as prohibiting same-sex relations in general. Instead, they cite favorably scholars who argue that "because these verses are immediately proximate to prohibitions against the cultic practices of other nations, they condemn only . . . male temple prostitution and idolatry" (Comstock, 1991:121). Whether accurate or not, the more literal translation has nonetheless been used to justify state policy (as in Bowers v. Hardwick) and anti-gay violence.

Anti-gay violence is consistently associated with biblical references. Offenders are frequently reported to refer to victims as "sinners," as "unnatural," as "violators of God's law," or as "going against the Bible" (Comstock, 1991; NGLTF, 1994, 1995, 1996). The contemporary mainstreaming of homosexuality through civil rights protections "shook the foundations of orthodox religious belief . . . The increasing acceptance of homosexuality . . . became a sign of godlessness and impending calamity" (Herman, 1997:4). The anti-gay backlash in recent years has been so intense as to be characterized as a "crusade" (Comstock, 1991:26). Perpetrators are socialized in an environment where homosexuality is derided and vilified (see Chapter 12). The religious ideologues who perpetuate these extreme images have

> . . . created an atmosphere of loathing and contempt for lesbian, gay and bisexual people by poisoning communities with rhetoric and misinformation that vilify and demonize lesbians, gay men and bisexuals as sexual predators and undeserving of basic human rights and protections against discrimination. Although many Far Right organizations distance themselves from anti-gay attacks, they are complicit in and often direct campaigns that fuel intolerance. (NGLTF, 1994:15)

That such an atmosphere engenders violence is obvious in the recent campaigns to restrict gay rights and protections that were discussed in Chapter 12. There we saw how scripturally grounded homophobic rhetoric was correlated with a heightened incidence of anti-gay violence. The key to breaking this link is to deconstruct damaging interpretations, as Comstock (1991) and Biery (1990) have done.

Christian Identity Churches and RAHOWA

Perpetrators of religiously motivated violence are often associated with Christian Identity theology, which identifies the enemies of God in very broad terms. The anti-Semitism, racism, and homophobia that characterize so many hate groups—and not just the Identity Churches—can be traced to the theocratic principle of Christian Identity. On the basis of a creative reading of biblical scripture, those advocating this perspective claim the white race to be the direct descendants of Ancient Israel, and therefore God's chosen people. Moreover, in contrast to the glorification of the white race, Jews are seen to be the source of all evil, spawned as they are by the Devil himself:

> WE BELIEVE that there are literal children of Satan in this world today . . . WE BELIEVE that the Canaanite Jew is the natural enemy of our Aryan (White) Race. The Jew is like a destroying virus that attacks our racial body to destroy our Aryan culture and the purity of our race. (www.aryan-nations.org)

As a corollary of this, the anti-Semites often portray African Americans as the pawns of the Jewish conspiracy. It is blacks who are forced into interracial mixing at the behest of Jews seeking to defile the white race. Black-on-white crime is also seen as a phenomenon orchestrated by Jews as a means of cowing whites. After Jews, then, blacks are perceived to be the greatest threat to the purity and safety of the white race:

> Today you can escape the terror of black ghettos and Brown Barrios. Your children and your children's children will have no refuge. The DEATH OF THE WHITE RACE is neither imaginary nor far off in the distant future. (www.aryan-nations.org)

The belief systems of Christian Identity lead many hate groups to a frightening conclusion: through organized action, the white race must reverse the trends represented by the myriad forms of white racial "suicide" and "genocide." All traces of the non-white presence must be erased from the United States through RAHOWA—RAcial HOly War—in which whites must be victorious. Representatives of the various hate groups are explicit in their call to arms. They do not shrink from violence. Consider the following illustrative exhortation on the World Church of the Creator's Website:

> WE BELIEVE that the White Race, its Biological and Cultural Heritage, is now under attack by our mortal racial enemies: Jews, niggers and the mud races. WE BELIEVE that RAHOWA (RAcial HOly WAr) . . . is the only road to the resurrection and redemption of the White Race. (www. churchofthecreator.org)

It is this call to RAHOWA that puts minorities most at risk, since it attempts to justify violence by appealing to God's will. According to the rhetoric, Jews and their allies have distorted the word of God, and in so doing, they threaten the white race. When it is believed that these "subhuman" and "soulless" races are closer to Satan than to God, it becomes acceptable to attack them in the name of ridding the world of evil. Supremacists claim a moral right to engage in violence as a means of restoring God's law and the white race to its rightful place in the United States' racial hierarchy. This is the ultimate discursive attempt to marginalize and disempower the perceived threats posed by women, homosexuals, and all people of color.

SERVICE PROVIDERS

In contrast to those organizations that exploit religious belief to justify oppressive violence against others are religiously grounded organizations that use their beliefs to further the interests of justice. One rallying point continues to be the struggle for religious freedom within the criminal justice system. The Religious Freedom Restoration Act (RFRA) of 1993 represents an uncertain victory in this arena. The Act seeks to significantly increase inmates' freedom to exercise their religious beliefs and rituals. Yet, this will not be an easy task:

> Engulfed in problems—prison gangs, overcrowding, violence and riots—and exacerbated by limited finances, outdated facilities, and a soaring inmate population, prisons must accommodate the demands of a panoply of faiths. Outside the prisons, religious adherents can select their own diets, places of worship, and religious leaders, but in prisons, these aspects of religious life must be supplied and regulated by the penal institution. (Solove, 1996:462–463)

Prison administrators have traditionally offered an array of untested assumptions to support their failure to recognize religious freedom: disruption of prison routine; elevated religious animosity between groups; loss of control and discipline over inmates; excessive costs; lack or resources, space and personnel.

Non-traditional—that is, non-Judeo-Christian—religions have been most significantly affected. Muslims and Buddhists have been refused the right to wear ritual symbols of faith, or denied the use of prison chapels. Rastafarians, Native Americans, and Orthodox Jews have been forced to shed their traditionally lengthy locks or beards. For the most part, the RFRA has failed to live up to its potential, largely because courts continue to be uninformed and insensitive about prisoners' religious rights and freedoms (Solove, 1996).

One area of particular concern in the context of freedom of religion has been the freedom of Native Americans to practice traditional ways of spirituality. In spite of the 1978 American Indian Religious Freedom Act and the 1993 RFRA, Native American inmates still face obstacles in their attempts to worship according to tradition. Four particular issues stand in their way. First, Native American prisoners are often incarcerated away from their homes, making it difficult to maintain contact not only with family and friends, but with spiritual leaders as well. Second, many prison officials continue to deny religious ceremonies such as Sweat Lodges. Third, Native Americans are generally denied access to sacred objects such as herbs, pipes, feathers, and long hair. Fourth, officials fail to recognize the natural, cyclical, rather than linear nature of the schedule of Native religious ceremonies.

There is nonetheless hope for progress. There is a growing recognition that freedom of religious practice may in fact serve the rehabilitative goals of corrections. In the debates preceding the RFRA, senators as disparate as Bob Dole and Edward Kennedy acknowledged the value of religion in prisons. Dole insisted that "If religion can help just a handful of prison inmates get back on track, then the inconvenience of accommodating their religious beliefs is a very small price to pay." Kennedy shared the sentiment: "We would encourage prisoners to be religious. There is every reason to believe that doing so will increase the likelihood that a prisoner will be rehabilitated" (cited in Solove, 1996:472).

Religious activists and to a lesser degree prison officials have recognized the utility of religious programming in the prison context. Consequently, a variety of prison ministries have emerged nationwide. An Internet search for "prison ministries" identified 20 predominantly Christian and non-denominational ministries, many of which are committed to helping inmates to "find Christ" and subsequently to helping them to reintegrate into their communities. Even the omnipresent 12-step programs—such as Alcoholics Anonymous—have found their way into prison rehabilitation programs. These, too, are grounded in spiritual notions of renewal:

> . . . a crisis of separation; a longing for faith; a sense of rescue by a higher power; a supportive and close-knit community; and ritual renewal combine in a format that also promises continuity and social reinforcement upon release from confinement. (Skotnicki, 1996:41)

On the other side of the prison fence are those religious organizations committed to preventing crime and breaking the links that contribute to crime and violence. Churches often see it as part of their mission to combat the violence, prejudice, and abuses that characterize their congregants and the community in which they live. While informed by religious precepts, such organizations are not limited to proselytizing. Many provide food to those who might otherwise steal it, training for those without job skills, rehabilitation programs for those addicted to drugs, or shelters for those victimized by domestic and family violence. Below is just a small sampling of such groups:

- Muslims Against Family Violence offers an educational campaign intended to make the community aware of, as well as eliminate the problem of, family violence (www.mpac.org/mafv).
- Islamic Relief of Los Angeles seeks to feed, clothe, and find employment for underprivileged Muslims, as well as providing an alternative to gangs and life in prison (amahelp.com/lamission.htm).
- The Social Concern Ministry of the Catholic Church operationalizes church teaching "as it relates to issues of human rights, justice and the empowerment of the poor and disenfranchised in our society" (www.cathcharitiesffldcty.com/SocialCo.html).
- Churches Taking a Corner is an Interfaith organization "fighting substance abuse, violence, racism and prejudice in every community where we work" (www.ctac-usa.org.html).

As the presence of such organizations suggests, religion has the potential not only to inspire violence, but also to inspire its opposite: peace, tolerance, and justice. As criminal justice practitioners, we might learn from the peacemaking efforts of the religions of the world.

References

Anti-Defamation League. 2006. Audit of Anti-Semitic Incidents, www.adl.org/main_Anti_Semitism_Domestic/Audit_2006.htm.

Aryan Nations Website. http://www.aryan-nations.org (last accessed May 06, 2008).

Biery, Roger. 1990. *Understanding Homosexuality.* Austin, TX: Edward-William Publishing.

Bowers v. *Hardwick,* 478 U.S. 186 (1986).

Boorstin, Daniel. 1992. *The Americans: The Colonial Experience.* New York, NY: Vintage Books.

Butler, Jon. 1990. *Awash in a Sea of Faith: Christianizing the American People.* Cambridge, MA: Harvard University Press.

Chin, Sharon. 2007. Anti-Muslim Prejudice Up In Bay Area, Group Says. CBS 5, July 5, http://cbs.5.com/local/local_story_187011716.html.

Colson, Nicole. 2007. *Socialist Worker Online,* September 21, http://www.socialistworker.org/2007–2/645/645_03_Racist.shtml.

Comstock, Gary. 1991. *Violence Against Lesbians and Gay Men.* New York, NY: Columbia University Press.

CAIR. 2006a. *Western Muslim Minorities: Integration and Disenfranchisement.* Washington, DC: www.cair-net.org.

CAIR. 2006b. *American Public Opinion About Islam and Muslims.* Washington, DC: www.cair.com.

CAIR. 2007. *The Presumption of Guilt: The Status of Muslim Civil Rights in the United States.* Washington, DC: www.cair.com.

Dinnerstein, Leonard. 1994. *Anti-Semitism in America.* New York, NY: Oxford University Press.

Eggen, Dan. 2007. Patriot Act Provisions Voided. *Washington Post,* September 26; page A-02.

Elliott, Andrea. 2006. Muslim Immigration Has Bounced Back. *Seattle Times,* September 10, http://seattletimes.nwsource.com/cgi-bin/PrintStory.pl.

Erickson, Kai. 1966. *Wayward Puritans.* New York, NY: John Wiley and Sons.

Friedlander, Blaine. 2004. Fear Factor: 44 Percent of Americans Queried in Cornell National Poll Favor Curtailing Some Liberties for Muslim Americans. *Cornell News,* December 17, http://www.news.cornell.edu/releases/Dec04/Muslim.Poll.bpf.html.

Friedman, Lawrence. 1993. *Crime and Punishment in American History.* New York, NY: Basic Books.

Ghazali, Abdus Sattar. 2007. September 13. American Muslims Six Years After 9/11. http://www.khabrein.info (accessed September 23, 2007).

Haught, James. 1990. *Holy Horrors.* Buffalo, NY: Prometheus.

Herman, Didi. 1997. *The Antigay Agenda: Orthodox Vision and the Christian Right.* Chicago: University of Chicago.

Maloney, Jennifer. 2007. Muslim Woman Victim of Hate Crime. Newsday.com, September 17, http://www.newsday.com/news/local/crime/ny-libias.

Mihesuah, Devon. 1996. *American Indians: Stereotypes and Realities.* Atlanta, GA: Clarity Press.

Miller, Leslie. 2006. At National Airport6, Prayers Against Profiling. Washingtonpost.com, November 28. http://www.washingtonpost.com/wp-dyn/content/article/2006/11/27/AR2006112701184_pf.html.

Newton, Michael and Judy Ann Newton. 1991. *Racial and Religious Violence in America: A Chronology.* New York, NY: Garland.

NGLTF. 1994. Anti-Gay/Lesbian Violence, Victimization and Defamation in 1993. Washington, DC: NGLTF Policy Institute.

NGLTF. 1995. Anti-Gay/Lesbian Violence, Victimization and Defamation in 1994. Washington, D.C.: NGLTF Policy Institute.

NGLTF. 1996. Anti-Gay/Lesbian Violence, Victimization and Defamation in 1995. Washington, DC: NGLTF Policy Institute.

Pipes, Daniel, and Khalid Duran. 2002. *Muslim Immigrants in the United States.* Center for Immigrant Studies. Washington, DC: www.cis.org.

Politove, Josh. 2007. Anti-Muslim Bias Complaints Increasing. *TBO News,* June 21, http://www.tbo.com/news/metro/MGBWJ66N63F.htm.

Prager, Dennis. 2006. America, Not Keith Ellison, Decides What Book A Congressman Takes His Oath On. Townhall.com, http://townhall.com/Common/Print.aspx, November 28.

Raman, Sheela. 2006. Muslim Gets Apology for April Spring Search. Tampabay. com, December 28, http://www.sptimes. com/ 2006/12/28/news_pf/Hillsborough/ Muslim_gets_apology_f.shtml.

Sabbagh, Suha. 1990. *Sex, Lies and Stereotypes: The Image of Arabs in American Popular Fiction.* Washington, DC: ADC.

Skotnicki, Andrew. 1996. Religion and Rehabilitation. *Criminal Justice Ethics* (Summer/Fall): 34–42.

Solove, Daniel. 1996. Faith Profaned: The Religious Freedom Restoration Act and Religion in the Prisons. *Yale Law Journal* 106: 459–491.

Stannard, David. 1992. *American Holocaust.* New York, NY: Oxford University Press.

Walker, Samuel. 1998. *Popular Justice: A History of American Criminal Justice.* New York, NY: Oxford University Press.

World Church of the Creator, www.churchofthe creator.org (last accessed May 06, 2008).

PART THREE

How Does Difference Matter?

CHAPTER 17

Undocumented Immigration as Moral Panic

Casting Difference as Threat

Michael Costelloe

INTRODUCTION

Public discourse concerning immigration and immigration policy often relies on the characterization and universalization of the threats that are posed by increasing immigration. That is, rather than engaging in rational discussions that acknowledge that immigration reform must strike a balance between the interests of current citizens and a recognition of the needs of those who risk their lives coming to the United States for a better existence, those who favor restrictive immigration policies tend to engage in rhetoric that refers to the widespread personal, social, and economic threats posed by undocumented immigration.[1] It is the specification of and reference to these threats that allows one to consider undocumented immigration as an ideologically driven "moral panic" and to examine how framing undocumented immigration in terms of threat influences public policy. Moreover, this chapter will examine how policies developed out of moral panics are often ineffectual and at times harmful and even deadly.

MORAL PANIC

Although the term "moral panic" was first used by Jock Young in 1971, Stanley Cohen (1972) is credited for analytically applying the concept in his seminal work on Mods and Rockers. Cohen noted that at certain times:

> a condition, episode, person or group of persons emerges to become defined as a threat to societal values and interests; its nature is presented in a stylized

and stereotypical fashion by the mass media; moral barricades are manned by editors, bishops, politicians and other right-thinking people; socially accredited experts pronounce their diagnosis and solutions; ways of coping are evolved or (more often) resorted to; the condition then disappears, submerges or deteriorates and becomes more visible. Sometimes the subject of the panic is quite novel and at other times it is something which has been in existence long enough, but suddenly appears in the limelight. (Cohen, 1972:9)

In short, the term "moral panic" defines the exaggerated social reactions to perceived deviance from and threats to societal values.

Based on Cohen's definition of moral panics, Kenneth Thompson (1998:8) outlines five significant aspects of moral panics:

- Something or someone is defined as a threat to values or interests.
- This threat is depicted in an easily recognizable form by the media.
- There is a rapid build-up of public concern.
- There is a response from authorities or opinion-makers.
- The panic recedes or results in social change.

Implicit in the term "moral panic" is the belief that "the threat is to something held sacred by or fundamental to the society" (Thompson, 1998:8). That is, what distinguish moral panics from other forms of public concerns are both the intensity with which the threat is felt and its potential effect on societal values and morals. The problem, left unchecked, portends to tear at moral fabric. In the United States, threats to such values as family (particularly aimed at children), culture, personal safety, and religion tend to have a greater probability of becoming moral panics than other types of concerns.

The term "moral panic" is a sociological concept; it is not itself a theory (Goode, 2000). It is a tool that can be employed by any number of diverse theories to aid in the examination of the similarities between seemingly different phenomena (Critcher, 2006; Goode, 2000). Moral panics have been employed within a number of different theoretical frameworks, including quite disparate theories such as Marxist theory (e.g., Hall et al., 1978) and structural functionalism (e.g., Lauderdale, 1976). However, if the term "moral panic" is to be a useful conceptual tool and not stretched to meaninglessness, then it should be applied to only those situations that commonly exhibit most of Thompson's previously mentioned five aspects of moral panics.

Goode and Ben-Yehuda note that "the concept of moral panics expands our understanding of social structure, social process, and social change." They argue that moral panics work to clearly define normative behaviors and the moral boundaries of society and to demonstrate that there are limits to how much diversity a society can endure (1994:29). Moreover, the study of moral panics demonstrates that development and implementation of suitable policies and responses to perceived deviance do not develop from rational discourse that draws on objective assessments of the potential harm. Instead, social reaction to moral panics springs forth from the real or imagined threat to certain "positions, statuses, interests, ideologies and values" (Cohen, 1972:191).

Those involved in the creation and maintenance of moral panics include the "five powerful Ps of moral panics" (Critcher, 2006:4):

- The press and broadcasting
- Pressure groups and claim seekers
- Politicians and government
- Police and law enforcement agencies
- Public opinion

When these entities come together on a particular issue, their power to arouse intense reaction is remarkable and often results in the creation of legislation that provides for oppressive social control measures to address the problem (Critcher, 2006). In other words, a "signification spiral" occurs where the actions of and interactions between these groups take a public concern and exaggerate it until it becomes disproportionate to the true threat.

A key component of moral panics is the identification of perpetrators as evil "folk devils," or those labeled as outsiders, deviants, and threats to entrenched and cherished values of society (Cohen, 1972). In moral panics, they are often identified as the source of concern and fear. These individuals or groups are perceived as being not only problematic, but also as at odds with the normative values and morals of the society in which the panic takes place. A core component of this process involves the use of stereotypes to paint quite disparate individuals with a broad brush simply based on group membership. The result is the creation of the perception that all group members have the same problematic characteristics, which then serve to accentuate and exaggerate the differences between "us and them" (Critcher, 2006:8). This process of demonization is an important stage in the development of expanded social control measures and punitive policies founded on difference.

Moral panics are generally a response to some newly perceived problem or a previous problem that is perceived as reemerging (Cohen, 1972). They tend to develop during times of increased uncertainty and anxiety. During these times there is support, and at times demand, for increased social control measures as we attempt to redefine moral boundaries, which have arguably become blurred because of rapid and dramatic social and economic changes. Political elites, the media, and special interest groups often then exploit these generalized anxieties in an attempt to define and frame particular problems. Problems are generally defined in overly simplistic and sensationalistic terms that suggest clear policy implications. For example, past moral panics over daycare centers in the United States suggested that our children were in danger at the hands of evil day care workers. Many have argued that this was a product of anxiety concerning women who were perceived to be forsaking their familial duties for increased participation in the labor force. Unfortunately, because the problem is exaggerated, distorted, misrepresented, or misunderstood, the responses that are initiated are rarely appropriate. In the case of daycares, many individuals were wrongly prosecuted and convicted based on the unreliable testimony of children, whose accounts of bizarre and harmful behaviors were often the product of highly inappropriate and suggestive interviewing techniques by supposed experts. Children were encouraged—in some cases even coerced—to provide statements about events and behaviors that never occurred, resulting in an amplification of deviancy that was not based in reality. It is this exaggeration and/or distortion of the problem that accompanies moral panics and illustrates the link between moral panics and ideology.

MORAL PANICS AS IDEOLOGY

Referring to two forms of ideology as explicated by Gouldner (1976) and Larrain (1983), Chiricos (1996) notes that moral panics are ideological in two senses. First, they are ideological in that they involve rational, partisan discourse that attempts to mobilize public action in the pursuit of some particular interest (1996:26). That is, a problem is identified, outlined, and explained in ways that intend to encourage public concern and demands for effective responses. This corresponds to what Gouldner (1976:23–66) regarded as the "positive" or neutral form of ideology. Moral panics are also ideological in that they involve reports about a problem that are accompanied by commands to do something of a public nature, and that there is a distortion or misrepresentation of the problem in pursuit of that objective (Chiricos, 1996). This is what Larrain (1983) referred to as the "negative" form of ideology. It is this distortion that links ideology and moral panics. Moral panics exaggerate the scope of the problem, and the media, politicians, and special interest groups attempt to exploit these events in order to achieve a particular end, which generally serves a narrower interest than is publicly acknowledged.

In regard to discussions concerning unauthorized immigration, both the positive and negative forms of ideology are readily noticeable. First, the discourse surrounding immigration involves reports about the problem that attempt to justify doing something about it, whether it is building a wall between the Arizona/Mexico border, involving local and state law enforcement in the enforcement of federal immigration statutes, or implementing a guest worker program. We can also readily note the negative aspect of ideology in that often the discourse about undocumented immigration is rooted in a distortion of the problem. One common distortion seems to entail the universalization of threat. That is, a great deal of immigration discourse attempts to describe, explain, and demonstrate the general nature of the risks that are posed as a result of a failure to control our national borders. The reference to the ubiquity of threat is an important component in ideological discourse. In fact, there are those who argue that all forms of ideology are negative in the sense that they attempt to mobilize public action and reach the greatest number of people by presenting the problem in overly generalized terms (Larrain, 1983). It is critical to convince as much of the public as possible that this problem in some way affects them or at least has the potential to affect them. In terms of immigration, then, it may be important to universalize the dangers that are thought to be posed by undocumented immigration. One way this is accomplished is by referring to and describing multiple types of threat such as cultural threat, economic threat, political threat, and criminal threat. The more threats referred to, the greater saliency for a broader social audience.

A DISCOURSE OF THREAT

In attempting to characterize the discourse of threat that surrounds immigration dialogue, it is important to note that this discourse is diverse and is expressed at a number of different institutional sites, by numerous groups and individuals, and for a range of purposes. However, because anti-immigration discourses exhibit similar patterns and support comparable policies, they are considered to belong to the same discursive formations (Thompson, 1998).

Currently, the estimated percentage of the total U.S. population that is undocumented stands at approximately 4%. In other words, 96% of the U.S. population is documented. These figures are important in that they provide some context in considering the description and extent of the problems that a relatively small number of undocumented migrants are purported to present.

Critcher (2006:2) notes that moral panics are, by definition, disproportionate reactions to perceived threats. As previously mentioned, a rather effective way to mobilize public action is to create a sense that the problem is more widespread and threatening than evidence would support. Anti-immigration discourse readily relies on descriptions of the threats that are the result of porous borders and that emphasize the generalized extent of these threats. References to these threats are expressed by a broad range of individuals that include politicians, political pundits, the media, and members of a variety of special interest groups. This section examines some of the more commonly referred threats, which include cultural, economic, and criminal threats.

Cultural threats involve the belief that immigrants somehow threaten "our way of life." That is, immigrants imbued with distinct cultural patterns, norms, values, and morals infiltrate our country, drastically altering American culture. These cultural concerns include the belief that undocumented immigrants, particularly Latinos, possess an inability to assimilate, are unintelligent, and lack proper work ethics and, thus, consequently live in habitual poverty. Furthermore, it is believed that these immigrant groups are less patriotic and remain more closely tied to their homeland rather than the United States. These supposed characteristics are then deemed to contribute to the demise of an "American identity." Perceived cultural threats also include concerns and opposition to such things as bilingual language, education, street signs, and election ballots or to the importance of making English the "official language." A reference to the cultural threat posed by undocumented immigration is aptly illustrated in the comment by noted Harvard political scientist Samuel P. Huntington (2004: 221), who describes the problem of Mexican immigration as "the leading cause of the deterioration of American society, because the constant influx of immigrants has socially, linguistically, and economically diluted American unity and identity."

What seems problematic about these arguments is that what is truly distinctive about U.S. culture is that its "identity"—assuming there is some distinct American identity—cannot be easily separated from its immigration past. Unless you are a member of an indigenous population or your family was brought here against their will as slaves, your family can be traced back to an immigrant population. Therefore, U.S. culture has, in part, been developed through a process of negotiation and accommodation between different ethnic and racial groups, who often have come to the United States (or who were already here) with distinct cultural patterns and beliefs that have eventually all contributed to the "American culture." The stance of anti-immigration groups is that Latino immigration is somehow different—that their size, shared language, and religion, and the fact that they tend to be concentrated in close proximity to the border, all mean that assimilation is more unlikely (Citrin et al., 2007:31). Citrin et al. (2007) also note that this argument suffers from the assumption that assimilation is more preferable than pluralism, which rather than eradicating difference, as assimilation attempts to do, accepts and celebrates it.

Additionally, recent research concludes that available data does not seem to support the assertion that Latino immigration poses a threat to American identity. A study undertaken by Jack Citrin and his colleagues (2007) attempted to "ground the debate over Huntington's prognosis . . . in a sustained empirical analysis of recent immigrants." Using data from the U.S. Census and several large national and Los Angeles opinion surveys, the study concludes that Hispanics acquire English and lose Spanish quickly starting in the second generation; they also are as religious and as committed to the work ethic as native-born whites. Furthermore, it found that Hispanics largely reject simple ethnic identification and demonstrate levels of patriotism that grow yearly and by the third generation are equivalent to native-born whites.

Immigrants are also portrayed as representing an economic threat. This threat can be described as being applicable at an individual level whereby people are encouraged to perceive the presence of undocumented individuals as a threat to their own or familial economic prosperity. This concern is expressed in a number of different ways, which may include references to increased competition for desirable jobs and the reduction in wages. Threats to individual economic security also manifest in concern for tax increases to pay for welfare, medical care, and education for undocumented immigrants. For many, immigration is seen as a zero-sum game, whereby the acquisition of benefits for some means a loss for others. Immigrants who get jobs, educational opportunities, and social services are seen as taking away the same resources from citizens.

Economic threat can also be couched in terms of broader concerns about the overall well-being of the U.S. economy. It is believed by some that undocumented immigrants are detrimental to the U.S. economy because they are often perceived as placing strains on jobs, resources, housing, and as disproportionately benefitting from social welfare programs (Espenshade and Hempstead, 1996).

It is not surprising that this threat seems to resonate with many people. There are two plausible explanations for this fact. The first is simply that we live in a society that overemphasizes wealth as a measure of success. Therefore, we are always concerned about how policies and behaviors may affect our overall economic well-being. The second reason that the economic threat posed by recent undocumented immigrants tends to resonate with many Americans, and the reason which helps make the terrain fertile for moral panics, is the economic changes, which have led to a general sense of anxiety and insecurity. That is, over the last 40 years, corporate attempts to recoup profits in the face of expanded global competition have involved a number of strategies, which have included deindustrialization, disinvestment, and downsizing (Barlett and Steele, 1996). The result has been a reduction in wages and benefits for many American workers and an increasing sense of economic insecurity.

There is little conclusive evidence about the effect of undocumented immigration on individual economic security or the well-being of the national economy. However, one study done by the Pew Hispanic Center, using Census Bureau state-level data from 1990 to 2004, found that increases in foreign-born populations are not correlated with negative effects on the employment of native-born workers (Kochhar, 2006). While the jury is still out as to the overall effect of undocumented immigration on the economy, what is probably true is that arguments about undocumented immigrants taking a disproportionate share of social services such as welfare and food stamps is highly suspect because recipients of these services are required to provide proof of citizenship. We should also remember that many undocumented immigrants pay into the pools that are used to subsidize such services through their payment of sales and property taxes.

The American public has long suspected that newly arriving immigrants are inherently crime-prone (see Chapter 7). Historically, immigrants have been thought to be disproportionately involved in drugs and violent crimes. Pat Buchanan (2006:27) echoes this perception of criminal threat in his recent book when in reference to inadequate controls at the border, he states, "How many American women must be assaulted, how many children molested, how many citizens must die at the hands of criminal aliens . . . before our government does its duty?" However, these threats are not strongly supported by empirical evidence. On the contrary, 2000 U.S. Census data of incarcerated males demonstrate that foreign-born people commit fewer crimes per capita than U.S. citizens, regardless of race and ethnicity. Those born in the United States commit crimes at a rate that is approximately four times that of their foreign-born counterparts. In fact, one study found that among men aged 18–40, native-born men were more likely to be incarcerated than immigrants (Butcher and Piehl, 1998a). In another study, the researcher found that recent immigrants had no significant effect on crime rates, and youth born abroad were less likely than native-born youth to be criminally active (Butcher and Piehl, 1998b). Additionally, according to Ramiro Martinez, (2002) research confirms that immigrants actually provide a stabilizing effect on their communities, reducing crime rates and increasing the area's economic viability.

A number of additional threats have been noted but have primarily played a more minor role in immigration discourse. For example, there have been references to environmental threats associated with undocumented border crossings, namely litter, destruction of the natural environment, and danger to wild animals. Medical threat has also been presented and includes stories about the spread of diseases such as AIDS, tuberculosis, and hepatitis.

One threat, however, that is notably missing in the above discussion and deserves greater attention is racial threat. Racial threat, which was expressed most aptly by Hubert Blalock (1967), who suggested that as the number of racial minorities within a particular area increases, opposition in various forms—including violence—also increases. However, rarely does public discourse about undocumented immigration explicitly refer to the racial characteristics of immigrants. This may be due not to a lack of concern about the racial ramifications of immigration, but may result from a desire to cloak racial concerns in more socially acceptable terms. Some, for example, have suggested that words like "welfare" and "crime" are simply code words for race. That is, instead of directly discussing race, which has become socially taboo, many use "race coding" to allude to perceived negative aspects of different races and ethnic groups (Gilens, 1996). Because of a perception of disproportionate minority involvement, words like "crime" and "welfare" and even references to "cultural dissimilarity" allow those who are so inclined to articulate negative feelings for minority groups without ever specifically mentioning race. Some suggest that these "code words" for race are particularly useful to political and economic elites who wish to tap and exploit negative racial perceptions and resentments among whites in the implementation of what are essentially race-based policies. In short, references to economic, cultural, criminal, and political threats of undocumented immigration may simply be serving as referents to racial concerns.

In describing the above threats, it is not suggested that these threats are entirely baseless or without some evidence. It would be difficult to argue that the presence of undocumented immigrants has had no effect on the economic and personal security of at least some Americans. In fact, ideologically based moral panics are always rooted in some form of evidence. As Cohen (1972:274) notes, it is not that there is nothing there but because the scope of the problem is distorted, exaggerated, or misunderstood, societal responses are primarily inappropriate. There is little doubt that some U.S. workers have been displaced by immigrant workers, some citizens have been criminally victimized by undocumented immigrants, and that American culture is changing (as it always has and will continue to do) in the face of changing demographics. It is the exaggerated degree to which these threats are presented as being problematic and the extent to which these threats are portrayed as universal that characterizes such discourse as an example of negative ideology.

Finally, it is worth remembering that the casting of immigrants in terms of threatening "others" is not new. Few immigrant groups (legal and illegal) were readily accepted when first arriving on U.S. shores, and most, in fact, were demonized as representing a threat to our culture, economy, and personal security in the same way that undocumented immigrants are today.

IMMIGRATION POLICY

Attempts at controlling (as well as punishing) undocumented immigration have resulted in a number of public policies as well as actions on the part of private citizens and interest groups. Some of these policies, because they are rooted in a misrepresentation or distortion of the problem, not only fail to address the problem in some meaningful and humane way, but have also had (or have the potential to have) rather dire consequences. This section examines some of these policies.

Historically, immigration control has been under the jurisdiction of the federal government. However, in light of the events of September 11, 2001, the perceived failure of the federal government to adequately control undocumented immigration, and the supposed criminality of undocumented immigrants, there has been a recent push for greater involvement of state and local law enforcement in controlling immigration. As a result, some states like Arizona require that police officers who apprehend undocumented immigrants for law violations turn them over to federal immigration officials (Menjivar and Bejarano, 2004). This sometimes results in the deportation of individuals for relatively minor offenses. Moreover, the role of local and state law enforcement in immigration control may be expanding even more to allow officers to ask about the residency status of those they come into contact with regardless of the reason.

In 2007, the Clear Law Enforcement for Alien Removal (CLEAR) Act (HR 842) was introduced in the U.S. House of Representatives (Library of Congress, 2007). This bill offers financial incentive for the involvement of local law agencies in the enforcement of federal immigration statutes. The consequences of increased involvement by local and state law enforcement have not been evaluated as this is still a relatively new phenomenon. However, there is fairly good reason to believe that while this may result in somewhat more effective immigration control, it will also have potentially detrimental effects. For example, due to the complexity of immigration law, it is more than likely that civil rights violations will occur. It often goes unnoticed that the U.S. Constitution, and the rights that it provides, applies to everyone on U.S. soil, regardless of their legal status. These types of policies are likely to increase the instances of racial profiling and police stops for "driving while Hispanic."

Perhaps even more worrisome is the effect of such enforcement on crime and public safety. These policies will seemingly undermine the efforts of police to gain the trust of the communities that they serve. Over the past few decades, there has been a strong move toward community policing. A core component of these policies is the development of trust and cooperation between the police and community members in developing joint solutions to crime problems. The concern is that if local and state police begin actively enforcing federal immigration statutes, then, those who are undocumented or may have friends and family who are undocumented may become reluctant to have any contact with police because of fear of the possible consequences, which may include deportation for themselves and/or their families. This would not only reduce the effectiveness of community policing, especially in communities with a greater proportion of immigrants, but also will presumably decrease the reporting of crime and suspicious behavior in certain neighborhoods. Criminals, therefore, may come to see undocumented immigrants and the neighborhoods in which they reside as easy and vulnerable targets.

The militarization of the border is another policy that has been adopted and widely supported. This involves the escalation of military involvement and technology in law enforcement. In 2006, President Bush detailed a series of enforcement measures including the deployment of 6,000 National Guard members to the border. These troops now provide support to the border patrol along the southern borders of Texas, Arizona, New Mexico, and California.

Strengthening of the border, either through its militarization or the construction of an 800-mile wall, is unlikely to deter those who are desperate to come to the United States. Instead, what is more likely to occur (and is occurring) is that immigrants will simply find different points of entry. Often this involves crossing the desert in areas that are less populated and more perilous. These border policies are, therefore, likely responsible for recent increases in the number of injuries and deaths that have occurred on the U.S.–Mexico border. The U.S. Government Accountability Office (2006) reported that since 1995, the number of border-crossing deaths increased and had more than doubled by 2005. The total number of border-crossing deaths increased from 241 in 1999 to 472 in 2005. The report goes on to note that this increase in deaths occurred despite the fact that there was not a corresponding increase in the number of unauthorized border crossings. The analysis also shows that more than three-fourths of the doubling in deaths along the southwest border since 1995 can be attributed to increases in deaths occurring in the Arizona (U.S. Government Accountability Office, 2006).

Another consequence of the militarization of the border is that more immigrants will simply turn to "coyotes" (human smugglers) as a means of crossing the border. This not only increases the peril of those who pay for this method of entry; it also means an increase in crime and a decrease in public safety that often accompanies organized criminal enterprises such as these. It is estimated that coyotes are a "two billion dollar a year" business that is often accompanied by violence, kidnapping, and human slavery (Wagner, 2006).

In addition to explicit policies meant to strengthen the border, numerous other policies have been suggested, or actually developed and implemented, in an effort to either deter those who aspire to come to the United States or punish those already here. Arizona's 2006 election provides a laundry list of policies that are unlikely to effectively direct immigration reform. In this election, Arizona residents overwhelm-ingly supported a variety of policies that speak to their concern over immigration. Some of the propositions that were passed included denying bail in certain situations to undocumented immigrants who are charged with crimes; barring those not in this country from legally collecting punitive damages for personal injuries; prohibiting undocumented immigrants from enrolling in adult education classes, receiving state-subsidized childcare, receiving scholarships, grants, tuition assistance, or in-state tuition rates at Arizona public schools and universities; and declaring English as the state's official language.

Some of these policies deserve some discussion. For example, declaring English as the official language has no practical impact. It is merely a symbolic gesture that does lit-tle more than accentuate the difference between "us and them," and to reassert an overly restrictive definition of American culture and identity. Denying educational opportunities also seems counterproductive. This would only serve to increase the soci-etal problems that tend to accompany a lack of education, such as crime and poverty.

To cast immigration concerns in terms of threat serves two purposes. The first is to overgeneralize the problem in an effort to mobilize public action, and the second is to cast undocumented immigrants as "others" and often as "dangerous others." Such portrayals allow us to more easily deny or ignore the humanness of those who risk their lives to seek a better life in the United States. In such instances, then, we more eas-ily succumb to what Dario Melossi (1985) called "vocabularies of punitive motive." Melossi suggests that during certain periods, a "discursive chain" of punitiveness and severity spreads across society, linking the attitude of "moral panic" expressed by busi-ness leaders and "moral entrepreneurs" to the ways in which citizens, police, courts, and correctional authorities perceive behavior as deviant and/or criminal (1985:183). These vocabularies of punitive motive then provide the justification for lawmakers to pass legislation that expand social control measures which are often punitive and harmful with little or no public opposition.

To couch immigration discourse in terms of these threats and others simply runs the risk of developing policies that are based on stereotypes, and that attempt to scape-goat certain populations, which in turn justify punitive responses. As long as we continue to frame these discussions in terms of threat and otherness, in terms of our dissimilarities rather than what we have in common, we will continue to fail to progress toward rational and commonsense solutions to this critically important issue.

Endnote

1. The choice to use the term "undocu-mented immigrants" rather than "illegal immigrants" is not an arbitrary one. The term is used so as to not attach the nega-tive and subjective connotations that accompany the word "illegal."

References

Barlett, Donald L., and James B. Steele. 1996. *America: What Went Wrong?* Kansas City, MO: Andrews and McMeel.

Blalock, Hubert M. 1967. *Toward a Theory of Minority Group Relations*. New York: John Wiley and Sons.

Buchanan, Patrick J. 2006. *State of Emergency: The Third World Invasion and Conquest of America.* New York: St. Martin Press.

Butcher, Kristen, and Anne Morrison-Piehl. 1998a. Cross-City Evidence on the Relationship Between Immigration and Crime. *Journal of Policy Analysis and Management* 17: 457–493.

Butcher, Kristen, and Anne Morrison-Piehl. 1998b. Recent Immigrants: Unexpected Implications for Crime and Incarceration. *Industrial and Labor Relations Review* 51 (4): 654–679.

Chiricos, Ted. 1996. Moral Panics as Ideology: Drugs, Violence, Race and Punishment in America. In *Race with Prejudice: Race & Justice in America*, ed. M. J. Lynch and E. B. Patterson, 19–48. New York: Harrow & Heston.

Citrin, Jack, Amy Lerman, Michael Murakami, and Kathryn Pearson. 2007. Testing Huntington: Is Hispanic Immigration a Threat to American Identity? *Perspectives on Politics* 5 (1): 31–48.

Cohen, Stanley. 1972. *Folk Devils and Moral Panics.* St. Albans: Paladin.

Critcher, Charles. 2006. *Critical Readings: Moral Panics and the Media.* Maidenhead: Open Press University.

Espenshade, Thomas J., and Katherine Hempstead. 1996. Contemporary American Attitudes Toward U.S. Immigration. *International Migration Review* 30: 535–570.

Gilens, Martin. 1996. "Race Coding" and White Opposition to Welfare. *American Political Science Review* 90: 593–604.

Goode, Erich. 2000. No Need to Panic? A Bumper Crop of Books on Moral Panics. *Sociological Forum* 15 (3): 543–552.

Goode, Erich, and Nachman Ben-Yehuda. 1994. *Moral Panic: The Social Construction of Deviance.* Oxford: Blackwell.

Gouldner, Alvin. 1976. *The Dialectic of Ideology and Technology.* New York: Oxford University Press.

Hall, Stuart, Charles Critcher, Tony Jefferson, John Clarke, and Brian Roberts. 1978. *Policing the Crisis: Mugging, the State and Law and Order.* London: Macmillan Press.

Huntington, Samuel. 2004. *Who Are We? The Challenge to America's National Identity.* New York: Simon and Shuster.

Kochhar, Rakesh. 2006. Growth in the Foreign-Born Workforce and Employment of the Native Born. *Pew Hispanic Center, Executive Summary.* August 10, 2006.

Larrain, Jorge. 1983. *Marxism and Ideology.* London: Macmillan Press.

Lauderdale, Pat. 1976. Deviance and Moral Boundaries. *American Sociological Review* 41: 660–676.

Library of Congress. 2007. *Thomas: Legislative Information from the Library of Congress.* http://thomas.loc.gov/

Martinez, Jr., Ramiro. 2002. *Latino Homicide: Immigration, Violence and Community.* New York: Routledge.

Melossi, Dario. 1985. Punishment and Social Action: Changing Vocabularies of Punitive Motive with a Political Business Cycle. *Current Perspectives in Social Theory* 6: 169–197.

Menjivar, Cecilia, and Cynthia L. Bejarano. 2004. Latino Immigrants' Perceptions of Crime and Police Authorities in the United States: A Case Study from the Phoenix Metropolitan Area. *Ethnic and Racial Studies* 27 (1): 120–148.

Thompson, Kenneth. 1998. *Moral Panics.* London: Routledge.

U.S. Bureau of Census. 2000. *Law Enforcement, Courts, and Prisons.* Washington, DC: U.S. Government Printing Office.

U.S. Government Accountability Office. 2006. *Border-crossing Deaths Have Doubled Since 1985; Border Patrol's Efforts to Prevent Deaths Have Not Been Fully Evaluated.* GAO-06-770, August.

Wagner, D. 2006. Phoenix's Hidden $2 Billion Industry – Human Smuggling. *The Arizona Republic* (Phoenix, AZ) 23, July 2006, A1.

Young, J. 1971. The Role of Police as Amplifiers of Deviancy, Negotiators of Reality and Translators of Fantasy: Some Aspects of Our Present System of Drug Control as Seen in Notting Hill. In *Images of Deviance*, ed. Stanley Cohen, 27–61. Harmondsworth: Penguin.

CHAPTER 18

Fairness in the Courts

Investigating and Addressing Race, Ethnic, and Gender Bias

Dennis Catlin

INTRODUCTION

By tradition, the courts have tried to remain what could been termed the "Invisible Third Branch of Government." They tried to do their business out of the spotlight of the public and the media. The fight to keep cameras out of the court and the tradition of judges not discussing the business of the courts in public are examples of the policies that were designed to support this goal. Efforts at accountability that had an impact on other branches of government were late coming to the judiciary. This disconnection from public scrutiny may have contributed to the lack of attention to issues of race, ethnic, and gender bias in the court. In preparation for the First National Conference on Eliminating Racial and Ethnic Bias in the Courts, the National Center for State Courts produced the manual "Establishing and Operating a Task Force or Commission on Racial and Ethnic Bias in the Courts" (National Center for State Courts, 1995:1). Its introduction suggests:

> For racial and ethnic minorities, the early history of the court was that of an institution that denied equal justice to minorities. Even our own precious Constitution and the Bill of Rights refused to embrace all manner of humankind in its guarantee of "freedom for all". Recently, both the federal and state courts have become more active in protecting and extending the rights of racial and ethnic minorities.

A major catalyst for the examination of the public's confidence in the court system was the 1977 Public Image of the Courts study (Yankelovich, Kelley, and White, Inc., 1977). It was the first national survey to focus on how citizens who were outside the system and the lawyers and judges inside the system viewed the courts. The study was undertaken in preparation for the 1978 National Conference on the State Judiciary: The Public Image of the Courts conducted by the National Center for State Courts. This study found that equality and fairness were major expectations by the public for the courts but that courts discriminate against the poor and blacks. Following this study and national conference, the state courts began to examine the wide range of issues related to the public's confidence in the courts. The creation of race, ethnic, and gender bias task forces and commissions to study the issues at the state level and to formulate responses to the findings of the task force studies were among the first priorities of the conference.

INVESTIGATING BIAS IN THE COURTS

Race, Ethnic, and Gender Bias Commissions and Task Forces

A major vehicle for investigating bias in the court was the creation of race, ethnic, and gender bias commissions or task forces by state court systems. In many cases, the first activity of these commissions and task forces was to conduct surveys to determine the extent of bias in the state's court system. The first state-level survey addressing bias in the courts occurred in Utah in 1978. Between 1977 and 1999, 25 states commissioned similar surveys to investigate bias in the courts (Rottman and Tomkins, 1999).

In 1999, another national survey, *How the Public Views the State Courts: A 1999 Survey*, was the first to comprehensively address how diverse social groups viewed the state courts (National Center for State Courts, 1999; Rottman and Tompkins, 1999). In addition to other public confidence issues, the study also looked at how ethnic and racial groups view the treatment they and other groups received from the courts, representation on juries, and how closely the courts were in touch with what was going on in the community. For example, this report found that (National Center for State Courts, 1999:8)

> Although most Americans (83%) feel that "people like them" are treated either better or the same as others, that perception is not shared by African-Americans. Two-thirds of African-Americans feel that "people like them" are treated somewhat or far worse than other people . . . Almost 70% of African-American respondents think that African-Americans, as a group, get "Somewhat Worse" or "Far Worse" treatment from the courts, whereas over 40% of White/Non-Hispanic and Hispanic respondents have that opinion.

Rottman et al. (2003:2–3) report that "Six national and 29 state surveys have been devoted in whole or large part to the study of public perceptions of state courts." While many of these surveys were used to inform the investigative work of commissions and task forces on race, ethnic, and gender bias in the courts, Rottman et al. (2003:3) suggest that

> The cumulative value of the data collected in these surveys is less than might be anticipated. Few state surveys have been analyzed to a point beyond displays of frequencies or simple cross-tabulations. There is little consistency in the questions they asked or the wording of questions. Also few state specific data sets were archived and thus are unavailable for secondary analysis.

Regardless of the statistical efficacy of these surveys, they drove much of the work of these task forces. They contributed to the recommendations and policies emanating from the task forces and commissions (Rottman et al., 2003).

The first such task force was created in 1982 when the New Jersey Supreme Court established a task force to study gender bias in its state courts (Resnik, 1996). Its mandate was "to investigate the extent to which gender bias exists in the New Jersey judicial branch and to develop an educational program (for the 1983 New Jersey Judicial College) to eliminate any such bias" (Wikler and Schafran, 1991:313). It is likely that the first task force dedicated to the study of gender bias was related to the high level of activity at the time of the National Association for Women's Judicial Education Project (Cortina, 2002) and the National Association of Women Judges (NAWJ). The NAWJ was created in 1979 and was "at the forefront in the establishment and implementation of gender bias task forces in both federal and state courts" (NAWJ website). By 2001, 45 states had created gender bias task forces (Schafran and Wikler, 2001). Table 18.1 presents a sample of public perceptions and findings of a sample of state court gender bias task forces.

New Jersey in 1985 and Michigan in 1987 were the first two states to establish task forces that addressed racial and ethnic bias in the courts (Resnik, 1996; http://www.ncsconline.org/Projects_Initiatives/REFI/MI1REB.htm). The New Jersey Supreme Court Task Force on Minority Concerns (http://www.ncsconline.org/Projects_Initiatives/REFI/NJ2REB.htm, para. 10) found that

- There is a perception of insensitivity or indifference to minority citizens who are in the criminal justice process.
- Many minorities express a lack of confidence in the court system and are reluctant to bring cases to court.
- The judiciary reflects many of the prejudices of the society it serves, and minorities often view the judiciary as working in concert with law enforcement.

In its 1989 report, The Michigan Supreme Court Task Force on Racial/Ethnic Issues in the Courts found that "There is a perception on the part of racial and ethnic minorities and also of many non-minorities of the justice system's discrimination and insensitivity.

TABLE 18.1 Sample of Public Perceptions and Findings of Gender Bias Task Forces

State	Task Force or Commission Title	Finding
Idaho	District of Idaho's Gender Fairness Committee	Gender bias exists in the District of Idaho.
New Jersey	New Jersey Supreme Court Task Force on Women in the Courts	Widespread perceptions of discrimination against women judges, lawyers, court personnel, litigants, and witnesses.
New York	New York State Judicial Committee on Women in the Courts	Gender bias against women litigants, attorneys, and court employees is a pervasive problem with grave consequences. Women are often denied equal justice, equal treatment, and equal opportunity.

TABLE 18.2 Sample of Public Perception Findings of Race and Ethnic Bias Task forces

State	Task Force or Commission Title	Finding
Connecticut	Connecticut Judicial Branch Task Force on Minority Fairness	Profound differences exist in the way minorities and non-minorities perceive the workings and attitudes of Connecticut's judicial system. In some instances, these perceptions mask the realities of the system's functioning; in others, the perceptions are so endemic that they become, in effect, the reality.
Minnesota	Minnesota Supreme Court Task Force on Racial Bias in the Judicial System	People of color often choose not to go to trial because of the perception that they will not receive a fair trial
Washington	Washington State Minority and Justice Task Force	Minorities believe that bias pervades the entire legal system in general and hence they do not trust the court system to resolve their disputes or administer justice even-handedly.

Source: http://www.ncsconline.org/Projects_Initiatives/REFI/SearchState.asp

There is evidence that such behaviors do exist" (http://www.ncsconline.org/ Projects_Initiatives/REFI/MI1REB.htm, para 7). Table 18.2 contains a sample of the public perceptions and findings of state court race and ethnic bias task forces.

Somewhat after the initiation of bias task forces on the state level, the federal court system took up the challenge of examining bias in the federal court (Carlisle, 1999; Cortina, 2002; Grubin and Walker, 1997; O'Connor, 1994; Resnik, 1996; Special Report: Report of the First Circuit, 2000). In 1990, the federal courts joined the effort to investigate bias in the courts when the District of Columbia Federal Court and the Ninth Circuit Court of Appeals established the first gender bias task forces (Cortina, 2002). The establishment and work of these task forces were not without controversy. As these task forces began to report the results of their studies in 1995, the future work of the task forces faced opposition from the then Republican majority in Congress (Coyle, 1996; Resnik, 1996). Resnik reported that

> Hostility toward these projects has also emerged, as a few vocal federal judges have mounted a sustained attack. In the spring of 1995, at the request of Senator Charles E. Grassley, the General Accounting Office launched an investigation into federal funds spent on task forces. In September of 1995, Senators Grassley, Phil Gramm, and Orrin Hatch recommended on the congressional record that no federal funds be spent on such task forces. In December, nine democratic senators and one member of the House of Representatives countered by voicing on the congressional record their support for such projects. (1996:953)

In the face of this funding stalemate, the federal courts used internal funding to support the work of the task forces (Cortina, 2002).

TABLE 18.3 State Approaches to the Creation of Task Forces

Task Force Typology	Number of States
Race/ Ethnic Bias Task Force Only	2
Gender Bias Task Force Only	3
Separate Race/Ethnic Bias and Gender Bias Task Forces	28
Combined Race/Ethnic/Gender Bias Task Force	11
Gay/Lesbian Task Force	2

Source: National Center for State Courts Racial Fairness Task Force Reports.
http://www.ncsconline.org/wc/CourTopics/statelinks.asp?id=75&topic=RacFai

As these task forces began to develop, some states chose to have separated task forces, one to address gender bias and one to investigate racial and ethnic bias. Other states chose to have a single task force to address all issues related to bias in the courts. In some instances, states that originally formed two task forces merged them into a single task force that addressed racial, ethnic, and gender bias issues. Table 18.3 reflects the way in which states chose to approach the creation of their task forces. This clearly indicates that most states created two separate task forces, one for gender bias and one for race/ethnic bias. Only two states, California and New Jersey, have created gay/lesbian taskforces.

SAMPLE FINDINGS, RECOMMENDATIONS, AND IMPLEMENTATION EFFORTS FROM SELECTED TASK FORCES

The number, diverse composition, missions, and reporting methods of the many state and federal court task forces and commissions make it impossible in this chapter to identify and compare all of their findings, recommendations, and actions. However, by looking at a sample of state and federal task forces, it is possible to get a picture of the process and progress in tackling the problem of bias. For the purpose of this discussion, three state court systems, New Jersey, Nebraska, and California, were selected as geographically representative examples.

New Jersey

The New Jersey Supreme Court Task Force on Minority Concerns was established in 1985 and published its final report in 1992. The findings and recommendations were organized into ten major areas: Perception, Access, Juries, Courtroom Experience, Legal Profession, Education, Criminal Justice, Court as Employer/Appointer, Jury Selection, Juvenile Justice, and Other Topics. The final report contained 68 findings and 63 recommendations (http://www.ncsconline.org/Projects_Initiatives/REFI/NJ2REB.htm). Table 18.4 reflects a sample of the findings and related recommendations.

Of the 63 Task Force recommendations, 53 "were approved in some form for implementation. In 1992, the New Jersey Supreme Court appointed the Standing Committee on Minority Concerns charged with monitoring the implementation of the court-approved recommendations of the Task Force on Minority Concerns and with the task of advising the Supreme Court on how the Judiciary may best assure

TABLE 18.4 Sample of Findings and Recommendation from the New Jersey Supreme Court Task Force on Minority Concerns Report

Major Area	Findings	Recommendations
Public Perception	There is a perception of insensitivity or indifference to minority citizens who are in the criminal justice process.	The Supreme Court should require annual sensitivity training to address racial and ethnic bias for all judge and court support employees.
Judicial Selection	There is a paucity of minorities on the New Jersey Supreme Court, Superior Court, and Tax Court. There is a dearth of minority judges on the municipal court level.	The Supreme Court should consider presenting to the Governor and the State Legislature the finding of the Task Force that there is widespread concern about the underrepresentation of minorities on Supreme, Superior, and Tax Court benches.

fairness, impartiality, equal access, and full participation of ethnic and racial minorities in the Judiciary" (http://www.judiciary.state.nj.us/hudson/minority/minority.htm, para 1). Since its creation, the Standing Committee on Minority Concerns has issued regular reports of the court's implementation activities.

By 2007, numerous initiatives were being implemented to meet the Minority Concerns task force report. The Code of Judicial Conduct, the Rules of Professional Conduct, and the Code of Conduct for Judiciary Employees were amended to prohibit discrimination on the basis of language. A research project was designed to assess the impact of bail practices on minorities and persons of color (New Jersey Supreme Court Task Force on Minority Concerns, 2002). A research was also initiated to examine minority representation in the jury pool. A significant focus of the original task force recommendation was on the training of key judicial system personnel, with a number of implementation initiatives addressing these recommendations. Examples of these curriculum development, training, and education initiatives include (New Jersey Supreme Court Task Force on Minority Concerns, 2007:155–157)

- Workshops for judges: " 'Please Don't Let Me Be Misunderstood': Providing Interpreting Services for Linguistic Minorities in Court Proceedings."
- Workshops for judges: "Fair in Theory, Fair in Practice: Developing Effective Strategies for Managing Culturally Diverse Participants in the Courtroom."
- Workshops for judges: "Exploring the Intersections of Religion, Culture and the Rule of Law."
- Workshops for court personnel: "The Impact of Ethnic and Cultural Differences on Attitudes towards Domestic Violence."
- Workshops for court personnel: "Understanding Islam."

Another major initiative designed to promote access to justice was the creation of an ombudsman program. This program was originally envisioned as a way "to promote equal justice by monitoring problems such as enforcement of judicial orders in domestic violence cases and bringing community perspectives to the judiciary by working with community organizations such as rape crisis centers and battered women's shelters" (New Jersey Supreme Court Task Force on Minority Concerns, 2007:38). A pilot program that has the expanded responsibility of handling complaints by court users of bias, discrimination, and unfair treatment was implemented in 1996 and was eventually expanded statewide in 2001.

Nebraska

The Nebraska Minority and Justice Task Force was created in 1999 as a joint effort of the Nebraska Supreme Court and the Nebraska State Bar Association. Its final report was issued in 2003 (Nebraska Judicial Branch, 2003, 2005). The final report contained 68 findings and 75 recommendations (Nebraska Judicial Branch, 2003; http://www.ncsconline.org/Projects_Initiatives/REFI/NE1REB.htm). The Task Force found that "minorities are overrepresented as defendants in the criminal and juvenile justice system; minorities are underrepresented in Nebraska's legal profession and as court employees and jurors; and a substantial portion of the responding public, Nebraska lawyers, and court personnel perceive that bias exists in the Nebraska justice system" (Nebraska Judicial Branch, 2003:xiii). The Task Force's general recommendation was "that the Nebraska justice system commit itself to a morally searching, permanent, institutional effort to study, address and change those practices and procedures that may disadvantage minorities, whatever the cause of those practices" (Nebraska Judicial Branch, 2003:xiii). Table 18.5 reflects a sample of the findings and related recommendations.

To insure implementation of the recommendations, the Nebraska Minority and Justice Implementation Committee (Implementation Committee) was established in 2003 (Nebraska Judicial Branch, 2005). In its 2005 report, the Implementation

TABLE 18.5 Sample of Findings and Recommendation from Nebraska Minority and Justice Task Force Report

Major Area	Findings	Recommendations
Juries	The majority of Nebraskans believe that it is important that juries reflect the racial and ethnic make up of the community. However, many respondents, especially minority respondents, believe that juries in general are not representative of their communities.	Juries should be more reflective of the diversity of the community, and source lists for juries should be expanded to ensure such diversity.
Courtroom Experience	Over half of Nebraska's counties have no public defender. Nebraska's minorities are substantially more likely than whites to use a public defender or assigned counsel.	Nebraska should adopt and enforce mandatory standards for the operation of county indigent defense systems that comply with the American Bar Association's "Ten Principles of a Public Defense Delivery System."

Sources: http://www.ncsconline.org/Projects_Initiatives/REFI/NE1REB.htm; Nebraska Judicial Branch (2003, January).

Committee reported significant progress. To promote fair access to justice and to insure that defendants receive a trial of their peers in an ethnically balanced process, a Civil Procedure Bill was passed that requires the annual updating of jury pool information. In addition, it was proposed that the jury source list be drawn from both the voter registration and driver's license lists. The use of a standardized juror questionnaire that would allow for collecting race and ethnicity information was proposed. Further, to provide for fair proceeding for those who are not English speakers, the Implementation Committee developed a Legal Service via Technology (LIST) proposal that would provide for access to legal interpreters by telephone (Nebraska Judicial Branch, 2005).

In order to strengthen the public defenders system, the Task Force joined with the Nebraska Commission on Public Advocacy to assess the current status of the public defender system. The Task Force worked with the Commission on Public Advocacy to implement a pilot project to provide counties with 40% of the cost of implementing a set of standards of indigent defense system (Nebraska Judicial Branch, 2005).

California

Created in 1991 by the California Judicial Council (also known as the Judicial Council of California), the California Judicial Council Advisory Committee on Racial and Ethnic Bias in the Courts (The Advisory Committee) was "directed to (1) study the treatment of racial and ethnic minorities in the state courts, (2) ascertain public perceptions of fairness or lack of fairness in the judicial system, and (3) make recommendations on reforms and remedial programs, including educational programs and training for the bench, the bar, and the public" (Judicial Council of California, 1997:1–2). The Advisory Committee held public hearings around the state of California, from which it concluded that (Judicial Council of California, 1997:54)

- Some minorities and non-English-speaking persons believe that judges are not held accountable for conduct demonstrating insensitivity toward racial, ethnic, and linguistic minorities.
- Some minorities and non-English-speaking persons believe that judges are not held accountable for the actions of court staff that evidence bias toward racial, ethnic, and linguistic minorities.
- Some members of the public believe that the justice system shows favoritism toward whites.

The Advisory Committee's Final Report contained 68 findings and 60 recommendations (http://www.ncsconline.org/Projects_Initiatives/REFI/CA1REB.htm). Table 18.6 reflects a sample of the findings and related recommendations from the Advisory Committee's final report.

In 1994, the Judicial Council of California charged the Judicial Council's Access and Fairness Advisory Committee with the responsibility of insuring that the recommendations of the Advisory Committee were implemented. A sample of the Access and Fairness Advisory Committee's accomplishments include (Judicial Council of California, 2007:2–5)

- Proposed rule 10.625 of the California Rules of Court that requires courts to maintain a database of demographic information on every prospective grand juror and every seated grand juror.

TABLE 18.6 Sample of Findings and Recommendations from the California Judicial Council Advisory Committee on Racial and Ethnic Bias in the Courts

Major Area	Findings	Recommendations
Courtroom Experience	An essential component of judicial demeanor is manifest respect for everyone involved in the court system. Such respect demands that judges foster an atmosphere of fairness and neutrality in the courts for litigants, witnesses, and other court users, whether minority or non-minority.	Pursuant to Section 1 of the Standards of Judicial Administration, judges should monitor their courtrooms and intervene when instances of racial bias are manifested. Accordingly, judges should consider referring court personnel who manifest biased behavior to diversity training.
Education	Judges and court personnel may benefit from cultural competency training; therefore, judges should be encouraged to participate in CJER (Center for Judicial Education and Research) fairness programs. Comparable programs should be developed for court personnel.	The Judicial Council should encourage the judiciary to participate in periodic cultural competency training. Tribal court judges should be included as faculty in diversity training programs and be permitted to attend CJER education programs.
Minority Women	The Advisory Committee concludes that women of color encounter dual barriers of racism and sexism in the justice system and legal profession; The Advisory Committee concludes that too often the unique situation and negative experiences of women of color are neglected or inadequately addressed in studies of bias and discrimination in the courts.	The Advisory Committee recommends recognition of the double disadvantage of being a woman of color involved in the justice system— whether as litigant, lawyer, judge, witness, court personnel, or law student. The Advisory Committee recommends inclusion of more women of color in all aspects of the planning of future conferences on bias in the courts.

Sources: http://www.ncsconline.org/Projects_Initiatives/REFI/CA1REB.htm; Judicial Council of California (1997).

- Drafted rule 10.611 of the California Rules of Court and standard 10.21 and amendments to standard 5.40 of the Standards of Judicial Administration relating to nondiscrimination in court appointments.
- Convened educational roundtables to explore issues related to Native Americans, women of color, child care, and court security.
- Hosted a statewide conference, The New Millennium: Women of Color as Court Leaders and Managers, in spring 2000.
- Cosponsored a summit, Continuing a Legacy of Excellence: A Summit on Diversity in the Judiciary, in June 2007 with the California State Bar's Diversity Pipeline Task Force's Subcommittee on Government and the Public Sector.

- Produced *Summary Judgments,* an educational video for judicial officers and court staff that addresses sexual orientation, racial, ethnic, and gender fairness; and collaborated with CJER's (California Judicial Education and Research) Fairness Education Committee.
- Developed a pilot curriculum on sexual orientation fairness and preventing sexual harassment.

The California Administrative Office of the Courts and the Judicial Council of California have continued to explore the most effective ways to make the California Judicial System more responsive to the needs of the public it serves. In 2005, the Trust and Confidence in the California Courts Project began with a Public Trust and Confidence Survey. The six themes from that survey included receiving and seeking information from the courts, experience in court cases—incidence and consequences, barriers to taking a case to court, diversity and the needs of a diverse population, fairness in procedures and outcomes, and expectations and job performance. Recommendations from this ongoing effort continue to address the issues of fairness in the courts (Judicial Council of California/Administrative Office of the Courts, 2006).

PUBLIC TRUST AND CONFIDENCE IN THE COURTS: THE CONTINUING CHALLENGE

It has been over 25 years since the first bias task forces began their work. In most cases, the process of implementation of these task force recommendations has been the responsibility of various state court standing committees on task force recommendation implementation. Over time, it became clear to the leaders of the state court systems that a constant reexamination of the courts' interactions with the public is required to insure fairness in the courts and also to insure the relevance of the courts to the changing cultural, social, and legal environment. The Trust and Confidence Project in California is a reflection of this reality.

Following the 1999 national survey "How the Public Views the State Courts," the National Center for State Courts convened the National Conference on Public Trust and Confidence in the Justice System. The conference was attended by 500 members of the state and federal judiciary, the bar, the media, and the public. The conference attendees identified issues affecting public trust and confidence. Several of these issues reflected the need to continually address issues that were identified by the preceding race, ethnic, and gender bias task forces. The top-ranking issue identified by the conference was unequal treatment in the justice system (Leben, 1999). In her comments to the conference, U.S. Supreme Court Justice (Retired) Sandra Day O'Connor addressed the identified issue of bias and stated, "But concrete action must be taken to insure that court services do not operate in ways that perpetuate racial or gender bias" (O'Connor, 1999:11).

A national action plan emerged from this conference with strategies to address the identified public trust and confidence issues. One of the primary strategies was to "Implement the recommendations of the task forces on gender and racial bias in the courts" (National Conference on Public Trust and Confidence in the Courts, 1999:21). Many state court systems have, like California, reenergized their commitment to fairness in the courts by creating Public Trust and Confidence Projects.

CONCLUSION

If anything has been learned by those responsible for the judicial system in the United States during the last 20 years of examining and responding to the public perception of racial, ethnic, and gender bias, it is that the credibility of the judicial system is dependent on the public's trust and confidence in the courts. In discussing the implications of a lack of trust and confidence, Benesh and Howell suggest that "At the extreme level, a lack of confidence in 'normal' channels may lead to attempts at individualized justice in the form of political connections, bribery, taking the law into one's own hands, and other means to circumvent the system" (Benesh and Howell, 2001:200–201). Trust and confidence in the courts is essential to a fair and just system in a democratic society. In the words of Frank A. Bennack, President and Chief Executive Officer of the Hearst Corporation, "But the courts—that's something different. Here trust is essential. Here, knowledge is essential. Here, society and institution come together in ways that really define who we would like to think we are as a society—fair, open, and protective of the rights of every individual" (National Conference on Public Trust and Confidence in the Courts, 1999:9).

References

Benesh, Sara C., and Susan E. Howell. 2001. Confidence in the Courts: A Comparison of Users and Non-Users. *Behavioral Sciences and the Law* 19: 199–214.

Carlisle, Jay C. 1999. Perspectives: Synopsis of the Report of the Second Circuit Task Force on Gender, Racial, and Ethnic Fairness in the Courts. *Pace Law Review* 19: 431–441.

Cortina, Lilia. M. 2002. The Study of Gender in the Courts: Keeping Bias at Bay. *Law and Social Inquiry* 27 (2): 199–204.

Coyle, Pamela. 1996. Taking Bias to Task. *ABA Journal* (April): 63–67.

Grubin, Sharon E. and John M. Walker. 1997. Report of the Second Circuit Task Force on Gender, Racial, and Ethnic Fairness in the Courts. *New York School of Law Annual Survey of American Law:* 11–115.

Judicial Council of California. 1997. *Final Report of the California Judicial Council Advisory Committee on Racial and Ethnic Bias in the Courts.* http://www.courtinfo.ca.gov/reference/documents/rebias.pdf (accessed October 12, 2007).

Judicial Council of California/Administrative Office of the Courts. 2006. *Trust and Confidence in the California Courts: Public Court Users and Judicial Branch Members Talk About California Courts.* San Francisco: Judicial Council of California.

Judicial Council of California. 2007. *Fact Sheet: Access and Fairness Advisory Committee.* http://www.courtinfo.ca.gov/reference/documents/factsheets/accfair.pdf (accessed October 12, 2007).

Leben, Steve. 1999. Public Trust and Confidence in the Courts: A National Conference and Beyond. *Court Review* 36 (3): 4–7.

National Center for State Courts. 1995. *Establishing and Operating a Task Force or Commission on Racial and Ethnic Bias in the Courts.* Williamsburg, VA: National Center for State Courts.

National Center for State Courts. 1999. How the Public Views the State Courts: A 1999 National Survey. Williamsburg, VA: National Center for State Courts.

National Conference on Public Trust and Confidence in the Courts. 1999. *National Action Plan: A Guide for State and National Organizations.* Williamsburg, VA: National Center for State Courts. http://www.ncsconline.org/WC/Publications/

Res_AmtPTC_NatlActionPlanPub.pdf (accessed October 31, 2007).

Nebraska Judicial Branch. 2003. *The Nebraska Minority and Justice Task Force Final Report.* http://www.supremecourt.ne.gov/community/adminreports/mjtf_report.pdf (accessed October 12, 2007).

Nebraska Judicial Branch. 2005. *Minority and Justice Implementation Committee: Progress Report February 2005* http://ppc.nebraska.edu/program_areas/documents/mjtf/MJTF-2005Progress_ Report.pdf (accessed October 12, 2007).

New Jersey Supreme Court Task Force on Minority Concerns. 2002. *2000–2002 Report* http://www.judiciary.state.nj.us/reports/minconpart1.pdf (accessed October 12, 2007).

New Jersey Supreme Court Task Force on Minority Concerns. 2007. *2004–2007 Report* http://www.judiciary.state.nj.us/reports 2007/minority_concerns.pdf (accessed October 12, 2007).

O'Connor, Sandra Day. 1994. The Effects of Gender in the Federal Courts: The Final Report of the Ninth Circuit Gender Bias Task Force. *Southern California Law Review* 67: 745–1063.

O'Connor, Sandra Day. 1999. Public Trust as a Dimension of Equal Justice: Some Suggestions to Increase Public Trust. *Court Review* 36 (3): 10–13.

Resnik, Judith. 1996. Asking About Gender in Courts. *Signs: Journal of Women in Culture & Society* 21: 952–991.

Rottman, David. B, and Alan J. Tomkins. 1999. Public Trust and Confidence in the Courts: What Public Opinion Surveys Mean to Judges. *Court Review* 36 (3): 24–31.

Rottman, David B, Randall Hansen, Nicole Mott, and Lynn Grimes. 2003. *Perceptions of the Courts in Your Community: The Influence of Experience, Race and Ethnicity.* Williamsburg, VA: National Center for State Courts.

Schafran, Lynn Hecht, and Norma Juliet Wikler. 2001. *Gender Fairness in the Courts: Action in the New Millennium.* Alexandria, VA: State Justice Institute

Special Report: Report of the First Circuit Gender, Race and Ethnic Bias Task Forces. 2000. Special Report: Report of the First Circuit Gender, Race and Ethnic Bias Task Forces. *The Boston Public Interest Law Journal* 9: 173–371.

Yankelovich, Kelley, and White, Inc. 1977. *Public Image of the Courts.* Washington, DC: United States Department of Justice.

Wikler, Norma Juliet, and Lynn Hecht Schafran. 1991. Learning from the New Jersey Supreme Court Task Force on Women in the Courts: Evaluation, Recommendations and Implications for Other States Women's Rights. *Women's Rights Law Reporter* 12 (4): 313–379.

CHAPTER 19

Wrongful and Unlawful Conviction

Robert Schehr

If the wrong person is put in prison, the actual perpetrator of harm is free to commit more violent crimes. This phrase encapsulates the shared wisdom of the international Innocence Network, as well as those working in the criminal justice system who are knowledgeable about wrongful and unlawful convictions. When the wrong person is put in prison we systemically generate two sets of victims—the actual victim(s) of the original crime, and the victim of a wrongful or unlawful conviction that sends men and women to prison for crimes they did not commit.

LEGAL TERMINOLOGY

In the United States, when scholars speak of wrongful and unlawful conviction they are referring to the conviction of a person who is *actually innocent* of the crime for which they have been charged. Simply put, they didn't do it; someone else did.

It is important at the outset to make a few relevant legal distinctions with regard to the matter of wrongful and unlawful conviction and the notion of "innocence." The general public may freely use the concept innocence without careful consideration of its meaning. In legal circles, however, innocence has a very precise meaning depending on its context. Attorneys and judges may refer to a defendant as either *legally* innocent or *actually* innocent. The distinction is by no means a trivial one. The accused in a criminal case can be considered *legally* innocent if he/she has been found not guilty by a judge or jury. That is, a jury could not determine *beyond a reasonable doubt* that the defendant was responsible for committing the crime of which he/she was accused. To attain the level of certainty necessary to convict a defendant beyond a reasonable doubt, a jury must determine, based on careful review of all evidence presented, whether the evidence is so persuasive that any reasonable person would come to the conclusion that the defendant is responsible for the crime he/she has been charged with. This standard does not require the jury to be certain, only that the evidence presented would lead any reasonable person to come to the same conclusion.

THE PREVALENCE OF WRONGFUL CONVICTIONS
IN THE UNITED STATES

It is convenient to believe that because so much attention has been directed at exonerations over the course of the last decade, but with significantly greater media attention beginning in the early twenty-first century, conviction of the actually innocent is a recent phenomenon. Nothing could be further from the truth. In the box insert, I have provided one classic case of wrongful and unlawful conviction for review—the Boorn brothers case. Occurring in 1812, the Boorn brothers case is the oldest documented case of wrongful conviction and includes virtually every known cause.

We do not actually know how many people have been wrongfully convicted and have been, or still are, serving time in prison, or still worse, have been executed

---

THE BOORN BROTHERS CASE

The facts of the Boorn brothers case are as intriguing today as they must have been at the time. The Boorn brothers worked on their family farm with their brother-in-law, Russell Colvin. It was widely known throughout the small town of Manchester, Vermont, that the Boorn brothers viewed Colvin with considerable contempt. When Colvin disappeared in 1812, the Boorn brothers came under immediate scrutiny. Seven years passed before Colvin's disappearance produced charges against the Boorns. According to Wilkie's account of the story, an uncle of the Boorns was visited by a ghost in a dream. The ghost indicated that the Boorns had killed Colvin and buried his body in a cellar hole on the family farm. When the Boorns' uncle shared his story with authorities, the site was excavated, but no body was located. Not long after, however, a dog unearthed bones thought to be those of Russell Colvin. It was at this point that an official investigation was initiated by police. Jesse Boorn was taken into custody, but Steven had since moved to New York.

Jesse Boorn shared a jail cell with a man named Silas Merrill. Merrill pursued police to tell them that during conversations in their jail cell, Boorn confessed to the crime. When Merrill agreed to testify against Boorn at trial, he was released from jail. When police confronted Boorn with the physical evidence taken from the old cellar (the bones dug up by the dog), and with Merrill's willingness to testify against him in court, he confessed to participating in Colvin's death. However, Jesse also indicated that, while he was present, it was his brother, Steven, who actually committed the crime. It is believed by historians that Jesse was convinced his brother Steven was far enough away from Manchester that he couldn't be located by authorities. He was wrong. Manchester, Vermont, police organized a posse which located Steven in New York, arrested him, and returned him to Manchester to face charges. When Steven was questioned by police he, too, confessed to the murder of Russell Colvin.

Prior to the Boorns' trial, physicians examining the bones thought to be those of Russell Colvin changed their minds. They realized that the bones were actually animal bones, not human bones as was originally thought. But with the pending testimony of jailhouse informant Silas Merrill, and confessions to the crime from both Jesse and Steven, prosecutors went forward with the trial. Both Jesse and Steven Boorn were convicted of Colvin's murder and sentenced to death. Later, the Vermont legislature intervened to commute Jesse's sentence to life in prison, but Steven's death sentence was left intact.

In 1820, as Steven Boorn neared his execution by hanging, Russell Colvin was found very much alive and living in New Jersey. He returned to Manchester, Vermont, to clear his brothers-in-law of the crimes for which they had been convicted.

for crimes they did not commit. In the social sciences we refer to this as a "statistical unknown," or "a dark number." The reason is, in order to generate a sense of all the possible wrongful convictions that have taken place in the United States we would have to conduct what is called *postmortem* review of every criminal conviction. What we do know is the problem of wrongful conviction has troubled legal scholars and jurists for nearly a century.

In 1931, the National Commission on Law Observance and Enforcement *Report on Lawlessness in Law Enforcement,* otherwise known as the Wickersham Commission, reported on the significant role played by law enforcement in the generation of wrongful convictions (Wickersham Commission, 1931). The following year, Edwin Borchard wrote about the inherent danger of convicting the innocent through the use of coerced confessions (Borchard, 1932). In 1934, Justice Roscoe Pound followed these reports with a call for the recording of custodial interrogations. In the remaining decades of the twentieth century, from the 1950s on, only a handful of publications attempted to address the problem of wrongful conviction (Drizen and Reich, 2004), often appealing to matters relating to indigent defense and coerced confessions. These scholarly attempts to dramatize the undue influence of law enforcement practices leading to coerced confessions led to two significant court cases—*Escobedo* v. *Illinois* (1964) and *Miranda* v. *Arizona* (1966). Of the two, it was the Miranda case that had the most dramatic influence on discussions of wrongful conviction, coerced confessions, and criminal investigation. And still, criminal justicians claimed that wrongful convictions were at best an aberration.

In the United States, the 1990s marked the dawn of the science of DNA and its application to the determination of culpability in violent crimes. In many ways, the influence of DNA science on practitioner and public acknowledgement of wrongful conviction speaks to what may be viewed as a uniquely American reliance on scientism. Despite two century's worth of experiential evidence establishing the fact of wrongful conviction, Americans—especially law enforcement officers, prosecutors, and judges—required more proof (Jones, 2004). To date, DNA testing has resulted in 217 documented exonerations in the United States (Innocence Project website). But it is important to know that DNA exists only in about 10% of all criminal cases. That means that in 90% of criminal cases the defendant is convicted based on something other than physical evidence (e.g., eyewitness identification, false confessions, snitch testimony, police and prosecutorial misconduct). So for most people accused of crimes they did not commit, the challenge for attorneys and members of innocence projects working to exonerate them is that they must traverse enormous procedural hurdles put in place by federal and state legislatures, the most recent being the 1996 Anti-Terrorism and Effective Death Penalty Act (AEDPA), often with little or no success.

Radelet, Bedau, and Putnam's (1992:17) important study of twentieth-century homicide and rape convictions indicated that 416 were wrongfully convicted of murder or capital rape; twenty-three of the actually innocent were executed. According to the Death Penalty Information Center's 2004 report on death row exonerations, since the reinstatement of the death penalty in the United States in 1976 (Death Penalty Information Center website),

> One hundred and sixteen people have been freed from death row after being cleared of their charges, including 16 people in the past 20 months. These inmates cumulatively spent over 1,000 years awaiting their

freedom. The pace of exonerations has sharply increased, raising doubts about the reliability of the whole system.

Importantly, the report goes on to add that the average amount of time taken for exoneration is nine years.

Recent scholarship assessing both death penalty and non-death penalty cases indicates that in the United States since 1989, 368 factually innocent people have been exonerated (Gross *et al.*, 2005).

Let's say for the sake of argument that *only* 2% of all inmates presently incarcerated in the United States are wrongfully convicted. I have selected this conservative number based on unpublished research conducted by D. Michael Risinger (2006), Professor of Law at Seton Hall University. Let's also agree that the current number of people incarcerated in the United States is 2 million. If 2% of 2 million people incarcerated in the United States are wrongfully convicted, then criminal justice authorities have placed 40,000 people in prison who shouldn't be there. Equally problematic is the fact that if we have placed 40,000 people in prison who shouldn't be there, we also have not captured the true perpetrator of harm in those 40,000 cases. That means that the public remains at risk for possible re-offense, and we have generated 40,000 new victims in the wrongfully convicted who have lost virtually everything considered meaningful in their lives by current cultural standards.

THE DEMOGRAPHICS OF WRONGFUL AND UNLAWFUL CONVICTION

African Americans represent about 12% of the U.S. population, and about 19% of the population of the South. An analysis of 350 cases of wrongful and unlawful conviction conducted by Radelet, Bedau, and Putnam (1992) indicated that 43% (150) were black, and that blacks were more likely than whites to be wrongly convicted of capital crimes. Scheck, Neufeld, and Dwyer, (2000) examined 62 wrongful and unlawful convictions and found that 29% were white, and 57% were black. Radelet, Lofquist, and Bedau (1996) reviewed 68 death row cases and found that 45.6% of whites, 41.2% of blacks, and 13.2% of other minorities were wrongfully and unlawfully convicted. Harmon's (2001) study of 68 cases emerging from 1970 to 1998 found that 58% of minorities had been wrongfully and unlawfully convicted. Important to her study was the revelation that only 10% of the victims were minorities. Parker, DeWees, and Radelet (2003) analyzed 107 death row exonerees since 1973. They found that nationally 45% were black, 42% were white, and 13% were other minorities. In the South, 63% of death row exonerees were black.

EXPLICATION OF THE KNOWN CAUSES OF WRONGFUL CONVICTION

A decade of legal and social scientific scholarship has exposed the leading causes of wrongful conviction in the United States. The methodology practiced by scholars interested in understanding the leading causes of wrongful and unlawful conviction has, with a few exceptions, been based on legal case analysis.

Beginning in the late 1990s, scholars began collecting cases of known wrongful convictions, typically based on discovery of DNA, and conducted *postmortem* review.

Through this process of "working backwards," that is, taking a known exoneration and working from the post-conviction review (PCR), back through all the appeals, sentencing, and finally through all documents relating to the trial (e.g., police and forensic reports, witness statements, jury instructions, etc.), scholars are able to determine those moments where a case began to go wrong.

A concerted effort has been made by the national Innocence Network to gather exoneration cases state by state. These cases are being collected and posted at the Northwestern University Law School's Center on Wrongful Conviction website (http://www.law.northwestern.edu/depts/clinic/wrongful/links.htm). The purpose behind the collection of exoneration cases is to have researchers conduct *postmortem* review so that a database can be generated which documents the prevailing causes of wrongful convictions nationally. What has emerged from analysis of these cases, in addition to other sophisticated studies based on the case analysis method (Liebman and Fagan, 2000), is identification of the following predominant explanations for why wrongful and unlawful convictions occur: police and prosecutorial misconduct, false eyewitness identifications, false confessions, faulty forensics (junk science), jailhouse informants (snitches), and poor indigent defense.

To this list can be added a host of additional structural and process-related causes. For example: (1) police interrogation tactics (not necessarily misconduct, but police training in Reid School tactics designed to generate confessions) (Drizin and Leo, 2004; Leo *et al.*, 2006, Weisberg, 1961); (2) limitations brought on by the pretrial process (pretrial release, jury selection, delays, government disclosure, and pretrial discovery access, etc.) (Leipold, 2005); (3) jury perceptions of defendant guilt based on the fact that they are defendants in a trial; (4) the direct connection doctrine (making it difficult for defendants to introduce evidence of third-party suspect(s); (5) admissibility of eyewitness identification (Sullivan, 2004); (6) post-conviction procedural hurdles following the enactment of the Anti-terrorism and Effective Death Penalty Act; (7) system-wide "tunnel vision" that hones in on specific suspects to the exclusion of other possible suspects leading to interpretation of all evidence as being consistent with police and prosecutorial claims of inculpation, or ignoring or delegitimating evidence that does not fit the official theory of the case (Findley and Scott, 2006).

Since space limitations prohibit discussion of each of the known causes of wrongful and unlawful conviction, I will limit my attention to prosecutorial misconduct. I have selected this particular issue because of the extraordinary power vested in prosecutors to make cases, or dismiss them.

PROSECUTORIAL MISCONDUCT

Prosecutors have an ethical duty to the truth. Following Gershman (2001), this is largely due to the prosecutor's responsibility not only to convict the guilty, but equally as important *to protect the innocent*. That is, a prosecutor is supposed to expose both inculpatory *and* exculpatory evidence of a suspect's involvement with an alleged crime. This is important because it is often the case that the person first arrested for a crime is not the actual perpetrator of it. A 2006 Orleans Parish, Louisiana *amicus curiae* brief ("friend of the court" brief) seeking changes that would enhance the disclosure of exculpatory evidence at preliminary hearings provides a case in point. According to the Metropolitan Crime Commission (2005),

> In Orleans, prisoners serve an average of 41 days of DA [district attorney] time before a decision is made on their case. Many of those serving DA time are improperly detained. For those arrested on felony charges in Orleans there is a less than 50% chance that charges will be accepted by the DA at all, and only a one in four chance that they will eventually be found guilty. Only 7% of all those arrested are ultimately sentenced to incarceration.

Similarly, in 1993 the Bureau of Justice Statistics published "a survey of criminal dispositions in the seventy-five largest counties in the United States [which] reported that 42% of all violent crime felony defendants—those who presumptively survived the screening for innocence—had their cases dismissed in 1990. . . . Only slightly more than half (53%) of violent felony defendants were convicted of a crime. More than 90% of convictions for violent felonies reported in the seventy-five county survey were the result of a guilty plea. Of those defendants who chose to go to trial, slightly more than half (57%) were convicted of a violent felony, 15% were convicted of a misdemeanor, and 28% were acquitted. A look at the most serious violent felony, murder, reveals figures that are even more surprising: of the defendants who went to trial for murder, a majority (57%) were acquitted" (Givelber, 1997).

There are many reasons advanced to explain why prosecutors overcharge defendants, withhold exculpatory evidence, and refuse to consider claims of innocence, each of which is likely to produce acquittals. Burke (2006) contends that the most prescient explanations are: (1) confirmatory bias; (2) selective information processing; (3) belief perseverance; and (4) avoidance of cognitive dissonance. Briefly, *confirmatory bias* speaks to a single-minded belief that the suspect in custody is the most likely perpetrator of harm. This is problematic because confirmatory bias blocks out all other possible suspects from consideration. *Selective information processing,* argues Burke, occurs because human beings are incapable of "evaluating the strength of evidence independent of their prior beliefs" (1597). Thus, when prosecutors receive a suspect in a particular case they are likely to believe that the suspect is the actual perpetrator (confirmatory bias), which leads them to interpret all subsequent evidence consistent with that presumption. The opposite is also true; any exculpatory evidence presented to prosecutors that may challenge their original theory of the crime will tend to be dismissed as irrelevant. This is called *belief perseverance.* With belief perseverance prosecutors will, despite evidence to the contrary, adhere to their original theory of the crime. Finally, to avoid the psycho-emotional discomfort caused by *cognitive dissonance*—the gap between what we believe to be true, and what is actually true—prosecutors will convince themselves that their belief about the theory of the crime, and the accused, is salient.

What Burke's analysis demonstrates is that prosecutors, like all human beings, process information consistent with their prior beliefs and values, and when confronted with discordant information are reluctant to reassess those beliefs because to do so would generate cognitive dissonance and a strong sense of psycho-emotional instability.

The prosecutor's near monopoly over the facts of the case, and his/her ability to shape those facts signify the prosecutor's role as one of supreme authority. Prosecutors wield extraordinary power. In fact, they represent the single most powerful group of actors in the criminal justice system. Prosecutors determine who to charge with a crime, what to charge them with, whether to offer plea agreements or go to trial, and they recommend the appropriate sentence upon conviction. With all this power lies the ability to significantly influence the outcome of all criminal proceedings. In its 2003 national study of the incidence of prosecutorial misconduct going back as far as 1970, the Center for Public Integrity interviewed judges and appellate court panels and found that prosecutors in 2,341 jurisdictions were guilty of engaging in prosecutorial misconduct when "dismissing charges at trial, reversing convictions or reducing sentences in at least 2,012 cases" (Center for Public Integrity website). In an additional 513 cases, appellate judges offered dissents or concurrences in which they found prosecutorial misconduct. When analyses of prosecutorial misconduct are raised on appeal, they are typically viewed by appellate court judges as "harmless error." That is, appellate judges may acknowledge that a particular violation has occurred, but will consider the violation in lieu of determining whether, absent the violation, the jury would have come to a different conclusion regarding the verdict. An analysis of 187 DNA exonerations revealed that 56 of them were cases where serious constitutional errors were made at trial, but where appellate courts ruled those errors were harmless (Short, 2007). Again, each was later exonerated.

There are many ways that prosecutors can violate ethical rules of the court, as well as constitutionally protected due process rights. A list of the most common forms of prosecutorial misconduct includes: confirmatory bias or tunnel vision (prematurely focusing attention on a specific suspect to the exclusion of other possible suspects); charging without sufficient evidence of guilt; in capital eligible cases, forcing plea agreements by using the threat of the death penalty if convicted at trial; improper behavior during grand jury proceedings (e.g., speaking to alleged facts that have not been confirmed with documentation for a grand jury to review); knowingly allowing police officers to commit perjury while testifying at trial (known as "testilying"); making inappropriate or inflammatory comments in the presence of a jury; introducing or attempting to introduce inadmissible, inappropriate, or inflammatory evidence; charging and prosecuting solely on the basis of eyewitness identification, suspect confessions, and/or snitch testimony; manipulation of state police crime lab technicians to generate forensic results consistent with prosecution's theory of the case; uncritical acceptance of forensic experts; uncritical acceptance of forensic "sciences," including DNA, but especially fingerprint, ballistic, tool mark, tire, footprint, hand writing, and bite mark (odontology) testimony; mischaracterizing the evidence or the facts of the case to mislead a jury; committing violations pertaining to the selection of the jury (e.g., selecting specific race/ethnicity or gender, or only jurors who support the death penalty—they are more likely to convict); mishandling of physical evidence, especially exculpatory evidence (what is known as a Brady violation following the *Brady* v. *Maryland* case); threatening, badgering, or tampering with witnesses; harassing, displaying bias toward, or having a vendetta against the defendant or the defendant's counsel; making improper closing arguments; and failure to re-open and reinvestigate cases where a wrongful conviction has occurred and the assailant is potentially still on the street.

Given the overwhelming authority wielded by prosecutors with regard to the outcome of criminal trials, it is imperative that attention be directed at ways to curb the practices listed above. Most important, some of the most egregious manifestations of prosecutorial misconduct are shielded from public view. That is because nearly 95% of cases are plea-bargained and never make it to trial. No doubt the competitive "us versus them" adversarial environment that constitutes criminal due process is largely the reason behind many of the activities listed above. Prosecutors, like defense attorneys, must "win at all costs." In both high profile and run-of-the-mill cases, prosecutors are pressured by crime victims and their families, law enforcement, political interest groups like those that speak on behalf of crime victims, the public, the media, and their professional culture into generating a result, regardless of their duty to the truth. Often it is the case that concerns about offending these organizations and interests, along with the fear of appearing to be too lenient with regard to defendants, and their own intellectual dishonesty and arrogance, send prosecutors down a path, not of truth-finding, but of saving face.

There are many examples of prosecutors who have rebuked the "win at all cost" culture and have, instead, worked to serve in the interest of truth. These prosecutors demonstrate considerable moral courage as they must deflect criticism from others in the criminal justice system keen to close a case and get a conviction. They are careful to avoid easy answers, and are characterized by their commitment to carefully testing their case hypotheses in lieu of ever-present newly discovered evidence. [Former] The United States Supreme Court Justice Robert H. Jackson articulates his vision of an ideal prosecutor:

> The qualities of a good prosecutor are as elusive and as impossible to define as those which mark a gentleman. And those who need to be told would not understand it anyway. A sensitiveness to fair play and sportsmanship is perhaps the best protection against the abuse of power, and the citizen's safety lies in the prosecutor who tempers zeal with human kindness, who seeks truth and not victims, who serves the law and not factional purposes, and who approaches his task with humility. (In Gershman, 2001:15)

Despite Justice Jackson's plea, until the dominant cultural emphasis on adversarial due process abates the likelihood of attaining anything near a commitment to "human kindness," "humility," and a sense of "fair play" are likely to remain pipe dreams. This is largely because there are no significant punishments for prosecutors who behave in unethical and unlawful ways. Prosecutors are largely immune from prosecution for their acts of misconduct. Without civil and criminal sanctions to accompany misconduct, it is unlikely that the behaviors listed above, and that are clearly associated with wrongfully and unlawfully convicting innocent men and women, will change in any significant way.

REMEDIES

Response to the known causes of wrongful and unlawful conviction includes legislation at both the federal and state levels. At the federal level has been passage of the Justice For All Act Factsheet in 2004 (http://www.ojp.usdoj.gov/ovc/publications/

factshts/justforall/fs000311.pdf). This Act provides for the right to petition for DNA testing when it can prove exculpatory; the implementation of evidence preservation procedures, and proof of the establishment of oversight bodies responsible for making certain these procedures are being adhered to; and better training and compensation for death penalty attorneys. At the state level has been implementation of double-blind and sequential procedures for eyewitness identification; video-taping suspect interviews; independent auditing of state police crime laboratories; and better training and funding of indigent defense attorneys.

A number of states have implemented innocence commissions that independently review cases where viable questions of actual innocence have been established, and recommend policy changes for ways to improve due process. Innocence commissions are typically comprised of bi-partisan interdisciplinary associations of judicial and law enforcement experts, members of the community, politicians, and academics (Schehr, 2005; Schehr and Sears, 2005). The North Carolina Actual Innocence Commission signifies a model constituting *postmortem* case review with the mandate to report recommended changes to due process, educate commission members, and consider implementation costs (Mumma, 2004). The Illinois Death Penalty Commission established by then-Governor George Ryan was charged with investigating the state's death penalty conviction, and sentencing process and articulated 85 recommended changes to its state death penalty procedure. However, the Illinois Death Penalty Commission, like the Arizona *Capital Case Commission* (http://www.ag.state.az.us/CCC/FinalReport. html), was established for the specific purpose of cross-sectional research. Following completion of their work, each commission was disbanded. The innocence commission for Virginia, established in 2003, is structured to investigate known cases of wrongful conviction to identify those areas most frequently cited as being prone to generating error. Finally, in 2004 the California General Assembly established the California Commission on the Fair Administration of Justice (http://www.ccfaj.org/). The purpose of the Commission is to investigate the causes of wrongful conviction, and to recommend changes necessary to improve due process to avoid generating wrongful and unlawful convictions.

But much more must be done if we are to realize the kind of institutional changes necessary to limit the errors we are presently aware of that lead to wrongful and unlawful convictions. Here are but a few of many necessary improvements we must invest in:

• Changes must be made to improve the funding of the indigent defense system. If U.S. citizens are committed to an adversarial process they must meaningfully fund those responsible for generating an adequate defense of the indigent accused. That means more funds to hire and retain qualified attorneys in significant enough numbers to reduce caseloads and provide for quality case investigations, and we must provide the funding necessary for defense attorneys to hire private investigators, forensic scientists, and mitigation experts.
• We must invest in high-quality training for first responders to crime scenes. Police officers must be trained in best practices for evidence procurement and preservation.
• States must pass stringent evidence-preservation laws.

- States must invest in independent crime laboratory oversight.
- Defense attorneys must be given greater access to pretrial discovery.
- Prosecutors must be committed to seeking the truth. That means objectively interpreting evidence of *both* inculpatory *and* exculpatory evidence.
- We should severely limit the use of jailhouse informant testimony (they serve only one interest—their own).
- We should allow expert legal and social science scholars to testify at trial to the potential error involved in eyewitness identifications and suspect confessions.
- We should change the way suspect interviews are conducted so that we minimize the likelihood of false confessions, especially in cases where the suspect is young, and/or mentally ill. Changes would include video-taping suspect interviews, and changing our methods for obtaining suspect information by moving away from the psycho-emotional manipulating methods presently employed by most law enforcement agencies.
- We should minimize the coercive tactics employed by prosecutors to induce suspects to plea bargain to crimes they did not commit. Plea bargaining accounts for roughly 95% of convictions nationwide.
- We should be conscious of race/ethnicity-biased venire (jury pool). States should follow the lead of California which has required prosecutors to demonstrate that prospective jurors removed for cause were so removed for race-neutral reasons (*Uttecht v. Brown*, 2007).
- Procedural bars to raising *habeas* appeals need to be removed for those who have actual innocence claims. The current timelines established in many states, and for federal appeals, make it nearly impossible for defendants to raise claims of innocence in a timely way. This is because of the time it takes to generate newly discovered evidence of actual innocence (e.g. *Bowles v. Russell*, 2007).
- State and federal courts should return to their previous harmless error analysis. That would mean that violations of constitutional due process rights would no longer be passed on as harmless error.
- We must systematically abolish both the state and federal death penalty. More than enough evidence exists to indicate that wrongfully and unlawfully convicted defendants have been, and likely will be executed. Enhanced *habeas corpus* restrictions, problems with racially/ethnically-biased venire, the likelihood that juries empanelled in death-eligible cases will more often convict, the use of the death penalty to threaten suspects into plea bargaining to lesser charges, and the likelihood of convicting in cases where defendants are minorities and victims are white each suggest that the death penalty must be eliminated. Moral positions aside, the prevalence of wrongful and unlawful convictions suggests that police and prosecutors cannot be certain they have the actual perpetrator of harm in custody. That simple truth in a system of laws founded on the principle that all must be presumed innocent means that we cannot retain the hubris necessary to execute.
- State and federal courts and the U.S. Supreme Court should recognize comity with international law, where appropriate, by drawing upon international statutes and case law to remedy domestic wrongful and unlawful convictions. This practice has long been a part of American jurisprudence and is consistent with the U.S. Constitution's Supremacy Clause (Schehr, 2008).

CONCLUSION

Wrongful and unlawful conviction is a fact of jurisprudence in the United States. The most conservative estimate indicates there are likely 40,000 wrongfully and unlawfully convicted people presently serving time in the U.S. prisons. Data also suggest that among this population is a disproportionate number of poor and working class whites and African Americans, with African Americans overrepresented based on their overall numbers in the population as a whole. This is largely due to the inability to procure quality legal representation, and the continued race/ethnic bias associated with charging practices, venire, and institutional racism. With increasing recognition of the proliferation of wrongful and unlawful conviction in the United States, consequent state and federal changes to crime scene investigation and criminal due process signify a new civil rights movement directed at improving application of the administration of justice.

References

Borchard, Edwin. 1932. *Convicting the Innocent: Sixty-Five Actual Errors of Criminal Justice.* New Jersey: Garden City Publishers.

Bowles v. *Russell.* No. 06–5306 (2007).

Bureau of Justice Statistics. 1993. *Sourcebook of Criminal Justice Statistics,* 649, Table 6.89. Washington, DC: U.S. Department of Justice

Burke, Alafair S. 2006. Improving Prosecutorial Decision Making: Some Lessons of Cognitive Science. *William and Mary Law Review* 47: 1587.

California Commission on the Fair Administration of Justice website, http://www.ccfaj.org/.

Capital Case Commission Report. 2002. Office of the Attorney General of Arizona. http://www.ag.state.az.us/CCC/FinalReport.html.

Center for Public Integrity website, http://www.publicintegrity.org/pm/.

Death Penalty Information Center (DPIC) website, http://www.deathpenaltyinfo.org/article.php?scid = 45&did = 1149.

Drizen, Steve, and Marissa Reich. 2004. Heeding the Lessons of History: The Need for Mandatory Recording of Police Interrogations to Accurately Assess the Reliability and Voluntariness of Confessions. *Drake Law Review* 52 (4): 619–646.

Drizin, Steven A. and Richard A. Leo. 2004. *The Problem of False Confessions in the Post-DNA World.* 82 *N.C. L. Rev.* 891–1007.

Escobedo v. *Illinois,* 378 U.S. 201 (1964).

Findley, Keith, and Michael Scott. 2006. The Multiple Dimensions of Tunnel Vision in Criminal Cases. *Wisconsin Law Review* 2: 291–397.

Gershman, Bennett. 2001. The Prosecutor's Duty to Truth. *Georgetown Journal of Legal Ethics* 14: 309. [Accessed through Lexis-Nexis.]

Givelber, Daniel J. 1997. Meaningless Acquittals, Meaningful Convictions: Do We Reliably Acquit the Innocent? *Rutgers Law Review* 49: 1317–1396.

Gross, Samuel, Kristen Jacoby, Daniel Matheson, Nicholas Montgomery, and Sujata Patil. 2005. Exonerations in the United States. *Journal of Criminal Law & Criminology* 95 (2): 523–553.

Harmon, Talia. 2001. Predictors of miscarriages of justice in capital cases. *Justice Quarterly* 18: 949–968.

Innocence Project website, http://www.innocenceproject.org/ http://www.innocenceproject.org/docs/NC_Innocence_Commision_Mission.html.

Jones, Nancy. 2004. Scientism or Luddism: Is Informed Ethical Dialogue Possible? *American Journal of Bioethics* 4 (1): 18–20.

Justice for All Act Factsheet. 2004. http://www.ojp.usdoj.gov/ovc/publications/factshts/justforall/fs000311.pdf.

Leipold, Andrew. 2005. How the Pre-trial Process Contributes to Wrongful Convictions. *American Criminal Law Review* 42 (4): 1123–1165.

Leo, Richard, Steven Drizin, Peter Neufeld, Bradley Hall, and Amy Vatner. 2006. Bringing Reliability Back In: False Confessions and Legal Safeguards in the 21st Century. *Wisconsin Law Review* 2: 479–539.

Liebman, James, and Jeffrey Fagan. 2000. A Broken System: Error Rates in Capital Cases, 1973–1995. http://www2.law.columbia.edu/instructionalservices/liebman/

Metropolitan Crime Commission. 2005. *Performance of the New Orleans Criminal Justice System 2003–2004.* August, New Orleans, Louisiana. http://www.metropolitancrimecommission.org/html/2Perf_of_the_NO_Criminal_Justice_System_2003–2004l.pdf.

Miranda v. *Arizona,* 384 U.S. 436, 467 (1966).

Mumma, Chris. 2004. The North Carolina Actual Innocence Commission: Uncommon perspectives Joined by a Common Cause. *Drake Law Review* 52 (4): 647–656.

Northwestern University Law School's Center on Wrongful Conviction website, http://www.law.northwestern.edu/depts/clinic/wrongful/links.htm.

Parker, Karen. F., Mari A. DeWees, and Michael Radelet. 2003. Race, the Death Penalty, and Wrongful Convictions. *Criminal Justice Magazine* 18 (1): 48–54.

Radelet, Michael, Hugo Bedau, and Chris Putnam. 1992. *In Spite of Innocence: Erroneous Convictions in Capital Cases.* Boston: Northeastern University Press.

Radelet, Michael, William Lofquist, and Hugo Bedau. 1996. Prisoners Released from Death Rows Since 1970 Because of Doubts About Their Guilt. *Thomas M. Cooley Law Review* 13: 907–966.

Risinger, D. Michael. 2006. Unpublished Conference Presentation. National Innocence Network Conference, Harvard Law School, March, 2006.

Scheck, Barry, Peter Neufeld, and Jim Dwyer. 2000. *Actual Innocence.* New York: Doubleday.

Schehr, Robert. 2005. The Criminal Cases Review Commission as State Strategic Selection Mechanism. *American Criminal Law Review* 42 (4): 1289.

Schehr, Robert. 2008. Shedding the Burden of Sisyphus: International Law and Wrongful Conviction in the United States. *Boston College Third World Law Journal* 28 (1).

Schehr, Robert, and Jamie Sears. 2005. Innocence Commissions and Accountability in Wrongful Convictions. *Critical Criminology* 13 (2): 181–209.

Short, Ligia. 2007. The Harmless Error Doctrine: The Dilution of the Defendant's Constitutional Rights. Unpublished Master's thesis research. Department of Criminology and Criminal Justice, Northern Arizona University.

Sullivan, Thomas. 2004. Police Experiences with Recording Custodial Interrogations. Special Report Presented by the Northwestern Center on Wrongful Convictions, No. 1. http://www.law.northwestern.edu/wrongfulconvictions/issues/causesandremedies/falseconfessions/Sullivan Report.pdf.

Uttecht v. *Brown.* No. 06–413 (2007).

Weisberg, Bernard. 1961. Police Interrogation of Arrested Persons: A Skeptical View. *Journal of Criminal Law, Criminology & Police* 52 (21): 44–45.

Wickersham Commission on Law Observance and Enforcement. 1931. Part 1: Records of the Committee on Official Lawlessness. Samuel Walker (Consulting Editor). Amicrofilmproject of University Publications of America. 4520 East-West Highway, Bethesda, MD. http://www.lexisnexis.com/documents/academic/upa_cis/1965_WickershamCommPt1.Pdf.

PART FOUR

Reframing
Difference

CHAPTER 20

Educating for Change

The Effect of Laws and Training

Larry A. Gould

Amendment 14 to the United States Constitution—
Citizenship Rights

1. All persons born or naturalized in the United States,
and subject to the jurisdiction thereof, are citizens of the
United States and of the State wherein they reside. No
State shall make or enforce any law which shall abridge the
privileges or immunities of citizens of the United States;
nor shall any State deprive any person of life, liberty, or
property, without due process of law; nor deny to any
person within its jurisdiction the equal protection of the
laws. Ratified June 28, 1868.

42 UCS § 1983. Civil action for deprivation of rights

Every person who, under color of any statute, ordinance,
regulation, custom, or usage, of any State or Territory or the
District of Columbia, subjects, or causes to be subjected, any
citizen of the United States or other person within the
jurisdiction thereof to the deprivation of any rights,
privileges, or immunities secured by the Constitution and
laws, shall be liable to the party injured in an action at law,
suit in equity, or other proper proceeding for redress, except
that in any action brought against a judicial officer for an act
or omission taken in such officer's judicial capacity,
injunctive relief shall not be granted unless a declaratory

decree was violated or declaratory relief was unavailable. For the purposes of this section, any Act of Congress applicable exclusively to the District of Columbia shall be considered to be a statute of the District of Columbia.

Solutions to discriminatory, harassing, insensitive, and/or uncivil behavior occur as the result of social change and initiatives, changes in the law through judicial findings or legislation, and finally through training or education. This a very complex set of interactions in which courts often reverse themselves, legislative bodies attempt to protect the powerful (Katznelson, 2005), and then through social pressure and activism change the laws (Katznelson, 2005; Rothenberg, 2004) and finally through training and education. It is often the case that amendments to the Constitution, legal decisions, executive orders, and changes in the law are not immediately enforced. In fact, such changes are often resisted to great extent such as was the case with integration of the military and *Brown* v. *Board of Education* (347 U.S. 483, 1954). It is the case, however, that ignoring any of the factors or points of change noted above will cost justice agencies in terms of litigation, loss of status in the community, loss of employee productivity, and loss of diversity, leading to continued insensitivity on the part of the organization. Through the use of a multi-pronged approach, which addresses the needs of the diverse group of service providers, victims and offenders, the likelihood of success is increased.

This chapter focuses on four related and interconnecting areas concerning the applicability of cultural diversity education in criminal justice. First is a brief review of some of the relevant laws and court decisions followed by a review of the historical context that relates the problems of the past to those of today. Third, there is a review of some of the points of resistance to cultural diversity training, and finally, there is a review of some of the techniques used in overcoming that resistance.

When discussing diversity training it is important to consider much more than just race and gender; however, equality in the areas of race and gender tend to be in the forefront of change in other areas of unequal or disparate treatment. In fact, to focus only on race and gender will simply serve to alienate those whom you most need to reach, thus dooming the training to inevitable failure. In this chapter, as is the case with the remainder of the book, the term "diversity" is used in its broadest sense so as to include age, socioeconomic status, culture, gender, race, sexual orientation, religion, ethnicity, and so on. The overall focus involves recognition of how similar we are, while not forgetting that we should also be respectful of our group and individual differences. This means that, to effect any change, we must use a multi-pronged approach to addressing those issues that continue to keep us separate and thus mistrustful and disrespectful of each other.

This chapter starts with five overlapping assumptions, which have been drawn from previous research. The first is that a diverse justice system is a more effective justice system. The second assumption is that an increased understanding of diversity issues can begin with education or training that, in part, asks people to question how and why they have come to hold certain opinions. The third assumption is that the method of achieving a justice system that is sensitive to diversity is equally as important as the message that is being conveyed. The fourth assumption is that, in teaching diversity, one may at times speak in general terms; however, particular attention must be paid to teaching not only about the differences *between* groups, but also about the differences *within* groups. The fifth assumption is that attitudes concerning cultural sensitivity/diversity can be changed if the methods and techniques of delivering the message are appropriate. This assumption focuses on those factors and/or characteristics of the audience to whom the message is directed. The impact of these five assumptions on the teaching of cultural diversity will be more fully discussed after a brief, historical review of the attempts to sensitize justice systems personnel to the different cultures in which they work.

RELEVANT CHANGES TO THE U.S. CONSTITUTION, PRESIDENTIAL EXECUTIVE ORDERS, LAWS, AND COURT DECISIONS

This chapter opens (above) with two of the most relevant, sometimes controversial, and, in their early history, ignored legal changes (the Fourteenth Amendment to the U.S. Constitution and 42 USC Section 1983) in the area of civil rights. It is important to note that the protection of civil rights and the representation of people through universal suffrage is one of the first steps in guaranteeing diversity. As noted in Gould's earlier chapter, in the case of *Elk* v. *Wilkinson*, citizenship was based on an interpretation by the U.S. Supreme Court of the Fourteenth Amendment. That decision, which was overturned within three years by the same Supreme Court, held that Native Americans were not citizens; thus, could not vote. If anything, this exemplifies the sometime complex and certainly torturous route of the development of civil rights, thus the development of diversity in our country. A discourse on judicial decisions and legislative changes in the United States would consume a space at least twice the length allotted for this whole book. Even the two laws mentioned above are pre-dated by a long history of social movement and change. For example, the term "due process" is mentioned in the Magna Carta of 1215 A.D. In Chapter 39 of the Magna Carta, King John of England promised as follows: "No free man shall be taken or imprisoned or seized or exiled or in any way destroyed, nor will we go upon him nor send upon him, except by the lawful judgment of his peers or by the law of the land."

Thus, of more current interest to the issues discussed in this chapter are:

- *McCulloch* v. *Maryland* (17 U.S. 316, 1819).
- Amendment XV (the Fifteenth Amendment to the U.S. Constitution, ratified February 3, 1870).
- Amendment XIX (the Nineteenth Amendment to the U.S. Constitution, ratified August 18, 1920).
- *Brown* v. *Board of Education* (347 U.S. 483, handed down May 17, 1954).
- The integration of the military by President Truman (Executive Order 9981, July 26, 1948).
- Creation of affirmative action in employment issued by President Kennedy, (Executive Order 10925, March 6, 1961).
- The National Voting Rights Act of 1965.
- President Lyndon Johnson's "To Fulfill These Rights Speech" at Howard University, June 4, 1965 (Katznelson, 2005).
- Title VII of the Civil Rights Act of 1964.
- The Americans with Disabilities Act of 1990.

Each of these cases, executive orders, speeches, or laws has become part of the cumulative, mutually supportive, and continuing effort to insure equal protection, which in turn recognizes diversity.

Interestingly, the much older case that allowed the Supreme Court the authority to decide the issue of supremacy of federal powers over those powers held by the states is based on the supremacy clause of the U.S. Constitution (*McCulloch* v. *Maryland*, 17 U.S. 316, 1819). In McCulloch, Chief Justice John Marshall asserted that the laws adopted by the federal government, when exercising its constitutional powers, are generally superior to any conflicting laws adopted by state governments. The primary legal issues settled in this case concerned powers of Congress under the Constitution, and whether the states possess certain powers to the exclusion of the federal government even if the Constitution does not explicitly limit them to the States. In sum, the result of the case was the ability of Congress to implement laws that were in conflict with state laws. This eventually signaled the end of the Jim Crow laws in the South (1876 – 1965), which specified how the separate but equal ruling in *Plessy* v. *Ferguson* (163 U.S. 537, 1896) was to be operationalized. In *Plessy* v. *Ferguson* (1896), the U.S. Supreme Court found that a Louisiana law mandating separate but equal accommodations for blacks and whites on intrastate railroads was constitutional. This decision provided the legal foundation to justify many other actions by state and local governments to socially separate blacks and whites (Katznelson, 2005).

The Fifteenth Amendment (ratified on February 3, 1870) established the following:

> Section 1. The right of citizens of the United States to vote shall not be
> denied or abridged by the United States or by any State on account of
> race, color, or previous condition of servitude. Section 2. The Congress
> shall have power to enforce this article by appropriate legislation.

Even with this amendment to the Constitution, the vote was still withheld from most southern blacks and from non-white minorities in the United States, from the post-Reconstruction era through the 1960s.

Amendment XIX (the Nineteenth Amendment) to the U.S. Constitution provides that neither the individual states of the United States nor its federal government may deny a citizen the right to vote because of the citizen's sex. American women were pioneers in the women's suffrage cause, advocating women's right to vote from the 1820s onward. Some early victories were won in the territories of Wyoming (1869) and Utah (1870), although Utah women were disenfranchised by the U.S. Congress in 1887.

Another seemingly small but yet very important point of change occurred when President Harry Truman supported a civil rights bill and desegregated the army. "WHEREAS it is essential that there be maintained in the armed services of the United States the highest standards of democracy, with equality of treatment and opportunity for all those who serve in our country's defense:

> NOW THEREFORE, by virtue of the authority vested in me as President
> of the United States, by the Constitution and the statutes of the United
> States, and as Commander in Chief of the armed services, it is hereby
> ordered as follows:
> 1. It is hereby declared to be the policy of the President that there
> shall be equality of treatment and opportunity for all persons in the
> armed services without regard to race, color, religion or national origin.
> This policy shall be put into effect as rapidly as possible, having due

regard to the time required to effectuate any necessary changes without impairing efficiency or morale.

Again we see that even though there was a mandate to integrate the military, it was not until the troop strength in all white units had dropped to critical lows in the Korean War, while at the same time troop strength in all black units was over staffed, that military leaders actually started to integrate units on a regular basis (MacGregory, 1985).

Brown v. *Board of Education of Topeka*, 347 U.S. 483 (1954),[1], a landmark decision of the U.S. Supreme Court, overturned earlier rulings going back to *Plessy* v. *Ferguson* in 1896. The Court declared state laws establishing separate public schools for black and white students unconstitutional because black children were denied equal educational opportunities. The Warren Court, in an unanimous (9–0) decision handed down on May 17, 1954, found that "separate educational facilities are inherently unequal." As a result, *de jure* racial segregation was ruled a violation of the Equal Protection Clause of the Fourteenth Amendment. While the Civil Right Movement was well underway by the time of this decision, it nevertheless had a major impact that furthered support for both integration and equal treatment of blacks.

President Kennedy in Executive Order 10925 decreed in March 1961 that "The contractor will take affirmative action to ensure that applicants are employed and that employees are treated during employment without regard to their race, creed, color or national origin." From this decree comes the term *affirmative action*. The exact meaning of affirmative action was not clear, many people thinking that it meant the use of quotas, target of opportunity hiring, incentives to organizations for hiring people with certain characteristics or career counseling. It could mean any of these things; however, its intent is to protect people based on categories such as race, creed, color, gender, national origin, age, marital status, and childbearing status from discrimination. In fact employers must be more than just passively non-discriminatory; they must be proactive in their hiring, pay, and retention practices. This does not mean that a person of a protected category can be hired in lieu of a more qualified person not in a protected category.

In his landmark speech at Howard University, President Johnson inquired as to what should now be done since we had achieved the imminent passage of national voting rights legislation. "To this end," Johnson insisted, "equal opportunity is essential, but not enough, not enough." His remarks suggest that now that the playing field is level, how do we insure that the centuries of past exclusion and racism do not prevent the players from gaining the field so that they can play.

The National Voting Rights Act of 1965 (42 U.S.C. § 1973–1973aa-6)[1] was the beginning of the end of the violence and intimidation that were concomitant with Jim Crow laws that included literacy tests, poll taxes for blacks, while grandfathering in otherwise disqualified white voters whose grandfathers voted (thus allowing some white illiterates to vote). Of course, the ultimate aim of restricting who could vote was the prevention of blacks from having political and economic power.

Another means of disempowering people is to deny access to gainful employment because of age, race, religion, disabilities, sexual preference, gender, or country of origin. Title VII of the Civil Rights Act of 1964 authorized the creation of the Equal Employment Opportunity Commission (EEOC). Title VII of the Civil Rights Act was later amended by the Age Discrimination Act of 1975, the Pregnancy Discrimination Act of 1978, and the Americans with Disabilities Act of 1990. As is the case with many of the other laws and judicial decisions mentioned in this chapter, this issue involves the creation of a level playing field for people who have been economically, politically, culturally, or socially disadvantaged. Certainly each point of disadvantage decreases the likelihood of employment in the justice system, while increasing the likelihood of disparate treatment by that same justice system. As noted later in this chapter, Title VII, in many settings, carries with it an extension set of training and educational outcomes.

In sum, the development of civil and other rights has a direct impact on the criminal justice system and a relative impact on issues of diversity. Until a person or a people are allowed to exercise their natural rights, they are more likely to be excluded from participation in the justice system as employees, recognized as victims, or suffer at the hands of government for the violation of socially constructed laws that are contrived to disadvantage a group of people.

HISTORICAL CONTEXT

It is of vital importance to note that training and education (discussed later) is one of the natural results of changes in the laws; however, before addressing training and educational issues, it is also important to draw a connection between the general discussion of laws and the actual impact they have had on the criminal justice system. It is certainly a historical truism that various groups of service providers, victims, and offenders have all suffered disparate treatment as a result of a lack of sensitivity to differences by members of the dominant group(s) in the justice system. Whether those differences result from gender, race, ethnicity, religion, region of the country, or any of the other things that make us different as groups, research suggests that the negative impact of groupings could be reduced, if not eliminated, through the use of proper training or education for justice system service providers at the appropriate time. It is also true that the methods by which we have brought attention to diversity issues and the methods by which we have set about providing solutions to these issues have changed over time.

Historically, the various components of the justice system are replete with failed attempts to increase the sensitivity level of the service providers toward minority groups[1], through either education or training. It should be noted at this point that the term "justice system" refers not only to police, corrections, and the courts, but also to other members of the system, including lawyers, social workers, and victims.

Until recently the police, courts, and corrections have been largely unsympathetic to the differing needs not only of the various "client" communities they serve, but also of many of the employees within the system. This is often referred to as "gatekeeping." Katznelson (2005), and Jurik and Martin (2006) all report on the various means by which minorities and women in particular have been the victims of disparate and outright discriminatory behavior by the justice system at the levels of the courts, corrections, and police.

It has often been the case that the three parts of the justice system have been openly hostile to those individuals or groups, who have either sought membership in or needed the services of the justice system (Jurik and Martin, 2006; Skolnick and Fyfe, 1993). Walker (1992:166) points out that "Special training in race relations was virtually unthinkable in an era when most police departments offered no formal training of any sort."

While diversity considerations in the training of justice system personnel have varied in importance since the mid-1800s, the message to justice personnel has also changed over time. For instance, it was not that long ago that police departments had police–community relations units. These units usually consisted of two or three officers in a medium-sized department. One of the stated goals of these units was to achieve a more harmonious relationship with minority communities through contact with the community leaders. It should be emphasized that there was little effort on the part of the members of these units to contact members of minority communities other than the supposed leaders. Another of the stated goals of such a unit was to help other officers to transcend the differences between the individuals they were sworn to protect by reducing the separation between the police and the community (Miller and Braswell, 1983). This remains one of the goals of community-based policing today; however, the methods of achieving that goal today are much different than in the past. A third stated goal was to apprize the community leaders of the reason for certain police actions in the community. In other words, to inform the community leaders of the police side of any story, in a sometimes thinly veiled attempt to deflect criticism of the department. It was very rarely the role of the police–community relations unit to attempt to understand the inner workings of the community. In short, information control was paramount. It is not being suggested here that the police–community relations units have been completely abandoned; they have not. Their role has, however, changed over time to the point that they are now more involved in planning and research concerning issues of police responsiveness to community needs.

The justice system continues to suffer from a tendency to look for quick and simple solutions to problems that are deeply rooted in our social structures and communities (Hennessy, 1994). By this we mean that the justice system has a tendency to be reactive and responsive to problems using short-term solutions rather than attempting to be proactive and providing longer term problem-solving. Thus, attempts on the part of justice agencies to make the necessary changes which would lead to a true understanding of diversity were, of course, doomed to failure.

There were five major errors made by the agencies. The first was their failure to truly understand diversity. Protection of the status quo, or of a particular and narrowly defined standard of living, was often at the forefront of enforcement efforts. A part of this problem was that the police were more interested in "bringing" members of the minority community "up" to the standards of the white community, as opposed to understanding that being different does not necessarily equate with being "wrong." As I heard so many officers say time and again in the 1970s and 1980s, "Why can't you people learn to act more like white people?" or, equally offensive, "Let's find a way to keep the 'natives' happy."

The second error was the inability to distinguish between one minority community and another; that is, to recognize that there may be different communities of blacks, Hispanics, or other minority groups. This often resulted in one or two so-called "community leaders" being identified as the spokespeople for a large number of people, who were really of different communities. This often led to a "one approach fits all problems" method of problem-solving.

The third error concerned the method used in training the new service providers. The course of study was often structured in such a way as to afford various minority representatives an opportunity to address rookie trainees or in-service officers. This meeting usually took place in a training seminar in which there was either a one-way monologue delivered by the minority representative or a confrontational dialogue between the minority representative and the trainees. The goal was to induce a change in trainee attitudes by having them learn more about the minority representatives' points of view (Hennessy, 1994). This approach usually resulted in a strident and emotional challenge to participants, which often led to a deepening of their anger and resentment (Work, 1989). Even when possible avenues for discussion developed, discussion did not occur because the various participants had by then become too emotionally entrenched in their own views.

The fourth error was and continues to be that administrators in general, and justice system administrators in particular, have made the mistake of primarily using minorities and women to teach cultural diversity. It is important that the best people are used, regardless of their race or gender (Hennessy, 1994). It is also important to prevent the perception of "a vested interest" on the part of these groups.

The fifth error often made by administrators has been to rely simply on the development of rules and on punishment for violation of the rules. Hemphill and Haines (1997) suggest that diversity training has failed to eliminate discrimination and harassment because it has focused on *awareness, understanding, and appreciation* of differences. They do acknowledge that it is useful to recognize and acknowledge unique differences, but they contend that it is far more essential to address effective and appropriate workplace behaviors, often through enforcement of rules by use of punitive measures. Given the general psychological profile of justice agency workers, particularly that of the police officers, Hemphill and Haines' (1997) suggestions hold some interest. While some disagree (Barlow and Barlow, 1993, 1994; Gould, 1996) with Hemphill and Haines' single-track approach, there are some useful tactics to be learned from their research, in terms of errors that have been often been credited to the failure of cultural diversity courses. Hemphill and Haines (1997:5–6) suggest that the failure of the current form of cultural diversity training results from:

- participants found many training programs to be divisive, disturbing, and counterproductive;
- diversity trainers were often inexperienced and ineffective;
- minority groups' expectations were raised, and then disappointed;
- white males were often stereotyped and blamed;
- there was reverse discrimination and reverse stereotyping;
- sensitive and personal issues were brought out in hostile public settings;
- participants experienced unnecessary anxiety and emotional upheaval;
- increased distrust was engendered;
- many participants were resistant to attending further diversity training programs; and,
- little or no transfer of learning took place from teaching about differences to changing discriminatory and harassing behaviors.

THE EFFECT OF PSYCHO-SOCIAL DEVELOPMENT ON MINORITY RELATIONS

Police, courts, and corrections are generally conservative in nature and they tend to have a status quo orientation, both of which are reflected in the culture of the organization and, to a certain extent, the culture of the dominant members of society.

It is important to any attempt at changing the attitudes and behaviors of justice system personnel to understand the organization and individual cultures with which a trainer or educator will be dealing. Failure to take the psycho-social variables into consideration in developing an approach to teaching cultural diversity will certainly decrease the likelihood of success and may even decrease the likelihood of success for later attempts.

There are three major theoretical approaches to the question of the possible existence of an identifiable organizational culture that impacts the individual development and individual personality that a person brings to the job. For the purposes of this discussion, the development of the police personality will be used as an example of psycho-social development. This discussion could also be applied to correctional officers, probation/parole officers, judges, prosecutors, and even defense attorneys.

The first approach to understanding the police personality views police departments as organic social systems created by and composed of human beings: They are microcosms of the society at large and provide a socio-cultural milieu in which people interact with and influence one another as they pursue common goals and objectives (Moore, 1992). The individual police officer is the fundamental subsystem around which the police organization is built. Individuals consist of interdependent physiological and psycho-social systems that work in concert with environmental factors to produce distinctive behavior. The dynamic interdependence between the human police officer and the environmental factors (the public and the department) helps to account for the complexity of the behavior of the officer (Roberg and Kuykendall, 1990).

According to this approach, officers bring an already existing set of attitudes to their work, but those attitudes have not necessarily been set in actual behavior. It is the interaction between the officers and their environment that generates the actual behavior of the officers.

The second approach explains cynical, bigoted, indifferent, racist, authoritarian, and/or brutal behavior on the part of police officers by positing that policing attracts individuals who already possess these qualities (Balch, 1992; Smith, Visher, and Davidson, 1984). The adherents to this view suggest that the "power of the badge" attracts those individuals seeking power, having a poor self-image, or having hidden agendas.

The third approach explains aberrant police behavior by a combination of the previous two theories. Those advocating this position suggest that some individuals who seek to become police officers already possess those qualities which make them cynical, bigoted, indifferent, authoritarian, and/or brutal in nature, while other police officers adopt one or more of these qualities as a result of the policing environment (More and Unsinger, 1987; Roberg and Kuykendall, 1990). This body of research further suggests that those individuals possessing these qualities prior to beginning a career in policing generally become even more negative as a result of the policing experience (Moore, 1992; Roberg and Kuykendall, 1990). It should be noted, however, that these officers are also more likely to drop out of policing in the first five years of the job experience (Evans, Coman, and Stanley, 1992; Terry, 1981; Wright *et al.*, 1980).

Consistent with any of these explanations for poor police attitudes, particularly toward minority groups, is research which suggests that the problem which exists between the public and the police is the result of a growing view, on the part of the police, that the public *is* the problem (Walker, 1992; U.S. Commission on Civil Rights, 1990). Researchers have also reported that police officers are typically suspicious, aloof, cynical, and authoritarian in their dealings with the public, particularly minorities (Evans, Coman, and Stanley, 1992; Kroes, 1985; Violanti and Marshall, 1983). As far back as 1967, Niederhoffer suggested that police officers were more cynical than the public in general. This cynicism, according to Niederhoffer, explains in part the indifference, alienation, bigotry, and brutality with which the police sometimes treat the public. It should be noted at this point that a "healthy" dose of cynicism is necessary for the survival of the officer, both mentally and physically. It is when the level of cynicism reaches such a point that it has almost complete control over how the officer views the world that the cynicism becomes a problem. Niederhoffer was criticized for not considering other explanations and for not properly controlling for the length of service of the officers in his research. Recent research suggests, however, that cynicism remains one of the critical variables in determining police behavior (Balch, 1992). The more cynical officers are, the less likely they are to be willing to change their perception of the world. If anything, they are going to be heavily invested in maintaining the status quo with which they have become comfortable.

Continuing to use police officers as an example, recent research into Myers-Briggs Cognitive Styles, based in Jungian Personality Type Theory and data from other cognitive studies, suggests that the majority (65%) of police officers prefer to take in information and process it through their five senses rather than through intuition. This means that they are "bound in reality;" they are not likely to be convinced by anything but reasoning based on tangible facts. This is one reason that appeals to the heart, a method often used in older forms of teaching police–community relations, may appear to be too "touchy-feely" (Hennessy, 1994).

To fully understanding how the solutions can work to improve the levels of sensitivity to cultural diversity, it is necessary to understand the emotions surrounding this issue. Gould (1996) found that more experienced white male officers and to some extent black male officers felt that cultural diversity training was an attempt to emasculate policing or to turn police officers into social workers. The intensity of these feelings was expressed in a series of intensive interviews. As one black male officer said, "Sure, I will try this stuff for a while: if it works, fine if not, screw it." A white male officer was a bit more vehement in his view, "This is bunch of crap. Will it be useful? Hell no. While I am doing this social work shit on somebody, they are trying to figure out how to fuck me or the system. What you people need to do is spend more time making the asshole learn the rules. I already know them." Another experienced officer (white male) commented,

> "Yeah, I am informed. I am informed that nobody cares about us. It is also clear to me that some of the other people here liked to hear this stuff."
>
> INTERVIEWER: "Which other people?"
>
> OFFICER: "The blacks and the women."
>
> INTERVIEWER: "What stuff do they like to hear?"

> OFFICER: "That policing should be something other than what it is. Man, we are supposed to throw people's asses in jail, not treat them like a social work case."
>
> INTERVIEWER: "Who doesn't care about you?"
>
> OFFICER: "The people, the female cops and the blacks."

It appeared that many of the white male and some of the black male officers felt that their position and behavior as an officer was being challenged and/or changed not only by having to take this class, but by some of the actions of the black and female officers also attending this class. As part of a successful solution to getting people to understand the need for cultural diversity training, it is important to remember that some individuals will be asked to redefine who they are in the context of their jobs. As previously noted, some individuals come to a career with a preconceived notion of what the job is about. These notions or images are defined in part by the individual's personality. Other individuals develop much of their "working personality" on the job; that is, their personality is impacted by their experiences on the job. When the correctness of some of the negative behaviors that are a part of the individual's working personality are called into question, the individual has to either continue to suffer criticism or change the behavior, thus redefining who they are.

It should be noted that Gould (1996) found that cadets, less experienced officers, and female police officers (both black and white) were much more receptive to cultural diversity training and they also recognized that the training could have some very positive outcomes for them as police officers. For example, one white female officer stated,

> "Of course the course will be useful to me as an officer. I learned two things. First, I learned that just because a person is different does not mean that they are wrong. Second, I learned that I don't have to act like the meanest person on the block to get many of the people that I deal with to do what I want them to do. I just have to figure out how to understand them and get them to understand me."
>
> INTERVIEWER: "What else did you learn that might be useful?"
>
> OFFICER: "I guess that I learned that I don't have to be one of the guys to be a good cop. I can be me."

A black female officer, who apparently had been the brunt of some abuse on the job, commented,

> "Those motherfuckers just don't get it, this is for them."
>
> INTERVIEWER: "Which motherfuckers are you referring to?"
>
> OFFICER: "Those dumb white boys."
>
> INTERVIEWER: "What is it that they don't get?"
>
> OFFICER: "That this training is for them. It will help them if they would let it work. They are the reason that we are here, the way they treat people."

INTERVIEWER: "How else would it help?"

OFFICER: "If those guys got enough of this training they would quit treating people bad. Maybe they would even be nicer to me."

Given the wide range of responses of the officers quoted above, it should be apparent that an understanding of the personality of the justice system service provider is vitally important to the success of any program of study intended to change the attitudes of the service provider toward minority groups (Gould, 1996). Gould (1996), based on a study of the effect of a training course on cultural sensitivity, suggests that the teaching of cultural diversity also means the "unteaching" of some already existing culturally insensitive attitudes and behaviors. A change in behavior will not generally result from sitting through one cultural diversity course. Gould's work suggests it would be easier to teach tricks to a "new pup" (new police officers) than to an "old dog" (experienced police officers) unless the trainer and educators learn to respect the needs of the "old dog." The respect comes from an understanding of the life experiences of the established criminal justice service provider. Gould (1996) suggested that, as a matter of policy: (1) the training of experienced officers should include the training of administrators in the same classroom setting; (2) experienced officers' training should include more time for venting of frustrations centering on the cultural diversity training; (3) cultural diversity training should begin early in an officer's career; (4) the training should be reinforced throughout the officer's career; and (5) the training should be aimed toward explanation and discovery concerning cultural differences, rather than appearing simply to place blame for police–community conflict on the individual officer.

THE BEGINNING OF A SOLUTION

Barlow and Barlow (1993, 1994) and Gould (1996) found patterns of behavior similar to those discussed in the previous section, in response to cultural diversity training among police officers; however, they viewed the criticisms as a springboard for refining rather than discarding the training. In particular, Barlow and Barlow (1993, 1994) and Gould (1996) suggest that channeled venting, which results from the criticisms listed by Hemphill and Haines (1997), actually leads to healthy discussion in which behavior can be changed.

Despite the limited view presented by Hemphill and Haines (1997), they do provide useful additions to the "tool belt" of the diversity trainer. First, it is necessary to stop denying that discrimination and harassment, based on some ascribed or achieved characteristic(s), exists within justice organizations or between justice organizations and other groups. Second, in addition to a focus on awareness, understanding, and appreciation of differences, there should be a focus on changing workplace behaviors. Third, there must be a commitment to a plan of action which at a minimum includes: (1) the establishment and enforcement of a zero tolerance policy for discrimination and harassment practices, not only within the organization, but also as employees come in contact with both victims and offenders; (2) development of organization-wide behavior standards that provide specific guidelines concerning acceptable and unacceptable behaviors; and (3) the establishment of a continuing workplace relationship skills training program.

Barlow and Barlow (1994) noted that there is no "silver bullet" solution to the problem of teaching cultural diversity issues; however, they do provide a set of goals which are critically important to even the partial success of any program intended to improve the level of sensitivity of justice personnel toward minority issues. These goals include: (1) understanding the importance of power and image in maintaining a professional reputation for justice organizations; (2) understanding the contributions and life styles of the various racial, cultural, and economic groups of the served communities; (3) recognizing and dealing with biases, discrimination, and prejudices that affect both the organizations and the citizens served; (4) understanding professional behaviors of justice system employees which contribute to the development of the self-esteem of the community residents and which establish positive interpersonal relations within organizations; and (5) respecting diversity and personal rights.

Success in teaching a course of study on cultural diversity starts with the formula suggested by Barlow and Barlow (1994). There should be six clearly defined components: "selling the course," examination of prejudices, dissemination of information, development of personal strategies, discussion of supervisory issues, and ventilation periods. The first block of instruction is intended to explain why the course is important to the officer and the police department. The second block involves definition and examination of personal prejudices. The third block involves dissemination of information on the current state of police–minority relations and includes a historical-to-present view of the relations. The fourth block involves the development of personal strategies directed at increased understanding of cultural diversity. The fifth block is directed at supervisory and management issues. The final block involves a ventilation period in which the officers can respond to either the material presented during the course or to the course itself.

While there is no such thing as a cookbook for the delivery of a course on cultural diversity or cultural sensitivity to justice professionals, it is possible to synthesize the works of Hennessy, Barlow and Barlow, Work, and Gould. By synthesizing these works, it becomes possible to categorize the necessary parts of training into three areas: (1) Those components necessary for any type of cultural diversity training, such as avoiding accusatory language; (2) Those components that are specifically about communication and adult learning, such as allowing the students to bring their life experiences into the classroom; and (3) Those components specific to justice system personnel, such as discussing the image of power that the police bring to any meeting with members of the community. In general terms, these components emphasize the need in cultural diversity training for awareness, understanding, and appreciation of individual and group differences, rather than for the type of approach suggested by Hemphill and Haines (1997), which focuses on behavioral changes on the part of practitioners resulting in part from the development and enforcement of rules (punishment). Hemphill and Haines' (1997) approach will be discussed in greater detail in the following section.

GENERAL COMPONENTS OF CULTURAL DIVERSITY TRAINING

One of the first steps that should be a part of any course of study on cultural diversity or cultural sensitivity training is to assist the participants in examination and consideration of how their perceptions about other cultures and people were developed, and how this affects their own behavior (Work, 1989). This can be done by asking the participants to assess their own ancestry and/or by an examination of how stereotyping works to create perceptions of both individuals and groups. Before getting too far into a discussion of cultural diversity or the effect of stereotyping, it would be helpful to remember that the very discussion of cultural differences may cause some people to be offended, thus a discussion concerning the rules of conduct in the class, such as mutual respect, is important.

Another key to teaching cultural diversity is a recognition that learning about individuals and groups cannot take place when the participants refuse to discuss or acknowledge both differences and similarities between and among cultures. Usually it is best to start a discussion along the lines of those things that the various participants (whether present or not) have in common. A discussion of common interests, shared goals, and shared means often helps a class to learn to discuss issues in a less heated manner.

Virtually every writer on the topic of cultural diversity training has commented that administrators and managers must make a long-term commitment to offering courses on cultural diversity. In particular, line personnel often become frustrated with one-shot training, which is viewed as punishment by the officers, thus little is actually accomplished in terms of changing behavior (Gould, 1996; Hennessy, 1994).

The instructor and administrators/managers must be aware that success in changing either an attitude or a behavior only comes in small increments and that actual change occurs over long periods with repeated reinforcement; thus, the need for repeated training that continually re-enforces previous periods of training. It is important to remember that simply getting participants, particularly those in the justice system, to think about some of the issues presented in a cultural diversity class should be considered a significant success.

The instructor must work with managers to ensure that their subordinates will be held responsible for their actions (Gould, 1996; Hemphill and Haines, 1997; Hennessy, 1994). Organizational policy regarding bias and prejudice must be clear and enforceable, and must be vigorously enforced and supported throughout the agency (Hennessy, 1994).

One tactic that has proven to be successful is to conduct classes that include a cross section of all ranks within the agency (Gould, 1996). This allows for the discussion of problems and potential solutions while many levels of participants are present.

COMMUNICATION/LEARNING TRAINING

To be successful in understanding the nuances of cultural diversity, justice system personnel must be afforded the opportunity to understand the dynamics of cross-cultural communication. Thus, there is a need to develop an awareness of communicative, analytical, and interpretive skills that will aid in maintaining communications with both the current and changing populations. The process of understanding how to communicate with other cultures often begins with an understanding of how our behavior is perceived by other people. Thus, it is important that some time be spent on discussing the ways in which our presentation of self can facilitate or inhibit our communication with others. To facilitate this discussion, instructors need to pay particular attention to helping course participants achieve an understanding of how both large and small behaviors can positively or negatively affect outcomes (see Chapter 4 by Nielsen and Maniglia).

The instructor should facilitate discussion on the need to understand the difference between intentions and behavior. Police, probation/parole officers, and correctional officers have all been immersed in the idea that their jobs are dangerous. There is nothing false in this position; however, it is important to note that within different cultures, the same behaviors may take on different meanings; thus, when the officer behaves in a manner intended to protect himself/herself, that behavior may elicit misunderstandings in others. The officers are not expected to change their behavior, but should be trained to understand and sometimes expect negative responses.

A brief review of Mehrahian's (1987) work on nonverbal communication would be of value to the cultural diversity class. Mehrahian (1987) suggests that body language sends about 55% of a message, that tone of voice sends about 38% of a message, and that actual words send only about 7% of a message. The instructor could use videos and other tools to provide examples of how this works.

At all times it must be remembered that the students in a cultural diversity education class are adults. Adults communicate ideas and learn much differently than do children, teenagers, or even young adults who have not had much life experience. A review of Arnold and McClure (1994) provides many of the keys to the principles of adult learning, some examples of which are provided here:

- The trainer must be willing to challenge the participants' tendency to think in ways that may cause hard feelings.
- The use of small groups and work exercises often facilitates the flow of ideas. Discussion between group participants is an important part of the learning phase.
- Life experiences are an important part of the adult learning process; thus, it is important to use these experiences to the advantage of the learning process.
- Don't set the instructor up as the "expert." The instructor should be a facilitator of communication and a communicator of knowledge.
- Adult students tend to learn best when the subject matter is kept focused. In the case of teaching police officers for example, the instructor should focus on how additional information might provide insights and knowledge into different cultures, which in turn could make their jobs easier.

It is not uncommon for justice system personnel to see cultural, ethnic, religious, or gender structures with which they come into contact as being dysfunctional because of differences in the way, in which communication occurs between cultures and among individuals within the culture. For example, many police officers are at a loss to understand the extended family structures commonly found among some of the racial and ethnic groups with which they come into contact. To help officers understand the importance of other cultures' extended family structures, it might be of value to discuss how the officers feel when they hear that another officer has been injured or killed.

CRIMINAL JUSTICE SPECIFIC TRAINING

In developing tactics that are specific to justice personnel it is necessary to understand who they are and to some extent how they have been socialized. In other words, it is necessary to be sensitive to the social and psychological characteristics of the audience.

For the most part, justice system personnel are businesslike and, if forced to choose between tact and truthfulness, they usually choose truthfulness. Likewise, justice system personnel are usually not convinced by anything other than reasoning based on solid facts. In view of the above, when teaching cultural awareness or gender issues it is important to remember that the information must be presented in a factual, rational, concrete, and practical manner for it to be considered for discussion. In other words, justice system personnel need to be informed in a pragmatic, logical, and objective manner of the importance of learning about other cultures (Hennessy, 1992).

The instructor must take into consideration that justice systems personnel make decisions in vastly different ways than do other groups. This means that the police, for example, tend to view a situation in a much different light than do the media, the community, or even other justice system personnel (Hennessy, 1992). It is important that the instructor have as much information as possible on the way in which police differ from other groups, thus increasing the likelihood that the police will see the instructor as being legitimate.

The instructor must be aware of the fact that justice system personnel, particularly police officers, frequently feel that they are alone as the primary protectors of justice and that the other components of the justice system are working at cross-purposes with the police (Walker, 1992). The instructor must encourage students to have the courage to speak out against the derogatory comments and discriminatory actions made by other members of the justice system that bring discredit to the criminal justice system.

The instructor must be aware that asking justice system personnel to examine and possibly change closely held beliefs and prejudices will mostly likely result in an emotionally negative situation. Thus the venue must allow for venting of emotion and frustration (Gould, 1996).

Because of the way in which many police officers tend to think, it is important to note that change in a community is continual. This means that information on cultural diversity must be provided on a continual basis (Hennessy, 1994). It is of equal importance that the officers understand that the specifics they learn today may be of little value some years from now, but that the concepts of cultural sensitivity instruction are applicable far into the future (Gould, 1996).

Even a cursory review of either the plan of attack favored by Barlow and Barlow (1993, 1994) or by Gould (1996), as compared to that favored by Hemphill and Haines (1997), suggests much overlap and certainly some complementary components. Adopting pertinent parts advocated by both groups increases the likelihood of a successful implementation of a multi-pronged approach.

While the focus has thus far been on the police, it should not be forgotten that only through court orders have prisoners been allowed to practice in a limited way some of their religious beliefs, and until recently, women probation officers were rarely allowed to work on cases other than those of juveniles or other women, and that women and minorities could not attend many law schools, and therefore could not be judges. Criminal justice agencies have systematically discriminated against women and minorities in employment, assignments, promotions, and social acceptance. Many white males have not, and do not, consider women and minorities to be their equals in terms of either capabilities or competencies (Roberg and

Kuykendall, 1997). These attitudes are based on myths that can only be debunked through education and training. The remaining vestiges of these attitudes can now only be attributed to the control of power that is so closely associated with membership in the justice system.

While there is no single solution to discriminatory, harassing, insensitive, and/or uncivil behavior, training or education of the type described in this chapter will advance the efforts of justice agencies to become more sensitive to these issues thus reducing their cost to justice agencies in terms of time and resources. As mentioned in the chapter introduction, not addressing the issue will continue to cost justice agencies in terms of litigation, loss of status in the community, loss of employee productivity, and loss of diversity, leading to continued insensitivity on the part of the organization. The multi-pronged approach described above increases the likelihood of successfully addressing the needs of the diverse group of service providers, victims, and offenders. Ignoring the totality of concerns that have been outlined in this chapter and favoring one set of solutions over another will certainly reduce the likelihood of success. Cultural diversity trainers/educators must emphasize awareness, understanding, and appreciation of individual and group differences, particularly of the participants, while paying attention to the more tactical solutions of stopping the denial that discrimination and harassment exist, while developing a plan of action that promotes a focus on changing behavior and a commitment to the development of a zero tolerance policy. The policy must include the development and "training to" of standards of acceptable and unacceptable behavior and relationship skills training.

While much of this chapter has focused on training as opposed to education, it should be remembered that it is important for future justice system administrators, such as students taking this course, to be constantly and consistently exposed to the concepts discussed in this chapter. The type of insensitivity, hatred, and misunderstanding of others that leads to a lack of tolerance for diversity is intergenerationally transmitted during the socialization of new justice system personnel by older justice system personnel. To break this cycle, the problem of insensitivity to differences must be brought to light and discussed in the college classroom, as well as in justice system training sessions. Additionally, the information contained in this chapter should have forewarned and thus prepared students for some of the problems they will face as potential justice system personnel.

Endnotes

1. For the purposes of this chapter the author is content with the definition of *minority group* provided by Louis Wirth (1945:347): "A group of people who, because of their physical or cultural characteristics, are singled out from others in the society in which they live for differential and unequal treatment and who therefore regard themselves as objects of collective discrimination." The author recognizes that there may be some problems with this definition; however, those arguments are better left for other discussions.

References

Arnold, W. E., and L. McClure. 1994. *Communication Training and Development.* Prospect Heights, IL: Waveland Press.

Balch, R. W. 1992. The Police Personality: Fact or Fiction? *The Journal of Criminal Law* 63 (1): 106–119.

Barlow, D., and M. Barlow. 1993. Cultural Diversity Training in Criminal Justice: A Progressive or Conservative Reform? *Social Justice* 20: 3–4.

Barlow, D., and M. Barlow. 1994. Cultural Sensitivity Rediscovered: Developing Training Strategies for Police Officers. *Justice Professional* 9: 2.

Brown v. *Board of Education* of Topeka (347 U.S. 483, 1954).

Evans, B. J., C. J. Coman, and R. O. Stanley. 1992. The Police Personality: Type A Behavior and Trait Anxiety. *Journal of Criminal Justice* 20: 420–441.

Gould, L. A. 1996. Can Old Dogs Be Taught New Tricks? Teaching Cultural Diversity to Police Officers. *Police Studies* 19: 122–147.

Hemphill, Helen, and Ray Haines 1997. *Discrimination, Harassment, and the Failure of Diversity Training.* Westport, CT: Quorum Books.

Hennessy, Stephen M. 1992. *Thinking Cop-Feeling Cop: A Study in Police Personalities.* Scottsdale, AZ: Leadership Press.

Hennessy, Stephen M. 1994. Cultural Sensitivity Training. In *Multicultural Perspectives in Criminal Justice and Criminology,* ed. James E. Hendricks and Byran Byers, 234–267. Springfield, IL: Charles C. Thomas.

Jurik, Nancy C., and Susan E. Martin. 2006. *Doing Justice, Doing Gender: Women in Legal and Criminal Justice Occupations,* 2nd edn. Los Angeles, CA: Sage Publications.

Katznelson, Ira. 2005. *When Affirmative Action Was White: An Untold History of Racial Inequality in Twentieth-Century America.* New York: W.W. Norton & Company.

Kroes, W. H. 1985. *Society's Victim—The Policeman—An Analysis of Job Stress in Policing,* 2nd edn. New York.

MacGregory, Morris J. 1985. *Integration of the Armed Forces 1940–1965.* Washington, DC: Center for Military History.

Mehrahian, A. 1987. Communication Without Words. In *Readings in Cross-Cultural Communication,* ed. B. Weaver, 2nd edn., 142–184. Lexington, MA: Ginn Press.

Miller, Larry, and Michael Braswell. 1983. *Human Relations and Police Work.* Prospect Heights, IL: Waveland Press.

Moore, M. H. 1992. Problem-Solving and Community Policing. In *Modern Policing,* ed. M. Tonry and N. Morris, 57–87. Chicago: University of Chicago Press.

More, H. W., and Peter C. Unsinger. 1987. *Police Managerial Use of Psychology and Psychologists.* Springfield, IL: Charles C. Thomas.

Roberg, Roy, and Jack Kuykendall. 1997. *Police Management,* 2nd edn. Los Angeles, CA: Roxbury.

Roberg, R., and K. Kuykendall. 1990. *Police Organization and Management: Behavior, Theory and Process.* Pacific Grove, CA: Brooks/Cole.

Rothenberg, Paula. 2004. *White Privilege: Essential Readings on the Other Side of Racism.* New York: Worth.

Skolnick, J., and J. Fyfe. 1993. *Above the Law: Police and the Excessive Use of Force.* New York: The Free Press.

Smith, D., C. Visher, and L. Davidson. 1984. Equity and Discretionary Justice: The Influence of Race on Police Arrest Decisions. *Journal of Criminal Law and Criminology* 75: 234–249.

Terry, W. C. 1981. Police Stress: The Empirical Evidence. *Journal of Police Science and Administration* 9 (1): 61–73.

U.S. Commission on Civil Rights. 1990. *Who Is Guarding the Guardians?* Washington, DC: U.S. Government Printing Office.

Violanti, J. M., and J. R. Marshall. 1983. The Police Stress Process. *Journal of Police Science and Administration* 11 (4): 389–394.

Walker, S. 1992. *Popular Justice: A History of American Criminal Justice.* New York: Oxford University Press.

Wright, R.D., D. G. Christie, G. D. Burrows, J. P. Coghlan, and K. L. Milte. 1980. *Occupational Health in the Police Force.* Unpublished manuscript, University of Melbourne.

Work, J. W. 1989. *Toward Affirmative Action and Racial/Ethnic Pluralism.* Arlington, VA: Belvedere Press.

CHAPTER 21

Irreconcilable Differences? Understanding the Crime Victim/Justice Worker Relationship

Lynn Jones

Phoebe Morgan

Barbara Perry

Throughout this book we have explored how cultural, social, and economic structures produce varying expectations of and actions by actors within the criminal justice system. While the actions of law enforcement officers, prosecutors, and judges are the most visible, their decisions to act or not to act depends in large part upon the choices that crime victims make. Crime workers rely on the cooperation of victims to do their jobs. In fact, without the willingness of victims to report crimes, assist investigations, or to provide testimony, the criminal justice process as we know it would not exist (Gottfredson and Gottfredson, 1988). In turn, without the aid of criminal justice agents, crime victims would be forced to seek justice on their own terms.

At the same time, crime victims are often "used" in the pursuit of justice as prosecutors act "in the interests of victims" and politicians hold up examples of victimization to justify justice policies. However, victims in general, and particularly victims in minority statuses, remain largely forgotten as their voices and the diversity of their experiences are not accurately portrayed or truly understood by those who serve them. Rights of crime victims and the improved service delivery to underserved populations are relatively new areas of attention in the criminal justice system. Whether and how those rights are implemented and enforced, informed to victims, and whether victims themselves exercise those rights depends greatly on their early interactions with justice workers, on perceptions of the criminal justice system, and on expectations of how the justice system treats members of their group (Muscat and Walsh, 2007; Sherman, 2002). Thus, the legitimacy and effectiveness of any criminal justice organization rests upon its ability to foster and sustain positive working relationships between crime victims and those whose job is to assist them.

The impact on the victim in terms of satisfaction, further victimization by system, future victimization, and the process of healing or positively dealing with the experience of victimization all relate to how justice professionals respond. Even though culturally sensitive victim services have expanded, there still remains the need for attention to interaction between victims and justice professionals who are not specifically designated as "victim" service providers. In one study, Latina women were less likely to seek help for their victimization than others, and it was suggested that there needs to be "culturally accessible and supportive resources" made available to improve reporting and help-seeking behavior (Block, 2003).

Even with training to improve interaction with victims, in most cases relations between the crime victims and crime workers are fraught with tension and discord. Few crime victims have a completely positive experience inside the criminal justice system, and trust in justice professionals varies across group identities (Sherman, 2002). Often they blame the individuals who processed their cases for their disappointments and aggravations. Similarly, crime workers regularly complain that crime victims are uncooperative, manipulative, or just plain "bogus."

Observing relations between domestic violence victims and the law enforcement officers who respond to their calls for aid, Ferraro and Pope (1993) theorized that what underlies the tensions between these two groups are the differing expectations and conflicting needs that individuals bring to the relationship. They argue that differences between victims and workers are shaped not only by discordant personality styles and disparate individual values, but also by differences in cultural backgrounds, contrasting legal roles, and organizational constraints. Knowing more about how these external pressures affect the internal workings of this type of relationship is the key to expanding our understanding of how interactions between crime victims and crime workers can serve to either advance or erode justice.

In the following pages, we take the highly personal relationships that exist between individual crime victims and criminal justice workers and place them within their larger cultural, legal, and organizational contexts. We begin by examining the ways in which relations between crime victims and crime workers are not only interpersonal, but intercultural as well. Next, we identify some of the key differences between the roles that crime victims and crime workers play and discuss how those differences can foster tension between the individuals who assume them. We also examine the ways in which the organizational goals of criminal justice agencies fail to meet expectations fueled by media images, public education, and social change. We conclude by proposing various strategies for managing the tensions that arise from the differences between crime victims and criminal justice workers.

WHEN RELATIONS BETWEEN CRIME VICTIMS AND CRIME WORKERS ARE INTERCULTURAL

As we have seen throughout this volume, there is a disparate distribution of racial, ethnic, cultural, and gender identities across the FBI's crime index (Federal Bureau of Investigation, 2007). According to the Bureau of Justice Statistics website, in 2005, Latinos were victims of violence at a rate higher than non-Latinos, and ethnic groups (Latinos and African Americans) experienced higher levels of property crime. Craven's (1994) analysis of the National Victimization Survey data reports that women are five times more likely than men to be victimized by their families and loved ones. And, while for the past ten years, violent crime has been disproportionately perpetrated on young black males, the rate of victimization among young black women is growing at a much faster rate (*Sourcebook of Criminal Justice Statistics*, 2005). While victimization rates are high for black women, Native American women experience higher rates of victimization than any other group of women (Dugan and Apel 2003; *Sourcebook of Criminal Justice Statistics*, 2005).

While the targets of property and personal crimes tend to be young, poor, and people of color, those most likely to process their claims are not. Rates of criminal justice employment of women and people of color, for example, have not paced their rates of victimization. Criminal justice work continues to be the province of working-class white males (Martin and Jurik, 2006). Consequently, the claims of many crime victims are handled by criminal justice agents of a different gender and racial or ethnic background. In those cases, interactions between crime victims and crime workers are as much intercultural exchanges as they are interpersonal ones. As we have seen throughout this book, age, gender, race, ethnicity, sexuality, and religion not only create variations in social identities, but also differences in the values and practices that go with them.

Crime Workers' Responses to Minority Victims

All else being equal, defendants who are poor, unemployed, or who are members of minority racial groups are more likely to receive full prosecution than their well-to-do or white counterparts (Black, 1976). Along the same lines, reports made by women, those with brown skin, or who are gay or lesbian too often receive less vigorous prosecution than those made by victims who are male, heterosexual, white, or of the upper classes (McKean, 1994; U.S. Commission on Civil Rights, 1990). How does this disparity in prosecution occur?

Social psychologists note that regardless of our intentions, it is harder to connect with and sustain empathy for those who are visibly different from ourselves (Goffman, 1967). For that reason, crime workers often create emotional distance between themselves and victims who are of a different social class, gender, skin color, or sexual orientation (Kidd and Chayet, 1984). When victims appear to think in a different way or make different choices, it becomes easy to assume they are somehow less rational and therefore less deserving of legal assistance than those whose demeanor and behavior more readily meet a crime worker's expectation (Frohmann, 1991).

Once a crime worker labels a victim as "different" from himself/herself, then it becomes easier to take the next step and blame them for their plight (Ryan, 1976). This is especially evident in male crime workers' responses to women's reports of intimate victimization. Frohmann's (1991, 1998) studies of prosecutorial decision making, for example, find that prosecutors regularly employ extralegal factors such as the victim's unusual dress or irrational demeanor to justify their failure to bring sexual assault charges. Along the same lines, observing interactions between lower court personnel and battered women, Merry (1990a) noticed that judges and court clerks dispensed moral lectures rather than orders of protection when the choices made and actions taken by victims did not correspond to their own personal preferences. In sum, when relations between crime workers and crime victims are intercultural, crime workers are more likely to *distance* themselves from the victims, *blame* them for their plight, and subsequently, *fail to meet victim expectations* of justice.

Minority Victims' Responses to Crime Workers

Given the perceived antipathy of crime workers for minority victims, it is not surprising that so many minority victims are hesitant to engage the aid of crime workers. Moreover, once they have enlisted the aid of crime workers, minority victims of crime are more likely to express hostility and resentment for the treatment they receive. Research consistently finds, for example, that relative to white respondents, people of color hold more unfavorable views toward criminal justice personnel (Mann, 1993). In public opinion research, 60% of whites report having a great deal or quite a lot of confidence in police, while only 32% of non-whites hold such feelings (*Sourcebook of Criminal Justice Statistics*, 2007). More specifically, minorities rate crime workers more negatively than whites on such dimensions as fairness (Mann, 1993), quality of service and responsiveness (Smith, Graham, and Adams, 1991; U.S. Commission on Civil Rights, 1992), use of force (Greene, 1996), and handling of citizen complaints (Walker, Spohn, and DeLone, 2006). Certainly such disaffection among minorities is at least in part fostered by experiences of disparate treatment by law enforcement. More importantly, even if they have not experienced discrimination first hand, simply the expectation of differential treatment contributes to minority victims' general reluctance to contact or cooperate with crime workers (Sherman, 2002).

In addition to differences in culture, language differences also place pressure on an already strained relationship. When criminal justice workers and crime victims do not speak the same language, victims tend to avoid the criminal justice process altogether (Muscat and Walsh, 2007; U.S. Commission on Civil Rights, 1992). As a Latina woman explained in her native tongue: "Yes, we are very limited because we don't speak the language. If something happens to us, we cannot even ask for help" (Madriz, 1997:349). Consequently, when crime victims and crime workers speak different languages, it is even harder to develop and sustain a good working relationship (Murdaugh *et al.*, 2004).

According to a recent study (Obinna *et al.*, 2006), sexual assault victims who are deaf experience a unique set of issues that are not encountered by the hearing. When reporting assault, deaf rape victims experience stereotypes "about being a sexual assault victim *and* being deaf" (Taylor and Gaskin-Laniyan, 2007). Also, deaf victims may hesitate to report the assault due to the typically small and close-knit nature of the deaf community, which can "compromise a victim's anonymity and erode privacy" (Taylor and Gaskin-Laniyan, 2007). Finally, a lack of awareness of deaf culture among the hearing, and the absence of TTY (teletypewriter) services or someone skilled in using it are further barriers to service delivery to these unique victims.

For immigrants, reticence due to language differences is compounded by their fear of abuse by authorities, and of deportation. Some immigrants come to the United States to escape persecution and genocide perpetrated in the name of justice. As a result, their distrust of the intentions and motivations of criminal justice workers is high, making it difficult for them to trust agents of the American criminal justice system. Sadly, while a disproportionate number of undocumented workers become victims of personal and property crimes, fear of deportation also makes it difficult for them to come forward and request assistance (see Chapter 7).

CONTRASTING EXPECTATIONS BETWEEN CRIME VICTIMS AND CRIME WORKERS

While cultural differences make it more difficult for crime workers and crime victims to establish mutually supportive relationships, not all tensions between crime victims and workers involve intercultural dynamics. Differing expectations about what interactions will be like, as well as what victims and workers should accomplish can make the establishment of a working partnership difficult. At times, the goals of crime victims are not only different from crime workers, but in direct contrast (Conley and O'Barr, 1990).

Contrasting Definitions of Justice

Since the late 1970s, various civil rights movements have considerably heightened the expectations for justice of many crime victims (Karmen, 2007). Increasing numbers of women, poor people, gays, lesbians, and members of minority racial groups are entering the justice system with a sense of self-worth and entitlement to justice that prior to 1965 was simply unimaginable. No longer willing to silently endure victimization, battered women, targets of hate crimes, and victims of institutionalized poverty and racialized violence are now more committed than ever to claiming their right to justice (Friedman, 1994).

In addition, the emergence of a victims' rights movement has raised even further the expectations that crime victims have, consequently increasing both the number and range of demands they place on the criminal justice system (Karmen, 2007; McShane and Williams, 1992). Changes in expectations about the treatment victims feel they are entitled to are producing a new class of crime victims who are placing increasingly higher demands on crime workers. While the victims of the 1990s are entering the criminal justice system with heightened expectations for justice, a corresponding expansion of defendant rights and increasing concern for liability has made it more difficult than ever for criminal justice authorities to realistically and consistently fulfill victims' demands for justice.

Unable to meet victims' demands for a more total justice (Friedman, 1994), while at the same time fully honoring the constitutional rights of those accused, criminal justice workers either consciously or unconsciously categorize and then rank order claims made by "real" victims (i.e., helpless or innocent) and those that are "bogus" (i.e., claims made by criminals or perpetrators of violence) (Frohmann, 1998). Complaints made by "real" victims receive vigorous processing while the bogus victims are "cooled out" or ignored completely (Blumberg, 1967). Within this typology, "authentic" victims are those deemed to be innocent or especially helpful, and "bogus" victims are those who themselves violate the law or have the means to intimidate or bully others. Most of those who report crimes fail to meet the criteria for a "real" or "authentic" victim. Engagement in a criminal lifestyle puts one at significantly greater risk of victimization. An occupational hazard of working in the sex trades, for example, is a higher risk of sexual assault (Pettiway, 1996). Thus, a significant portion of those who report crimes are themselves criminals. Thus, drug addicts, sex workers, and thieves fail to meet many crime workers criteria for authenticity. Who is deemed "worthy" of our attention and sympathy, and who we define as "real" victims, is absolutely wrapped up in the complex web of constructing difference. In the end, the rights to justice of many legitimate victims are denied.

In addition, for the many who are trapped inside violent families and marriages, justice becomes a revolving door through which victims enter repeatedly—at times assuming the role of plaintiff and at other times the role of defendant (McShane and Williams, 1992). As with criminals, when batterers become the battered, crime workers often label their complaints as "bogus" and dismiss them. Such disparate treatment in turn engenders frustration and disappointment. With each subsequent trip through the revolving door of justice, these victims return with either greater resolve to exercise their right to see justice done or lowered expectations for fairness and justice.

Contrasting Definitions of Service

The heightening of victims' expectations for justice has taken place in tandem with an increase in consumerism. Since World War II, consumerism has encouraged an increasing conflation of the process of criminal justice with the commercial transaction. As a result, consumer-oriented victims perceive their relationships with crime workers as analogous to those between paying customers and sales clerk or paid servant. Regardless of the facts of their case or the system's current caseload, consumeristic victims expect timely service and deferential treatment by the civil servants they encounter, and then readily complain when the service is not to their liking.

The highly sensationalized coverage of the two-year-long prosecution of O. J. Simpson suggested to millions of television viewers that those who can most afford it are most likely to get "full service" by court personnel. Justice has a price. In reality, however, the criminal justice system operates more often as a bureaucracy than as a service-oriented business. As bureaucrats, the primary mandate of police and court personnel is not provide "good service," but to clear caseloads quickly and efficiently. Thus, victims and their complaints are queued up and moved down the assembly line of justice (Brickey and Miller, 1975). In busy jurisdictions where caseloads are high, victims of serious crimes are fortunate to get even one full day in court and victims of misdemeanors are more likely to get only about seven minutes (Bonsignore *et al.*, 2005). As a result, rich and poor victims alike, feel their time before the bench is too brief. Unable to get what they feel is their money's worth, those seeking to purchase justice leave the court feeling shortchanged.

Relations between crime victims and criminal justice workers are at risk of becoming dysfunctional when expectations about service conflict. Many of those who perform crime work do so because they find the call to serve especially compelling (Coles, 1993). College, law school, and academies instill idealistic values of what it means to "serve and protect" (Gould, 1997). Graduates see themselves as "human service workers" rather than commercial "dispensers of justice." As a result, crime workers find the expectations of consumer-oriented victims repugnant and offensive (Merry, 1990b).

DIFFERING RIGHTS AND RESPONSIBILITIES

Unlike other working relationships, relationships between crime victims and criminal justice workers are determined not by personalities but by statute and legal precedent. In short, the law greatly constrains what crime workers and crime victims can actually accomplish together. In fact, the law purposefully allocates differing amounts and types of rights and responsibilities between victims and workers.

The Victim's Prerogative

As citizens of the state, victims enjoy certain prerogatives that crime workers do not have. Much to the frustration of criminal justice practitioners, victims are under no legal obligation to press charges, produce evidence, provide testimony, or even to appear in court. Fear of retaliation by those they accuse causes many women to drop charges, or to fail to appear in court (Ford, 1991). To avoid secondary stigmatization or victimization, minorities and the socially deviant may abandon their quest for justice before the case has been closed. It is a rare moment when a victim stays the course and participates in all phases of the criminal justice process. Most often, victims exit the criminal justice process before the prosecutions of their claims are complete.

But, while victims can opt out of the prosecution and adjudication processes at any time, crime workers cannot. No matter how frivolous a complaint may be, criminal justice workers are legally mandated to respond. As citizens of the state, victims have a legal right to demand protection and prosecution, and it is the duty of police, prosecutors, and court personnel to process those requests, regardless of their personal feelings regarding them. When victims choose to exercise their prerogative and not to file charges or to provide testimony, those charged with the responsibility to process their claims feel betrayed and exploited.

Yet it is important to remember that for many crime victims the decision not to file charges or to not appear in court is not made on a whim but out of necessity. Most seek assistance from the criminal justice system, and even become dependent upon such aid because they have so little autonomy or control over abusive or violent relationships in their personal lives (Merry, 1990b). Although fear for one's life or the lives of their children compels victims of interpersonal violence to call the police, fear of retaliation often results in the dropping of charges or the refusal to testify (Ford, 1991).

Victims who do file charges find that meetings with prosecutors and court appearances can be lengthy and that postponements can extend a trial for months. Those with little job security or who do not accrue paid leaves of absence are often forced to choose between earning wages and participation in the prosecution of their own cases. Rather than relinquishing what little control they might still have over their plight, victims who are poor or working class abandon the pursuit of justice, leaving crime workers with a formidable load of open or unwinnable cases.

Criminal Justice Workers' Discretion

Victims have little power to decide who will process their claims, much less how they will do so. They lack the authority to participate in most of the decisions that move their complaints through (or out of) the justice system (Erez and Roberts, 2007). Victims' rights have been adopted by every state and the federal government, and expansion of these rights continues each year and in every jurisdiction. However, even in those jurisdictions that have strong protections for victims, these rights for victims are still largely underutilized and unenforced (Howley and Dorris, 2007), and victims have little if any power to determine the fate of their claims (Weed, 1995).

In contrast, crime workers possess extraordinary amounts of discretionary power. How quickly a case moves down the assembly line of justice depends upon the willingness and ability of crime workers to mobilize resources and to activate authorities (Emerson, 1983). Thus, the whims of police officers, victim assistance volunteers, prosecutors, and even court clerks greatly affect a victim's ability to achieve justice. Without the authority to demand a different case worker or prosecutor, victims often feel helpless when their cases are placed in the hands of indifferent or prejudiced workers.

Acts of prerogative and discretion can spark accusations of exploitation. Unable to control the course or direction of their claims or their participation in the processing of them, victims often feel like helpless pawns in the game of justice and complain about feeling discounted, ignored, and otherwise "jerked around" (Davis and Smith, 1994). Likewise, without authority to make victims follow through, crime workers feel betrayed and let down by the very people they seek to assist. Ironically, each feels powerless to affect the cooperation of the other.

THE CONSEQUENCES OF CONFLICT IN THE CRIME VICTIM/CRIMINAL JUSTICE WORKER RELATIONSHIP

Considering the cultural and structural context in which relationships between crime workers and crime victims function, it is no wonder that so many of them turn sour. The lived experiences of those who have actually been in or are currently in a crime victim/criminal justice worker relationship stand in stark contrast to the romantic portraits that the media, our public schools, and political figures so readily paint (Erez and Roberts, 2007). In real life, relations between crime victims and those whose job it is to handle their claims are at best strained, and are more likely to be downright contentious. So, on an almost daily basis, at crime scenes and police stations (Stenross and Kleinman, 1989), in the offices of prosecutors (Frohmann, 1991), inside courtrooms (Merry, 1990a, 1990b), and even at the doors of the social service agencies providing shelter and solace (Ferraro, 1995), crime victims and agents of justice commonly battle *each other* for autonomy and control (see also Ford, 1991). When relations with crime victims becomes difficult, criminal justice agents blame the victims they serve, calling them "assholes" (Van Maanen, 1978) and accusing them of being "overly emotional" (Stenross and Kleinman, 1989), "insincere" (Ferraro, 1995), or without "self control" or "common sense" (Merry, 1990a). With each negative interaction with a victim, crime workers become increasingly *cynical* about the needs and motivations of those who request their aid.

Along the same lines, victims justify their dissatisfaction with entire justice system by blaming those who happened to have handled their cases for being "inept", "lazy," "petulant," "power hungry," "insensitive," or just plain "cold-hearted" (Madigan and Gamble, 1989). With each disappointment, victims grow more disaffected with the criminal justice system and those who work in it. The consequences of such cynicism and disaffection are not without consequence.

The Price We Pay For Cynicism

The price the community pays for cynicism among its criminal justice workers is significant. Cynical workers too easily abandon the goal of justice and simply settle for the processing of cases. With little compassion or creativity, they move victims and their problems along a dehumanizing assembly line of justice (Brickey and Miller, 1975). Research shows that the cynicism is a formidable barrier to sensitivity training (Gould, 1997). Research also shows that such cynicism and tension in the relationship between victims and criminal justice workers contribute to stress, burnout, and compassion fatigue among criminal justice workers (Jones, 1997; Jones and Woods, 2007). The spillover effect is significant. Frustration with uncooperative or difficult victims is easily transferred onto others. One study, for example, reports that the families of law enforcement workers are at a significantly higher risk of domestic violence than others (*Arizona Daily Sun*, 1998).

Perhaps more insidiously, cynicism opens the door to the abuse of authority and power. As the videotaped beating of Rodney King so vividly illustrated, pent-up frustrations from negative experiences with victims and defendants alike can become lethal. However, on a day-to-day basis, police officers, court clerks, and prosecutors abuse their discretion in much smaller ways—by harassing, intimidating, or otherwise aggravating victims (and those who are, for whatever reason, associated with them) who have made their lives difficult.

Victims frequently report feeling violated a second time when crime workers fail to take their claims seriously. Madigan and Gamble (1989:3) make the convincing argument that "women who report a rape are again raped by a system composed of well-intentioned people who are nevertheless blinded by the myths of centuries." In their zeal to file charges and close cases, investigators, prosecutors, and judges re-traumatize victims when they take testimony and collect evidence without providing sufficient support or expressing empathy. Gay victims of crime also fear the courtroom experience. In Chapter 12, Perry noted the increased use of the homosexual panic defense, whereby "homosexual advance" is interpreted as a mitigating circumstance in bias motivated assaults. We have also seen in many of the chapters in this volume, and earlier in this chapter, how minority victims of crime often derive "less justice" from the courts, than do their white counterparts.

Workers at all levels of the criminal justice system engage in secondary victimization, or "derivative deviance" (Berrill and Herek, 1992). This is behavior that further stigmatizes or, in fact, revictimizes victims of crime because of their identity. Gay men and women, prostitutes, and drug dealers, for example, are often held responsible for their own victimization because of their "deviant" identities; people of color, women, and immigrants are often revictimized because of their perceived "difference." These perceptions, if held by crime workers with whom they come in contact, leave minority victims of crime vulnerable to castigation, harassment, and even violence. The King beating in Los Angeles and the alleged sodomization of Louima in New York City are extreme illustrations of broader patterns whereby people of color and poor people, in particular, bear the brunt of crime worker frustrations. In addition, on average 20% of gay lesbian victims of hate crime report victimization at the hands of police (Berrill and Herek, 1992; see also Comstock, 1991). Women, too, are vulnerable to sexual violence at the hands of criminal justice personnel. Sexual harassment is especially prevalent, as male officers attempt to preserve the traditional masculinity of the field (Messerschmidt, 1997).

The Price We Pay for Victim Alienation

Secondary victimization disempowers victims, who perceive themselves to be without legal redress. It instills, or in fact reinforces, distrust of the crime workers, who are seen as the "enemy" rather than as advocates. Consequently, many victims exit the justice system feeling *revictimized* by their contact with the criminal justice system (Jones and Woods, 2007; Madigan and Gamble, 1989; Kelly, 1984). Even in the absence of revictimization, dissatisfaction with either the process or the outcome engenders a sense of injustice, which in turn fosters disaffection with the entire justice system. The disaffected often lack sufficient motivation to report crimes or to cooperate in either criminal investigations or prosecutions.

   Given the stress and trauma that reporting a crime can entail, it is little wonder that victims of crime are reluctant to come forward; but, there is even less incentive for those who have been marginalized from power and then victimized for it by crime workers. Less than 20% of hate crimes against gays and lesbians are ever reported to police (Dean, Wu, and Martin, 1992). Fear of being hassled or demeaned for being different, immigrants, the homeless, and people of color are also hesitant to seek aid from criminal justice authorities (Muscat and Walsh, 2007; U.S. Commission on Civil Rights, 1992; see also Walker, Spohn, and DeLone, 2006). Because they fear that they will not be taken seriously, women also tend to keep violations by husbands and lovers to themselves (Belknap, 2007; Warshaw, 1994).

   In sum, the cynicism that so often infects crime workers also has implications for crime victims. The frustration experienced by so many police officers, prosecutors, victim advocates, and judges is often played out in the context of their interactions with victims of crime. The risk is that those victims will, at best, be underserved, and at worst, be revictimized.

RECONCILING DIFFERENCE?

Are the differences between victims and workers truly irreconcilable? Is the crime victim/criminal justice worker relationship doomed to be one of conflict and contention? Is disaffection with and cynicism about criminal justice an inevitable byproduct of such a partnership? While the romantic portraits as painted by the media may be unrealizable and even undesirable, we can at least consider some strategies for making the relationship more empowering if not effectual. Some of these strategies might be implemented inside the criminal justice system, and some might be more effective independent of its bureaucratic structures. The following are but a few techniques that might help to empower both crime victims and crime workers.

Crime Victim Empowerment

Looking at what we have learned from our analysis it is important for criminal justice workers to keep in mind that while in *theory* the crime victim/criminal justice worker relationship is conceptualized as a partnership between equals, in *reality*, it often is not. The individuals who step into the victim role do so because they lack the personal or social power to resolve problems and right transgressions on their own (Merry, 1990a, 1990b). It is no accident that a disproportionate number of crime victims are women, non-white, and poor as these groups are in greatest need of social and legal empowerment. Those without the means to terminate violent relationships, those without insurance to replace stolen goods, and those without access to trauma counseling seek a relationship with criminal justice workers because it is the most viable source of empowerment available to them. It is imperative, therefore, that as criminal justice workers, we seek to engage in strategies that will help, rather than harm, crime victims. What follows are but a few possible strategies and promising practices that we might keep in mind.

1. *Interpreters.* Given the earlier argument that language barriers (or hearing impairments) often limit the access of non-English speakers to the criminal justice system, it is important that interpreters be available at all stages of the criminal justice process (Murdaugh *et al.*, 2004; Taylor and Gaskin-Laniyan, 2007). If there is a paucity of language-trained police or court personnel, jurisdictions should contract with multiple interpreters in the area so that the problem of availability is alleviated. This should extend not only to non–English speaking interpreters, but American Sign Language experts as well.

2. *Victim advocates.* One of the factors that contributes to victim dissatisfaction is the disjuncture between expectations and experiences of the criminal justice system. The use of victim advocates would mitigate this. Advocates should be involved as early as possible in the process. They would thus be available to inform victims what to expect at every stage, and to educate victims about their rights. Advocates would also be responsible for keeping victims informed about the ongoing status of the case, so that victims do not feel distanced from the process. Advocates should be trained in cultural sensitivity and in any issues of difference relevant to their geographic region and/or populations to be served (Jones and Woods, 2007).

3. *Counseling.* Victims of violent crimes such as assault or sexual assault may be in particular need of counseling to assist them in coping with their victimization. This is especially true where they have experienced secondary victimization or revictimization by criminal justice workers. They may need to be reassured that they are in fact victims, not offenders. Beyond that, many victims often need assistance in coming to terms with their experiences in a way that helps to mitigate the trauma. It is also important to bring awareness of difference into the arena of counseling and treatment of victims.

4. *Crisis centers or advocacy organizations.* Victim advocates or counselors might be activated through crisis centers designed to respond immediately to reported victimizations. These entities would be expected to provide a range of services, usually to specific classes of victims such as victims of hate crime, victims of domestic violence, victims of sexual assault, or victims of property offenses.

More recently, we have "discovered" victims of difference in new categories, so there needs to be greater expansion of organizational services for these victims, including the elderly, immigrants, and the homeless (Jones and Woods, 2007; Muscat and Walsh, 2007). These organizations would assist with advocating for the rights of victims and helping through all stages of the criminal justice process, including reporting the crime, guiding victims through the process, helping to file insurance or victim compensation claims, or orders of protection.

In the wake of the victims' rights movement, many models of intervention aimed at victims have been introduced across the nation. We have offered very broad suggestions about some of the more common types of strategies employed both inside and beyond the criminal justice system.

Criminal Justice Worker Empowerment

Crime workers are not to be forgotten in our efforts to enhance the worker–victim relationship. They too encounter obstacles in their efforts to engage with victims. Moreover, crime workers are not immune to the emotional toll that the criminal justice process takes on those involved with it. It is important, then, that we address the needs of crime workers. It is also important to recognize that all levels of the criminal justice system are subject to the types of problems identified: cynicism, distrust, or burnout, for example. Consequently, the types of services suggested here should be available to judges, prosecutors, and police officers alike.

1. *Counseling services.* Like victims of crime, crime workers often have difficulties coping with criminal justice processes. Police officers and correctional officers, for example, experience relatively high levels of emotional exhaustion and burnout. Counseling may ameliorate these effects. Crisis counseling should also be made available to those who have experienced especially traumatic emergencies, such as a police shooting of a civilian, or the death of a colleague. We should not assume that crime workers can cope with these traumas any better than civilians can cope with their victimization.

2. *Language training.* If crime workers are to interact effectively with their victim counterparts, they must be able to communicate with them. Consequently, workers should be given the opportunity to learn languages that are relevant to their work. If there is a sizable population of Vietnamese immigrants in a community, for example, police officers and court workers should be rewarded for efforts to learn the appropriate dialects. This would help to minimize the frustration often experienced by both groups.

3. *Cultural awareness training.* Understanding of and sensitivity toward local communities also facilitates the process of communication and cooperation. Criminal justice personnel should therefore be encouraged, if not required, to engage in periodic cultural awareness training. To do so only once at the beginning of one's career is insufficient, since communities change demographically over time. Workers should always be "in touch" with the diversity of their clientele.

4. *Problem solving/conflict resolution training.* An important element in the successful negotiation of the worker–victim relationship is the ability to render a satisfactory decision. This does not necessarily mean that someone "wins" and

someone "loses" in a dispute situation. Rather, it suggests the ability to achieve some compromise whereby all parties are satisfied with the process of the decision, if not the decision itself. In an era of community policing, this particular tool is becoming more highly valued relative to traditional adversarial means of dispute resolution. Here, criminal justice workers might learn from peacemaking initiatives.

Promising Practices for the Relationship Between Crime Victims and Criminal Justice Workers

This chapter has argued throughout that at the heart of the criminal justice system lies the partnership between crime victims and criminal justice workers. Consequently, to be most effective, strategies aimed toward victims and workers as separate entities should be embedded in a criminal justice system that is more attuned to the fact that the two groups are involved in a relationship. Those strategies which seek to negotiate that relationship will be paramount in our efforts to minimize conflict and dissatisfaction.

1. *State Victim Assistance Academies.* The Office for Victims of Crime (OVC) created a grant opportunity to fund the development of a fundamental level training for victim assistance providers and criminal justice professionals that is rooted in the needs of the diverse populations of individual states (Office for Victims of Crime, 2005). Included in these trainings are topics on rural and urban crime victims, tribal victims, hate crime victims, elderly victims, as well as an emphasis on diversity across all areas of criminal justice service delivery to victims. These academies typically involve victims, academics, and justice workers in the education of victim assistance workers, thus offering a positive model for how to build a strong justice community that is *inclusive* of victims. While these academies were initially funded through grant initiatives, many of these state academies are suffering from funding problems and should be considered for greater funding from the states themselves.

2. *Community and cultural liaisons.* One very important means of bridging the gap between crime workers and crime victims is the establishment of community liaisons. These trained officers of the court, or police department, or other agency are responsible for making sustained contact with the community, thereby creating a relationship that is mutually beneficial. On the one hand, it gives the community a voice; on the other, it helps the criminal justice agency to make itself welcome in that community.

3. *Mediators.* Sometimes, liaisons are not enough, or do not exist in a particular area. Where this is the case, and a conflict arises between the crime worker and the community, mediators may play a useful interim role. For example, if the community should become alarmed about what they perceive to be as discriminatory treatment of its members, a mediator may be called in to seek some resolution. Both (or all) parties would be brought to the table, given an opportunity to voice their concerns and perceptions. The intent of this particular form of dispute resolution would be to provide a neutral process of reconciliation between the community and the criminal justice system.

4. *Citizen advisory boards.* Where communities are especially mistrustful of the operation of the criminal justice system, increasing demands are being made

for the establishment of citizen advisory boards. Such bodies are assigned varying degrees of oversight with respect to the agency in question. These are most common in the field of policing; however, we are beginning to see boards which oversee sentencing practices, for example. Such bodies are intended to democratize the criminal justice system, by allowing civilian input in the decision-making process. By times, however, they have had the unintended effect of creating resentment on the part of the criminal justice agency in question (Miller and Hess, 1998).

5. *Community policing.* Many of the strategies listed above are best employed within the context of community policing. As the label suggests, this approach to policing is explicitly concerned with forging closer links between diverse communities and the police who serve them. It is a philosophy that is finding increasing support among workers and victims alike. Implemented effectively, community policing has the potential to enhance the voice of the public—and victims in particular—while simultaneously making the work of criminal justice easier. It is itself an effort to overcome both the cynicism of the worker and the disaffection of the victim.

At the outset of this chapter, we argued that the actions of crime workers are often contingent on the decisions reached by crime victims and that both are shaped by the relationship between the two groups. We also argued that the crime victim/criminal justice worker relationship is fraught with tension and conflict. However, it is important to bear in mind that that tension is not generated by the personalities in question, but by the cultural and structural differences between these two groups. The concluding section of this chapter was intended to suggest that those tensions are not irreconcilable. We took the first step in this process of reconciliation when we recognized that problems exist. We took the second step when we suggested potential means by which the tensions could be negotiated. The next step is yours, as future or present criminal justice workers: that is, it is up to you to implement these reforms.

References

Arizona Daily Sun. 1998. October 11. Police home violence a silent ill?

Belknap, Joanne. 2007. *The Invisible Woman: Gender, Crime and Justice.* New York: Wadsworth.

Berrill, Kevin, and Gregory Herek. 1992. Primary and Secondary Victimization in Anti-Gay Hate Crimes: Official Responses and Public Policy. In *Hate Crimes: Confronting Violence Against Lesbians and Gay Men*, ed. Gregory Herek and Kevin Berrill, 289–305. Newbury Park, CA: Sage Publications.

Black, Donald. 1976. *The Behavior of Law.* New York: Academic Press.

Block, Carolyn Rebecca. 2003. How Can Practitioners Help an Abused Woman Lower Her Risk of Death? *NIJ Journal* 250 (November): 4–7.

Blumberg, Abraham. 1967. Law as a Confidence Game: Organizational Co-optation of a Profession. *Law and Society Review* 1: 15–39.

Bonsignore, John J., Ethan Katsh, Peter d'Errico, Ronald Pipkin, Stephen Arons, and Janet Rifkin. 2005. *Before the Law: An Introduction to the Legal Process*, 8th edition. Boston, MA: Houghton Mifflin Company.

Brickey, Stephen, and Dan Miller. 1975. Bureaucratic Due Process: An Ethnography of a Traffic Court. *Social Problems* 22: 688–697.

Coles, Robert. 1993. *The Call to Service: A Witness to Idealism.* Boston: Houghton Mifflin Company.

Comstock, G. 1991. *Violence Against Lesbians and Gay Men.* New York: Columbia University Press.

Conley, John, and William O'Barr. 1990. *Rules Verses Relationships: The Ethnography of Legal Discourse.* Chicago: University of Chicago Press.

Craven, Diane. 1994. Sex Differences in Violent Victimization. U.S. Department of Justice, Bureau of Justice Statistics online document.http://www.ojp.gov/bjs/pub/pdf/sdvv.pdf.

Davis, Robert, and Barbara E. Smith. 1994. Victim Impact Statements and Victim Satisfaction: An Unfulfilled Promise? *Journal of Criminal Justice* 22 (1): 1–12.

Dean, L., Shanyu Wu, and J. L. Martin. 1992. Trends in Violence and Discrimination Against Lesbians and Gay Men. In *Hate Crimes: Confronting Violence Against Lesbians and Gay Men*, ed. Gregory Herek and Kevin Berrill, 46–64. Newbury Park, CA: Sage Publications.

Dugan, L., and R. Apel. 2003. An Exploratory Study of the Violent Victimization of Women: Race/Ethnicity and Situational Context. *Criminology* 41 (3): 959–979.

Emerson, Robert. 1983. Holistic Effects in Social Control Decision-Making. *Law and Society Review* 17 (3): 425–455.

Erez, Edna, and Julian Roberts. 2007. Victim Participation in the Criminal Justice System. In *Victims of Crime*, ed. Robert C. Davis, Arthur J. Lurigio, and Susan Herman, 3rd edn., 277–297. Los Angeles, CA: Sage Publications.

Federal Bureau of Investigation. 2007. *The Uniform Crime Reports.* http://www.fbi.gov/ucr/ucr.htm.

Ferraro, Kathleen. 1995. Cops, Courts and Woman Battering. In *The Criminal Justice System and Women*, ed. Barbara Raffel Price and Natalie Sokoloff, 262–271. New York, NY: McGraw-Hill.

Ferraro, Kathleen, and Lucy Pope. 1993. Irreconcilable Differences: Battered Women, Police and the Law. In *The Legal Responses to Wife Assault*, ed. N. Zoe Hilton, 96–123. Thousand Oaks, CA: Sage Publications.

Ford, David. 1991. Prosecution as a Victim Power Resource. *Law and Society Review* 25 (2): 313–334.

Friedman, Lawrence. 1994. *Total Justice.* New York: The Russell Sage Foundation.

Frohmann, Lisa. 1991. Discrediting Victims' Allegations of Sexual Assault. *Social Problems* 38 (2): 213–226.

Frohmann, Lisa. 1998. Constituting Power in Sexual Assault Cases: Prosecutorial Strategies and Victims' Constrained Agency. *Social Problems* 45 (3): 393–407.

Goffman, Erving. 1967. *Interactional Ritual: Essays on Face-to-Face Behavior.* New York: Anchor Books.

Gottfredson, Michael, and Don Gottfredson. 1988. The Victim's Decision to Report a Crime. *Decision Making in Criminal Justice*, 15–45. New York: Plenum Press.

Gould, Larry. 1997. Can An Old Dog Be Taught New Tricks? *Policing: An International Journal of Police Strategies and Management* 20 (2): 339–356.

Greene, Helen Taylor. 1996. Black Perspectives on Police Brutality. In *African American Perspectives on Crime Causation, Criminal Justice Administration and Crime Prevention*, ed. Anne Sulton, 109–122. Boston, MA: Butterworth-Heinemann.

Howley, Susan, and Carol Dorris. 2007. Legal Rights for Crime Victims in the Criminal Justice System. In *Victims of Crime*, ed. Robert C. Davis, Arthur J. Lurigio, and Susan Herman, 3rd edn., 299–314. Los Angeles, CA: Sage Publications.

Jones, Lynn C. 1997. Both Friend and Stranger: How Rape Crisis Volunteers Build and Manage Unpersonal Relationships with Clients. In *Social Perspectives on Emotions: Real Life Applications*, ed. Rebecca J. Erickson and Beverley Cuthbertson-Johnson, 125–148. Greenwich, CT: JAI Press.

Jones, Lynn C, and Kathryn Woods. 2007. Crisis Response. Module 11 in *Arizona Victim*

Assistance Academy: Participant Manual. Arizona Coalition for Victim Services. AVAA.

Karmen, Andrew. 2007. *Crime Victims: An Introduction to Victimology,* 6th edn. Belmont, CA: Thomson Wadsworth.

Kelly, Deborah. 1984. Victims' Perceptions of Criminal Justice. *Pepperdine Law Review* 11: 15–21.

Kidd, Robert, and Ellen Chayet. 1984. Why Do Victims Fail to Report? The Psychology of Criminal Victimization. *Journal of Social Issues* 40 (1): 39–50.

Madigan, Lee, and Nancy Gamble. 1989. *The Second Rape: Society's Continued Betrayal of the Victim.* New York: Lexington Books.

Madriz, Ester. 1997. Images of Crime and Victims: A Study on Women's Fear and Social Control. *Gender and Society* 11 (3): 342–356.

Martin, Susan, and Nancy Jurik, 2006. *Doing Gender Doing Justice: Women in the Law and Criminal Justice Occupations,* 2nd edn. Thousand Oaks, CA: Sage Publications.

McKean, Jerome. 1994. "Race, Ethnicity and Criminal Justice. In *Multicultural Perspectives in Criminal Justice and Criminology,* ed. James Hendricks and Bryan Byers, 85–134. Springfield, IL: Charles C. Thomas.

McShane, Marilyn, and Frank Williams. 1992. Radical Victimology: A Critique of the Concept of Victim in Traditional Victimology. *Crime and Delinquency* 38 (2): 258–271.

Merry, Sally Engle. (1990a). *Getting Justice, Getting Even.* Chicago: University of Chicago Press.

Merry, Sally Engle. (1990b). Law as Fair, Law as Help. *New Directions in the Study of Justice, Law and Social Control,* 167–186. New York: Plenum Press.

Messerschmidt, James. 1997. *Crime as Structured Action: Gender, Race, Class, and Crime in the Making.* Thousand Oaks, CA: Sage Publications.

Miller, Linda, and Kären Hess. 1998. *The Police in the Community: Strategies for the 21st Century.* Belmont, CA: West/Wadsworth.

Murdaugh, C., S. Hunt, R. Sowell, and I. Santana. 2004. Domestic Violence in Hispanics in the Southeastern United States: A Survey and Needs Analysis. *Journal of Family Violence* 19 (2): 107–115.

Muscat, Bernadette T., and Jeffrey A. Walsh. 2007. Reaching Underserved Victim Populations—Special Challenges Relating to Homeless Victims, Rural Populations, Ethnic/Racial/Sexual Minorities, and Victims with Disabilities. In *Victims of Crime,* ed. Robert C. Davis, Arthur J. Lurigio, and Susan Herman, 3rd edn., 315–336. Los Angeles, CA: Sage Publications.

Obinna, J., S. Krueger, C. Osterbaan, J. M. Sadusky, and W. DeVore. 2006. *Understanding the Needs of the Victims of Sexual Assault in the Deaf Community.* Final report submitted to the National Institute of Justice. NCJ 212867. Washington, DC.

Office for Victims of Crime. 2005. *Report to the Nation 2005.* Washington, DC: U.S. Department of Justice. http://www.ojp.usdoj.gov/ovc/welcovc/reporttonation2005/welcome.html.

Pettiway, Leon. 1996. *Honey, Honey, Miss Thang: Being Black, Gay and On the Streets.* Philadelphia: Temple University Press.

Ryan, William. 1976. *Blaming the Victim.* New York: Vintage Books.

Sherman, Lawrence W. 2002. Trust and Confidence in Criminal Justice. *NIJ Journal* 248: 22–31.

Smith, Douglas, Nanette Graham, and Bonney Adams. 1991. Minorities and the Police: Attitudes and Behavioral Questions. In *Race and Criminal Justice,* ed. Michael Lynch and Britt Patterson, 22–35. Albany, NY: Harrow and Heston.

Sourcebook of Criminal Justice Statistics. 2005. Victimization webpages. http://www.albany.edu/sourcebook/pdf/t3102005pdf.

Sourcebook of Criminal Justice Statistics. 2007. Public opinion webpages. http://www.albany.edu/sourcebook/pdf/t2122007.pdf.

Stenross, Barbara, and Sherryl Kleinman. 1989. The Highs and Lows of Emotional Labor: Detectives' Encounters with Criminals and Victims. *Journal of Contemporary Ethnography* 17 (4): 435–452.

Taylor, Lauren R., and Nicole Gaskin-Laniyan. 2007. Study Reveals Unique Issues Faced by Deaf Victims of Sexual Assault. *NIJ Journal* 257: 24–26.

U.S. Commission on Civil Rights. 1990. *Intimidation and Violence: Racial and Religious Bigotry in America.* Washington, DC: U.S. Government Printing Office.

U.S. Commission on Civil Rights. 1992. *Civil Rights Issues Facing Asian Americans.* Washington, DC: U.S. Government Printing Office.

Van Maanen, John. 1978. The Asshole. In *Policing: A View from the Street*, ed. Peter K. Manning and John Van Maanen, 221–238. Santa Monica, CA: Goodyear Publishing.

Walker, Samuel, Cassia Spohn, and Miriam DeLone. 2006. *The Color of Justice*, 4th edn. Belmont, CA: Wadsworth.

Warshaw, Robin. 1994. *I Never Called It Rape: The Ms. Report on Recognizing, Fighting, and Surviving Date and Acquaintance Rape.* New York: Harper Perennial.

Weed, Frank. 1995. *Certainty of Justice: Reform in the Crime Victim Movement.* New York: Aldine De Gruyter.

PART FIVE

Conclusion

CHAPTER 22

Reinvestigating Difference

Lynn Jones

Barbara Perry

Marianne O. Nielsen

Difference matters. Each of the chapters in this book has demonstrated that fact. The authors have encouraged readers to think about how difference is constructed and how difference is handled in the context of criminal justice. In particular, we have seen how the effects of difference have been and continue to be informed by privilege, power, and discrimination within the criminal justice system. However, it is not enough to identify the negative consequences of difference. Consequently, each of the authors has also drawn attention to the ways in which the damaging effects of difference might be ameliorated. This concluding chapter seeks to pull those threads together so that, as criminal justice practitioners, readers will be empowered to reinvestigate difference. The goal of this chapter, then, is to consider strategies by which the effects of the social construction of difference can be challenged in the interests of not just criminal justice, but social justice.

DECONSTRUCTING AND RECONSTRUCTING DIFFERENCE

One of the themes that unifies the discussions in this volume is that difference is socially constructed. The mechanisms by which this is accomplished are many and varied: stereotypes, language, legislation, and differential experiences with the criminal justice system are but a few. You have read, for example, how stereotyping Native Americans as "savages," or criminalizing the sexuality of gay men and lesbians, or excluding Asians from citizenship have served to maintain the stigmatized outsider identity of these Others. You have read how these "Others" have been defined negatively in terms of their relationship to some dominant norm—that is, how "black" is defined as inherently inferior to "white," Jewish to Christian, gay to straight. You have read how the criminal justice system has been a primary site for enacting these differences, as well as acting on them, by differentially enforcing the law along the lines of race, class, gender, age, ability, sexuality, and religion.

However, as Wonders points out in Chapter 2 of this volume, there is reason for hope: since difference is socially constructed, it can also be socially reconstructed. In other words, as a society, we can redefine the ways in which difference "matters." We can strive for a just and democratic society in which the full spectrum of diversity addressed here is re-evaluated in a positive and celebratory light.

We would do well to heed Young's (1990) advice that we embrace a positive politics of difference. This would involve much more than efforts to assimilate those who are different, or merely "tolerate" their presence. Rather, it challenges us to celebrate our differences. Of course, this requires that much of our current way of ordering the world would be radically altered. It means that we must cease to define "different" as inferior and see it instead as simply not the same.

To engage in such a powerful political activity is to resist the temptation to ask everyone to conform to an artificial set of norms and expectations. It is to reclaim and value the "natural" heterogeneity of this nation rather than force a false homogeneity. It is to refuse to denigrate the culture and experiences of black people, women, or gay men, for example. It is to learn and grow from the strength and beauty that alternate cultures have to offer.

Given the historical and contemporary processes uncovered in this book, reconstructing the meaning and value associated with difference will be no easy task. It will require dramatic changes in attitudes and behavior throughout society. However, as current or potential criminal justice practitioners, you, as students, will have a crucial role to play in this transformation, since the criminal justice system has all too often been complicit in enforcing a negative politics of difference. We now turn to a consideration of concrete strategies by which criminal justice workers might lead the way in empowering those who have traditionally been weakened.

LAW AS A MECHANISM OF EMPOWERMENT

An important first step in empowering the disempowered is to question and critically evaluate the role of the legal structure in perpetuating unequal relations of power. Most authors in this volume have drawn attention to the material and ideological means by which law has contributed to the subordination of minority groups. The law itself can effectively exclude or restrict the participation of particular groups in the ongoing activities and processes of society—just as immigration and naturalization laws have historically prevented many Asians from entry, or from attaining citizenship. Law can—by its silences—exclude groups from protections afforded to others, such as in the failure to include gays or women in hate crime or civil rights legislation, for example. Law can also marginalize others: "immigration sweeps" stigmatize and victimize Latinos, in particular; legal distinctions between crack and white powder cocaine incarcerate more African Americans than other groups; anti-abortion policies limit women's autonomy; social security restrictions endanger and exclude immigrants; the federal government's Indian policy marginalizes Native American populations; the military's "Don't ask, don't tell" policy silences gays. In their own way, each of these cases serves to marginalize or subordinate the groups in question. They raise questions about the particular group's legitimacy and place in U.S. society; in some cases, they explicitly define their "outsider" status. In other words, law is a dramatic form of political and cultural expression which "draws the boundaries that divide us into groups, with momentous effects on our individual identities" (Karst, 1995:2). It is an integral part of the field in which difference is constructed and reaffirmed. At the same time, the law can protect and encourage difference.

Consequently, if we are to democratize the criminal justice system, legislation which is unjust and discriminatory in its content or effects must be eliminated, to be replaced by legislation which promotes justice and equity. This is not the place to catalog all of these legislative reforms. It is, rather, the place to encourage criminal justice workers to investigate the legislation they are asked to enforce for signs of injustice, and then act on those findings. Consider these examples: status offenses hold youth to different and unreasonable standards of behavior—lobby for the elimination of this class of offenses; domestic violence legislation trivializes the harm to female victims—lobby for reform of the legislation; death-penalty case processing create pressures that lead to wrongful convictions—lobby to reform investigation and prosecution procedures.

The law is not an immutable behemoth. It is vulnerable to the impact of ongoing struggles between groups. It has been used effectively in the past to extend the rights and protections afforded to women, people of color, children, and disabled persons. The Americans with Disabilities Act, for example, has been crucial in enhancing the mobility and independence of those who are differently abled. The Violence Against Women Act has dramatically expanded the services available to battered women, and it was recently renewed with funding. Successive civil rights acts—at the national and state levels—have been crucial to the recent political and economic advances of women and people of color in particular. It is not unreasonable, then, to encourage legislative reform as a means of minimizing the negative and exclusionary effects of difference.

PREJUDICE REDUCTION

The legal regulation of difference has often been grounded in broader social and cultural perceptions of difference. Across time and across the country, we have seen repeatedly how the "Other" is demonized and stigmatized both within the criminal justice system and beyond. These processes have informed the criminalization and the victimization of those deemed both different and inferior. Stereotypes of the "promiscuous woman," for example, consistently served to enable violence against women; stereotypes of gay men as pedophiles consistently served to enable legislation criminalizing their sexuality; stereotypes of irresponsible adolescents consistently served to enable both their victimization and criminalization. In each of these illustrative cases, the stereotypes disempower those who are different, since their difference is assumed to be immutable and deviant. Consequently, the key to empowerment is to eliminate the "discriminatory and/or privileging effects attached to difference" (Wonders, Chapter 2).

This is a task that will be most effective if it is attained in a broad array of contexts. Prejudice and hostility toward those who are deemed different inform every level of society. Consequently, anti-prejudice initiatives will also be broadly disseminated. The most effective starting point will be the elementary and high schools. In fact, recent years have seen a dramatic growth in education-based anti-prejudice programs. The most compelling of these is the Southern Poverty Law Center's *Teaching Tolerance* project, which includes *Teaching Tolerance* magazine and a website full of ideas for the positive reframing of difference (www.tolerance.org). This preventative initiative assists educators in designing curricula, which encourage students to recognize, understand, and value difference. Here in Flagstaff, the Northland Family Help Center includes a youth theater troupe called the P.E.A.C.E. Project (Prevention Education And Creative Expression), which educates through performances and dialogue with their peers that highlight issues of gender and relationship violence, prejudice, and the positive ways to reconstruct difference (P.E.A.C.E. website).

It is to be hoped that such interventions break the connections between difference and intolerance, so that subsequent generations will be less vulnerable to the messages of hate propagated by the hate movement. To the extent that educational activities—in the schools and in the community—are able to deconstruct damaging and divisive stereotypes, they will continue to be effective mechanisms by which to counteract prejudice and discrimination. Although not all educators or students will be receptive to the alternative messages of tolerance, "for every school child and young adult that we can and do reach, we shall be influencing a world beyond our own" (Kleg, 1993:260).

The messages transmitted in our public schools will have little long-term impact unless they are accompanied by subsequent repetition in society at large. Media campaigns aimed at deconstructing popular misconceptions, and community organizations devoted to minimizing negative imagery are useful local initiatives. Moreover, as individuals, we also have a responsibility to recognize and eliminate prejudice within ourselves. For most of us, the learning of prejudicial (e.g., racist, sexist, ageist) ideas was an unavoidable outcome of our early socialization and learning. Whatever its source, prejudice hinders our ability to adapt to our increasingly diverse social environment. Prejudice is like a communicable disease (Skillings and Dobbins, 1991). Consider tuberculosis for example. It is a serious disease which anyone could contract quite by accident. However, once we become aware that we have it, we are obliged to have it treated so that we do not infect others. So it is with prejudice: once we realize we have been "infected," we are obliged to have it "treated" so that we do not pass it on and harm others. Treatment can vary from increased self-analysis of one's own perceptions, to seeking out opportunities for meaningful intercultural communication, to individual counseling in extreme cases. In addition to these mechanisms, the goal of prejudice reduction should be kept in mind in the context of hiring and training practices.

CRIMINAL JUSTICE EMPLOYMENT AND TRAINING

Criminal justice agencies that are representative of the communities they serve will almost invariably be more aware of the particular problems of these communities. However, as the authors in this book have indicated, minority groups are dramatically underrepresented as service providers in the criminal justice system. As the

United States becomes even more diverse, it will become increasingly important for agencies to recruit those who are "different." It is these recruits who will bring with them an understanding of their clientele, as well as slightly different approaches to their jobs. Latino/a police officers, for example, will bring insights into the specificity of domestic violence among Latinos/as; women bring dialogic rather than aggressive tactics into emotional confrontations; physically challenged persons bring attention to the barriers implied by the physical environment. In other words, hiring those who are different is a way to invest in and take advantage of diversity.

There are a number of distinct advantages to employing a culturally heterogeneous workforce within criminal justice. Officers and personnel drawn from the communities they represent may play the formal or informal role of liaison between the public and the criminal justice system. They may have a better understanding and greater empathy for the people with whom they interact. The potential benefit to be derived from this bridging of the distance is a less hostile, more cooperative community. Ultimately, stronger community relations may engender greater safety for all justice workers.

There is also considerable value in members of diverse groups designing and operating their own services, such as the battered women's shelters or rape crisis centers that were first established by groups of concerned women. Similarly, Native Americans have the unique legal right to establish criminal justice organizations to provide services in their own Nations. The Navajo Nation, for example, has its own police, courts, probation services, and peacemakers devoted to traditional justice practices. Immigrant organizations have been especially useful as advocates for newly arrived residents; and immigrant rights organizations often merge with victims' rights advocates to enhance reporting and improve the service delivery to immigrant victims of crime.

However, there are often problems associated with members of subordinated groups working within the criminal justice system. Police officers, for example, may experience "double marginality," wherein they are seen as outsiders by their predominantly white (male, straight) colleagues and as traitors by their non-white (female, gay) community. The distance from their fellow criminal justice practitioners may in fact be exacerbated by the tendency to marginalize minority officers by giving them primary responsibility for serving their own community, or serving in "culturally sensitive" roles (e.g., women in juvenile justice; people of color in communities of color).

Moreover, hiring and promoting women, or people of color, or people with disability, or anyone else within criminal justice agencies is no guarantee that those agencies will necessarily be more sensitive to cultural diversity. There are, for example, gay men who are racist, women who are sexist, and Latinos/as who are classist. Ignorance and prejudice cut across difference. Consequently, regardless of the makeup of criminal justice agencies, cultural awareness training will have a crucial role to play in sensitizing its members to the experiences, values, and needs of the communities they serve. As global differences continue to become part of our experiences, the criminal justice system, like other institutions in society, must continue to grow and reflect the changing demographics of those being served. Gould's chapter (Chapter 20) on cultural awareness training highlights the rationales and content of effective training modules. In particular, such training, whether at the point of hire or in-service, should address key cultural differences in such areas as values, communication, patterns of interaction, and the importance of family.

SPEAKING OF DIFFERENCE

No amount of cultural awareness training or employment of minority personnel will bridge cultural differences if problems of communication persist. Nielsen and Manglia's chapter (Chapter 4) on intercultural and interpersonal communication explicitly identifies a number of potential barriers to effective communication between individuals and between groups. The most obvious obstacle is language difference. One of the prime indicators of the diversity of the United States is the fact that hundreds of languages and thousands of dialects are spoken within the nation's borders. Obviously, this can pose problems for predominantly English-speaking agents who come in contact with non-English-speaking clients. Ogawa (1999:3) tells the story of a police officer who offended a number of Latinos at an accident scene by asking them (erroneously) why no one spoke English. An African American man responded that, if the officer intended to serve the community, it was his responsibility to be bilingual. Increasingly, police departments and other criminal justice agencies are acknowledging this responsibility to serve their communities in the appropriate and relevant language.

Regions and cities across the United States—especially on the coasts—contain heavy concentrations of people whose first language is not English. Many, for example, have large Latino/a populations; some have high proportions of Native Americans; a growing number of communities host large Asian populations. With changing demographics and the increasing globalization of the economy, bi- or multilingualism will become a source of strength. Moreover, if criminal justice personnel, specifically, are to serve the needs and interests of all people, it is vital for them to provide services in languages other than English (including American Sign Language). Hiring bilingual officers is one solution. However, this is not always possible or feasible. The alternative, then, is to have ready access to translators who help bridge the linguistic gap.

Even where language differences are absent or mitigated in some way, interpersonal and intercultural barriers to communication may still be present. Like most other professions, those in criminal justice often have a language of their own. Acronyms and numerical codes prohibit civilian comprehension; jargon creates barriers to service or understanding. More broadly, however, even people who share a common language may use the language differently. In Canada, neither "Grits" nor "Waffles" would be eaten for breakfast, since these terms refer to political parties. These interpretive problems are often accompanied by nonverbal communication patterns. Depending upon one's cultural experience, nodding one's head could mean either yes or no; silence could imply either great respect or great disrespect. Also, even communicating to authorities that a behavior is victimization depends on cultural understandings and difference. Muscat and Walsh (2007) note there are many victimization behaviors that are recognized in the United States that may not be considered harmful in some cultures, such as verbal abuse, sexual harassment, and neglect. Again training in the communication patterns of local populations can minimize the misunderstandings that emerge out of these differences.

It is not only the community that benefits from such considerations. Police officers and other justice workers often voice frustration when they are unable to communicate with the people with whom they interact. This is understandable, because such barriers may make it difficult to investigate a crime, or provide services to victims of crime, for example. Knowledge of the local language and other patterns of communication opens up the lines between criminal justice personnel and their communities. In fact, their jobs are made easier rather than more difficult when they are able to engage in a meaningful dialogue with victims, witnesses, and offenders.

COMMUNITY OUTREACH

One means by which criminal justice agencies might gain familiarity with the communication patterns, and values and needs of diverse populations is the establishment of community outreach or liaison programs. Some police departments, for example, have attached outreach officers to their community policing strategies. In line with the police–community partnership philosophy, such departments have created local substations, and encouraged officers to become active in the communities they serve. These initiatives are intended to minimize the cultural and organizational distance between police officers and their publics. This is particularly important in immigrant communities, where newcomers are reluctant to report crime. Law enforcement agencies have sought to overcome the fear and reticence by mounting a friendly presence in such communities. They attempt to overcome language barriers by offering translation services, multilingual emergency/telephone hotlines, and community–criminal justice alliances.

Many such alliances have been formed in cities hosting large non-English speaking populations. Oakland California's Asian Advisory Committee on Crime (AACC) is constituted by a coalition of criminal justice officials and Asian community leaders. It has representatives from such local organizations as the Center for Southeast Asian Resettlement, the Buddhist Church of Oakland, and the Lao Iu Mien Culture Association. An innovative Boston project addresses the special fears of senior citizens through its alliance of the police department and the Department of Public Health, and senior programs such as the Council of Elders and the Commission on Affairs of the Elderly. The program offers home crime prevention advice, as well as strategies intended to respond to street crime. Such collaborative efforts are attempts to break the "us vs. them" mentality so common to criminal justice personnel. The initiatives seek instead to foster trusting, positive relationships between criminal justice agencies and their diverse publics.

Communities are empowered when they feel some connection to criminal justice agencies. They are also empowered when they feel they are allowed some input into the operation of those agencies. Consequently, the institutionalization of civilian review boards goes a long way in bridging the gap between the two "sides." These are particularly effective—perhaps necessary—where there is a history of criminal justice abuse or corruption, or a newly discovered social problem. Robert Schehr in his chapter on wrongful conviction (Chapter 19) discussed a compelling example of how difference matters in the criminal justice system, and innocence commissions are an important positive step. Increasingly, community members are demanding more open and democratic oversight of investigations into police abuse, brutality, or corruption.

It is hoped that such scrutiny would have the dual effects of minimizing abuse and maximizing public confidence in the investigative process. Again, the overarching goal is to strengthen the criminal justice–community relationship.

COMMUNITY ORGANIZING

Many authors in this volume have also highlighted the importance of communities organizing for themselves. The criminal justice system is not always willing or able to address the specific needs of the diverse communities it serves. Consequently, recent years have seen incredible growth in organizations like the National Asian and Pacific American Legal Consortium (NAPALC) and Gay and Lesbian Advocates and Defenders (GLAD). These organizations are grassroots associations dedicated to civil rights and legal advocacy for their specific communities.

Equally important are umbrella organizations dedicated to monitoring and confronting violence—especially ethnoviolence—directed at minority communities. Perhaps the most effective means of confronting hate crimes, for example, is through the maintenance and support of anti-violence projects which do battle against them—in the courts, in the media, and in public forums. Organizations like the Southern Poverty Law Center (SPLC), the Anti-Defamation League (ADL), and the Prejudice Institute perform an invaluable service for the public in their roles as monitors, litigators, and educators. Antiviolence projects are also crucial for their activities that respond to hate groups and hate crimes directly. The Prejudice Institute, for example, supplements its research activities with direct technical assistance to communities which have been victimized, and with program and policy design. The ADL has been instrumental in shaping public policy responses to hate crime and hate groups. In fact, most states have adopted legislation inspired by the ADL's model hate crime legislation.

These sorts of organizations play a critical educational role as well. Many regularly publish and distribute newsletters to members, police departments, and educational institutions. These resources highlight the threats posed by hate-group activities, and what can be done to dilute the threats. These regularly scheduled publications are supplemented by more specialized documents, such as the ADL's *Hate Crimes: Policies and Procedures for Law Enforcement Agencies,* Klanwatch's *Ten Ways to Fight Hate,* or the Prejudice Institute's *The Traumatic Effects of Ethnoviolence.*

Such agencies can also be important exercises in coalition building. As Wonders (Chapter 2) argues, differences are overlapping and intersecting. That is, each of us occupies multiple identities; for example, as a woman, and a Latina, and a lawyer. Consequently, each of us has an interest in bridging difference. Moreover, the groups written about in this volume have often experienced a similarity (but not sameness) of oppression. In other words, African Americans, Jews, Asians, homosexuals, the disabled, and others have all suffered various degrees of discrimination and victimization. Consequently, the interethnic alliances necessary to minimize interethnic conflicts rest on practices that empower all minority groups. In other words, such strategies must be "transformative rather than simply effective in reducing tensions or addressing particular problems" (Okazawa-Rey and Wong, 1996:35). Energies must be devoted to the identification and acknowledgment of what these communities share and what they can accomplish together.

VICTIM SERVICES

Ogawa (1999:4) succinctly describes the quandary facing victims who have come in contact with the criminal justice system: "All victims of crime are susceptible to being mistreated by uncaring, misinformed or antagonistic individuals and/or an overburdened, ponderous and jaded criminal justice system. These are insensitivities or injustices that victims of every race and ethnicity have endured." Our task as criminal justicians, then, is to mitigate the negative effects of difference for not only communities, but also for individual victims of those communities. The experience of victimization is traumatic for all people; however, it can be doubly, triply so for those whose difference leaves them even more vulnerable and at the mercy of a "jaded criminal justice system." Furthermore, different communities may in fact experience the trauma of victimization in different ways. Research has shown the importance of asking how victimization is viewed in their culture (Muscat and Walsh, 2007) and validating victims' thoughts, feelings, and beliefs *in the context of their cultures* (Dugan and Apel, 2003; Murdaugh *et al.*, 2004). Victim services and outreach to culturally diverse victims "must include resources that are specific to their needs" (Office for Victims of Crime, 1998:157).

Jones, Morgan, and Perry (Chapter 21) explicitly address the issue of victim services. Our purpose here is not to repeat that discussion, but to highlight its significance. The criminal justice response to serving the needs of victims has been varied and broad, ranging from legislation (e.g., Federal Victim and Witness Protection Act of 1982; Victims of Crime Act of 1984; Crime Victims Rights Act (CVRA) of 2004) to the establishment of victims' bills of rights which defines victim participation in the criminal justice system. As of 2005, 33 states had victims' bills of rights constitutions (Howley and Dorris, 2007) and the 2004 CVRA became the legislative compromise to failed efforts at a crime victims' rights amendment to the federal constitution (Karmen, 2007). The most common and well-known approach, however, consists of the array of services known as victim-witness programs (Figure 22.1 summarizes the most common types of services offered in this context).

These services cross the boundaries of difference. They serve the general needs of victims, regardless of what "category of difference" they may occupy. However, those victimized because of their difference, or those who experience victimization differently because of their difference, or those who are uncomfortable with the criminal justice system because of their difference, often require culturally sensitive services. The Violence Against Women Act acknowledges this in the context of the specificity of the victimization of women. The act is an exploitable resource for victims, offering legal redress as well as funding for programs, services, and shelters intended to confront violence against women. The Office for Victims of Crime (OVC) funds technology, training, and programs that promote best practices in serving victims' needs.

The OVC places particular emphasis on meeting the needs of underserved populations, including victims with disability, victims in rural areas, Native American victims, and new victims of internationally based crimes such as telemarketing fraud and trafficking (Office for Victims of Crime, 2005).

Awareness and knowledge of how crimes affect diverse communities allows criminal justice decision makers to implement services that are appropriate to localized

Emergency Aid

24-hour crisis hotline
Information on victims' rights and services
Referrals for emergency financial aid
Accompaniment to hospital for rape examination
Referrals for short- and long-term counseling
Emergency restraining or protection orders
Information and assistance on recovery of stolen property
Information and assistance on document replacement
Interpreter services

Counseling and Advocacy

Crisis intervention services
Short- and long-term counseling
Access and referrals to self-help support groups
Group counseling

Investigation

Regular updates on status of investigation
Notification of suspect arrest
Basic information on the criminal justice system
Interpreter services
Protection from intimidation and harassment
Notification of pretrial release of accused

Prosecution

Orientation to the criminal justice system
Regular updates on the status of the case
Accompaniment to court
Notification of plea negotiations
Victim consultation in plea decisions
Child care services

Sentencing

Notification of right to submit a victim impact statement
Victim impact statements
Notice of sentence

Post Disposition

Information/notification of appeal
Notification of parole hearing
Victim impact statement on parole
Notification of violation and revocation of parole/probation
Notification of revocation of parole/probation
Advance notification of release

FIGURE 22.1   Victim Services

Adapted from Office of Victim Services 1998, 192–193.

dynamics. For example, communities experiencing high rates of victimization of the elderly may implement transportation and escort services, legislation criminalizing elder abuse, or foster-grandparent programs. None of these would be an appropriate response, however, where the paramount problem is violence against gay men and lesbians. In those cases, media and educational campaigns against homophobia, or the creation of a local gay and lesbian advocacy panel would be effective interventions.

The key to effective delivery of victim services is sensitivity to the needs of the victim's community. The very meaning and goals of "justice" often differ across communities. Consequently, the same Western-based philosophy of intervention does not work equally well in all communities. Accordingly, service providers are encouraged to recognize and value the disparate practices and beliefs that shape cultural, religious, and other responses to victimization. Ogawa (1999:155–156) discusses an illustrative example from Albuquerque, New Mexico. The local chapter of Mothers Against Drunk Driving (MADD) conducts regular victim-impact panels. However, people from different cultures are encouraged to express themselves in very different ways. Navajo members engage in storytelling, and set up family circles intended to share responsibility for "healing." Latinas'/os' reverence for their religion is reflected in panels that integrate the Rosary or other rituals. This example demonstrates how a particular program might be adapted and modified to allow for diversity.

OFFENDER SERVICES

Offenders share with victims' disproportionate representation from disadvantaged groups—youth, the poor, and ethnic and racial minorities in particular. Many of the authors in this book demonstrate the overrepresentation of minority groups in the "official" crime statistics. Why this is the case is, of course, the focus of considerable debate. Is it the result of different rates of offending? Is it a result of how we have defined crime? Is it a result of disparate treatment within the criminal justice system? The answers to these questions are complex. Nonetheless, it is important to bear in mind that the offender population is diverse and, in general, disadvantaged. Thus, criminal justice service providers must also be aware of the particular problems and needs of these communities if they are to serve them appropriately.

It is beyond the scope of this chapter to provide an exhaustive overview of potential interventions which might assist offenders. What is offered is a concise discussion of a multicultural approach to offenders in the context of crime prevention and treatment, and equity in criminal justice processing of offenders.

Prevention and treatment

In spite of the fact that minorities, and especially minority youth, are overrepresented in the criminal justice system, the vast array of crime prevention and treatment strategies have largely been devoid of a multicultural component that takes into account the social and cultural milieu in which offenders find themselves (Corley and Smitherman, 1994). One of the dangers of this is that "attempts to offer youths of color (for example) non-delinquent activity alternatives, skill development, power enhancement and/or other delinquency prevention without knowledge of cultural specifics may further alienate diverse group members" (Corley and Smitherman, 1994:282). Successful prevention and treatment strategies will be those that are attuned to the culture and heritage of the individual in question. For example, Newark, New Jersey's Soul-O-House Drug Abuse Program seeks to prevent and overcome drug abuse through a variety of strategies including parent meetings, school after-care, and athletics. However, what makes it uniquely appropriate and effective is that "program participants are counseled from an African American perspective within an extended family . . . Knowledge of one's culture and history and cultural pride are associated with positive self-concept" (Miller and Hess, 1998:549). Integrating culturally specific skills and knowledge helps to reconnect youth, in particular, to their community.

Equally important, however, is the need to (re)connect diverse communities as a means of reducing hate crime, in particular. If this divisive form of violence is to be minimized, differences between groups must also be bridged. It is not enough to provide services for the victims of such hostility. The other side of the equation must also be addressed, so that the pool of offenders is reduced through treatment and prevention strategies. As a condition of probation, some judges across the country have attempted to prevent secondary offending by helping the offender to see the humanity of the victims' community. This is often accomplished by requiring that the offender engage in community service with an element of the victim community: an anti-Semite might work with the ADL; a gay-basher may work with a local gay and lesbian advocacy group (Levin and McDevitt, 1993).

As a means of preventing hate crime, anti-prejudice, and anti-violence projects have begun to spring up across the country. Elementary and secondary schools have been the preeminent site of such interventions. The *Teaching Tolerance* project and the P.E.A.C.E. project, mentioned earlier in this chapter, provide valuable models.

Although ethnoviolence is grounded in cultural animosities, most crime finds its roots in the life conditions in which offenders find themselves. Smith (Chapter 8) explicitly addressed the ways in which poverty and the inequitable distribution of resources enhance the likelihood of criminal justice contact for African American males. The same could be said for most minority groups. Consequently, crime prevention necessitates the amelioration of those disparities.

Equity in Criminal Justice Processing of Offenders

Rectifying disparities in economic and educational opportunities will not necessarily eliminate all disparities in the criminal justice system, since differential treatment is systemic—it is embedded in the criminal justice system itself in the form of differential sentencing for crack and white powder cocaine, in differential applications of the death penalty, and in differential access to treatment programs, for example. If the criminal justice system is to dispense justice, then, it must be purged of systemic bias. There is no better way to make this point than to quote at length from Tonry's *Malign Neglect*, the thesis of which is that the criminal justice system should at least do no harm:

> First, think about the foreseeable effects of crime control policy decisions on members of minority groups; when policies are likely to burden members of minority groups disproportionately, reconsider the policies. Second, to guard against racial bias in sentencing and against unjustly severe penalties in general, establish systems of presumptive sentencing

guidelines for ordinary cases that set maximum penalties, scaled to the severity of offenders' crimes. Third, recognize the prudence and compassion of our predecessors, and throughout the justice system reestablish presumptions that the least punitive and least restrictive appropriate punishment should be imposed in every case. Fourth, empower judges at sentencing to mitigate sentences for all defendants, irrespective of race, ethnicity, or sex, to take account of individual circumstances. Fifth, celebrate the decent instincts of our predecessors, and reinvest in corrections programs that can help offenders rebuild their lives and enhance their own and their children's life chances. Sixth, most important of all, be honest; for as long as cynical and disingenuous appeals continue to be made by politicians to the deepest fears and basest instincts of the American people, the prospects of reducing racial disparities in the justice system will remain small. (Tonry, 1995:181)

The movement toward criminal *justice* would include utilizing community programs and treatment, especially for nonviolent offenders (Tonry, 1995). The United States has the highest incarceration rate of all Western industrialized nations, due largely to the harsh sentencing practices associated with drug offenses. The relatively long prison terms associated with these should be replaced by rehabilitation and training efforts. The emphasis would be on providing the skills and incentive necessary to escape the cycle of criminality—life skills, employment skills, financial management skills, and so on. In this way, offenders reenter or remain part of their community armed with enhanced personal resources.

As Tonry suggests, the elimination of harsh sentencing guidelines for drug offenses would have dramatic impact on incarceration, especially for those disadvantaged by race, class, and gender. The historical consequences of drug enforcement are seen in the enduring overrepresentation of people of color and poor people in juvenile and adult correctional institutions. Prison will not make these offenders less likely to offend; prisons do not focus on educating and training inmates. The vast majority of inmates do not complete college or acquire marketable employment skills, and their years in prison are in many ways a waste of time. In addition, when they leave they carry the disadvantaged status of convicted felon. For many reasons, and on many levels, incarceration is not an effective response to crime. Alternatives that enhance offenders' community integration must be tested. For example, many Native American communities are experiencing considerable success with more traditional peacemaking initiatives. African American communities are strengthening the discipline and self-esteem of at-risk youth with Afro-centric programs. The value of such programs is that they build on difference in positive ways, rather than constructing it as a pathology or inherent stain.

CRIMINAL JUSTICE / SOCIAL JUSTICE

As the preceding discussion implied, *criminal* justice will continue to be elusive in the absence of *social* justice. In a just society, difference would not be the foundation of criminalization, marginalization, or disparate sentencing. On the contrary, difference would be the foundation of inclusion and equity in all areas of social life. This reconstruction—referred to at the beginning of this chapter—will require social action both within and outside the criminal justice system. To engage in a positive politics of difference, all of those means of bridging difference discussed throughout this chapter must be embedded in social, economic, and cultural practices that empower rather than disempower diverse groups. This is a principle the 1967 President's Commission on Law Enforcement and the Administration of Justice acknowledged (but was never to realize): "crime flourishes where the conditions of life are the worst." The response, even then, was seen to be "an unremitting national effort for social justice."

Coincident with social action for reform of legislation, victim services, and criminal justice training, as criminal justice practitioners we also have a responsibility to work toward social change which mitigates the negative effects of difference. Access to adequate housing and medical care, education, full-time employment, income support, child care, and other crucial social services should be acknowledged as the inalienable rights of all rather than the privilege of a few. At bottom, "the goal should be to make sure that every child, whoever his or her parents and whatever their race or class, has a reasonable chance to live a satisfying, productive and law-abiding life" (Tonry, 1995:208). Only then can we say that this is a truly just society in which difference is not denigrated.

Recognition of social and economic rights must also be accompanied by efforts to *include and integrate difference* into our cultural repertoire. Culturally specific programs for victims and offenders were suggested earlier. However, the values and practices of alternate cultures have value beyond the criminal justice system. At the outset, this chapter suggests that we could learn and benefit from the strengths that other cultures might have to offer:

> Black Americans find in their traditional communities, which refer to their members as "brother" and "sister," a sense of solidarity absent from the calculating individualism of white, professional, capitalist society. Feminists find in the traditional female values of nurturing a challenge to a militarist world-view, and lesbians find in their relationships a confrontation with the assumptions of complementary gender roles in sexual relationships. From their experience of a culture tied to the land, American Indians formulate a critique of the instrumental rationality of European culture that results in pollution and environmental destruction. (Young, 1990:205)

Yes, difference matters. And it's a good thing, too!

References

Corley, Charles, and Geneva Smitherman. 1994. Juvenile Justice: Multicultural Issues. In *Multicultural Perspectives in Criminal Justice and Criminology*, ed. James Hendricks and Bryan Byers, 259–290. Springfield, IL: Charles C. Thomas.

Dugan, L., and R. Apel. 2003. An Exploratory Study of the Violent Victimization of Women: Race/Ethnicity and Situational Context. *Criminology* 41 (2): 959–979.

Howley, Susan, and Carol Dorris. 2007. Legal Rights for Crime Victims in the Criminal

Justice System. In *Victims of Crime*, ed. Robert C. Davis, Arthur J. Lurigio, and Susan Herman, 3rd edn., 299–314. Los Angeles, CA: Sage.

Karmen, Andrew. 2007. *Crime Victims: An Introduction to Victimology*, 6th edn. Belmont, CA: Thomson Wadsworth.

Karst, Kenneth. 1995. *Law's Promise, Law's Expression*. New Haven, CT: Yale University Press.

Kleg, Milton. 1993. *Hate Prejudice and Violence*. Albany, NY: SUNY Press.

Levin, Jack, and Jack McDevitt. 1993. *Hate Crimes: The Rising Tide of Bigotry and Bloodshed*. New York, NY: Plenum Press.

Miller, Linda, and Kären Hess. 1998. *The Police in the Community: Strategies for the 21st Century*. Belmont, CA: West/Wadsworth.

Murdaugh, C., S. Hunt, R. Sowell, and I. Santana. 2004. Domestic Violence in Hispanics in the Southeastern United States: A Survey and Needs Analysis. *Journal of Family Violence* 19 (2): 107–115.

Muscat, Bernadette T., and Jeffrey A. Walsh. 2007. Reaching Underserved Victim Populations—Special Challenges Relating to Homeless Victims, Rural Populations, Ethnic/Racial/Sexual Minorities, and Victims with Disabilities. In *Victims of Crime*, ed. Robert C. Davis, Arthur J. Lurigio,

and Susan Herman, 3rd edn., 315–336. Los Angeles, CA: Sage.

Office for Victims of Crime. 1998. *New Directions from the Field: Victims Rights and Services for the 21st Century*.

Office for Victims of Crime. 2005. *Report to the Nation 2005*. Washington, DC: U.S. Department of Justice. http://www.ojp.usdoj.gov/ovc/welcovc/reporttonation2005/welcome.html.

Ogawa, Brian. 1999. *Color of Justice: Culturally Sensitive Treatment of Minority Crime Victims*. Boston, MA: Allyn and Bacon.

Okazawa-Rey, Margo, and Marshall Wong. 1996. Organizing in Communities of Color: Addressing Interethnic Conflicts. *Social Justice* 24 (1): 24–39.

P.E.A.C.E. website, http://www.northlandfamily.org/ce_peace.html.

Skillings, Judith H., and James E. Dobbins. 1991. Racism as a Disease: Etiology and Treatment Implications. *Journal of Counseling and Development* 70: 206–212.

Tolerance.org website, http://www.tolerance.org.

Tonry, Michael. 1995. *Malign Neglect: Race, Crime and Punishment in America*. New York, NY: Oxford University Press.

Young, Iris Marion. 1990. *Justice and the Politics of Difference*. Princeton, NJ: Princeton University Press.

CONTRIBUTORS

FACILITATORS/CO-EDITORS

Lynn Jones earned her Ph.D. in Sociology from the University of Arizona in 1999 and is currently an associate professor in the Department of Criminology and Criminal Justice at Northern Arizona University. Her research interests focus on cause lawyers; social movements and activism using the law; and crime victim services. Since 2001, she has worked with the Pennsylvania Commission on Crime and Delinquency (PCCD) and the Arizona Coalition for Victim Services (ACVS) to create, administer, and evaluate a State Victim Assistance Academy. These academies, initially funded through the Department of Justice Office for Victims of Crime, aim to standardize training to victim service providers and improve service delivery to the diverse crime victims of a state, with particular emphasis on overcoming the geographic and cultural barriers in service delivery. She serves on the editorial advisory board of the journal *Law & Society Review,* and is co-organizer of the Law and Social Movements Collaborative Research Network (CRN) for the Law and Society Association.

Marianne O. Nielsen received her Ph.D. in 1991 from the University of Alberta, Canada, and is a professor in the Department of Criminology and Criminal Justice at Northern Arizona University. She has worked for indigenous organizations and done comparative research on indigenous justice issues in the United States, Canada, Australia, and New Zealand. She is co-editor with Robert Silverman of *Aboriginal Peoples and Canadian Criminal Justice* (Harcourt Brace, 1992) and *Native Americans, Crime and Criminal Justice* (Westview, 1996); and with James W. Zion of *Navajo Nation Peacemaking: Living Traditional Justice* (University of Arizona Press, 2005). She was one of the two lead editors for the first edition of *Investigating Difference: Human and Cultural Relations in Criminal Justice* (The Criminal Justice Collective of Northern Arizona University, Allyn and Bacon, 2000), and for this edition as well. Her writings on indigenous issues have appeared in numerous books and scholarly journals.

THE CRIMINOLOGY AND CRIMINAL JUSTICE COLLECTIVE

Alexander Alvarez earned his Ph.D. in Sociology from the University of New Hampshire in 1991 and is a professor in the Department of Criminology and Criminal Justice at Northern Arizona University. From 2001 until 2003, he was the founding Director of the Martin-Springer Institute for Teaching the Holocaust, Tolerance, and Humanitarian Values. His main areas of study are in the areas of collective and interpersonal violence, including homicide and genocide. His first book, *Governments, Citizens, and Genocide,* was published by Indiana University Press in 2001 and was a nominee for the Academy of Criminal Justice Sciences book of the year award in 2002, as well as a Raphael Lemkin book award nominee from the International Association of Genocide Scholars in 2003. His other books include *Murder American Style* (2002), and *Violence: the Enduring Problem* (2007). He has also served as an editor for the journal *Violence and Victims,* was a founding co-editor of the journal *Genocide Studies and Prevention*, was a co-editor of the H-Genocide List Serve, and is an editorial board member for the journals *War Crimes, Genocide, and Crimes Against Humanity: An International Journal* and *Idea: A Journal of Social Issues*. He has been invited to present his research in various countries such as Austria, Bosnia, Canada, Germany, the Netherlands, and Sweden. Dr. Alvarez also gives presentations and workshops on various issues such as violence, genocide, and bullying.

Cynthia Baroody-Hart is an associate professor in the Justice Studies Department at San Jose State University (SJSU). She received her Ph.D. in 1990 from the State University of New York at Buffalo. Her research has included the study of art worlds in prison, inmate-artists' and jailhouse-lawyer's networks, gender differences in social support among inmates, as well as access issues for inmates with disability and elderly inmates. As a consequence of her participation in an international conference on paratransportation, her work on disability also includes the proposed development of a national paratransit network providing meaningful inclusion for the disabled and elderly at all levels of the workforce—in urban, suburban, and rural areas, regardless of the regional economy.

Dennis W. Catlin is an associate professor in the Department of Criminology and Criminal Justice at Northern Arizona University's Tucson campus. Dr. Catlin served as a police officer, Special Agent for the Federal Bureau of Investigation, and Training Supervisor for the Michigan Law Enforcement Officers Training Council. He was Executive Director of the Michigan Judicial Institute, an agency of the Michigan Supreme Court. Dr. Catlin has consulted on "rule of law" and judicial reform projects in Egypt, Botswana, Croatia, Bulgaria, the Philippines, Barbados, Slovakia, and Armenia. He received his master's degree in Criminal Justice and his Ph.D. in Administration and Higher Education from Michigan State University. His areas of teaching and research are justice system organization and administration, education and training of justice system personnel, comparative justice systems, criminal justice ethics, and human and cultural relations in criminal justice.

Michael Costelloe is currently Assistant Professor of Criminology and Criminal Justice at Northern Arizona University. He received his Ph.D. in Criminology and Criminal Justice in 2004 from Florida State University. His current research interests include punitive attitudes, issues of social control and social justice in late modernity, immigration as moral panic, and policing immigration. He is also the Assistant Director of the Northern Arizona Justice Project and plans on commencing a research agenda pertaining to wrongful convictions. He has previously published research in the areas of punitive attitudes, drug issues, and policing.

Luis A. Fernandez holds an M.A. in Political Science and a Ph.D. in Justice Studies from Arizona State University, and is currently an assistant professor in the Department of Criminology and Criminal Justice at NAU. He has worked for several research institutions, including the National Council on Crime and Delinquency and the Morrison Institute for Public Policy. He serves on the board of directors for the Society for the Study of Social Problems. His research interests include protest policing, securitization, and militarization of borders. Most recently, he is the author of the book *Policing Dissent: Social Control and the Anti-Globalization Movement*.

Larry A. Gould is Associate Vice President and Campus Executive Officer for Northern Arizona University-Yuma. After a career in law enforcement, Dr. Gould graduated from Louisiana State University in 1991, with a Ph.D. in Sociology and a minor in Criminal Justice and Experimental Statistics. His primary research areas include drug and alcohol issues and law enforcement–related issues. Dr. Gould has been one of the leading researchers on Native American policing. Recent research projects include studies of Native American law enforcement and assaults on National Park Service Rangers. His most recent publications include an edited volume entitled *Native Americans and the Criminal Justice System*, a research report concerning the *Analysis of Assaults Upon National Park Rangers: 1997–2003* and an article entitled "Developing the Interface Between the Navajo Nation Police and Navajo Nation Peacemaking," along with Marianne O. Nielsen.

Karla B. Hackstaff earned her Ph.D. in Sociology from the University of California, Berkeley, in 1994, and is currently Associate Professor of Sociology at Northern Arizona University in Flagstaff, Arizona. Her research and teaching focus on the areas of family, gender, feminisms, social psychology, and qualitative research methods. She is the author of the book *Marriage in a Culture of Divorce*. Her work on gender and marriage in divorce culture has been published in *Family in Transition*, *Families in the U.S.*, *The Family Experience*, and *International Journal of Marital Spirituality*. She is interested in the politics of inequality and knowledge construction and is currently working on a research project examining the genealogical constructions of race and family relations; an article on this topic is forthcoming in *Qualitative Sociology*.

Carole Mandino is the Director of the Northern Arizona Regional Gerontology Institute, Senior Companion, and Foster Grandparent Programs at NAU. Carole has a doctorate in Educational Leadership from Northern Arizona University and has worked in the field of aging for 25 years. She is an adjunct faculty member to the department of Sociology and Social Work and has also instructed courses for Educational Leadership. She was a governing board member of Coconino Community College for four years and has served on the board of the National Senior Corps Association for the past four years, the past two as treasurer.

Rebecca Maniglia is an assistant professor in the Criminology and Criminal Justice Department at Northern Arizona University. As a private consultant, Rebecca has also provided training and technical assistance to over 45 states on issues related to juvenile justice and juvenile female offenders. She holds a Ph.D. from the University of Illinois at Chicago in Criminal Justice and is the author of many articles and national reports on gender responsive services for female delinquents.

Meghan G. McDowell is a graduate student in the Department of Criminology and Criminal Justice at Northern Arizona University. Her research interests include race and space, (im)migration, the prison-industrial complex, and critical race theory. She also worked as a graduate assistant for the Northern Arizona Justice Project.

Raymond J. Michalowski, Ph.D., is a sociologist and Arizona Regents Professor in the Department of Criminology and Criminal Justice at Northern Arizona University. He is the author of *State-Corporate Crime: Wrongdoing at the Intersection* *of Business and Government; Crime, Power and Identity: The New Primer in Radical Criminology; Run for the Wall: Remembering Vietnam on a Motorcycle Pilgrimage;* and *Order, Law and Crime: An Introduction to Criminology.* He has served as Chair of the American Society of Criminology Division on Critical Criminology and the Society for the Study of Social Problems Crime and Delinquency Division, Executive Counselor for the Society for the Study of Social Problems, and is a member of the editorial boards of *Social Problems, Criminology, Humanity and Society,* and *Social Pathology.* He currently serves as editor for the *Critical Issues in Crime and Society* series at Rutgers University Press, and is a member of the U.S.–Mexico Border and Immigration Task Force. His current research projects focus on the legal, political-economic, and cultural dimensions of immigration along the U.S.–Mexico frontier, and the crimes of globalization and empire. In 2006 Dr. Michalowski was honored with the Lifetime Achievement Award from the American Society of Criminology Division on Critical Criminology, and the W.E.B. Dubois Award for Contributions to Race and Ethnic Studies in Criminology from the Western Society of Criminology.

Phoebe Morgan, Ph.D., is Professor of Criminology and Criminal Justice at Northern Arizona University. She teaches courses about women, crime and justice, research methods, justice policy, and the War on Terror. With James Gruber, she edited *In the Company of Men: Male Dominance and Sexual Harassment* (Northeastern University Press). Her research also appears in The *Law and Society Review,* the *Journal of Law, Culture and the Humanities,* the *Journal of Criminal Justice Education, The Women's Studies Association Journal, Affilia Social Work Journal,* the *Sourcebook for Violence Against Women, Classic Papers on Violence Against Women, Everyday Sexism in the Third Millennium,* and *The Gendered Economy.* Her current research interests include the globalization of U.S. sexual harassment policy and the U.S. War on Terror's impact on American education and the status of women.

Barbara Perry, Ph.D., is Professor of Criminology, Justice and Policy Studies at the University of Ontario Institute of Technology. She has written extensively in the area of hate crime, including two books on the topic: *In the Name of Hate: Understanding Hate Crime;* and *Hate and Bias Crime: A Reader.* Most recently, she has conducted interviews with Native Americans on their experiences of hate crime. The findings of this research will soon appear in print in two books: *Silent Victims: Hate Crime Against Native Americans* (University of Arizona Press) and *Policing Race and Space: Under- and Over-policing Native American Communities* (Lexington Press). She is also completing a British Home Office project on anti-racism programming in England and Wales. Dr. Perry was in the Department of Criminal Justice at NAU from 1996 to 2004. She continues to work in the area of hate crime, and has begun to make contributions to the limited scholarship on hate crime in Canada. Here, she is particularly interested in anti-Muslim violence, and hate crime against First Nations people.

Paula K. Rector was an instructor in the Department of Criminology and Criminal Justice at Northern Arizona University from 2002 to 2007, where she taught undergraduate courses in theory and cultural relations. She received her M.S. from Northern Arizona University in 2000. She is currently an instructor at Missouri State University. Her research interests include the intersections of race, class, and gender and social inequality. Specifically, she has researched the criminal justice treatment of pregnant drug users and is published in the book *Victimizing Vulnerable Groups: Images of Uniquely High-Risk Crime Targets*, edited by Charisse Tia Maria Coston (Praeger). Her current work focuses on pregnant women who use methamphetamines and the social and criminal justice responses to them.

Linda Robyn, Ph.D., is Associate Professor of Criminology and Criminal Justice at Northern Arizona University. She has published articles on a variety of indigenous issues including indigenous knowledge, environmental injustice, resistance to colonialism and white collar crime, and victimization of Indian people through forced removal. She is involved with the Northern Arizona Justice Project, and future research will include wrongful conviction of American Indians. Her current research interests also include white collar crime, government, and state-corporate crimes. Her current research is on the effects of uranium mining on Native Americans as state-corporate crime.

Robert Schehr is Professor of Sociology in the Department of Criminology and Criminal Justice at Northern Arizona University. He is the Executive Director of the Northern Arizona Justice Project, a live client clinical actual innocence project operated out of the College of Social and Behavioral Sciences at Northern Arizona University, and is a member of the United States National Innocence Network Board of Directors. Dr. Schehr is a frequent invited lecturer in the United States, and in Europe and Australia, on the known causes of wrongful conviction, and ways to establish an innocence project. He presently serves on the Board of Directors for the Innocence Project United Kingdom. Dr. Schehr's primary research interests include (1) comparative criminal law and criminal procedure and its applications to domestic wrongful conviction; (2) comparative constitutional law and policy development; and (3) critical pedagogy and live client clinic innocence projects.

Brian J. Smith has a Ph.D. in Justice Studies from Arizona State University. He is an associate professor in the Department of Sociology, Anthropology, and Social Work at Central Michigan University. His research, writing, and publications focus on social inequalities, marginalized youth, and education; his current field research project explores the intersections of social control ideologies and social inequalities during juvenile court processes. In 2007 he received Central Michigan University's Excellence in Teaching Award and was also named Professor of the Year by CMU's Honors Program. He was a visiting professor in the Department of Criminal Justice at NAU from 1997 to 1998.

Michael R. Stevenson, Ph.D., was appointed Dean of Social and Behavioral Sciences at Northern Arizona University in 2007, after serving the Miami University and Ball State University communities for over 20 years. A fellow of the American Psychological Association, he has also served as a Fulbright Senior Scholar, a Senior Congressional Fellow, a Malone Fellow, and an American Council on Education Fellow. Trained in Developmental Psychology at Purdue University, his scholarly work has consistently appeared in a wide variety of books, interdisciplinary periodicals, and psychology journals. He is the founding editor of *The Journal of Diversity in Higher Education* and has offered lectures, workshops, and seminars for professional and lay audiences in Asia, Canada, the Middle East, South Africa, and across the United States. His current work focuses on diversity policy in higher education and the application of research findings in the development of public policy.

Nancy A. Wonders, Ph.D., is a sociologist, as well as Professor and Chair of the Department of Criminology and Criminal Justice at Northern Arizona University. Her research and teaching focus on the relationship between social inequality, difference, and justice, with an emphasis on underrepresented and vulnerable populations. She has published numerous high-profile journal articles and book chapters on the relationship between structural inequality and justice, and has achieved national recognition for innovation in teaching about difference and under-represented groups. Dr. Wonders is internationally recognized for her research on globalization and migration and has been an invited speaker at universities and institutes in the United States, the Netherlands, Italy, and Spain. Dr. Wonders is a past Chair of the American Society of Criminology's Division on Women and Crime and recipient of the Western Society of Criminology's June Morrison-Tom Gitchoff Award for significant improvement of the quality of justice.

INDEX